The Blackwell Guide to Kant's Ethics

Blackwell Guides to Great Works

A proper understanding of philosophy requires engagement with the foundational texts that have shaped the development of the discipline and which have an abiding relevance to contemporary discussions. Each volume in this series provides guidance to those coming to the great works of the philosophical canon, whether for the first time or to gain new insight. Comprising specially commissioned contributions from the finest scholars, each book offers a clear and authoritative account of the context, arguments and impact of the work at hand. Where possible the original text is reproduced alongside the essays.

Published

1. The Blackwell Guide to Plato's *Republic*, edited by Gerasimos Santas
2. The Blackwell Guide to Descartes' *Meditations*, edited by Stephen Gaukroger
3. The Blackwell Guide to Mill's *Utilitarianism*, edited by Henry R. West
4. The Blackwell Guide to Aristotle's *Nicomachean Ethics*, edited by Richard Kraut
5. The Blackwell Guide to Hume's *Treatise*, edited by Saul Traiger
6. The Blackwell Guide to Hegel's *Phenomenology of Spirit*, edited by Kenneth Westphal
7. The Blackwell Guide to Kant's Ethics, edited by Thomas E. Hill, Jr.

Forthcoming

The Blackwell Guide to Heidegger's *Being and Time*, edited by Robert Scharff

THE BLACKWELL GUIDE TO

Kant's
Ethics

EDITED BY THOMAS E. HILL, JR.

WILEY-BLACKWELL

A John Wiley & Sons, Ltd., Publication

This edition first published 2009
© 2009 Blackwell Publishing Ltd

Blackwell Publishing was acquired by John Wiley & Sons in February 2007. Blackwell's publishing program has been merged with Wiley's global Scientific, Technical, and Medical business to form Wiley-Blackwell.

Registered Office
John Wiley & Sons Ltd, The Atrium, Southern Gate, Chichester, West Sussex, PO19 8SQ, United Kingdom

Editorial Offices
350 Main Street, Malden, MA 02148-5020, USA
9600 Garsington Road, Oxford, OX4 2DQ, UK
The Atrium, Southern Gate, Chichester, West Sussex, PO19 8SQ, UK

For details of our global editorial offices, for customer services, and for information about how to apply for permission to reuse the copyright material in this book please see our website at www.wiley.com/wiley-blackwell.

The right of Thomas E. Hill, Jr. to be identified as the author of the editorial material in this work has been asserted in accordance with the Copyright, Designs and Patents Act 1988.

Wiley also publishes its books in a variety of electronic formats. Some content that appears in print may not be available in electronic books.

Designations used by companies to distinguish their products are often claimed as trademarks. All brand names and product names used in this book are trade names, service marks, trademarks or registered trademarks of their respective owners. The publisher is not associated with any product or vendor mentioned in this book. This publication is designed to provide accurate and authoritative information in regard to the subject matter covered. It is sold on the understanding that the publisher is not engaged in rendering professional services. If professional advice or other expert assistance is required, the services of a competent professional should be sought.

Library of Congress Cataloging-in-Publication Data

The Blackwell guide to Kant's ethics / edited by Thomas E. Hill, Jr.
    p.   cm. – (Blackwell guides to great works)
Includes bibliographical references and index.
ISBN 978-1-4051-2582-6 (hardcover : alk. paper) – ISBN 978-1-4051-2581-9
    (pbk. : alk. paper)
1. Kant, Immanuel, 1724–1804. 2. Ethics. I. Hill, Thomas E.
    B2799.E8B53 2009
    170.92–dc22
            2008054105

A catalogue record for this book is available from the British Library.

Set in 10/13pt Galliard by SNP Best-set Typesetter Ltd., Hong Kong
Printed and bound in Malaysia by Vivar Printing Sdn Bhd

01   2009

Contents

Acknowledgements

Many people have helped to make this volume possible. I am grateful to the Paar Center for Ethics and the Philosophy Department at the University of North Carolina at Chapel Hill for providing funds for a workshop on Kant's ethics, which was held for the contributors in the fall of 2004. The Kenan Foundation contributed significantly as the project progressed, especially by supporting research assistants to help with editing and correspondence.

The authors contributing to this volume have taken the time to share their understanding and insights as much as possible in a form accessible not only to scholars but also to students and other serious readers. I am grateful for their willingness to write original essays on the topics suggested to make the volume a systematic guide to Kant's moral philosophy (broadly construed). Thanks are due too for the authors' patience with our editorial suggestions, my mistakes when sending drafts back and forth, and regrettable delays in bringing the project to completion.

As our contributors would readily agree, we are all indebted to many other astute scholars and critics of Kant's work. Some of these are mentioned in notes and bibliographies, but it would be impossible to give a complete list. Despite disagreements, Kantian scholarship has increasingly become a cooperative enterprise and we have all benefited as a result.

The Blackwell editors and staff have been encouraging, cooperative, and patient as well as efficient. In addition, I was fortunate to have the help of two research assistants who are themselves excellent philosophers well grounded in Kant's practical philosophy. Justin Jeffrey assisted with the initial workshop and reviewed all of the essays to bring them more in line with the publisher's guidelines. Adam Cureton prepared the final manuscript, doing intense proof-reading and last-minute problem solving that avoided further delays. Their help was invaluable and working with them a pleasure.

As always, I am especially grateful for the constant help and support of Robin. She primarily organized and managed the workshop and, most important, while also doing her own social work, she kept me healthy and happy during this long process.

Notes on Contributors

Marcia Baron is Rudy Professor of Philosophy at Indiana University. She is the author of *Kantian Ethics Almost without Apology* (1995), and co-author, with Philip Pettit and Michael Slote, of *Three Methods of Ethics: A Debate* (Blackwell, 1997), as well as articles on Kantian ethics, Hume's ethics, and philosophical issues in criminal law.

Stephen Darwall is Andrew Downey Orrick Professor of Philosophy at Yale University. He has written widely on moral theory and the history of ethics. His books include *Impartial Reason* (1985), *Philosophical Ethics* (1998), *Welfare and Rational Care* (2002), and *The Second-Person Standpoint* (2006).

Richard Dean is an Associate Professor at the American University of Beirut, but will join the faculty of California State University, Los Angeles in fall 2009. His current research interests include Kantian ethics, applied ethics, and recent empirical approaches to moral philosophy.

Melissa Seymour Fahmy is Assistant Professor of Philosophy at the University of Georgia. Her current research focuses on the cultivation of moral feelings and the moral significance of personal happiness. Recent publications include "Active Sympathetic Participation: Reconsidering Kant's Duty of Sympathy," forthcoming in the *Kantian Review*, and "Widening the Field for the Practice of Virtue: Kant's Wide Imperfect Duties," Proceedings from 10th International Kant Congress (2008).

Richard Galvin is currently Betty S. Wright Chair in Applied Ethics in the Philosophy Department at Texas Christian University, where he has been a faculty member since 1982. His publications include "Legal Moralism and the U.S. Supreme Court," in *Legal Theory, Reasoning and the Law* (with Elias Savellos), and "Slavery and Universalizability," in *Kant-Studien*. Currently, he is working on articles titled "The Practical Contradiction Interpretation Reconsidered,"

"Rounding Up the Usual Suspects: Varieties of Kantian Constructivism in Ethics," and "The Fact of Reason."

Sarah Holtman is Associate Professor of Philosophy at the University of Minnesota, Twin Cities. Holtman works mainly on issues of justice in the areas of moral, political, and legal philosophy and on interpretive questions in Kant's practical philosophy. Articles include "Kant, Ideal Theory, and the Justice of Exclusionary Zoning" (1999), "Kantian Justice and Poverty Relief" (2004), and "Justice, Mercy, and Efficiency" (forthcoming).

Thomas Hill, Jr. is Kenan Professor of Philosophy at the University of North Carolina, Chapel Hill. He previously taught at UCLA and Pomona College and, on visiting appointments, at Stanford University and the University of Minnesota. His essays on moral and political philosophy are collected in *Autonomy and Self-Respect* (1991), *Dignity and Practical Reason in Kant's Moral Theory* (1992), *Respect, Pluralism, and Justice: Kantian Perspectives* (2000), and *Human Welfare and Moral Worth: Kantian Perspectives* (2002). With Arnulf Zweig he co-edited a new edition of *Kant's Groundwork for the Metaphysics of Morals* with extensive notes (2002).

Robert N. Johnson is Associate Professor of Philosophy at the University of Missouri. He is the author of many papers on ethical theory and Kant's ethics journals such as *Ethics*, *Philosophical Quarterly*, *Philosophical Studies*, and *Pacific Philosophical Quarterly*. He is also the author of the entry "Kant's Moral Philosophy" in the *Stanford Encyclopedia of Philosophy*.

Samuel J. Kerstein is Associate Professor of Philosophy at the University of Maryland, College Park. He is the author of *Kant's Search for the Supreme Principle of Morality* (2002) and several articles on Kantian ethics. He is currently working on an elaboration and defense of Kant's Formula of Humanity.

Thomas Pogge writes and teaches on moral and political philosophy and Kant. He is Leitner Professor of Philosophy and International Affairs at Yale University and Research Director at the Oslo University Centre for the Study of Mind in Nature (CSMN). His recent publications include *John Rawls: His Life and Theory of Justice* (2007), *Freedom from Poverty as a Human Right*, edited, (2007), *World Poverty and Human Rights* (2008), and *A Companion to Contemporary Political Philosophy*, co-edited, (Blackwell 2007). With support from the Australian Research Council, he currently heads a team effort toward developing the Health Impact Fund, an organization intended to improve access to advanced medicines for poor people worldwide.

Nelson Potter made his career in the Philosophy Department of the University of Nebraska-Lincoln, where he served for a time as department chair. His research and publication has been almost entirely on Kant's ethical theory, though he also has broader interests in the history of early modern philosophy and aesthetics. He served for four years as president of the North American Kant Society.

Arthur Ripstein is Professor of Law and Philosophy at the University of Toronto. He is the author of *Equality, Responsibility and the Law* (1998) and *Force and Freedom: Kant's Legal and Political Philosophy* (2009).

Allen Wood is Professor of Philosophy at Indiana University. His most recent book is *Kantian Ethics* (2008).

Arnulf Zweig, translator of *Kant's Correspondence* (1999) and of *Kant's Groundwork for the Metaphysics of Morals* (2002), which he co-edited with Thomas E. Hill, Jr., teaches as an Adjunct Professor at Baruch College and the Graduate Center, City University of New York. A native of Essen, Germany, he graduated from the University of Rochester and pursued graduate studies at Yale and Stanford, receiving his doctorate in philosophy and humanities from the latter. At Stanford, he assisted C.I.Lewis and wrote a dissertation under Donald Davidson. Aside from philosophy, he was for many years a bassoonist with the Eugene Symphony and performed also with the Boston Civic Symphony.

Abbreviations of
Kant's Works

In this volume, citations of Kant's works include reference to the standard German edition, *Kants gesammelte Schriften*, which was edited under the auspices of the Konigliche Preussische Akademie der Wissenshaften (Berlin: Walter de Gruyter, 1908–13). This edition of Kant's works is commonly called the *Akademie* (or Academy) edition and sometimes abbreviated "Ak". The relevant citations in this volume, which usually appear in parentheses, refer to the appropriate volume and page numbers of this Academy text in the from, for example, "4:421" for volume 4, page 421. The volumes of Kant's German works sometimes contain several of Kant's essays or books, but the most frequently cited works in this volume are listed below. To simplify, when these books and essays are cited in the text, the volume number is preceded by an abbreviation that indicates the particular work cited, unless otherwise specified. For example, as indicated below, "(MM 6:221)" refer to *The Metaphysics of Morals*, Academy volume 6, page 221. The list provides, in order, the title of an available English translation and its date of publication, the title and date of publication of the original German edition, and the Academy edition volume and page numbers. For reference information on Kant's other works, see the notes in particular chapters. When authors quote substantially from a different translation or provide their own, this is indicated in their notes.

A   Anthropology from a Pragmatic Point of View, trans. Robert Louden (Cambridge: Cambridge University Press, 2006). Translated from *Anthropologie in pragmatischer Hinsicht* (1798) in *Kants gesammelte Schriften* (7:119–333).

CPR   *Critique of Pure Reason*, trans. Norman Kemp Smith (New York: St. Martin's Press, 1965). Translated from *Kritik der reinen Vernunft* (1781, 1787) in *Kants gesammelte Schriften* (first or "A" edition, 4:1–252; second or "B" edition, 3:1–594).

CPrR *Critique of Practical Reason*, trans. Mary Gregor (Cambridge: Cambridge University Press, 1997). Translated from *Kritik der praktischen Vernunft* (1788) in *Kants gesammelte Schriften* (5:1–163).

CJ *Critique of the Power of Judgment*, trans. Paul Guyer and Eric Matthews (Cambridge: Cambridge University Press, 2000). Translated from *Kritik der Urtheilskraft* (1790). The Cambridge edition includes Academy pagination correlating to *Kants gesammelte Schriften* (5:167–485).

G   *Groundwork for the Metaphysics of Morals*, trans. Arnulf Zweig, ed. Thomas E. Hill, Jr., and Arnulf Zweig (Oxford: Oxford University Press, 2003). Translated from *Grundlegung zur Metaphysik der Sitten* (1785), in *Kants gesammelte Schriften* (4:387–463).

LE *Lectures on Ethics*, trans. Peter Heath and J. B. Schneewind (Cambridge: Cambridge University Press, 1997). Translated from *Kants gesammelte Schriften* (27:3–732).

MM *The Metaphysics of Morals*, trans. Mary Gregor (Cambridge: Cambridge University Press, 1996). Translated from *Die Metaphysik der Sitten* (1797–8), in *Kants gesammelte Schriften* (6:203–491).

PP *On Perpetual Peace*, trans. Mary Gregor in *Practical Philosophy* (New York: Cambridge University Press, 1996), pp. 311–52. Translated from *Zum ewigen Frieden: Ein philosophischer Entwurf* (1795), in *Kants gesammelte Schriften* (8:341–86).

R   *Religion within the Boundaries of Mere Reason*, trans. Allen Wood and George di Giovanni (Cambridge: Cambridge University Press, 1998). Translated from *Die Religion innerhalb der Grenzen der blossen Vernunft* (1793–4), in *Kants gesammelte Schriften* (6:1–202).

TP On the Common Saying: "This May Be True in Theory, but It Does Not Apply in Practice," trans. Mary Gregor in *Practical Philosophy* (New York: Cambridge University Press, 1996), pp. 273–310. Translated from *Über den Gemeinspruch: Das mag in der Theorie richtig sein, taugt aber nicht für die Praxis* (1793), in *Kants gesammelte Schriften* (8:275–313).

Introduction

Thomas E. Hill, Jr.

From 1785 through the 1790s Immanuel Kant published influential and controversial works of moral philosophy. Even his critics acknowledge that these works represent the serious and sustained efforts of one of the most profound thinkers of the modern age. In recent years there has been a resurgence of interest in Kant's philosophy and a corresponding increase in the amount, range, and quality of Kant scholarship. This includes not only new interpretations of Kant's classic work, the *Groundwork for the Metaphysics of Morals* (1785), but also important studies of Kant's later ethical writings, especially *The Metaphysics of Morals* (1797–8). We have seen more attention to Kant's ideas about law, justice, and international relations and about how these ideas fit with his ideas about ethical duty and virtue. Renewed interest in Kant's works, not surprisingly, has prompted new and better focused objections. Probably no Kant scholar endorses everything that Kant wrote, and many are careful to distinguish essential features of Kant's theory from misguided applications and other inessential accompaniments. In addition, contemporary moral philosophers have continued a long tradition of attempting to develop, modify, and extend Kant's basic theory in various ways, but all should agree that first we need to take seriously what he actually wrote.

This is the background for our *Blackwell Guide to Kant's Ethics*, which presents new essays on Kant's practical philosophy by both younger and more established scholars. The chapters address a wide range of topics that are important for understanding Kant's fundamental moral principles and their implications. Kant discussed these topics as parts of an inter-connected system of practical philosophy. The chapters in this volume are meant not only to illuminate particular topics but also to place them within Kant's larger framework of ideas. They also address questions that are relevant to philosophical and practical discussions today.

This collection of original chapters on Kant's ethics has a dual purpose. It is meant to introduce students and general readers to Kant's moral philosophy and to offer new perspectives on texts that have been too often neglected or misunderstood. The authors explain the main features of Kant's views on their topics but also give their own interpretations and assessments. Some of the topics will be less familiar and more difficult than others for the general reader, but they are nevertheless important aspects of Kant's "ethics," or moral philosophy, in a broad sense. Some chapters emphasize basic understanding, while others focus more on developing and assessing Kant's ideas. All offer new insights into familiar texts, but some aim to make more accessible texts that are less often studied. The essays are based on careful scholarship and serious philosophical reflection, and they often challenge commonly accepted interpretations. Together they provide basic explanations, original commentary, and an invitation to do further reading.

A special feature of this *Guide to Kant's Ethics* is that it includes chapters on aspects of Kant's work beyond those usually considered in introductory books and courses. For example, these chapters discuss not only Kant's idea of a good will and formulations of the Categorical Imperative, but also virtue, duties to oneself, justice, punishment, international relations, and Kant's arguments for the Categorical Imperative. They highlight issues that Kant addressed systematically in his later writings, especially *The Metaphysics of Morals*. The relation between Kant's theory of *justice* (*Rechtslehre*) and *ethics* in a narrower sense (*Tugendlehre*) remains controversial, but it is undeniably important. Both belong to Kant's systematic presentation of the rational principles of morality in a broad sense (a "metaphysics of morals"), and he maintained that it is an indirectly *ethical* duty to respect *juridical* duties. The chapters also draw from Kant's *Critique of Practical Reason, Religion within the Limits of Mere Reason*, and other essays on morals, politics, and history.

The authors include well-known Kant scholars, for example, Marcia Baron, Nelson Potter, Allen Wood, and Arnulf Zweig, as well as younger, increasingly prominent scholars: Richard Dean, Richard Galvin, Sarah Holtman, Robert Johnson, Samuel Kerstein, and Melissa Seymour. Some distinguished authors, for example, Stephen Darwall, Thomas Pogge, and Arthur Ripstein, may be best known for their contributions to contemporary discussion, for example, on practical reason, law, and international justice. Here they comment on Kant's work in their areas of concentration. I have come to know and respect all of the authors from professional associations as well as through their writings. Some of them have served as critics of my work, as sometimes I have of theirs. I was privileged to know Dean, Holtman, and Johnson as doctoral students, and to work with Arnulf Zweig as co-editor of Kant's *Groundwork* for Oxford University Press. There are, of course, other distinguished and worthy commentators on Kant's ethics from whom we have all learned. I am especially pleased, however, that that the group assembled here has contributed new and original chapters that combine helpful explanation and thought-provoking commentary over an unusually broad range of topics. For further reading, Kant's writings and the work of other commentators are cited in the introductory material and in bibliographies at the end of each chapter.

The chapters are presented here in more or less the order of Kant's major discussions of the topics they cover. Although obviously not every significant issue can be treated here, the order of topics also reflects Kant's conviction that philosophical questions should be treated systematically. The first four chapters, drawing primarily from Kant's *Groundwork* I and II, focus on the special value of a good will and acts from duty and then Kant's famous formulations of the fundamental moral principle ("the Categorical Imperative") – the formulas of universal law, humanity as an end in itself, and autonomy and kingdom (or commonwealth) of ends. The next two chapters address Kant's arguments for the Categorical Imperative: his attempt in *Groundwork* I and II to "derive" or identify the only possible supreme moral principle and his attempt in *Groundwork* III to justify the supreme principle as rational to accept. The last set of chapters takes up themes in *The Metaphysics of Morals*, first justice, punishment, and international relations, and then love, respect, and duties to oneself.

The coverage here, though limited, is more comprehensive and complex than is typical in introductory presentations of Kant's moral philosophy. This approach may help the reader to overcome the common but unfortunate impression that the moral philosophy mainly consists of excessive admiration for acts from duty and over-simple procedures expected to determine decisively how we ought to act in all cases.

Here is a brief preview of the chapters in this volume and a brief explanation of the context and how they are connected.

In the Preface to the *Groundwork* Kant's declared his aim as "to seek out and establish the supreme principle of morality" (G 4:392). In other words, he wanted to identify and explain the most basic and comprehensive principle presupposed in common morality and then to defend that principle against certain sources of possible doubt. These tasks, he insisted, required an a priori method of rational reflection as opposed to empirical studies and "impure" methods that mix empirical and rational considerations. He begins by discussing what is most worth having in life (a good will) and how this could be manifest in practice (by acting from duty).

The Special Value of a Good Will and Acts from Duty

Among the most familiar but controversial aspects of Kant ethics are his initial assertions that only a "good will" is good without qualification and that only acts "from duty" have moral worth. In an extended essay on *Groundwork* I, Robert Johnson offers an interpretation of these claims and how they fit together. Kant's aim is not to state comprehensive criteria for moral praise-worthiness or desert but rather to reveal the supreme principle of morality implicit in ordinary moral commitments. Too often interpretations of Kant's claims about a good will and moral worth fail to make sense of them as steps in Kant's overall argument in *Groundwork* I. Johnson offers a new interpretation that promises to overcome this problem and show Kant's claims to be more plausible than is commonly thought. Here are some main points.

A person's *will* is "a power to choose on the basis of principles" and a *good will* is a disposition "to adopt and act on the right sorts of policies." These are conceived as policies or *maxims* that any rational agent would or could have. An unqualifiedly good choice is a choice based on some principle that makes that choice good under any circumstance. That it is good under any circumstance implies that its principle has some essential property that it would retain no matter how circumstances might be changed around it. So the essential feature of a good will's principle cannot be that acting on it always produces desired results. Instead, if we consider what actions *express* an unqualifiedly good will, the only principle that qualifies is "to do my duty." As the argument unfolds, this amounts to the formal requirement: "I ought never to act except in such a way that I could not also will that my maxim should become a universal law" (G 4:402). This principle of a good will is a preliminary version of what later appears as the formula of universal law (FUL) of the Categorical Imperative.

Johnson also offers explanations of Kant's core concepts that are important apart from their role in the argument of *Groundwork* I. For example, he explains Kant's idea that to be good is to be the necessary object of a rational will. Goodness or value, then, is not a metaphysical property that is independent of rational choice and could ground it. Rather, what has value is determined by what it is necessarily rational to choose. Regarding Kant's claim that only acts from duty have moral worth, Johnson argues that this is the claim not that only such acts are praiseworthy or reliably lead to right action but rather that only such acts *express* a good will in action.

A few comments on the connection between Johnson's discussion of *Groundwork* I and the next set of chapters may be helpful here. Later chapters offer further discussion, and different perspectives, on some of the themes that Johnson addresses, notably the unqualified goodness of a good will (see especially Richard Dean's chapter) and the argument of *Groundwork* I (see especially Samuel Kerstein's chapter). As Johnson explains, the climax of *Groundwork* I is the "discovery" that persons with a good will are prepared to submit their policies and intentions to the test " 'Can you will that your maxim become a universal law?' If not, that maxim must be repudiated . . . because it cannot fit as a principle into a possible universal legislation" (G 4:403). This is essentially what Richard Galvin in the next chapter labels as "the principle of a good will" (PGW), otherwise expressed as "I ought never to act in such a way that I could not also will that my maxim should become a universal law (G 4:402)." As Galvin explains, this is more or less the same as the formula of universal law (FUL) that in *Groundwork* II Kant identifies as the basic principle inherent in the concept of duty (G 4:421). Kant offers several other "ways of presenting the principle of morality" that, he says, are "only so many formulations of precisely the same law" (G 4:436). These include the formula of the universal law of nature (FULN), a variation of FUL that Galvin discusses (G 4:222), the formula of humanity as an end in itself (FH or FHE) that Richard Dean discusses (G 4:429), and the formula of autonomy (FA) that Sarah Holtman discusses (G 4:431–2). As Holtman notes, Kant's discussion of a moral commonwealth, or "kingdom of ends," offers a principle that may be regarded either as a variation or as a new formula (FKE) (G 4:433–4).

Categorical and Hypothetical Imperatives

The context for all these discussions includes the distinction Kant makes early in *Groundwork* II between *categorical* and *hypothetical imperatives* (G 4:413–20). The various formulations of the supreme moral principle, after all, are supposed to be formulas of the Categorical Imperative. Also the arguments of *Groundwork* II and III rely on Kant's thesis that non-moral "ought" judgments purport to express hypothetical imperatives, whereas moral "ought" judgments purport to express categorical imperatives. Our volume does not include a separate chapter on this distinction, but some summary explanation may be helpful as background for later chapters.[1]

Rational beings are distinct in that they can act on the idea of laws or principles of reason even though they sometimes fail to do so (G 4:412). For such imperfectly rational persons as we human beings are, principles of reason take the form of *imperatives*. In other words, they say what is good to do, either as a means or in itself, but in words, such as "ought" and "must," that express the idea that for us rational principles "necessitate" our acting as they direct (G 4:413–14). That is, imperatives are "ought" judgments appropriately regarded as expressing rational *constraints* to which we are *subject*.

In everyday life we do not usually articulate our principles explicitly, but we take ourselves to be doing things for reasons. In explaining our reasons fully, Kant seems to assume, we would eventually need to appeal to a general principle of practical reason. This would be a principle that helps to makes sense of why certain particular facts count as good reasons for acting and other facts do not. As a philosopher, Kant was especially interested in articulating the most *fundamental* principles that explain why, given certain facts, a particular choice is rationally *necessary*. Ordinary judgments about what we rationally *must* do are of several kinds (G 4:416). Some express "rules of skill" that say what we must do in order to achieve an end we may happen to have. Others are "counsels of prudence" that indicate what (normally) we must do in order to be happy – or to approximate more closely our rather indeterminate ideal of lasting contentment and the satisfaction of all our desire-based ends (G 4:415–16). Examples of a rule of skill might be "If you aim to avoid bleeding gums, you ought to floss your teeth regularly" and "If you aim to get into medical school, you must study biochemistry." Counsels of prudence might be "For the sake of one's own happiness, one ought to avoid behavior that needlessly offends others" and "To be happy, you must stop and smell the roses."

Both rules of skill and counsels of prudence, Kant argues, express what is only conditionally rational to do. That is, they say what we what we must do as a means if and because we will to achieve (or to more closely approximate) a certain end, but leaving open the possibility that for good reasons we might give up that end or at least suspend our pursuit of it. The underlying principle seems to be something like "It is rationally necessary to take the necessary and available means within your power to achieve your ends – or else to give up those ends or at least temporarily suspend your pursuit of them." (This principle is sometimes referred to as "the Hypothetical Imperative" because it is the basis for specific hypothetical imperatives.) Since we can fail to live up even to this minimum requirement of rationality, we can express it in the language of constraining imperatives, using words such as "ought," "must," and so on.

Moral "ought" judgments, Kant argues, are not conditional in the ways hypothetical imperatives are. Particular moral judgments are based on unconditional or *categorical* imperatives, which are "commandments" of reason as opposed to mere rules of skill and counsels of prudence (G 4:416). Consider, for example, "You ought not to make false promises to borrow money you have no intention of repaying" (Kant's example) or "You should not kill or torture people for profit or amusement." These principles seem to express constraints that do not depend on whether your conforming to them will serve your particular ends or make you happy. Nevertheless, it is commonly supposed that there is good and sufficient reason to conform to these principles so that violating them would be unreasonable, if not irrational. But why? The general principle behind hypothetical imperatives ("the Hypothetical Imperative" mentioned earlier) does not support such unconditional requirements. There must be, Kant assumed, a different general principle of reason that we presuppose as the basis of all specific unconditional moral imperatives. This would be the only principle that is a categorical imperative in the strictest sense and so appropriately labeled "the Categorical Imperative." (Kant sometimes uses the plural "categorical imperatives" to refer to more specific non-optional imperatives that are based on the fundamental moral principle, the Categorical Imperative.)

This, in brief, is the background for Kant's discussion of the several formulas of the Categorical Imperative. As Kerstein explains, Kant has an argument in *Groundwork* I and II that there *can be only one* Categorical Imperative (in the strict sense) and that it is expressed in his formula of universal law and its equivalents. As Darwall explains, Kant later argues that it is *rationally necessary* for us to presuppose that moral imperatives are really supported by a valid Categorical Imperative. With this background in mind, let us turn now to Kant's several formulations of the Categorical Imperative.

The Universal Law Formulas

In *Groundwork* II Kant restates the supreme moral principle in several ways. Richard Galvin examines critically interpretations of two of these: the famous formula of universal law (FUL), *Act only on that maxim by which you can at the same time will that it should become universal law*, and a variation, the formula of the law of nature (FULN), *Act as though the maxim of your action were to become by your will a universal law of nature* (G 4:421). Kant offered four examples of how the latter might serve to guide moral deliberation, and many have tried to interpret and supplement his basic idea so that it can plausibly extend to other cases. Objections have prompted new interpretations, which in turn have generated further criticisms and defense. The result is a complex controversy that is hard to summarize and assess. Galvin takes up these difficult tasks, patiently distinguishing leading interpretations, noting recurring objections and misunderstandings, and offering critical commentary and a proposal.

There are many questions of interpretation here: What are *maxims*, and how general are they supposed to be? What is the difference, if any, between willing a maxim to be a *universal law* (in FUL) and willing it to be a *universal law of nature* (in FULN)? How are we to understand Kant's distinction between contradictions in *conceiving* a maxim as a universal law and in *willing* it as a universal law? Are the relevant inconsistencies logical or practical? What is the role of these formulas in Kant's moral theory? Are they, for example, meant to provide a comprehensive and independent decision guide for all cases? Are they supposed to show whether or not acts are objectively right or merely that we have deliberated properly on the basis of our perception of the facts?

Hegel raised objections that set much of the agenda for further discussion of the universal law formulas; he charged that they would condemn good actions and fail to condemn bad ones. Galvin painstakingly reviews many Kantian responses to these and other problems. The most persistent problems, he concludes, stem from the facts that maxims can be described in different ways, that the formulas apparently lead to conflicts of duty, and that independent standards are needed for what we can *rationally* will as a universal law. The formulas would be more plausible, he suggests, if they were understood as only a test for what is prima facie or defeasibly wrong.

The Formula of Humanity as an End in Itself

Kant's next formulation of the Categorical Imperative is this: *Act in such a way that you treat humanity, whether in your own person or in any other person, always at the same time as an end, never merely as a means* (FHE) (G 4:429). In his chapter Richard Dean begins by examining different interpretations of "humanity." Because Kant equates *humanity* in this context with "rational nature," Dean infers that Kant's principle would not include human beings in a permanent vegetative state as ends in themselves. It would, however, include non-human rational beings if there are any. A crucial question is how to interpret "rational nature." Dean argues on textual grounds that this is not the same as economic rationality, or a mere capacity to set ends, or even the capacity for morality. Rather, it is "the entire rational nature of a being, but only on the condition that the being is committed to accepting the force of moral demands." This interpretation, he argues, makes the most sense of Kant's *arguments* for the humanity formula, of Kant's use of humanity as an *ideal* to strive for, and of Kant's treating respect for persons as fundamentally the same as respect for the moral law.

Two especially important, though controversial, features of Dean's chapter are his explanation of Kant's conception of value and his analysis of Kant's arguments for the humanity formula. Value in Kant's theory, as he explains, is the object of rational willing. As Johnson also argues, this means that intrinsic value or goodness is not an independently discernable metaphysical property that could ground ultimate claims about rational willing. Kant's arguments for the humanity formula as a rational requirement, like the rest of *Groundwork* II, presuppose the common understanding of moral duties as rational requirements, a presupposition that Kant does not defend until *Groundwork* III. The texts are often cryptic and puzzling, but the best reconstruction, Dean argues, does not derive the humanity formula from a metaphysical claim about the value of persons independent of the common moral understanding that Kant tries to analyze in *Groundwork* II.

In his final sections Dean draws out some practical implications of his interpretation of the humanity formula and responds to an apparent objection. If only those with a good will are ends in themselves, one might suppose that we may do as we please with people that we think are immoral. As Dean explains, there are several reasons why this does not follow.

Autonomy and the Kingdom of Ends

Kant argues that to make sense of morality we must assume that autonomy (or freedom in a positive sense) is a property of the will of all rational beings. It is, he says, the will's "property of being a law to itself," and the error of all previous moral theorists was to fail to understand this crucial point (G 4:440–2). At the end of *Groundwork* II he declares in bold letters that autonomy is "the supreme principle of morality," but initially he presents the idea in a new formulation of the Categorical Imperative that he says follows from the previous two (FUL and FHE) (G 4:431–2; 440). Put into imperative form, this formula of autonomy (FA) apparently would say, *Always act in harmony with "the Idea of the will of every rational being as a will that legislates universal law"* (G 4:431). Instead of discussing examples, as he did for previous formulas, Kant models the idea of autonomy by describing an ideal commonwealth or *kingdom of ends* (G 4:433–4). This he describes as a community of rational autonomous agents, who are authors of their common moral laws and subject to them.

Sarah Holtman's chapter aims to explain the main ideas here and why they are important. She comments on the idea of autonomy, the relation of the formula of autonomy to the previous formulas, the elements and structure of a kingdom of ends, and Kant's distinction between two kinds of value, *dignity* and *price*. She then addresses several sources of worry about these ideas. For example, how can we understand the claim that moral laws bind us only because we give them to ourselves? Can we make sense of Kant's idea that practical reason guides moral decisions? These claims become less puzzling, Holtman suggests, if we try to understand the formula of autonomy through the associated idea of rational legislators in a kingdom of ends. We give ourselves moral laws, in a sense, by adopting an "attitude of autonomy," which is a readiness to rein in self-interest and adopt principles suitable for a community of beings with the capacity for morality.

By using the kingdom of ends as a way of interpreting the formula of autonomy, this formula can be seen to have action-guiding as well as metaethical implications. The ideal of legislating for a moral commonwealth has been developed or extended in different ways, and arguably it at least affirms "the importance of insuring that certain fundamental interests, pre-requisite to realizing and maintaining rational capacities, are protected in each agent." Particular applications, however, may inevitably rely on some contingent facts and values that are not strictly a part of Kant's basic moral theory.

In her final section Holtman sketches some implications of Kantian autonomy. For example, it gives us a conception of morality broadly construed that shows why slavery is wrong even apart from the physical and psychological consequences for its victims. She also explores further implications regarding national and global citizenship, for example, cosmopolitan rights and Kant's "definitive articles" towards perpetual peace.

Deriving the Supreme Moral Principle from Common Moral Ideas

The next two chapters are devoted to Kant's defense of his central claims about the formula of universal law: that *it is the only possible supreme moral principle* and that *we are rationally bound to follow it*. The chapter by Samuel Kerstein takes up Kant's defense of the first claim. More specifically, it reconstructs and discusses critically Kant's argument that, if there is a supreme principle of morality, the formula of universal law is the one and only principle that expresses its content. This argument or "derivation" is supposed to show that the universal law formula, and no other non-equivalent principle, meets Kant's criteria for being a supreme moral principle.

These criteria are supposed to be inherent in common moral thought. Kerstein argues that three criteria are implicit in the three main propositions in *Groundwork* I. These criteria are that a supreme moral principle must be "practical, absolutely necessary, [and] binding on all rational agents." The argument, however, requires a further criterion, which Kerstein identifies as the requirement that a supreme moral principle "would serve as the supreme norm for the moral evaluation of action." Examining Kant's derivation critically, Kerstein finds that it establishes less than Kant had hoped but more than critics generally concede.

Kerstein's reconstruction of Kant's derivation is important because it takes seriously Kant's attempt to justify his strong claim that he has found and articulated the only principle that could be the supreme principle of morality. Previous commentators have tended to dismiss Kant's derivation as fallacious, obscure, or woefully incomplete. Drawing from a fuller discussion in his book, *Kant's Search for the Supreme Moral Principle*, Kerstein fills in apparent gaps in Kant's explicit argument in a way that promises to make Kant's texts more comprehensible and his argument more interesting.

For a somewhat different approach to Kant's argument in *Groundwork* I, see Robert Johnson's chapter in this volume.

Why Kant Needs the Second-Person Perspective

Kant argues not only that the moral law is implicit in ordinary moral ideas but also that it is a necessary principle of practical reason. In the preceding chapter, Kerstein reviewed Kant's argument for the first, weaker thesis in *Groundwork* I and II. Kant argues for the second, stronger thesis in *Groundwork* III. Later, in his *Critique of Practical Reason*, he apparently abandons that argument, but still maintains that consciousness of the moral law is "a fact of reason." Stephen Darwall analyzes critically Kant's argument for the second thesis, concluding that it is insightful but ultimately unsuccessful. Several contemporary philosophers have proposed reconstructions of the *Groundwork* III argument that re-affirm its basic thesis that the rationality of the moral law is a necessary condition for the possibility of acting for reasons. Again, Darwall argues that the arguments fail, and he proposes a diagnosis of the problem and a solution.

The problem, according to Darwall, is that merely acting for reasons does not commit a person to the moral law or equal dignity. I can deliberate from a first-person perspective about what *I* ought to do without assuming that rational nature is an end in itself. In deliberating we must assume that we are free in some sense but not that we have autonomy of the will in Kant's sense. Darwall grants that even rational egoists must assume there is a rationally binding practical law, but he argues that they need not assume that this is a law of morality as we understand this.

The source of the problem, in Darwall's view, is that moral obligation has an essentially interpersonal or *second-person* aspect that is not necessarily assumed in all deliberation. The solution, Darwall suggests, is to see this second-person perspective as committing us to the moral law and equal dignity. Although taking this perspective and acknowledging second-person reasons is not a necessary feature of all deliberation, he maintains that it is an essential aspect of full engagement with others in practical reasoning.

The preceding chapters have focused primarily on themes from Kant's *Groundwork for the Metaphysics of Morals* and (to a lesser extent) from his *Critique of Practical Reason*. In these works Kant presents and defends his idea of the supreme moral principle and its relation to autonomy of the will and practical reason. He followed these foundational works with a "metaphysics of morals," or, in other words, a systematic presentation of more specific principles of (non-instrumental) practical reason regarding different areas of concern. Part I of *The Metaphysics of Morals* presents and applies principles regarding justice, law, and enforceable obligations in general (matters of "right"), and Part II develops a set of principles about obligatory moral ends and duties to oneself (matters of virtue and "ethics" in a narrow sense). The remaining chapters in this volume are primarily focused on these topics in this later work, *The Metaphysics of Morals*. The next three chapters focus on Part I: law, property, and political authority (Arthur Ripstein), punishment (Nelson Potter), and international justice (Thomas Pogge). These are followed by two chapters on themes from Part II: beneficence, gratitude, and self-perfection (Marcia Baron and Melisa Seymour) and duties to oneself and duties of respect for others (Allen Wood). In the final chapter Arnulf Zweig offers reflections on what is of lasting value in Kant's moral philosophy.

Kant on Law and Justice

Arthur Ripstein offers an interpretation of Kant's theory of "right" as sharply distinct from his theory of "ethical" duties. The former concerns "rightfully" enforceable relations of private property and public law, whereas the latter concerns ethical maxims that as individuals we should adopt and conscientiously follow. The theory of right concerns "external" freedom as a kind of independence rather than autonomy as the "inner" capacity to govern oneself by moral principles. Ripstein explains the basic principle of right as *independence* such that in a fully rightful condition no person would be subject to the will of another. Coercion by the state and other individuals can be justified, and so we are obviously not "free" to do as we please. Nevertheless, in a rightful condition enforced by legitimate state power everyone would be free from the *arbitrary* will of others. Ripstein's chapter is an attempt to explain how this is possible and what it implies about law and political authority.

The chapter traces Kant's development of this idea of independence in several stages. It begins with the innate right to humanity in one's own person, and then extends to rights over things, between persons, and (in a sense) *to* persons. These are entitlements of Private Right corresponding to the traditional categories of property, contract, and status. The right of humanity is innate in the sense that it does not need to be established by any public or private act. It is an equal right to one's own person and reputation but extended through a "postulate" to justify (provisional) property rights even in a state of nature. The basic presupposition behind the right to acquire property is that it must be possible that usable things can be rightfully used. Ripstein also explains the nature and limits of contractual rights and status rights (regarding family relations, for example) as ultimately based on the idea of equal independence.

Public Right is required for complete independence and equality because of the possibility of disputes about matters of private right. Unlike Hobbes and Locke, Kant does not rest the legitimacy of state coercion on empirical claims about the brutality or inconveniences of a state of nature. Rather, for persons to be related to each other in a fully rightful condition it is *a priori* necessary that there be an authoritative process for making provisional rights determinate and for adjudicating disputes. Ripstein attempts to show how Kant develops these basic ideas to explain the ground and limits of legitimate state authority and the need for separation of legislative, executive, and judicial powers. He analyzes Kant's arguments against revolution, arguing that they do not entail that it is wrong to resist or even rebel against rogue regimes such as the Nazis. Ripstein also offers an explanation of why Kant thought that "inequalities of wealth and power are consistent with the innate equality of all persons" and that the state's duty to help the poor is grounded in principles of right, rather than personal charity or utilitarian concern for the general happiness.

Kant on Punishment

Why should we have criminal law? What gives the state the authority to punish? What principles should determine the kind, amount, and limits of punishment? Focusing on these questions, Nelson Potter reviews the long-standing dispute between retributive and teleological views of punishment and then argues that Kant, despite his reputation as the arch-retributivist, combines elements of both. Potter argues that, nevertheless, Kant's theory of punishment is not inconsistent or at odds with his basic moral theory. Criminal law uses punishment to deter potential violations, but the nature and kind of punishment is determined by the *lex talionis* – roughly, the return to the criminals of the deprivation or harm that they unlawfully imposed on others. As Potter puts it, "[t]he teleological result of criminal deterrence is a sort of side-effect of imposing such punishments, though it is an indispensable such effect, because it provides the incentive for obeying the law that is necessary for its functioning as a law" (p. 7).

Kant was aware of objections to his retributive principle (*lex talionis*) and qualified his position to meet some of them – for example, we cannot use punishments that degrade humanity. Also the principle cannot be applied strictly to rape, fraud, and sex with children. And as Potter explains, Kant was aware of how distinctions of social class can be relevant in determining what specific punishments are appropriate. Small fines mean less to the rich than to the poor.

In the final section Potter examines critically Kant's strong endorsement of capital punishment for murder and treason. Various factors, Potter argues, qualify Kant's apparently inflexible position and make it more understandable, even if it is ultimately unacceptable. His emphasis on respect for persons – both the criminal and victim – has inspired contemporary writers. As Potter explains, it even suggests a possible Kantian argument against capital punishment of the sort presented by Supreme Court Justice William Brennan.

Kant's Vision of a Just World Order

Kant was also deeply concerned with justice beyond the borders of the state, in questions about cosmopolitan rights and relations among states, especially regarding war and peace. Should we aim for an international order modeled on the juridical state with its strict requirements for clarity of laws, authoritative interpretations, effective enforcement, and absolute sovereignty? Is a federation of nations the ideal or only a second best, endorsed for strategic reasons? Thomas Pogge examines Kant's treatment of these subjects with a close attention to the relevant texts and critical eye for contemporary implications.

He first explains Kant's strict requirements for a juridical condition and how they seem to require a world government. In an ideal juridical condition each person's rights are fully determinate, clear, and secure under a sovereign authority that is subject to no higher authority. Kant argues that in a state of nature everyone would have a duty to leave the state of nature to create a juridical condition, coercing others to join if necessary. The ideal is rule of law within a strictly governed nation state, in which the rights of its citizens are well defined and enforced within its borders. The problem, Kant realized, is that no one's rights are fully determinate or secure in a world where different "sovereign" states dispute among themselves and even threaten war. The solution, it seems, would be to establish one world government with ultimate authority over all local governments, but Kant argued instead for a voluntary federation of sovereign nation states. Scholars have been puzzled by the tension in Kant's writings on this issue. Reviewing the ambivalent texts, Pogge argues that Kant's ideal was in fact a sovereign world government but that he endorsed a looser federation of states as a necessary first step.

Pogge argues further that, although arguably it was Kant's ideal, satisfaction of Kant's strict binary criteria for a juridical condition is impossible at the international level. Nevertheless, as the historical examples of the European Union and the federal system of the United States illustrate, absolute sovereignty and determinate authoritative resolution of *all* legal controversies is an unnecessary and unwarranted standard. These examples show that "a high degree of juridicality" is compatible with limited authority and "vertical" (federal) separation of powers. Some passages suggest that Kant was partly aware of this, despite his strict criteria for a juridical condition. Pogge concludes, "Kant at least caught a glimpse of the kind of multi-layered political structure that is emerging in the European Union and that, if globalized, may well be the best chance for achieving what Kant so ardently sought: lasting peace for humankind."

Beneficence and Other Duties of Love

The demands of law and justice are enforceable and do not require morally worthy motives, but the duties of virtue are ethical requirements for adopting and pursuing moral ends. The chapter by Marcia Baron and Melissa Seymour addresses a major set of these ethical duties: beneficence, gratitude, and sympathetic feeling. It explains how ethical duties differ from juridical duties and why the obligatory ends are the perfection of oneself and the happiness of others. They show how Kant opposed paternalism in at least two ways – arguing that, in dealing with adults, it is not our business to try to make them virtuous and we should not impose our conception of happiness on them. Regarding the duty of beneficence, the authors point out ways in which Kant was more sensitive than commonly thought to the importance of our attitude, manner, and tone in trying to help others. For example, we must guard against making others feel obligated to us and, if wealthy, we should see aid to the very needy as more like a requirement of justice than as meritorious charity.

Baron and Seymour also take up a persistent controversy about how much latitude Kant's duty of beneficence allows. Reviewing many relevant texts closely, they favor with qualifications a rigoristic interpretation that permits latitude of several kinds in choosing how to promote others' happiness but does not allow us to refuse to help others so that we can do just what we please. The duty is not restricted to helping those in dire need but extends broadly to assisting others with personal projects.

Turning to other duties of love, the chapter explains Kant's striking ideas about the duty of gratitude and sympathetic feeling. The duty of gratitude, it seems, can never fully be discharged, and neither duty (of love and gratitude) is accompanied by a moral requirement to have appropriate feelings. Feelings cannot be acquired at will, and our moral duty, strictly speaking, is to choose acts and policies of the right kind. Sympathetic feelings, however, ought to be cultivated and used in our efforts to help others. Baron and Seymour conclude that Kant's treatment of duties of love, including the cultivation of morally useful feelings, shows that Kant did not think that rationality is the only morally important aspect of persons.

Duties to Oneself and Duties of Respect to Others

In the next chapter, Allen Wood examines Kant's account of duties to oneself and duties of respect to others. These include three of the four main categories of ethical (as opposed to juridical) duties that Kant discusses in *The Metaphysics of Morals*: duties to oneself, perfect and imperfect, and duties to others, respect and love. Wood orients Kant's discussion of specific duties within Kant's moral theory by first explaining how Kant distinguishes different types of duty and then how these duties are grounded in the Categorical Imperative to treat humanity in each person as an end in itself. Drawing from his fuller discussion in *Kant's Ethical Thought* (Cambridge University Press, 1999), Wood argues that the formal requirement expressed in Kant's formula of universal law is inadequate to ground and guide judgments about specific duties. For Kant, especially in *The Metaphysics of Morals*, the idea of humanity as an end in itself provides the "matter" or substantive value that, together with the fundamental formula of autonomy, is the ultimate basis of our duties to ourselves and duties of respect to others. To respect humanity we must adopt obligatory ends – our own perfection and the happiness of others. Our actions respect humanity insofar as they respond appropriately to the objective, unconditional value of humanity, and the appropriate response essentially depends on what our actions *express* rather than on what results they *produce*.

As Wood explains, *The Metaphysics of Morals* does not try to cover all ethical duties but only those "that are generated by applying the principle of morality to human nature in general." Special circumstances, including variable relations and institutions, affect our particular obligations, though these are constrained by universal moral principles. Also the particular content of our imperfect duties is to some extent up to us because the obligatory ends may be pursued in different ways and each path we choose may involve different obligations.

Wood addresses the apparent paradox in the idea of a duty to oneself. Kant's solution is that as an intelligible person one imposes obligations on oneself as a sensible person.[2] In Wood's view, however, this does not imply "the metaethical thesis that it is *we humans* who 'construct' the moral law or 'confer value' on things through our choices." Turning to specific duties to oneself, he reviews perfect duties arising from our animal nature (regarding suicide, 'unnatural' sexuality, gluttony, and drunkenness), then perfect duties regarding our moral nature (opposed to lying, avarice, and servility), and finally conscience as the fundamental duty to oneself. The role of conscience is not punishment for misdeeds but self-scrutiny ("know thyself") to improve one's attitudes and conduct. Next Wood reviews Kant's discussion of the mistake of taking duties to oneself to be duties to God, nature, or non-human animals. The final section concerns Kant's treatment of the duties of respect to others (and the contrary vices of arrogance, defamation, and ridicule). Throughout, the chapter tries to show how these (rather) specific duties follow from a proper respect for humanity as an end.

The Enduring Value of Kant's Ethics

In the final chapter Arnulf Zweig shares some reflections on what is of lasting value in Kant's writings on ethics. As translator of Kant's correspondence as well as a scholar, editor, and teacher of Kant's works, Zweig is well aware of Kant's brilliance and depth but also his humanity and limitations. He emphasizes that Kant's writings are diverse, inter-connected, and difficult to interpret. From the extreme diversity of interpretations, it even seems "there are many Kants." Acknowledging that it is "too early" to be sure which aspects of Kant's work, if any, will in fact continue to be influential, Zweig offers us some personal thoughts about which aspects *deserve* to be influential – and which do not.

For example, he admires Kant as a "critic of irrationalism, mysticism, and sanctimonious religiosity" and as a "defender of human rights, cosmopolitanism and political liberalism." In particular Zweig cites Kant's "diagnoses of the evils of colonialism," his proposal for a federation of nations to promote peace, and his idea that human beings have an irreplaceable value at odds with unconstrained cost/benefit thinking. On the positive side, too, Kant condemned "fantastic" devotion to virtue, which leads one to quibble over trivia, and moral "enthusiasm," which makes us sentimental about heroic deeds but leads us to ignore ordinary responsibilities. Zweig also notes that Kant's *application* of moral principles "shows a surprising degree of flexibility and pragmatism." Although Kant seems excessively confident on many points, he recognizes limitations of human knowledge that rule out knowing by divine revelation or intuitive insight into God's intentions.

Zweig also points to ways in which Kant was a "child of his times and background." For example, he had parochial attitudes about the wrongness of suicide and "unnatural" sexual practices, and, though he acknowledged human frailty, he allowed for very few excuses and none for hardships in a person's upbringing. His moral outlook is tough and stoical, and his veneration of duty can appear puritanical. Zweig finds that Kant's unwavering confidence in practical reason, autonomy, and universal principles is hard to sustain in our world today. Even so, Zweig expresses a cautious hope that Kant's ideals of critical thinking, human dignity, and equality may endure to inspire at least some in later generations to continue the fight against the evils of violence and exploitation.

Notes

1 Fuller interpretations of the distinction (and references) can be found, for example, in Thomas E. Hill, Jr. and Arnulf Zweig, *Groundwork for the Metaphysics of Morals* (Oxford: Oxford University Press, 2002), 51–65, and Mark Timmons, "Necessitation and Justification in Kant's Ethics," *Canadian Journal of Philosophy* (1992):223–61.

2 Kant's distinction between "intelligible" and "sensible" relies on controversial ideas that he develops in his *Critique of Pure Reason* (1781–7). In thinking of persons as "intelligible" we think of them through "Ideas" of reason, and in thinking of persons as "sensible" we conceive of them by means of empirical concepts. By contrast with what is sensible or "phenomenal," what is intelligible is "noumenal" and cannot be understood in ordinary spatial, temporal, and causal terms.

Part I
Basic Themes

1

Good Will and the Moral Worth of Acting from Duty

Robert N. Johnson

The first section of the *Groundwork* begins "It is impossible to imagine anything at all in the world, or even beyond it, that can be called good without qualification – except a *good will*" (G 4:393). Kant's explanation and defense of this claim is followed by an explanation and defense of another related claim, that only actions performed out of duty have moral worth. He explains that actions performed out of duty are those done from respect for the moral law, and then culminates the first section with a formulation of that law, "*I ought never to act except in such a way that I could also will that my maxim should become a universal law*". Kant dubs this fundamental principle of morality "the Categorical Imperative".

What does Kant mean by a "good will" and what is the meaning and significance of his claim that it is "good without qualification"? And how plausible is the position that only such a will possesses that sort of value? What is "acting out of duty alone" and what is the meaning and significance of the claim that this possesses "moral worth"? And how plausible is Kant's position that only acting out of duty alone possesses moral worth? Finally, what do these positions and arguments have to do with the stated aim of the *Groundwork*, to articulate and defend the fundamental principle of morality, the Categorical Imperative?

In what follows, I try to answer these questions. My answers will require me to take detours through moral psychology and metaphysics as well as to draw on theories of symbolic expression. My hope is that these efforts will produce a unified overall picture of the main point and purpose of Kant's discussion of the good will and the moral worth of acting from duty. My plan is this: In the first section, I discuss some initial puzzling claims that Kant makes about the unique value of a good will. I then turn to more basic topics. In section 2 I briefly discuss Kant's views on the nature of the will, and in section 3 I discuss his views concerning the principles according to which the will operates. In section 4 I take up Kant's general theory of value and in section 5, the more specific conceptions of unqualified and intrinsic value. I am then ready, in sections 6 and 7, to turn from the topic of the good will to the moral worth of acting from duty. I address successively two questions here, What is moral worth? and What is acting from duty? In these sections, I speculate about what role these topics have in the *Groundwork's* stated goal, uncovering and defending the fundamental principle of morality. Explaining the role of these topics leads me in section 8 to think about how actions "express" or "exemplify" the principles that motivate them. I end with a summary of how, given all of the above, the structure of the argument should be understood.

1. The Good Will

As a first approximation, to have a "good will" is in some sense to have a strong commitment to behaving morally. So Kant's claim that a good will alone has unqualified goodness amounts to the claim that only having such a commitment is of unqualified value. He appears to hold that having this strong commitment to behaving morally is what we ordinarily think of as being a morally good person (G 4:402). However, his position has some surprising consequences. For instance, Kant also holds that having a good will – indeed, having "the best will" – is compatible with lacking moral virtue (virtue, as he conceives of it, is the moral strength of will to overcome desires running contrary to what one ought to do) (MM 6:390, 408). So if possessing a good will is what makes one a morally good person, then it seems that Kant embraces the surprising position that one can be morally good, that one's will can possess "unqualified value", and yet lack moral virtue. Qualities such as courage and kindness play no part in giving our wills unqualified value and so no part in making us morally good persons. Further, Kant lists other qualities many associate with being a good person, qualities such as "moderation in affects and passions, self-control and calm reflection", and declares these and like qualities are "conducive to this good will itself" and that they "can make its work much easier" (G 4:393–4). These declarations, however, imply that the possession of a good will can survive their absence (though making its "work" more difficult). Indeed, Kant claims that a good will, because of the weakness of the character in which it is housed, might be utterly unable and unsuited to carry out any of its noble goals, goals such as fostering the wellbeing of those around her and improving herself and her own character (G 4:394). Nevertheless, and again surprisingly, the person possessed of such a will would be a morally good person.

Indeed, a person could apparently lack a good will yet possess the whole panoply of desirable qualities one might naturally associate with being a good person, qualities such as kindness, compassion, courage, moderation, strength of will and so on – the very qualities that Kant himself thinks make one able and suited to pursue the very goals that would be adopted by a good will. Since those are the very qualities of character and temperament that allow one to achieve these noble goals, it is even conceivable that someone might have all of these desirable qualities *and* achieve all of the noble goals a good will *would* have, yet *still lack a good will* and hence *still fail to be a morally good person*.[1] To be sure, Kant thinks that possessing such qualities and achieving such goals are good things. But Kant asserts that while we might have a favorable view of a being with such qualities, our esteem would be constrained by her lack of a good will (G 4:394). On the assumption that Kant thinks a good will is the lone source of a person's moral goodness, at least to many contemporary readers this is astonishing, since a person with such admirable character traits would strike many as being morally good *just because* she possesses those traits. But according to Kant, those traits apparently have nothing to do with whether she is a morally good person.

All in all, these considerations show that, whatever it is that Kant is thinking of as a good will, it is neither necessary nor sufficient for possessing any other qualities of character that one might reasonably have assumed are intimately connected to moral goodness. But if Kant's views are so far surprising, then it will be even more surprising to learn that Kant believes ordinary folk agree with him. He insists that the views he discusses in the initial pages of the *Groundwork* are nothing but data form from "ordinary moral consciousness", views any reasonable adult would agree with and recognize as reflecting her own views. No doubt, this position may be more plausible with regard to features such as intelligence, creativity or wit. Possession of these is surely ordinarily thought of as being neither sufficient nor necessary for moral goodness, nor are they thought of as having the special, unique value many of us think being a good person has. But it is much harder to believe that we ordinarily think that the traits of being strong-willed, compassionate, courageous, or thoughtful are not important parts of what makes someone a morally good person. We need to know, then, what exactly this good will is, given it does not require possessing the virtues or other desirable character traits, and then to evaluate whether his claim is at all plausible, as a view from ordinary moral consciousness or otherwise. That, in turn, requires us first to understand what it is to possess a will at all. And it is to this topic to which I will now turn.

2. The Will

Unlike events that operate according to natural laws, "only a rational being has the capacity to act *in accordance with the representation of laws*" (G 4:412). By this, Kant means the will is the capacity to choose to act on the basis of policies, plans, or (as Kant himself says) practical principles. Since reason is required to choose on the basis of such representations, such a will belongs only to a "rational being", such as ourselves (G 4:412). The capacity to act on the basis of some plan is different from the capacity simply to choose to act, which Kant thinks that animals also have.[2] Animals, for instance, do not choose to act on the basis of policies they come up with or because they have reasoned strategies behind their choices (MM 6:213–4). Their choices respond directly to their desires, and these responses, along with the operation of their desires, should in turn be wholly explicable by natural laws: their choices "work in accordance with laws." Human choices, as Kant sees it, never respond to desires in a way that are wholly explained by natural laws, though our desires do affect the formation and execution of the plans that guide our choices. This distinguishes the human will from a holy will, if there were such a thing. A holy will would make its choices on the bases of policies, as does the human will. However, it would lack any desires that could alter the formation and execution of policies that are rational to follow. Thus, a holy will would *necessarily* make rational choices, lacking as it does any basis for straying from such choices. The human will is thus different from both the non-rational power animals have to make choices directed immediately by desires, and the power a holy will would possess that would be necessarily rational. It is a power to act through choices on the basis of reasons *while affected, but not determined,* by non-rational desires.

Kant sometimes suggests (or at least many have read him this way) that his claim that our wills operate unlike everything else in nature is primarily a meta-physical claim, the claim that the will stands outside of the natural world but nev-ertheless affects it. In Kant's overall theory, there is a world insofar as it is an object of possible experience, and there is a world as it is "in itself", apart from its being an object of possible experience. And as with everything else that is observable, there is a way that the will is in itself, apart from how it appears to us in our observations of the actions agents (including our own actions). The puzzling sug-gestion is that this will as it is in itself nevertheless bears some sort of unique rela-tionship to the operations of the observable world, a relationship that will enable us to attribute observable events to the unobservable will as it is, in itself. If this is Kant's position, it is certainly difficult to make sense of, much less accept. It is difficult to even imagine a relationship between observable events in space and time – the operations of an observable act of choice and action – and something that does not exist in space and time and cannot characterized as being an "event" or an "operation."

However, suppose we were to reject Kant's metaphysical claims. It does not follow that we must reject the entirety of his views concerning the uniqueness of a rational will. One critical aspect of those views is that, as rational beings, we are related to the world in two distinct ways, as observers of the world as well as agents who change the world. We are beings who must think about not only what there is in the world and our place in it, but also about what to do with, to, or about that world. And discovering everything there is to discover about the world and our place in it will not answer the question how we are to change it. There is nothing that faces this question except a rational being with a will, and that makes it unique. We choose what to do guided by principles about what we ought to choose, not simply by what natural laws say we do or will choose. Kant describes this situation as our possessing wills that are not bound by natural laws. But we need not believe that we really *are* such a being to justifiably reason about how to affect events around us. At any rate, in attributing unqualified value to the good will, I assume that we are *not* attributing an extraordinary property to an unknow-able capacity that operates only in an unseen, non-natural world. The entire dis-cussion of the good will and its value – as well as the moral worth of actions from duty – is simply addressed to those facing the question of what to do, rational agents.

Kant does not make it clear in his discussion whether a good will is contained in a single choice, whether it consists of a collection of choices over time, or in a disposition to make choices of a certain kind. If he is talking about a single choice, he would be claiming that the only things with moral value are certain particular choices human beings make at particular times. But it is hard to believe that he thinks these isolated events are of such momentous value. It is hard to believe because it might be a fluke that a person makes a given choice for a given reason. Although we cannot rule out that this is what he is talking about, it would be more plausible to suppose he is talking about the collection of choices a person makes over some sufficiently long period of time. When we think of whether a given person has a good will, it seems as if we should be thinking about a whole set of choices, not just one, even if her good will is revealed in each choice. Yet even a set of choices is not the deepest fact about a person's agency. You may not really know the nature of a person's will even though you know what they have chosen and why over a long period of time. After all, she may not have faced any difficult circumstances during that stretch of time. So it seems to me that Kant most likely is talking about a *disposition* to make choices of a certain kind, a disposition to act on certain policies and not others, to pursue certain kinds of goals and not others, and so on. By "disposition" I mean whatever feature it is of a person that makes it true that, if she were in a range of circumstances, she would choose what to do on the basis of a certain sort of reason. Thus, even if she never had actually faced difficult circumstances, for instance, it would still be true of her that had she faced such circumstances she would have made her choices on the basis of the right principles. A good will is thus the disposition to choose courses of action on the basis of certain sorts of policies. This is most likely the thing that Kant believes has such dramatic value.

Kant is aware, however, that his readers could easily misunderstand his claim that this disposition is without qualification good. So early on he points out that he does *not* mean that human beings are necessarily better off for having this distinctive capacity. Indeed, he thinks we would be better off if nature had implanted in us instead an instinct to pursue our own happiness (G 4:395–6). Looking at human history, it may seem hard to argue with him. In any case, Kant argues that those who might think that the will has a natural purpose, and that this purpose is to make us happy, will have difficulty explaining why we would likely have been better off guided by an instinct whose purpose is to insure our happiness. Whatever the natural purpose of a will might be, it ought to be something the will seems reasonably well designed to produce, and it does not seem so well designed to produce our own happiness, indeed especially given that reason seems so often to counsel us *against* proposed ways of pursuing our happiness.

3. Principles, laws and maxims

I use terms such as "policies" or "plans" when talking about what Kant thinks directs human practical deliberation and choices. I use such terms because I believe they best connect Kant's concerns with our own way of thinking about moral psychology. But it is worth noting that Kant himself envisaged the nature of practical reason as quite complex. Kant distinguishes two sorts of practical principles. Kant dubs principles insofar as they are valid for some person or finite set of persons *subjective* practical principles or *maxims*. Principles that are valid for *every* rational agent he terms *objective* practical principles, or *laws*. We can understand this distinction in terms of plans: Plans to perform actions insofar as they happen to be my, your or some finite set of persons plans are one sort of plan. My plan to go to dinner and a movie tonight is this sort of plan. Plans that are valid for every rational agent are a different sort of plan. Every rational agent, for instance, plans to take the necessary and available means to her goals. We could say that the latter is in this sense an *objective* plan while the former is a *subjective* plan.

For instance, my plan to return a wallet to its owner might be oriented around my desire for a reward. Spelled out as a practical principle or maxim, that would be something such as "I return property when it will likely benefit me." It is the sort of thing a minimally rational agent might well say about returning a wallet, when truthful, articulate and self-aware, in response to a request for an explanation or justification of her action. This would obviously be a plan many other persons would have as well. But it is not a plan that everyone sees as something they have to adopt and act on insofar as they are rational. Some find a plan to be courteous more compelling, others plan to be honorable; neither need have any interest in a reward. Indeed, for the wealthy, a reward will likely not figure in any plans to return a wallet.

Now, contrast the above plans with the plan to return property to its owner (assuming an ordinary context where the person is not a fugitive from the law or some such thing). This would be a plan that is valid for anyone, to return a wallet to its owner, or at least Kant would argue, *even for those who have no interest that would be served by returning property to owners*. If it is a valid plan for anyone to return a wallet – that is, if there are any plans that apply to any rational agent in the circumstances – then we could say it is an objective plan. In the language of principles, we would say that the principle of returning things to their owners, which applies to anyone, is a *practical law*, while the principle "I do whatever will bring a reward," which applies to some, is only a maxim.

Sometimes, the policy some person is acting on in some circumstance could also be *anyone's* policy, as it would have been had my policy been to return property to its owner. In that case, I would have made my choice on the basis of what Kant refers to as a practical law, or at least my policy *could* be such a law.[3] Since the will in human beings is the power to choose on the basis of principles, to say that a will is *good* is to say that a disposition to exercise this power of choosing in a certain way is good. It is a disposition to adopt and act on the right sorts of policies. And the right sorts for Kant are or could be practical laws, policies that could or would be those of any rational agent. We shall return to these considerations when we take up the topic of actions from duty.

A *good* will, then, is a disposition to choose that is good because it is based on a principle that is or could serve as a principle for anyone. In order to determine the nature of the principles of a good will, we will need to understand better the nature of the extraordinary value that Kant is attributing to the good will. Kant begins the *Groundwork* by discussing the peculiar nature of the value of a good will in order to help us to locate what it is about the good will that is the source of this unique value. Thus, by understanding the nature of this value, we may be able to locate the nature of the principle that makes a good will good.

4. Kant's Conception of "Good"

Before I discuss the claim that a good will is unqualifiedly and intrinsically good, I need to explain Kant's conception of what goodness itself is. It will be of little use to try to understand what "qualified", "unqualified", "intrinsic" and "extrinsic" goodness are without first understanding what this property "goodness" is that these adjectives modify. In the *Groundwork* early on Kant appears to connect value with ideal approval. Happiness cannot be good without qualification because "an impartial rational spectator can take no delight in seeing the uninterrupted prosperity of a being graced with no feature of a pure and good will" (G 4:393). The idea would be that a thing is good if and only if an impartial rational spectator takes delight in it. But it is certainly not obvious that this is the analysis of goodness he is offering, especially since he does not explicitly offer it as an analysis. It could just be that good things are things in which impartial rational spectators take delight, but that is not what makes them good.

Later on, he does make substantive claims about value that look like a proffered analysis. For instance, he states that

> practical good . . . is that which determines the will by means of representations of reason, hence not by subjective causes but objectively, that is, from grounds that are valid for every rational being as such. It is distinguished from the *agreeable*, as that which influences the will only by means of feeling from merely subjective causes, which hold only for the sense of this or that one, and not as a principle of reason, which holds for everyone. (G 4:414)

Although one could read this as offering an analysis of the property of goodness itself, as I will explain in a moment, I believe Kant is speaking here, not of the property of goodness, but of the properties of the things that possess goodness, that is, the properties in virtue of which, or because of which, a given thing is good.[4] A good route to the airport, for instance, is a route that, other things equal, has the property of being quicker than other routes. It is in virtue of the property of being a quick route that the route is a good one. A good material for flooring is one that, other things equal, has the property of being durable. It is in virtue of the property of being durable that a flooring material is good. If, as I think, Kant is in this passage talking about such properties, then he is saying that the properties of something that make it good are those properties that determine the will by means of representations of reason.

By "representations of reason", Kant is referring to practical principles. Hence, the properties of something that make it good are, in his view, those properties that determine the will by means of being incorporated into practical principles. For instance, if I adopt a practical principle of taking I-70 to the St. Louis airport when traveling on the grounds that it's the quickest route, the property of being the quickest route is what determines my decision by being incorporated into that principle. By "determines the will", he means "provides a sufficient consideration for the will, insofar as it is rational, to issue in a volition". Thus, the properties of something that make it possess the property of goodness are, in his view, those properties that provide sufficient considerations for willing by means of practical principles or maxims. Finally, by "practical" good, Kant is here just distinguishing the account of moral and prudential goodness from other sorts of value, for instance, aesthetic value (as in a "good painting" or a "good symphony"), properties that are not sufficient consideration for actions, but perhaps considerations in favor having some attitude toward an object. That which is good (in this practical sense), then, is that thing which has properties that, through being incorporated into our practical principles, provide sufficient considerations in favor of willing it. Kant reasons that, because the properties of good things provide *objective* considerations in favor of willing, those properties provide considerations that are "valid for every rational being as such" or are "universally valid" for rational beings. Objectivity in practical matters at least is, for Kant, thus a matter of validity for every rational being in virtue of their shared rationality.

Thus, so far we do not have an analysis of "good", but we do know what sorts of properties a thing must have to possess goodness. The *Critique of Practical Reason*, however, contains an extended discussion of Kant's conception of the good, and helps to fill out the view. Here he states that by "the good", "one understands a necessary object of the faculty of desire [*Begehrungsvermögen*] . . . according to a principle of reason" (CPrR 5:58). Simplifying this a bit, we can say that the property of goodness is the property of being the necessary object of a rational will. An "object of the will" is simply whatever it is one wills – most immediately, an action. Thus, Kant states,

> good or evil is, strictly speaking, referred to actions, not to the person's state of feeling, and if anything is to be good or evil absolutely (and in every respect and without any further condition), or is to be held to be such, it would be only the way of acting, the maxim of the will, and consequently the acting person himself as a good or evil human being. (CPrR 5:60)

So to be good in the sense in which the good will is good is to be the object of a rational will. Moreover, it is to be the *necessary* object of a rational will. By this, Kant means that it is what a rational will *necessarily* wills to do. Because what is good is what is *necessary* for a rational will, it is what all rational wills, insofar as they are rational, will. Putting this together with the above account of the nature of properties that make a thing good, we get the view that goodness is the property of being, in virtue of possessing other properties that provide universally valid considerations sufficient for willing, the necessary object of a rational will. At the moment, this may seem quite abstract. However, put together with the rest of Kant's views, its importance for understanding those views will become clearer as we go along.

5. Kant's Conceptions of Unqualified and Intrinsic Goodness

Let us, then, return to Kant's first statements about the unique value of a good will. There is a range of things that we think of as being "good and desirable in many respects", he says, but which can also be "bad and harmful" (G 4:393). "Gifts of nature" such as intelligence and decisiveness, for instance, are not good when attached to a terrorist. Even "happiness" or "total wellbeing and content-ment with one's condition" can make a person "bold but consequently often reckless as well" or might be found in a "creature" that never feels "the slightest pull of a pure and good will". In these cases, Kant concludes, happiness is not good. In the former case, it seems Kant thinks happiness can be its own worst enemy, leading the person who enjoys it to recklessness that will undo it. In the latter case, a happy person who does not fall prey to the dangers of bliss still might not deserve their happiness. That a war criminal lives out his days undisturbed somewhere in South America is a terrible state of affairs, but it is made even worse, not better, if he is also happy.

It will be useful to compare Kant's position, that good things such as decisive-ness or intelligence become bad when combined with other characteristics, with the doctrine of organic unities, offered by the contemporary philosopher G. E. Moore. Moore's doctrine holds that the value of a given whole is not necessarily equivalent to the value of the sum of the values of each of its parts.[5] Thus, adding a good thing, such as pleasure, to a bad overall situation, such as a terrorist, does not necessarily make things better. Indeed, many have the strong intuition that adding a good thing makes the resulting whole even worse than the prior situa-tion. So far, this is consistent with Kant's view. However, there are a number of things we might want to say about what's going on in such cases. We might say that pleasure is good but loses that value when it is present in someone wicked, like a terrorist. Then the goodness of it, the pleasure, evaporates and pleasure comes to possess a new property, badness or perhaps neutrality. By contrast, we might say something quite different, namely that pleasure in fact retains its good-ness, even in a terrorist, but the resulting whole is not improved or is made worse by adding this good thing. I believe that Kant's position is the former and G.E. Moore's position is the latter. If that's right, then Kant's view has the advantage of being less paradoxical than Moore's. To be sure, Moore's view in a sense explains why the pleased terrorist is a worse whole than the neutral or displeased terrorist: a bad person is in possession of what is in fact a good thing.[6] It is precisely this that makes the former worse than the latter. However, what is paradoxical is that, if adding pleasure made the situation worse, surely the pleasure itself is what made the difference. So then it must not be good in this situation, but bad. How else could things get worse by adding it?

Whichever view of what is going on is correct, Kant's view appears to be that a thing's value is qualified just in case one could imagine some circumstance in which it is not good. If this is impossible to imagine, then it is good without qualification. Assume that something is possible when and only when there is some circumstance – actual or hypothetical – in which it can be conceived to exist or occur. It seems when Kant denies that one can imagine a good will failing to possess value, he is supposing this as a test of whether this is possible. Thus, if something is good without qualification, it is impossible for it to fail to be good; it is necessarily good. Kant's claim seems to be, first, that there is such a thing as being necessarily good, and second, that the only thing that has this property is the good will.

The very idea that anything could meet this standard should and no doubt will arouse skepticism. How could anything be good *no matter in what circumstances* in which we imagine it to exist? Surely we can imagine circumstances in which even a disposition to make choices based on objective considerations would not be good (indeed, no matter how we cash out the idea of a good will, it seems we should be able to do this). Imagine, for instance, that an evil all-powerful demon will cause eternal pain and suffering for everyone on the planet if you retain your good will. This disposition seems then not to be good for you to have. Outlandish as this fanciful idea is, it is *conceivable*. So it seems there is a possible circumstance in which being morally upright is not at all a good thing. For this reason, it seems likely that there will be conceivable circumstances in which *anything* is not good. So if this is what Kant's notion of "good without qualification" comes to, it appears to be in trouble from the outset.

Perhaps, then, Kant means something else. Perhaps he wants us to distinguish the valuable quality of having a good will itself – for argument's sake, the quality of being disposed to act on principles that are objectively valid – from its being possessed by someone – a particular person's actually having this disposition. Thus, while the quality of possessing this disposition in itself might be valuable no matter the circumstances, some particular person's actually *having* that quality is in some cases not valuable. This would allow us to claim that, in the demon case, it is that particular person's *possessing* a genuinely valuable quality – that of being morally upright – that is bad in the circumstance, not the quality itself. So Kant's claim would come to the claim that while the *quality* of being morally upright itself is good in any conceivable circumstance, *possessing* that quality would not be good under any conceivable circumstance.

What could it mean to say that some quality is good though not possessed by anything? Perhaps it means that it is "good in the abstract." Thus, "having a good will" is good in the abstract while "failing to have a good will" is bad in the abstract. Even if this makes sense, the problem would be that we seem bound to say the same thing of intelligence and all of the other qualities Kant cites as having only qualified value. For instance, we should not say that intelligence or pleasure is often a good thing, but not when it is in a criminal. Rather, we should instead say that though it is good in the abstract, it is not good for a criminal *to possess* it. And so on and so forth through all of the things Kant lists as qualified goods. That leaves us with no way to distinguish between qualified and unqualified values.

It may be that Kant means that while we can at least conceive of being intelligent, being happy, or any other putative good property as *in itself* failing to be good we cannot conceive of the property of having a good will as *in itself* failing to be good. The idea would rely on a general fact about many qualities: whether a thing possesses those qualities depends on what is going on around them. For instance, a table possesses the property "being next to the sofa" depending on what's going on around it – that is, where the sofa is relative to it. Put the table in front or in back or on the side of the sofa and it has the property; put it on the curb and it no longer has that property. Some qualities may change from being good to failing to be a good in the same way. Thus, the property of being good may change in most things depending on what's going on around the feature (such as intelligence) that is good. The claim, then, would be that unlike every other thing that is good, the property of goodness in a good will remains no matter what else is happening around the person who has it. In particular, it remains even if there is a horrific outcome – as, for instance, in the imagined demon case. We say that it is a bad thing that the person in the demon case possesses this good quality, rather than that the quality itself is no longer good in this circumstance. And this would then distinguish the good will from things such as intelligence and pleasure. It would do so because there are cases in which it is not only or merely that the person's possessing intelligence, and so on, is bad, but in which the intelligence itself would fail to be a good thing.

One might say this, for instance, of events that take place in the romantic novel *Frankenstein* (or at least it is one way of thinking about Mary Shelley's work of that title). Dr. Frankenstein's vast knowledge of what animates living beings loses its value because it is had in an unnatural degree. It is a good thing in quantities that fall short of that which Dr. Frankenstein had, perhaps. Somehow, knowledge can lose its value when it concerns altering the order of nature. Then, it is not merely that it is a bad thing that Frankenstein possesses this valuable thing, knowledge; knowledge itself has lost its value, and even has acquired a disvalue. That, at any rate, may be the way we are supposed to understand Kant's idea that the value of a good will is unique. There is a special sort of value that the good will has such that this value is not based on the circumstances in which the good will is placed. The view isn't simply that the good will has the same sort of value as other good things, and only differs from these other things in possessing that selfsame sort of value in every circumstance. It is instead that it possesses a value of an entirely different order, a sort of value the possession of which doesn't vary with circumstances. This would be a significant feature of the goodness of the good will, if the good will possesses it. But it is still unclear what the nature of this sort of value might be.

Kant also refers to unqualified goodness as *unconditional* goodness. Perhaps this idea will help us to understand his view better. The idea is not unfamiliar.

Something is conditionally good just in case there is some condition that must be met for it to be good. Its value depends on a condition, typically on the condition that some other thing is good. So a given good thing is conditionally good when some other thing's goodness is a condition of the given good thing's goodness. For instance, surgery is a good thing – but only on the condition that some other thing, the thing it produces, is good, such as health (assuming there is no such thing as recreational surgery). Money is a good thing – but, again, only on the condition that there are other valuable things, things that it can be exchanged for. Otherwise, it is just paper and metal, as it might become were one stranded on a deserted island with a fat wallet. A daub of color in a painting might be good, but only on the condition that some other thing, the painting of which it is a part, is good. In each case, there is some good thing – health, things to buy, a painting – whose value is the condition of the value of some other good thing – surgery, money, a daub of color. Kant claims that, in some such way, everything other than a good will has a condition of its goodness. The will's goodness, additionally, is supposed to be the condition of the goodness of *everything* that has value. That is, Kant believes that nothing is good unless the will of the person who possesses it is good. And, unlike every other valuable thing, there is no further condition of a good will's value. That is, there is no other thing distinct from the good will such that its value is the condition of the good will's value.

That a thing of qualified value has a condition under which it is valuable would explain why it is possible for it to lose its value, why it is only good in some circumstances but not in others. It is possible for it to lose its value because it is possible for the condition of that value to be missing in some circumstance. It is possible for surgery to be bad, for instance, because we can imagine the surgery without the circumstance of producing a benefit to our health. Think of the myriad of malpractice claims on this basis. That circumstance is the condition of surgery's having value. But the idea of being valuable only in some circumstance can still be distinguished from the idea of being only conditionally valuable. It can still be distinguished because the intuitive idea of a circumstance is the entire state of affairs surrounding a thing, but the condition of a thing's goodness seems to be only some constituent of that whole state of affairs, the particular constituent of the state of affairs upon whose value that thing's value depends.

Kant also claims that an unqualified good is good *in all respects*. That suggests that if a thing is of qualified value, then there is something about it that is not good, some respect in which it is perhaps even bad. The thought experiment of imagining a thing in a different circumstance could be thought of as a way of revealing respects in which it is not good.[7] Perhaps this is what Kant is thinking about the good will. We can discover, by doing these thought experiments, that there is nothing but a good will that is *all* good, so to speak. For instance, knowledge is supposed to be only of qualified value. When we imagine it in a Josef Mengele or Dr. Frankenstein, for instance, we think that intelligence isn't all good. There is some facet or respect in which it is not good. Now the respect in which knowledge is not good may not be apparent in the circumstances in which we judge it to be of value. But all that we have to do is to imagine it in different circumstances, and the respect in which it is bad will be plain. Shelly imagined forbidden knowledge, for instance, aberrant and unnatural. Perhaps she thought that at a certain point, knowledge can separate us too much from the rest of the natural world and that is a bad thing. Kant himself thought that intelligence can be "extremely bad and harmful when the will which makes use of [it] . . . is not good" (G 4:393). Part of what he is pointing to is a purely extrinsic feature of intelligence, its usefulness to pursuing purposes, good or evil. But as the fanciful case of the all-powerful demon indicates, there are extrinsic features of a good will that might be bad in this way too.

However, this now suggests that we have discovered an important difference between a good will and every other valuable thing: The person who possesses intelligence *can* use it in order to pursue his own evil purposes. There is nothing about the very nature of knowledge that bars its use by the wicked. But while some other person might make use of a person's good will for evil purposes – the demon, for instance – it is hard to imagine how the person who possesses a good will herself could ever, in any circumstance, use her good will for evil purposes. It seems that its very nature rules out this possibility, while the very nature of knowledge does not. This would make a good will unique – if, that is, every other thing or trait a person might possess could be used to pursue some evil end. If being good in every respect is at least part of the notion of unqualified goodness, then Kant's claim is that the good will alone is good *in every respect*. There is no respect in which it can be put to work in the name of something wicked by the person who possesses it. It seems, then, that for something to be unqualifiedly good no condition of its goodness should be lacking and it must be good in all respects.

Another aspect of Kant's views on the value of a good will is that it is *intrinsically* good, in the sense that it is "good in itself" (G 4:394). Is this the same thing as being unqualifiedly good? Kant's discussion gives the impression that he thinks that these concepts are different. He deliberately takes additional space to explain why an unqualifiedly good will is good in itself. Kant clarifies what he means in saying that a good will is good in itself by saying that it is good "only by virtue of its willing" (G 4:394). Being disposed to volition seems to be an intrinsic property of the will. So at least part of his meaning in saying that a good will is "good in itself" and "only by virtue of its willing" is that a will is intrinsically valuable when its intrinsic properties are what make it valuable.

A standard conception of an intrinsic property is of a property of the sort we have already characterized as the goodness of an unqualifiedly good will: A thing's intrinsic properties are those properties that it could still have regardless of how we might change the circumstances around the spatio-temporal region inhabited by the thing. For instance, no matter whether a baseball is in a glove, on the ground, in the air or in the stands, it is still spherical. Its sphericality does not change when the circumstances around the spatio-temporal region inhabited by the baseball change. But a given baseball would lose the property of "being inside of Busch stadium" once someone hits it out of the park. Its "being inside of Busch stadium" changes when the circumstances around the baseball change. So that property is an extrinsic property of a baseball. The property of being white is an intrinsic property of the baseball, since it is white wherever it is, but being smaller than a basketball is an extrinsic property, since a baseball would lack that property were there no basketballs. Intrinsic value, as Kant means us to understand it, seems to be the value a thing has in virtue of properties it could retain no matter how its surroundings might be changed. And the only intrinsic property of a will is the volition that characterizes it.

A caveat. Note that this understanding of intrinsic value does not yet require the property of value itself to be an intrinsic property. It is consistent with everything I have said so far that the property of value itself is in fact an extrinsic property of a thing that has it. For, in general, a thing can possess extrinsic properties in virtue of its intrinsic properties. For instance, a lamp may be expensive because of its shape. Or a shirt may be desired because of its color. Shape and color are paradigms of intrinsic properties. Expense and being desired are extrinsic properties. To be expensive is to cost a lot of money, but prices change based on market forces, supply and demand, and so on. A thing is desired if someone desires it. In the absence of someone's desiring it, the thing loses the property of being desired. In fact, intrinsic value might turn out to be like being desired: Things can be desired because of their intrinsic properties; in such a case, we think of them as intrinsically desired. The same might be true of intrinsic value for all that we have so far said about Kant's own conception of intrinsic value.

Now, the properties that make a thing valuable are conditions of its value. But they may not be the only conditions. Suppose a thing's being intrinsically good means that when it is good, it has intrinsic properties that make it good. Then those conditions of the thing's value would be present no matter how circumstances might shift around it. Nevertheless, there might be other conditions of that thing's goodness as well, conditions under which the good-making intrinsic properties of a thing will in fact make that thing good. For instance, what make pleasure valuable are its intrinsic properties. But it might also have some condition under which those intrinsic properties do not succeed in so doing. For instance, the intrinsic properties of pleasure that are the source of its goodness when it is in fact good might not make it good when a wicked person enjoys it. Even in the circumstance in which a wicked person enjoys pleasure, it retains the intrinsic properties that are the source of its value. There is just this further condition under which it is good, namely, that a wicked person is not enjoying it.

In any case, one thing seems clear: something that is valuable without qualification must also be intrinsically good. This just seems to follow from what we've learned about unqualified goodness. For an unqualifiedly valuable thing is valuable in any circumstance, and that means there is no circumstance in which the conditions of its value are lacking. But what remains across changes in the circumstances in which a thing exists will have to be that thing's intrinsic properties – properties that do not change across circumstances. And if that is so then whatever conditions there are of an unqualifiedly valuable thing's value, they must be that thing's intrinsic properties. So an unqualifiedly good thing must be good in itself. We've just seen, however, that the reverse is not true: that something is in itself good is consistent with its not being good without qualification. For a thing, for instance pleasure, can be good when it is good because of its intrinsic properties, yet have conditions under which those intrinsic properties fail to make it good.

There is a further reason why an intrinsically good thing need not be unqualifiedly good. This is that a thing's intrinsic properties are different from its *essential* properties, or properties a thing *must* have in order to be what it is. The sphericality of a baseball does not change as the circumstances around it change; but a baseball need not be spherical; the game might have evolved with oval balls or some other shape. A baseball is white, but it could have been brown or gold. A thing can lose its intrinsic properties – properties that do not change when the circumstances around it changes – and remain what it is. But if an unqualifiedly good thing is good no matter what the circumstances it is in then it must be not only intrinsic properties in virtue of which it is good, but also those properties must be essential properties as well, properties that must be present in order for the unqualifiedly good thing to be present.

This is a desirable outcome for a number of reasons. First, it seems that there are many things that are intrinsically good – valuable things about which it is true that what makes them valuable are their intrinsic properties – yet there are respects in which they are nevertheless not good. We've already noticed that pleasure appears to have this property. But many other things seem to have it as well. Beauty and knowledge for instance are good in themselves – that is, what makes them valuable are their intrinsic properties. But we do not think they are therefore unqualifiedly good, for they possess features that can, for instance, lead us to violate moral principles. They can be used by the person who possesses them to do evil things.

Second, most things appear to be, when good, in a number of different ways and also in some possible circumstances bad. And the circumstances in which things are good or bad appear to differ from each other in that some of these circumstances involve the intrinsic properties of the thing and some involve its extrinsic properties. The respects in which a diamond is valuable, for instance, seem to be mainly properties that do not change when the circumstances around the diamond changes – its beauty, for instance. But a diamond also is very hard and can be used to cut softer materials such as metal or glass. That hardness is a source of the diamond's extrinsic value, a value it would have only because it is related to some other thing of value – whatever might be achieved by cutting metal or glass. Indeed, it is the fact that most goods have such a mixture that is the source of the fact that they are not all good, not good in every respect.

With these details about unconditional and intrinsic value in place, let us consider again Kant's claim about the good will in full:

> A good will is not good because of its effects or accomplishments, and not by virtue of its adequacy to attain any proposed end: it is good only by virtue of its willing – that is, it is good in itself. (G 4:394)

Read literally, this appears to say that not only is a good will intrinsically good; it is *only* intrinsically good – *only* good by virtue of its volition or willing – and has no other value at all. But how can this be? Surely a good will can *also* be useful, indeed, might also be the best way of attaining some proposed valuable end. This seems odd, especially when we cast this, as I have, in terms of choice. Whether some choice you made was a good choice seems to depend on the value of the thing you chose as much or more than any intrinsic features of your choice itself. And surely no matter how good a choice is it might also be advantageous and hence good because of that as well.

However, here we have been talking about the value of an *unqualifiedly* good choice. A choice could not be good without qualification in virtue of the value of the outcome or any other extrinsic feature of that choice. This is because, for any choice and any outcome or other extrinsic feature of that choice, there will be changes in the circumstances that will not include that outcome or that extrinsic feature, but might still include the choice. Hence, as I argued above, if a thing is unqualifiedly good, then it is also intrinsically good. One thus need go no further than the intrinsic features of an unqualifiedly good will to find that in virtue of which it possesses this sort of value. This is why Kant says that a good will is good *only* by virtue of its willing; its willing is that intrinsic feature of a good will that makes a good will possess unqualified value.

As we've already seen, in Kant's view the will is our capacity as rational beings to perform actions by choosing them on the basis of principles or the "representations of laws" (or universally valid or acceptable plans). One way in which we exercise this capacity is when we choose on the basis of our representation of natural causal laws. For instance, suppose we choose to steer clear of the campfire in front of us because it will burn us otherwise. In that case, we have chosen on the basis of our representation of natural laws such as that fire burns human skin, and that by staying at a distance we avoid its burning our own. Indeed, were someone to ask why we were steering clear, we might well give as a reason "It will burn my arm otherwise." Here, we are making our choice (to steer clear, in this case) into a natural causal link to complete a causal chain that results in a desired outcome (avoiding burns). We are operating according to our representation of a certain chain of causes governed by natural laws. We represent those causal chains because we have a naturally occurring interest or desire for something (such as avoiding pain). We then conceive of that desired thing as something to be caused by our choices, and so conceive of our choices as causes of that thing's coming to be. This is practical reasoning about how to bring about goals that we have set for ourselves, and this is how it operates on the basis of principles.

Kant says that insofar as choices are based on such principles of reasoning, they are "in some way good" (G 4:414). By this, Kant means that they are good for achieving the goals we set ourselves to achieve. "That was a good choice," we might say about avoiding the campfire, for instance. We would mean it was a good choice because it was based on a good principle – to avoid campfires so that we don't get burned. Probably in some sense we might also think of a choice that just happened to result in a desirable outcome as a "good choice". But we wouldn't think it had genuine value as a choice. It would be good in the sense of being a lucky choice (although many, of course, would rather be lucky than good). A choice is in fact good only when it is good because the principle on which it was based is a good one. And what makes the principle in this case a good one is that it provides guidance to achieving a desirable goal, avoiding burns. Because this is what makes it a good principle, we would not, in saying that the choice based on it was good, mean that it was good in every sense. After all, there are things for which it is worth risking burns.

This is how we bring to bear representations of laws on our goals and thereby arrive at principles that apply to our situation and goals. And we also see the connection to the value of choices: it is because the choice is based on a good principle that we find the choice good. The same, moreover, is true of a good disposition to choose. A disposition toward a certain choice is good because of the goodness of the principle on which the choice would be based. But the good choice and disposition that we're interested in are not just good in any sense, but in an unqualified sense. Given that, they cannot be good because they are based on a principle that is good for achieving some desired results. This is because the condition under which such a choice will actually be good is the condition consisting of being in circumstances in which that choice leads to those desired results. But for any result we might want to achieve, the conditions will vary for achieving them. We may want to avoid getting burned by the campfire, so we avoid it. But it might be that avoiding the campfire requires walking through a hail of bullets. In that case, a choice on the basis of the principle of avoiding fires is not a good one.

What practical principle, then, makes a choice good, not because of its usefulness in achieving our goals, but no matter what the circumstances, and so makes the choice unconditionally good? Kant's answers this question in two steps:

1. "The pre-eminent good which we call 'moral' consists therefore in nothing but *the idea of the law* in itself . . . so far as that idea, and not an expected result, is the determining ground of the will" (G 4:401).
2. The "law . . . the idea of which must determine the will . . . if that will is to be called good absolutely and without qualification . . . is the [law of] universal conformity of actions to law as such" (G 4:402).

Change the circumstances around a given choice based on a principle such as "This will bring me more pleasure" or "That will make others happier", and that choice no longer is effective. So effectiveness in bringing about our goals cannot be essential to that choice. All you need to do is to imagine the circumstances are such that you no longer aim at pleasure or making others happy. Then, a choice based on that principle would provide you pleasure and make others happier, but wouldn't be good. Indeed, the value of choices based on all principles of instrumental reasoning depends on a property such as effectiveness, a property that is not essential to those choices. And that means that whatever the principle is that makes a good will good must be a non-instrumental principle. It must be a principle that makes a choice based on it unconditionally good, a principle such that no matter how circumstances are changed around the choice based on it, it still retains that property in virtue of which it is a good choice.

The claim that a good will is good without qualification thus at a first approximation means that under every conceivable circumstance in which it exists, a choice characterized by some principle, call it "M" (whatever M turns out to be), is good, and is good because it is characterized by M, and any other choice is good only if it is consistent with choices characterized by M. So, if there is a good will, then there is some feature of a motivating principle M such that it makes a choice based on it a good choice, and it would possess this feature under every circumstance.

Let me briefly summarize Kant's views as I have so far presented them. An unqualifiedly good choice is a choice based on some principle that makes that choice good under any circumstance. That it is good under any circumstance tells us to look for some property of the principle on which the choice is based that the principle would retain no matter how circumstances might be changed around it. It tells us to look for an essential property of that principle. We thus arrived at the question: What sort of motivating principle has a feature that makes a choice based on it good and is essential to that principle? We already know that it cannot be an instrumental principle, a principle whose value depends on achieving or being aimed at achieving certain results. The value of a choice based on that sort of principle is entirely dependent on the circumstances, and that means the property in virtue of which a choice based on it is good is effectiveness – an inessential property. So only a principle that is a non-instrumental principle makes a choice based on it good because of a property that is essential to that principle. To say more about that principle, we need to turn to the topic of the moral worth of acting from duty.

6. Moral Worth and Duty

Kant holds that if it is good that you to do some action, you can only think of this as what you *ought* to do, what you *must* do, or as he often puts it, as your moral *duty*. Kant believes human beings inevitably think in these terms because whenever some action would be good to do, we nevertheless are aware of the fact that we might not do it. We are rational agents, but also creatures with desires, and these desires are variable and contingent. I have desires you do not have and you have desires I do not have, both of our sets of desires change over time, and there is no desire everyone has had and no desire anyone always has. As a result, we have the potential to be motivated by desires that not everyone could be motivated by and fail to be motivated by desires others are motivated by, or we were once motivated by but are not now motivated by. So the thought of what it is good to do can only represent a constraint on what we will do. It is a constraint on what we want for ourselves or for others. The good, as a result, can only motivate us through the thought of duty. This is why Kant says that the concept of duty *contains* the idea of a good will under certain subjective limitations and hindrances (G 4:397). A good will *in us* is a will that might not do what is good, and so can be only motivated by duty rather than the good. This fact, the fact that the investigation of what motivates a good will in human beings must turn to a consideration of acts performed out of duty, has a side benefit: Kant believes that cases in which a person acts out of duty clearly exemplify the motivating principle behind the action. That in turn makes it easier to discover what the principle is that is the source of the extraordinary value of a good will.

Kant gives us four examples of persons acting in various ways to illustrate the point he wants to make. The first, a shopkeeper, gives correct change to a customer. The second preserves his own life. The third, a Samaritan, helps others. A fourth looks after his future happiness. In each case, Kant tells us that the action in question is a moral duty and asks us to imagine it being done for a variety of reasons. He does this because he wants us to compare the moral worth of the action when it is performed for these different reasons. In particular, he wants us to compare the case in which the person acts out of duty with when she does not. In each case, he believes we will see that it is only when the action is done because it is one's duty that it has what he calls "moral worth."

For now, let us set aside what Kant means by "acting from duty." What exactly does he mean by "moral worth," the property possessed only by an action done out of duty? Many readers will assume that "moral worth" is an ellipsis of "*worthy of*" something.[8] Kant's position would amount to this: only a person who acts from duty alone is praiseworthy, worthy of happiness or perhaps deserving of a special attitude such as esteem or respect. It is worth pointing out that if this is indeed what Kant means then his discussion of the moral worth of actions from duty is peripheral to the discovery and defense of fundamental moral principles, not central, in other words, to the discovery of what makes a good will good. It would not be central because what ordinary people think we are worthy of or deserve as a result of what we do would shed little light on what the principle is that tells us what we ought to do. Kant's claims about which actions have moral worth would only be of marginal interest, of interest because they are controversial pronouncements about how ordinary people think such things as esteem, praise or happiness ought to be doled out. However, I think that this is the wrong way of understanding the topic of moral worth. I'll explain why.

One common way of thinking about all of this is that to attribute moral worth to an action from duty is, for instance in Richard Henson's terms, to issue either a "battle citation" to or a "fitness report" on the agent.[9] A battle citation is due someone who victoriously overcomes inner opposition and does the right thing; a fitness report tells you that a person is ready to overcome that opposition, should it arise. Both appear to be forms of praiseworthiness. The idea is that an agent is morally praiseworthy in virtue of some duty she performs when and only when in performing her duty, she has overcome significant obstacles or was capable of doing so. But only when she performs her duty out of duty alone is either of these things true. So only when she acts out of duty alone is she praiseworthy.

If a praiseworthy action is an action that *ought* to be praised then this would be a deeply problematic view. For any moral theory, including Kant's, whether one *ought* to praise an action is a substantive moral question, since praising is an action and so is itself up for moral evaluation. In the case of Kant's theory, whether one ought to praise an action, including an action from duty, should depend on whether the Categorical Imperative tells one to praise in the circumstances, and it is not at all obvious that it will always or even typically do so. Indeed, it is all too easy to think of cases in which *prima facie* we ought to praise actions that were not done from duty or whose status is opaque. It might well show most respect for morality to encourage people to be moral even when we do not know why they did their duty. And it is equally easy to imagine that we ought not to praise an action that was performed from duty. For praising under certain circumstance can be disrespectful, for instance, because in the circumstance it would be ostentatious or unwelcome. After all, a person may well think it was only their duty to act as they did and that doing one's duty is not out of the ordinary for them, while praising them might under certain circumstances appear to imply that they did something out of the ordinary.

Of course, it might be that his position is that only such actions nevertheless *deserve* praise, and perhaps it is the deservingness that is important, not whether we ought to praise. This is certainly more plausible. But it is not consistent with what Kant himself says on the topic, even in these passages in the *Groundwork*. He explicitly and repeatedly asserts that many dutiful actions not from duty, such as those from sympathy and honor, *also* deserve praise and indeed can be morally meritorious.[10] And surely he was right to have said so. It is not contrary to any other element of his views. But it is also not true that Kant's views require that *all* actions from duty deserve praise, at least if we take him seriously when he says, in the *Doctrine of Virtue*, that weakness in overcoming obstacles to doing one's duty is something "childish and weak, which can indeed coexist with the best will" (MM 6:408). A person with such "childish weakness" might often enough have no other reason to act *save* the fact that it is his duty in some circumstances, and have no countervailing desires or interests. It is not at all clear why this childish and weak person who does his duty would deserve praise for doing it from duty in such a circumstance. It is only his duty, after all, and so he might not be deserving of praise for doing it for that reason alone. Nevertheless, it seems as if he could well act solely from duty and so it seems he could well have done something with genuine moral worth. Those who are critical of the position that all and only actions from duty deserve or ought to be praised are right; it is an indefensible position. But it does not appear to be Kant's.

"A good will" Kant wrote, "seems to constitute the indispensable condition even of worthiness to be happy" (G 4:393). This statement suggests an alternative possibility, that moral worth is to be taken as worthiness of a reward of some sort, such as happiness. Possessing a good will is indeed in Kant's view the condition of your worthiness to be happy. Are then all and only those who act from duty worthy of happiness? Is that what "moral worth" means? It would be surprising if Kant held that it was. Moral worth is an attribute of particular acts of will, and, however pure, a particular act of will is surely insufficient to make one worthy of happiness. Our worthiness to be happy more plausibly hangs on the moral character of our overall life. Moral worth seems concerned only with the condition of the will in discrete actions, or at any rate, that is the strong impression one gets from Kant's discussion.

Perhaps then one is worthy of happiness to just the degree this action contributes to the overall moral condition of our wills. The overall moral worth of our actions as a set may then constitute how deserving of happiness they make us. When a good willed person strengthens her will and increases her virtue, she appears to become by Kant's lights more worthy of happiness. But even if this is so, it does not seem to be what Kant is concerned with in the sorts of judgments that he asks us to consider. Judgments about our worthiness of happiness are apparently for God to make and must not form the basis for our attitudes toward others. Kant does not ask us how much of a boost to his deservingness of happiness the shopkeeper or philanthropist got for acting from duty alone. We are asked to consider only some quality of the will of the person acting, not of what that quality makes him deserving. All in all, Kant's term "moral worth" is not best understood as elliptical for "worthiness" of some reward either, even if possessing a good will constitutes one's worthiness to be happy.

Actions possessing moral worth deserve esteem; Kant makes this plain. Perhaps, then, for an action to have moral worth is just for it to be worthy – in the sense of deserving – of an attitude such as esteem.[11] Now if esteeming someone were understood as an action like praising her, then virtually all of the considerations regarding praise and rewards would also argue against taking moral worth to mean worthiness of esteem. The one consideration that would not is that moral worth *does* guarantee that the agent deserves esteem. However, it does not follow that if the agent deserves esteem for her action, her action has moral worth. If esteeming is not an action like praising, but an attitude, then it is a *response* to moral worth rather than what moral worth is. To "deserve esteem" is to be the fit object of the attitude of esteem; or, insofar as one is rational, one responds to such worthy things with esteem.[12] It is the moral worth of the action that makes it a fit object of esteem. So even if the idea of esteem-worthiness is relevant to which actions have moral worth and which do not, "moral worth" is not elliptical for "worthy of esteem." Esteem is the proper attitude toward actions with moral worth, and could serve as a guide to which actions possess it and which actions do not, but there is the additional matter of what makes actions deserving of this attitude.

The most telling consideration against understanding "moral worth" as "worthiness *of*" something is the absence of any rationale for its place in the first chapter of the *Groundwork*, a chapter in which he is initiating his search for the fundamental principle of morality. What the reader expects in a discussion that begins with the unique value of a good will and ends with a fundamental moral principle of action is not a discussion of who is worthy of what, but of the nature of moral value as it concerns the actions of human beings. If one is looking for the fundamental moral principle that is to guide human action, and one has begun with the assumption that this will be what makes a good will have its special value, then I believe it is most natural to expect a turn to a consideration of this value as it appears in discrete acts of will. In other words, "moral worth" seems best understood as just another name for moral value, in this case, as it is found in particular acts of will or volitions, as opposed to a general disposition of the will. And moral value may well be a property a will must have in order to qualify for or engender certain kinds of attitudes, such as moral esteem, but it is not equivalent to being so esteemed.

My proposal, then, is this: Kant's primary objective in discussing actions with moral worth is to discover that in virtue of which discrete acts of will, discrete willings if you will, possess moral value. That then raises the question of *why* certain acts of will are morally valuable and others not. That is, it raises the question, Which actions – the conception of which includes the principle characterizing the choice of this action, or the plan executed by the choice – have a value that would remain no matter how the circumstances might be changed around those actions? *These* willings possessing *this* property are the objects of esteem, the response that befits moral value. The principle behind these willings will be the fundamental principle of morality.

The connection between esteem and moral worth has to do with the fact that esteem is a form of respect, respect for *the person* as focused on the operation her will. Now Kant holds that "all respect (*Achtung*) for a person is actually only respect for the law (of righteousness, etc.,) that person exemplifies" (G 4:401n). The idea is that the source of the esteem we have for a person whose behavior displays before us the moral law is in fact just our respect for that law itself. The behavior displays or exemplifies that law when that law alone motivates it, and our esteem for such a person is really a response to the moral law itself. The person who exemplifies the moral law is living up to the standard set by the moral law. But our attitude is focused, not on that achievement as an achievement per se, but as an example of a law that draws the respect of rational agents. If esteem is the appropriate response to moral value, and what is of moral value is that which retains its value no matter how circumstances are altered around it, then esteem is the appropriate response to this intrinsic value of the thing exhibited by a good will. And that is the moral law itself.[13] That law is what our esteem focuses on. A given person's action has moral value, then, when and only when rational agents would esteem his willing of it, and they will do this when and only when willing his action exemplifies the law that rational agents respect. And that in virtue of which it has value is its intrinsic property, its principle or maxim.

7. Acting from Duty

We will take moral worth to be moral value, then, and now turn to the actions that alone supposedly have this value, actions from duty. Now a very common, perhaps even standard, way of reading Kant's discussion of acting from duty focuses on his claim that actions from other motivating principles such as sympathy are only "fortunate . . . to aim at something generally useful and consistent with duty" (G 4:398).[14] The idea behind this standard reading is supposed to be that actions chosen because we have concern for others' welfare or other seemingly desirable motivations have no moral worth because they only produce actions that conform to what is our duty by accident. Such principles aren't reliable in producing the right action, as determined by some, perhaps ordinary intuitive, standard. On the standard reading, we come to the examples with some conception of duties and of actions conforming to these duties, and Kant is supposed to want us to consider which motive is connected in the right way to that conformity. Thus, Kant tells us that helping others in need is a duty, but that doing so out of heartfelt concern for their plight has no moral worth. Indeed, it is only when we imagine a person who has lost all interest in her fellow human beings, but still helps them because it is her duty to do so, that we have the image of an action with genuine moral worth.

This picture has led some critics to claim that Kant's views have the absurd implication that we must come to dislike doing those actions that are our moral duty, in order that they might be done solely out of duty. There are several mistakes in such a criticism. As many have pointed out, it assumes that acting solely out of duty is incompatible with having sympathy and other emotions.[15] But Kant makes no such claim, and nothing he says requires this. So we can help others from duty and with sympathy, and *mutatis mutandis* with other duties and other feelings, attitudes and dispositions. Second, Kant does not say or imply that there is anything *wrong* with doing one's duty from other motives, nor that we should try to rid ourselves of such motives and replace them with a motive of acting from duty alone. Third, we have to keep firmly fixed before our eyes Kant's overall purpose, which is to discover what the fundamental principle of morality is, the principle that guides and motivates a good will. He picks the examples he does because in his view they clearly exemplify that principle. It is only when every other motivation counsels against doing one's duty that we can see and be sure that the person's sole motive was simply that it was his duty.

Much of this way of understanding Kant's point is right, I think. But this way of defending Kant and the criticisms that provoked those defenses are ultimately both flawed. If Kant's point is that acting from duty is acting from the only reliable motive in producing dutiful actions, then it is, again, difficult to understand what relationship the discussion of the moral worth of acting from duty (under this interpretation) would have to the primary point of the *Groundwork*, the discovery and justification of the fundamental principle of morality. Indeed, the discussion of acting from duty presupposes the existence of some principle that defines our duties. It presupposes this because it asks us to assume that the actions in question conform to such a principle, but are based on motives that are unreliably connected to producing this conformity. Moreover, the discussion, so understood, does not seem to connect to the discussion of the extraordinary intrinsic value of the good will, a value that could not be connected to its reliability in doing anything given that reliability is quite clearly an extrinsic property.

As I read Kant's examples and discussion, he assumes no independent gauge of right and wrong at work in these examples. In my view, Kant's point, and this is important, is simply that the principles motivating the shopkeeper, the philanthropist, and so on, are not principles that underlie an unconditionally and intrinsically good choice. The argument that they are not is based on the fact that in each case there are conditions on the value of the choice. Kant says that they only fortunately hit on something useful and dutiful because he wants to make the point that there is a condition of the value of such choices. It then follows that the principle on which these choices are based cannot be the principle of a good will. And if the principle on which these choices are based is not the principle of a good will, it also cannot be the fundamental principle of morality. For Kant's guiding assumption is that *whatever it is* that guides the choices of a good will, it will be the fundamental principle of morality, the very principle that he is trying to discover and justify.

Consider, then, an alternative understanding of Kant's discussion. Kant's claim that only actions from duty have moral worth, on this alternative understanding, amounts to the claim that, among the actions of human rational agents, only actions from duty express the unqualified value of a good will. If this is so then it appears that only the actions of someone with a good will possess moral worth. If I am right that a "good will" is an enduring disposition to act on the right principle or plan, and "the right principle" turns out to be "it is my moral duty" then this in turn implies that only someone with an enduring disposition to act because it is her moral duty to do so performs morally worthy actions. When her actions are the outcomes of her disposition to act because it is her moral duty to do so, then they have moral worth because they express the value of her good will.

I myself think that it is not an accident that Kant uses the examples he does to explain what it is to act from duty. Many philosophers, such as Hobbes, think that self-interest is a primary, even unitary, motivating principle behind all of our actions. If that were true then to justify moral principles – to show why we should perform them – would require showing that they are grounded in self-interest. Moral principles are those that ultimately serve your interest, such philosophers argue. The same is true for self-preservation and happiness. Sympathy, too, has been an element of the moral psychologies of some philosophers such as Butler and Hume. Moral principles are in their view somehow grounded in our sympathetic natures. Thus, in my estimation, each of Kant's examples is a challenge to each of his opponent's theories, theories that claim to ground moral principles in the motivation it illustrates. Is the fundamental principle of morality – the principle that explains and justifies our moral duties – at bottom the principle of self-interest? Is it a principle based on self-preservation, on our sympathetic natures, or on our desire for happiness? The discussion of moral worth is a shot across the bow for proponents of any such theories. Kant has already formulated a kind of test: If any such motivations are indeed the source of moral principles then they should make the will of the person acting unqualifiedly good. The principle of the shopkeeper is to act in his self-interest, so if moral principles are indeed those that serve self-interest, those actions should have genuine moral worth. In each case, however, Kant aims to point out that they obviously do not. It is only when the action is based on a choice whose principle gives that choice unqualified value that the action expresses an unqualifiedly good will and so has moral worth. The motive "It is my duty" is just a stand-in for this principle, and its value is quite different from self-interest and the rest of those motivations. Or so I think we should understand Kant's discussion.

Indeed, a pretty clear factor in favor of my understanding is Kant's own statement about these examples: "It is clear from our previous discussion that the objectives we may have in acting, and also our actions' effects considered as ends and as what motivates our volition, can give to actions no unconditional or moral worth" (G 4:400). He seems to be saying just what I have proposed, that in none of the examples he has given us is the will unqualifiedly good until the example is changed so that the person's choice is based on duty. In each case, the value of the choice is qualified by the value of some outcome or intended outcome. The shopkeeper's decision is good for his self-interest, but achieving one's own interest itself isn't always or unqualifiedly good. Even in the case of the person who helps out of sympathy, the value of her action depends on the value of her choice based on sympathy. Sympathetic choices are of value because a sympathetic maxim aims at furthering the welfare of some other person. But aiming or achieving that is not always worthwhile. As Barbara Herman points out,

> Suppose I see someone struggling, late at night, with a heavy burden at the back door of the Museum of Fine Arts. Because of my sympathetic temper I feel the immediate inclination to help him out. . . . We need not pursue the example to see its point.[16]

I might put the point in a slightly different way: The value of the welfare of the person at which her sympathy aims is a condition of the value of her choice to help out. But in some circumstances, that person's welfare is not good, for instance, a circumstance in which promoting it requires violating another person's rights. In that circumstance, a condition under which the choice to help would be good (that the promotion of the recipient's welfare is of value) fails to obtain. Indeed, any choice based on a sympathetic principle can be imagined in different circumstances in which the condition under which it is good does not obtain. So a choice based on that principle is not unconditionally good. The same is true in the other examples as well: choosing to preserve one's life based on the fear of death, and choosing on the basis of a natural inclination to happiness to prudently secure the means to it in the future. The value of the choices each person makes is conditional on the value of what the choice aims to accomplish. Since whatever motivates a good will is that principle which will serve as the fundamental principle of morality – the principle distinguishing right from wrong – none of the bases of these alternative choices can be that principle, since in none of these cases is a choice based on those principles good without qualification.

Now a key feature of this reading of Kant's examples is that it supposes that actions in some sense do or at least can exemplify the principles motivating them.[17] That is what draws the response of respect in us for the will of the agent and thereby grounds our judgment of the moral worth of the action. It is the expression of the moral law in the action of the person acting from duty that draws our esteem. It will be helpful to try to be explicit about what "expressing a principle" might amount to. Let's suppose that an action expresses the principle that moti-vates it by, in some sense, *exemplifying* those principles. Thus, "acting on princi-ple" expresses the principle on which you act in such a way that its expression engenders the appropriate attitude for the principle, so expressed, in others.

First off, an action that expresses a principle that motivates it must at least *conform* to the principle that motivates it. This would explain why Kant begins his discussion of moral worth by "passing over" "all actions that are already recog-nized as contrary to duty" (G 4:397). What he says is that "the question whether they might have been done *from duty* never arises." But we can also see that such actions could not in any case *exemplify* the moral principle on which they might be based (and so could not be objects of the relevant respect reserved for such principles). When someone does the wrong thing for the right reason, or the right thing for the wrong reason, as we say, their actions belie the principles that moti-vate them. Their actions do not exemplify their motivating principles. Let us assume that an action conforms to a principle when the act-description in that principle accurately describes the agent's action, and an action will be accurately described by a principle when it possesses the relevant features referred to in the principle. For instance, if a principle says to tell the truth and an act possesses the feature of being a truth telling then the action conforms to the principle.

Now many of our acts of speaking are truth tellings, just as much of our behav-ior trivially conforms to many other principles. However, little of that behavior actually *expresses* a principle. This is because that behavior does not provide an *example* of the principle to which it conforms. Imagine how one might use a bit of behavior as an example to explain a principle to someone, such as a child or someone learning a skill. One would not explain the principle of telling the truth by pointing to someone reading aloud out of an encyclopedia, for instance, or simply talking accurately about this or that set of facts. Nor would a scoutmaster point to just any person helping another to cross the street as an example of the scouting rule "be kind." In each case, it would be insufficient to provide an example of a principle to pick out someone who was merely conforming to the given principle or rule.

We can understand more precisely what is required for exemplification of a principle by drawing on some elements from Nelson Goodman's account of artistic expression, which involves, as he puts it, a kind of symbolic back-reference to the thing exemplified.[18] Goodman employs the example of a tailor's color swatch.[19] Not just anything of a particular hue of blue exemplifies that hue; a tailor's swatch, in addition to *being* blue, itself *refers* back to that blue. Likewise, my suggestion is that not just any action conforming to a principle exemplifies the principle. The action must additionally refer back to the principle to which it conforms, much as the tailor's color swatch not only *is* blue, but *refers* to that blue. Thus, an element beyond conformity to principle is required, something to make the action refer back to the principle or rule to which it conforms.

Color swatches refer back to the colors they possess because they are elements of a symbolic system within the tailoring practice in which they play this role. Perhaps they acquire this referential role because there exists a practice in which tailors use them to refer to a fabric color. Although actions that are performed on principle exemplify the principle, moral action is not in this way a part of a system of symbols (as it would be if, for instance, it were part of a ritual or theatre). But action on principle does refer back to the principle to which the action conforms. In teaching a principle, explaining what the principle is, and so on, we appeal to such actions, and not to actions that merely conform to the principle. The actions that exemplify a principle conform to a principle *because* the agent has chosen on the basis of that principle. Thus willing an action that conforms to a principle on the basis of the very principle to which it conforms refers back to the principle. The agent intends that his action conform to the principle, and in so intending, make his action an example of the principle. That reference back to the principle is missing when an action was not motivated and justified by the principle to which it conforms. Since actions cannot literally be examples of principles, however, I take it that they are metaphorical exemplifications or, as Goodman would term it, *expressions* of principles.

8. Overdetermination and Expressing the Moral Law

Obviously more needs to defend the sense of "expression" I delineated in the last section, but I hope it is clear enough so that from hereon we can simply assume that something such like this is the case in actions that are done *because* they conform to a practical principle. They express the principles on which they are based by, metaphorically speaking, exemplifying those principles. I take it the "because" in "acting because of conformity with a principle" includes both an explanatory and justificatory sense. But we can imagine that what explains a person's action (that is, motivates it) is one thing, while how she justifies it can be quite another. At any rate, that is how things often appear, so I shall assume that this does on occasion happen.

Now, suppose in some case someone's action is motivated by one principle that does not justify her action, but she regards it (correctly, we will assume) as justified by quite another principle. What motivates her to tell the truth in some case is the principle of telling the truth when there is a chance of being caught (adopted, say, because she is highly averse to being caught), but she believes her action is justified because she morally ought to do so. She embraces the moral principle of not lying, let's say, but that she embraces this principle is not why she tells the truth. She does it out of fear of being caught. Such an action, intuitively, does not fully express her will. It expresses her interest in avoiding embarrassment perhaps, but it does not express her embrace of the principle of not lying – even though it conforms to that principle. Such an action, it seems to me, does not express a good will in the sense in which Kant was talking of it.

Perhaps the reverse situation is conceivable, a situation in which a person justifies her action in non-moral terms but is wholly motivated by moral principle, although it is puzzling to me exactly how such a case might work, and so how to classify such an action. So, as a first approximation, then, let us say that some person S's action A expresses some (moral or non-moral) principle, M, only when

(i)   A conforms to M,
(ii) S's acceptance of M explains her choice of A,
(iii) S's justification for choosing A is that A conforms to M.

For instance, suppose S helps his grandmother around the house. S's helping exemplifies the Boy Scout principle "be kind" only if (A) the help was an act of kindness, (B) S chose to help because S embraced that scouting principle, and, finally, (C) that principle is what, by S's own lights, counted in favor of choosing to help. In a case of this kind, we shall say, S's act, because it expresses this scouting principle, has genuine "scouting worth." Those who likewise embrace scouting principles will, at least if they are not suffering from depression or some other abnormal psychological state, respond with scouting esteem to S's act. The principle they hold in high standing is there before them, exemplified by the action metaphorically speaking, and because that scouting principle is there before them, it engenders a response of esteem in them.

For moral principles, the same will apply *mutatis mutandis*. Suppose S helps his grandmother around the house. Suppose "help others" is a moral principle. S's helping exemplifies the moral principle "help others", only if (A) the help was an act of helping, (B) S chose to help because S embraced that moral principle, and, finally, (C) that principle is what, by S's own lights, counted in favor of helping. In a case of this kind, we shall say, S's act, because it expresses this scouting principle, has genuine "moral worth." Those who embrace that moral principle will, at least if they are not suffering from depression or some other abnormal psychological state, esteem S's act. The principle they hold in high standing is there before them, exemplified by the action, metaphorically speaking, and because that scouting principle is there before them, it engenders a response of esteem in them.

If my portrayal of this so far is correct, then moral worth is just a kind of value that is explained in the same way as many other sorts of value. For any system of practical rules (clubs, governments, orders) there will be actions that exemplify those rules, and those actions will have the relevant "worth" ("scouting worth", "civil worth", "military worth" etc.). The difference is that *moral* worth is a special kind of value because of the special nature of the principle that is expressed in action that is chosen on its basis, because of the supreme importance of the moral law and the special esteem we have for that law.

This leaves at least two important questions that need answering in order to be more precise about what acting from duty is. First, in order to express M, must S's acceptance of M *wholly* explain and be S's justification for A, or can these things cooperate with other principles motivating or favoring A? Second, practical principles of any kind can presumably require, forbid or permit a given action. Can an action that is not required by a practical principle, but is, say, only recommended, have any worth? The scouting rule "Be kind" for instance, requires us to help people struggling to cross the street, forbids us from making fun of someone's shortcomings, but may permit us to stay home and watch TV rather than work at the soup kitchen any given evening. Suppose M merely permits rather than requires A. If M does not *require* that S do A, then how can S's acceptance of M explain and justify her doing A? For instance, suppose we decide to go help at the soup kitchen this evening, though going is not required by the principle. In what sense might it be because we embrace the scouting rule "Be kind" that we do so? Does such an action have any scouting worth?

Consider these schemas of examples to answer these questions. Assume agent S (e.g., a boy scout) does some action A (e.g., tells the truth) that conforms to some principle M ("Be truthful").

Example 1:

(i)   M requires that S do A,
(ii) S's acceptance of M motivates her choosing to A,
(iii) S's justification for choosing A is that M requires it.
(iv) No other principle to choose A motivates S except M.

For instance, suppose the scouting principle "Be truthful" requires a boy scout to tell the truth to his parents on some occasion. And suppose it is the scout's acceptance of that principle as a guide to behavior that motivates him to tell the truth. Moreover, the principle that justifies his telling the truth, in his eyes, is that the scouting principle requires it of him. And finally, although the scout may recognize that other principles would counsel him to tell the truth, they play no role in his reasoning to do so. It was simply that scouting requires it.

Example 2:

(i)   M requires S to A.
(ii) S accepts some principle, N, to A other than that M requires it.
(iii) S's acceptance of M and N are together necessary to motivate her to A.
(iv) S's justification for A is that both M requires it and that N requires it.

Continuing with our scouting analogy, suppose the scout also knows that his parents are very good at detecting his lies, and offer stern punishment for lying. But S only cares some about avoiding punishment, and only cares some about the scouting rule "Be truthful". Alone, neither is enough to get him to tell the truth. But together, they weigh in favor of doing so, and so he tells the truth. Moreover, in justifying his actions to others, he will say genuinely that he tells the truth because together M and N are sufficient to make sense of doing so.

Example 3:

(i)   M requires that S do A.
(ii) S accepts some principle, N, to A other than that M requires it.

(iii) S's acceptance of M alone motivates her choice to A.
(iv) S's lone justification for choosing to A is that M requires it.

In this case, while he knows of the threat of punishment, it plays no role in motivating or justifying his action. It is only his embrace of the scouting principle that does. However, had M not required S to A, he would have done so anyway, because N also required it.

Example 4:

(i) M requires that S do A.
(ii) S accepts some principle to A, N, other than that M requires it that is sufficient to both motivate and to justify S's doing A.
(iii) S's acceptance of M and N motivates her choice of A.
(iv) S's justification for choosing A is that M and N require it.

In the final example, we have a classic case of "over-determination" of an action by motives. Unlike the second case, in which both principles are jointly sufficient for S to arrive at the choice, in this case, both principles are independently sufficient to arrive at it, both in the sense that they motivate and justify the action. Our scout, then, tells the truth both because he embraces the scouting principle *and* he fears his parents' retribution.

There are other schemas to consider, but these are enough to further the discussion. First note that in example 4, two contrary to fact conditionals are true: If the scout had not embraced the scouting principle "Be truthful", then he still would have told the truth (out of fear of punishment). And, by the same token, if the scout had not feared punishment, he still would have told the truth (because of his embrace of the principle). This is a difference between example 4 and example 2. In example 2, had he not been somewhat afraid of punishment, he would not have told the truth. Likewise, had he not embraced to some extent the principle "Be truthful", he would have lied. In case 4, unlike in case 2, he did not need the threat of punishment to conform to the principle. Likewise, in cases 1 and 3. In case 3, if there were no threat of punishment, it would make no difference to whether he was truthful, and in case 1, there is no such threat.

Now the actions that possess what we shall call "M worth" – that is, the sort of value I described as based on the fact that a given action expresses some practical principle or rule – are those which express the volitional principle M characterizing that will. Actions express their motivating principles when they exemplify those principles, metaphorically speaking. And they do this, as I have described above, when those actions not only conform to those principles, but also contain a reference back to the principle to which they conform. This is the way in which a swatch of fabric exemplifies a color, for instance. In the case of actions, the reference to the principle is contained in the fact that the person is conforming to the principle *for the sake of the principle* itself.

It seems to me that 1 and 3 are certainly the sorts of actions that would be expressions of principle M. They are the sorts of actions one might, for instance, use as examples, to explain or teach the principle, for instance. In example 2, by contrast, M is not expressed by the action, even if the action in 2 is explained in part by the fact that the agent embraces M. It would not be a genuine expression of the scouting principle, "Be truthful", for instance. It seems, instead, to express a will that half-heartedly embraces both a fear of punishment and scouting principles, such as "Avoid telling falsehoods" and "Avoid punishments." It is not the sort of action one would explain or teach the principle M with, and would not engender the esteem of those who hold this scouting principle dear. Finally, although in 4 the agent's embrace of M is sufficient for his action, in the sense that even if there were no other cooperating principles, he would have conformed to it, it is not clear whether the action expresses M or the cooperating principle because we don't stipulate which was the "real" explanation and justification for his conforming to M.

Suppose, then, that moral worth is simply moral goodness of the good will expressed in actions. And suppose further that moral goodness is being good in any circumstance. Then when M is the moral law, 2 and 4 do not express something that is valuable in every circumstance. In example 2, it is because the principle expressed would not be the moral law alone; it would be the moral law together with, for instance, fear of punishment. In example 4, however, there is no unqualified goodness expressed, not because what is expressed has conditional value, but because it is not an expression of any single principle of volition; it is an expression of two principles, and so is opaque. But it doesn't follow that 2 and 4 are bad actions. They are good in some, but not in all, respects.

As I see it, then, only 1 and 3 are examples of what Kant thinks of as "acting solely from duty". They turn out to be instantiations of a general schema that applies to a wide range of practical principles and actions (that can exemplify the principles on which they are based). Add this to the thesis Kant holds about our reaction to the moral law, when it is exemplified in a person's behavior, and we arrive at the following conclusion: Actions have moral worth when the principle they exemplify is the moral law, and this is so because the judgment of "moral worth" is nothing over and above our own reaction of respect toward that law, so exemplified.

9. Conclusion: From the Good Will to the Fundamental Principle of Morality

The connection between the good will, the moral worth of actions from duty, and the first formulation of the Categorical Imperative emerges once we properly understand what Kant is up to in each discussion. To be valuable is to be the object of a rational will. To be unqualifiedly valuable is to be unqualifiedly the object of a rational will. And to be an unqualifiedly valuable object of a rational will is to be willed by rational agents, insofar as they are rational, in any conceivable circumstance. The principle that is so willed will be expressed in the actions of a person with a good will. The good will in such actions expresses what is the object of rational willing under any conceivable circumstance, the moral law, and hence express what is unqualifiedly good.

The search in the *Groundwork* is for a motivating principle such that, when acted on, it would "make my volition morally good", that is, good without qualification. That, Kant assumes, must be the fundamental principle of morality, the principle he is trying to discover and justify. For it follows from the fact that a given choice has unqualified value that it is good because of some intrinsic property it has. But the intrinsic property of any choice is just the principle that motivates and justifies that choice. It is an extrinsic property of a choice that it furthers self-interest, sympathetic and eudemonic ends. Choices based on those principles are good because they further our interests, promote others' welfare or our own overall happiness. In each case, we can imagine circumstances in which the choice based on such principles is not good because what is furthered by such a choice is not good. That raises this question: If we want to find out what makes a will unqualifiedly good, since we must focus on the intrinsic property of the choice, its principle itself, and not what comes of that choice, such as the consequences of choosing on some principle, what sort of principle could be the object of rational willing no matter what the circumstances? That is, What sort of principle could be that in virtue of which a choice is unqualifiedly good? But then we are focusing simply on the form of that principle, not what it offers as an outcome of choosing on its basis.

If what is unqualifiedly good is what I could choose in any conceivable circumstance then the critical question for Kant's project is, Which principle could I rationally choose that I act on in any conceivable circumstance? I end with just Kant's own words, for Kant takes this question to be the same as asking

"Can you will that your maxim become a universal law?" If not, that maxim must be repudiated . . . because it cannot fit as a principle into a possible universal legislation, and reason forces me to offer my immediate respect to such legislation (G 4:403).

Notes

1 All except one, the goal of moral perfection, a goal the achievement of which would result in, naturally, having a good will.

2 Kant often refers to the human will with one umbrella term, *Wille*. But in fact he distinguishes two capacities implicit in the human will, *Willkür* or the capacity of choice (the capacity shared with animals), and (using the term in a narrower sense than above) *Wille*, the practical capacity of reason itself, the capacity to lay down laws of behavior for us.

3 There is quite a lot of difference of opinion about what exactly a maxim is, and, indeed, whether we are acting on a practical law when we act on a maxim that could be a principle every rational agent could act on. See, e.g., Allison, 1990.

4 I am here reading Kant as thus to some degree in agreement with T. M. Scanlon and others who are "buck-passers" about the good. See T. Scanlon, *What We Owe to Each Other* (Cambridge, Mass.: Harvard University Press, 1998), 95–100.

5 *Principia Ethica* (1903; rev. ed., Cambridge: Cambridge University Press, 1993), 78–80.
6 Michael Zimmerman argues this in Zimmerman 2001, p. 145.
7 Some inventors apparently work this way. In their mind's eye, they construct a given device, and then imagine how it would operate. When they first do it, they discover, in imagination, that there is a hitch, some gear missing, some different fiber that needs to be used, and so on.
8 For a notable exception, see Foot 1997, pp. 172–4.
9 Henson 1979, pp. 39–54. See also Herman, 1981, pp. 359–82.
10 See Johnson 1996, pp. 313–37, for a fuller discussion of some of these ideas.
11 For this reading, see, e.g., Wood, 1999, pp. 27, 30–33
12 "Before a humble common man in whom I perceive uprightness of character in a higher degree than I am aware of in myself *my spirit bows*, whether I want it or whether I do not and hold my head ever so high, that he may not overlook my superior position. . . . Respect (*Achtung*) is a *tribute* that we cannot refuse to pay to merit, whether we want to or not; we may indeed withhold it outwardly but we still cannot help feeling it inwardly" (CPrR 5:77).
13 "What I recognize directly as a law for myself, I recognize with respect, which means nothing more than the consciousness of my will's *submission* to the law, without the mediation of any other influences on my mind."
14 Both Henson and Herman think this idea is key to understanding Kant's position.
15 Herman, 1981. See also Baron, 1984, pp. 197–220.
16 Herman, 1981, pp. 364–5; see also Baron, 1984.
17 "All reverence for a person is properly only reverence for the law (of honesty and so on) of which that person gives us an example. Because we regard the development of our talents as a duty, we see too in a man of talent a sort of *example of the law* (the law of becoming like him by practice), and this is what constitutes our reverence for him" (G 4:401n).
 ". . . for their worth consists . . . in the attitudes of mind – that is, in the maxims of the will – which are ready in this way to manifest themselves in action . . . they exhibit the will which performs them as an object of immediate reverence" (G 4:435).
18 Thanks to Nelson Potter for suggesting that I consider Goodman's account.
19 Goodman, 1976, Ch. 2.

Bibliography

Allison, H. 1990: *Kant's Theory of Freedom*. Cambridge: Cambridge University Press.
Baron, Marcia. 1984: The alleged repugnance of acting from duty. *Journal of Philosophy* 81: 197–220.
Foot, P. 1997: Virtues and vices. Reprinted in R. Crisp and M. Slote (eds.), *Virtue Ethics*. Oxford: Oxford University Press.
Goodman, N. 1976: *Languages of Art: An Approach to a Theory of Symbols*, 2nd edition. Indianapolis: Hackett Publishing Company.
Henson, R. 1979: What Kant might have said: Moral worth and the overdetermination of dutiful action. *Philosophical Review*, 39–54.
Herman, B. 1981: On the value of acting from the motive of duty. *Philosophical Review*, 359–82.
Johnson, R. 1996: Kant's conception of merit. *Pacific Philosophical Quarterly 77*.
Wood, A. 1999: *Kant's Ethical Thought*. Cambridge: Cambridge University Press.
Zimmerman, M. 2001: *The Nature of Intrinsic Value*. Lanham, Md.: Rowman & Littlefield.

2

The Universal Law Formulas

Richard Galvin

Introduction

Although much of what Kant says in the *Critique of Practical Reason* and the *Metaphysics of Morals* has important implications for the "Universal Law Formulas," any discussion of those Formulas should begin with his treatment of them in the *Groundwork for the Metaphysics of Morals*. Commentators generally include both the Universal Law Formula itself ("Act only on that maxim by which you can at the same time will that it should become a universal law") and its close relative, the Law of Nature Formula ("Act as though the maxim of your action were to become by your will a universal law of nature"), as a single "Formula" of Kant's famous Categorical Imperative. In the *Groundwork* Kant devotes much of his attention to the derivation of those Formulas, as well his application of them to specific moral questions, such as whether it is contrary to duty to fail to develop one's talents. Although Kant discusses issues raised by the Formulas in other works, and introduces other principles that resemble the Universal Law Formulas in a variety of respects, in no other work does he so clearly and directly focus his attention on them.

In the preface to the *Groundwork* Kant identifies its sole aim as to "seek out and establish *the supreme principle of morality*." Commentators generally agree that the task of establishing that principle, in terms of providing a justification for its status as the unconditionally rational supreme principle of morality and establishing its authority over us, is something that Kant turns to in *Groundwork* III. The most natural way to construe the arguments in *Groundwork* I and II is as directed toward *seeking out* the supreme principle of morality, in the sense of trying to unearth what sort of principle our ordinary ways of thinking about morality commit us to, and providing some idea, however sketchy, of how Kant thought this principle could be applied to some situations that call for moral judgment. But although there are obvious differences in how the arguments proceed, the argument in *Groundwork* I seems to lead to the same principle that Kant famously identifies as the Categorical Imperative at the conclusion of the first series of arguments of *Groundwork* II. How so? The "motivational analysis" argument in *Groundwork* I, which begins with the claim that the good will is the only thing that is "good without qualification," leads Kant to conclude that the principle upon which a good will acts (PGW) is: "I ought never to act in such a way that I could not also will that my maxim should become a universal law."[1] In *Groundwork* II Kant argues that from the very idea of a categorical imperative, that is, one that commands the will to perform an action irrespective of that action's ability or inability to serve any of our inclination-based ends, we can know what the content of such a categorical imperative must be: It is necessary that the maxim of one's action conform to universal law as such. At this point Kant asserts that there can be one and only one categorical imperative, namely, "Act only on that maxim by which you can at the same time will that it should become a universal law," which Kant scholars usually refer to as Kant's Formula of Universal Law (FUL), or the Universal Law Formula of the Categorical Imperative.[2]

Anyone interested in Kant's moral philosophy might have hoped that having unveiled the supreme principle of morality, he would have turned immediately to the task of clarifying some important issues raised by his formulation of the principle itself, such as providing a comprehensive account of what a maxim is, how to identify the maxims of our actions, and how to understand crucial terms such as "will" and "universal law." But instead he introduces what he calls a "variation" on FUL: "Act as though the maxim of your action were to become by [some translations say "through"] your will a universal law of nature," which is commonly referred to as the Universal Law of Nature Formula (FLN).[3]

Immediately after introducing the Universal Law Formulas, Kant considers four examples designed to show how to derive duties from the Universal Law Formulas,[4] as well to conform to the "usual" division of duties into perfect and imperfect, and duties to oneself and to others. In each case Kant presents the reader with a proposed action whose maxim cannot be consistently willed as a universal law of nature. Although these examples have received extensive discussion in the literature on Kant's ethics, it is nonetheless helpful to begin by examining what Kant actually says in the text.

The first example concerns a person who has experienced a series of misfortunes and is contemplating suicide, because he believes that continuing to live would be intolerable. Still he wonders whether it would be "contrary to duty" to take his own life. Kant identifies his maxim as "I make it my principle out of self-love to shorten my life if its continuance promises more evil than it promises advantage," and argues that this maxim could not become a universal law of nature, because in such a system of nature, the very same feeling which is meant to promote life would actually destroy it.

Kant's second example involves someone who can get himself out of a difficult situation by borrowing money and promising to pay it back (realizing that's the only way he will get the money), even though he knows that he will never do so. Doing so would be morally permissible only if the maxim could be consistently willed as a universal law of nature. According to Kant his maxim would be "When I believe myself short of money, I will borrow money and promise to pay it back, even though I know that this will never be done." The agent must then ask: "How would things stand if my maxim became a universal law?" Kant argues that the maxim could never hold as a "self-consistent law of nature, but must necessarily contradict itself," and therefore it would be morally forbidden to act on that maxim.

In the third example we are asked to imagine someone who possesses a number of potentially useful talents but cares not to develop them, preferring to devote his life to "idleness, amusement, procreation – in a word, to enjoyment." Kant identifies the maxim as "neglecting his natural gifts" and says that even though we could imagine a world in which no one developed any of his talents, we could not consistently will that this maxim become a universal law of nature, or that it be "implanted in us as such a law by a natural instinct," since a rational being necessarily wills that his talents be developed.

Finally, Kant describes a person who is doing well, and could easily help others who are experiencing hardship. But he says to himself: "Let every one be as happy as Heaven intends or as he can make himself; I won't deprive him of anything; I won't even envy him, but I don't feel like contributing anything to his well-being or helping him in his distress." Although Kant does not specify what this agent's maxim would be, he concludes that even though we might be able to imagine a world in which the maxim that corresponds to this person's "attitude" or "principle" were a universal law of nature, we could not possibly will such a law of nature, since we might face situations in which we need assistance from others, and we would have willed that no one provide assistance to anyone else. Thus we would be left with a will that is "in conflict with itself," in that we would both will the help that we need from others, and also will that no help be given to anyone, including ourselves.

Having presented his four examples, Kant claims to have illustrated the two ways in which maxims can fail to be capable of being consistently willed as universal laws of nature: some cannot even be conceived as universal laws of nature. Raising the maxim to the status of a universal law of nature reveals what Kant calls an "inner impossibility." In such cases (including his suicide and false promising examples) universalizing the maxim yields a contradiction in conception. Other maxims, although capable of being conceived as universal laws of nature, cannot consistently be willed as universal laws; these (including the maxims in his rusting talents and nonbeneficence examples) entail a contradiction in the will. Kant then goes on to assert that maxims which cannot be conceived as universal laws violate strict or narrow duties, whereas those that can be conceived but not willed as universal laws violate wide or meritorious duties.

While there are few points on which all who have written on Kant's moral philosophy agree, there is a fairly broad consensus among both critics and sympathizers on some relatively fundamental issues. For example, Kant's FUL clearly requires that we test our maxims by determining whether we can consistently will them as universal laws (or universal laws of nature for FLN). Although there is much disagreement about how to formulate the maxim of an action, each of Kant's examples suggests that a maxim contains a description of the action-type (e.g., making a false promise) that the agent is considering performing. Beyond that, some (but by no means all) of Kant's examples contain a description of the circumstance that the agent finds herself in (when in need of money), the purpose or end that the agent aims at by performing the act (getting out of difficulty), and the motive for performing the act (from self-love), although none of Kant's maxims includes each of these elements. So a schematic of a maxim might look like this: In circumstances C, from motive M, I will perform act-type A to bring about purpose P, although we should reiterate that beyond the description of the act, none of the additional elements is included by Kant within each of his examples. We then take this maxim and "universalize" it, by creating its "Universal Counterpart" or "UC-maxim," which is identical to the original maxim, except for changing the "I will . . . " to "Everyone will. . . ."[5] Kant's FUL can now be seen as requiring agents to act only on maxims whose UC-maxims can be consistently willed as universal laws (as universal laws of nature for FLN).

But beyond the claim that some UC-maxims cannot be conceived as universal laws whereas others cannot be consistently willed as universal laws, there is very little agreement among Kant scholars about how the Universal Law Formulas' noncontradiction tests are supposed to operate. Scholars disagree about issues as basic and central to Kant's theory as how to formulate the maxim of one's action that is appropriate for moral appraisal. They also disagree on exactly how a contradiction is supposed to emerge when, for example, the maxim in the suicide example is raised to the status of a universal law of nature, and there is similar disagreement on exactly how a contradiction in the will emerges in trying to consistently will, for instance, the maxim of nonbeneficence as a universal law of nature. These disagreements concern pivotal features of Kant's view, and we shall see that scholars have attributed a wide range of views that are claimed to be "Kantian."

At this point I would like to make two disclaimers. First, this essay is necessarily selective in that it cannot address all or even the most important arguments and positions that commentators have developed on Kant's ethics, and that because of considerations of space, no argument or position will be able to receive the detailed, careful treatment it deserves. My aim is to provide an incomplete, but I hope accessible, overview of the major work that has been done on the Universal Law Formulas. Second, in the course of the essay I will be discussing what appear to be discrete topics related to the Universal Law Formulas, including questions about whether they are supposed to operate as first or third-person criteria, how to formulate the maxim properly, and interpretations of the noncontradiction tests. My aim in treating these topics separately, which is admittedly potentially misleading and somewhat artificial, is purely pedagogical and is not meant to deny their interconnectedness. There are obvious links between how one sees the test functioning, how the maxim is formulated, and how the noncontradiction tests are interpreted.

Some Common Misunderstandings

In the two centuries since Kant's death, some misconceptions about his moral theory, and most notably the Universal Law Formulas, have proved to be especially enduring. I shall examine a few that are among the more persistent and which, if uncorrected, would make it difficult if not impossible to obtain a fair and accurate hearing for Kant's moral philosophy.

Some critics have claimed that the Universal Law Formulas are merely tests for inconsistencies within the agent's maxim; hence the tests will reject only those maxims on which action would be incoherent, not those that indicate immorality. But this is not at all Kant's view. Rather, Kant clearly held that there are some maxims, which, although themselves internally consistent, cannot be consistently acted upon and also willed as universal laws of nature. The "inner impossibility" that Kant refers to in describing how some maxims entail a contradiction in conception is not within the agent's original maxim, but somehow between acting on the maxim and willing the maxim to be a universal law. We'll see shortly how various commentators have differed on the details of this relationship. But on any reasonable interpretation it is a mistake to hold that Kant's is a test for inconsistent maxims.

Others have argued, and some rather vehemently so, that the Universal Law Formulas, focusing as they do on whether our maxims are willable as universal laws, fail to account for the consequences of our actions, and especially the interests and well-being of others. Admittedly, this objection has more plausibility when directed at the Universal Law Formulas as opposed to Kant's moral philosophy taken as a whole, which includes, for example, the Formula of Humanity's requirement that we always treat others never merely as a means, but always as ends-in-themselves. But Kant also includes within the division of duties that emerges from the Universal Law Formulas, however tentative he may be about the details of that architectonic, duties of both strict and narrow obligation to others, including the duty of beneficence from the fourth example. Likewise, it is difficult to read Kant's argument that we have a duty (admittedly indirect) to pursue our own happiness, on the grounds that doing so is likely to make us better able to comply with the demands of duty, as being blind to the consequences of our actions. Granted, Kant does hold that the special moral value of a Good Will is independent of its consequences, that the justification of the Categorical Imperative must be *a priori*, and that as far as "objective practical laws" are concerned, "everything related to the empirical then falls away" (G 4:427). But none of this entails that Kant's view either ignores or undervalues the effects of what we do.

One line of argument maintains that despite Kant's claims to develop an account of ethics that is independent of our idiosyncratic inclination-based desires, insofar as the Universal Law Formulas require that our maxims be willable as universal laws, what we can and cannot will depends on our desires and preferences. Mill famously charged that rather than deriving any contradictions from universalized maxims, Kant has shown only that there are some universalized maxims whose consequences we would not choose to accept.[6] Granting that some of Kant's language in discussing the four examples might be taken as appealing to the agreeableness of the consequences of everyone's adopting a maxim (especially the rusting talents and nonbeneficence examples), it is hardly the most charitable or accurate reading of the text. For one thing, if there are any maxims that cannot be conceived as universal laws, the issue of how we would view the consequences of raising *them* to the status of a universal law would simply never arise for those maxims. As for maxims that can be conceived but cannot be consistently willed as universal laws, Kant's test is most plausibly understood as relying on some notion of rational willing, which minimally involves standards such as coherence and consistency, and which in any case does not reduce simply to what one would prefer. Kant's view should therefore be carefully distinguished from "Golden Rule" views, rule-utilitarianism and universal prescriptivism, despite any shared surface similarities.[7]

Still another common objection runs as follows: since FUL proposes a negative test, requiring that one not act on maxims that cannot be willed as universal laws, then if one proposes to perform some action, as long as there is some description of an action, and therefore some maxim, under which I can consistently will it as a universal law, then action on *that* maxim is permissible.[8] So to revisit one of Kant's own examples: Suppose I were considering not aiding someone who is need, and whom I could easily help. Given what Kant says in discussing the fourth example, it would be wrong of me to act on the maxim of "refusing to render aid." But suppose I could find another maxim on which I could act in those circumstances, perhaps a maxim containing the act description "heading to the bar for a drink," which I could rationally will as a universal law, but which would also result in my failing to render aid. Then I could act permissibly by acting on the maxim of "heading to the bar," even though I would also be failing to render aid. Although this objection raises numerous important questions about the description of an act, the maxim of one's action, and the application of Kant's Universal Law Formulas to one's conduct, it is simply not the case that Kant would allow such "maxim shopping," since for any action, no matter how morally reprehensible, there will inevitably be some true description of the action, and arguably some maxim incorporating that description, which one might claim to be "acting on," and which will sail through each of the noncontradiction tests. So whatever ends up being the most reasonable position attributable to Kant, it cannot be that we are morally permitted to perform some action just in case there is some maxim that I can claim to be "acting on" in performing that action and that I can consistently will as a universal law.

How Different Are PGW, FUL, and FLN?

One area of interest for Kant scholars concerns the relationship among the three formulas that I and others have grouped under the heading of FUL; are there any important differences between and among PGW, FUL and FLN? There seems to be no significant difference between PGW and FUL. Each proposes a negative test ("I ought never to act" vs. "Act only") and demands that I must be able to will that the maxim of my action should become a universal law. The only difference of note seems to be that the PGW stipulates that I act on my maxim and should "also" will it, and FUL that I act on it and will it "at the same time." Each seems to require that I be able consistently both to act on my maxim and to will it as a universal law.

A more difficult issue concerns FLN. Exactly what is the difference between FUL's requirement that we be able to will our maxims as *universal laws* as opposed to FLN's *universal laws of nature*? Kant's stated purpose in introducing FLN is to employ the model of laws of nature as a template of sorts in order to determine whether our maxims can hold and are willable as universal laws.[9] How so? Given that nature "as regards its form" concerns the "existence of things so far as this is determined by universal laws," we should first attempt to conceive of a possible world that contains our "universalized" maxim among its universal laws, and if we can conceive of such a world, to see if we can consistently will it. But exactly what is the test for the ability to conceive and consistently will such a possible world? Since the actual world is the one possible world that we are familiar with, and since the laws of nature function as its universal laws, one obvious way of determining whether a UC-maxim could hold as a universal law is to see if it mimics the laws of nature in our world in some basic and important respects. Still, there is one crucial respect in which the laws of nature differ from what results when we consider our UC-maxims as "universal laws": the laws of nature are causal laws whereas maxims are what Kant calls "laws of freedom." When I choose to act on a maxim, the maxim does not "cause" me to act in the way that, for example, magnetism causes one piece of metal to move toward another. But despite that important difference, Kant clearly maintains that we should use the lawfulness of the laws of nature as a guide for determining which UC-maxims can be conceived and willed as universal laws.[10]

Some scholars have argued for a stronger claim, citing the discussion of the "typic of Pure Practical Judgment" in the *Critique of Practical Reason*, that only perfectly rational beings would be able to use FUL, with its requirement that we try to conceive of our maxims as universal laws, since it cannot be applied to our experience in any direct way.[11] All of our experience is filtered through the category of causality, and is subject to the specific causal laws of the actual world. For imperfectly rational beings such as ourselves to be able to derive contradictions from any UC-maxims requires bringing in factors beyond what would be entailed by using the laws of nature as a mere template or guide for determining what can be conceived and willed as a universal law. Instead, we imperfectly rational beings must appeal to the causal laws of the actual world, including what we know about human behavior and laws governing natural occurrences, in applying FLN. Presumably such considerations would not be permitted within FUL, with its emphasis on whether a maxim can be willed consistently as a universal law *simpliciter*. So in essence the argument is that FUL is empty for finitely rational beings whereas FLN, insofar as it includes causal laws, is not.

However tempting this strategy may seem, we should be careful not to read too much into Kant's move from FUL to FLN. Although Kant admittedly does appeal to FLN more often than to FUL in discussing his examples, he does use FUL in his first analysis of the false promising case (G 4:403), and refers explicitly to "universal laws" in his discussion of the types of duties (G 4:424), which indicates that Kant himself did not see FUL as empty or inapplicable to imperfectly rational beings.[12] And the most plausible reading of both the passage in *Groundwork* II in which he introduces FUL and FLN, as well as the discussion of the "typic" in the *Critique of Practical Reason* supports a much more modest thesis, which I shall summarize. The appeal to the laws of nature does not give us license to bring new considerations to bear in FLN; if it is legitimate to bring a consideration in when testing a maxim using FLN, that consideration should also be legitimate when using FUL. Admittedly, the issue of what if any information must be included in testing our maxims according to FUL and FLN is a matter of heated debate. But in moving from FUL to FLN, and in the discussion of the typic, Kant appeals to nature "as regards its form"; FLN uses the lawfulness of the laws of nature in the actual world, in other words, their consistency and regularity, as a guide for determining whether a UC-maxim qualifies as a maxim that we can will as a universal law.[13] In no way should this be taken as indicating a significant difference between FUL and FLN in terms of the background information permitted within each formula.

The Role of the Universal Law Formulas

Although Kant's first two arguments that are explicitly directed at "seeking out" the supreme principle of morality yield the Universal Law Formulas, and although there are numerous references in Kant's own work to support the contention that the Universal Law Formulas were viewed by Kant himself as playing a crucial role in moral deliberation and judgment as well as providing a very important conceptualization of the Moral Law, some commentators have argued that the Universal Law Formulas represent only a preliminary step in Kant's development of the ultimate version of the supreme moral principle that, unlike the Universal Law Formulas, is mature and comprehensive, namely his Formula of Autonomy.[14] My strategy here will be to take Kant at his word in characterizing the Universal Law Formulas as, for example, "the universal principle of duty" and "the authoritative model for moral judging of action generally," and to treat them as expressing important features of Kant's views on moral deliberation and judgment, and as occupying an important place in Kant's ethical thought, even if they do not represent Kant's thinking in its fully mature state. Although, as we shall see, there is much disagreement among both defenders and critics of Kant's moral philosophy over nearly every aspect of the Universal Law Formulas, there should be little doubt that Kant's treatment of these formulas often suggests that we can establish whether a proposed action accords with the demands of duty by identifying the maxim of that action and then determining if I could both act on that maxim and consistently will it as a universal law.

Another important issue relies on a distinction between viewing FUL as providing a criterion of action to be used from the first-person point of view for deliberating about how to act, or which maxim to act on, as opposed to a criterion of assessment, whose function would be to provide an "objective" third-person criterion for evaluating the actions of moral agents. Criteria of action purport to supply agents with a first-person framework for moral decision-making, and render judgments for the agent, given the agent's best moral lights, about what she ought to do. Criteria of assessment purport to provide a perspective that is independent of limitations owing to the conditions of the agent's subjectivity. Criteria of action tell us "how to decide" whereas criteria of assessment tell us "whether acts are right."[15] Recall that FUL's noncontradiction tests operate on maxims, which Kant describes as "the subjective principles of a volition." Even though Kant's explicit account of the term "maxim" is less helpful than one might have hoped for, given that maxims are volitional principles, it is reasonable to suppose that maxims are related to, some even say they "describe," how an action is willed by an agent (although this should not be taken to imply that maxims must be present to the agent's consciousness). Understood as a criterion of action, FUL would instruct deliberating agents to act on only on those maxims that are consistently willable as universal laws. The agent surveys the available maxims and rejects those that fail FUL's noncontradiction tests.[16] As a criterion of assessment, FUL would judge actions to be, for example, morally permissible or forbidden insofar as the maxim that the agent acts on passes or fails the FUL's noncontradiction tests.[17] Each approach has its merits. Viewing FUL as a criterion of action coheres best with Kant's focus on actions as they are willed, whereas viewing FUL as a criterion of assessment makes good on Kant's repeated insistence that FUL yields actual duties. But although within Kant's ethics the "first-person" point of view has priority, there is also an undeniable element of the "third-person" point of view found in Kant's writing as well.[18]

A related discussion deals with Kant's focus on the inward requirements of duty, namely the demand that we act on a morally worthy motive and only on maxims that pass FUL's noncontradiction tests. The question is whether Kant's obvious concern with duty's inward requirements means that he is unconcerned with, or can say nothing about, the outward requirements of duty, which concern whether the actions that we perform, apart from questions regarding its motive and maxim, comply with or conform to the demands of duty. It seems clear that Kant did believe that duty is amenable to outward conformity questions (otherwise it would be difficult to make sense of the shopkeeper and friend of man examples from the *Groundwork*, and perhaps all of the *Rechtslehre*), and even that he believed that at least some answers to questions about outward conformity could be addressed using FUL.[19]

Issues Regarding the Maxim and
its Universal Counterpart

The relationship between actions and maxims has deservedly received much attention among commentators. Kant's own words suggest that he thought (or at least
presupposed) that one could speak of *the* maxim of an action, or at least that in
the context of employing FUL's noncontradiction tests, we could identify the
relevant maxim to test.[20] Clearly, since FUL tests maxims, its usefulness in any
context will require a method for determining exactly what the maxim of an action
is or, if actions can have more than one maxim, which maxim should be subjected
to FUL's noncontradiction tests. The problem with subjecting more than one
maxim of an action to the noncontradiction tests is, roughly, there is nothing to
rule out the test's giving mutually inconsistent results for those maxims. This in
turn would leave open the possibility, which would be troublesome to say the
least, that one and the same action (or "course of conduct") might be judged
right under one description or one maxim but wrong under another.

Some commentators argue that actions and maxims stand in a "many-to-many"
relationship, insofar as one action can be performed from any number of maxims,
and a single maxim can be acted upon in any number of ways.[21] Applying FUL
would then require determining which is the relevant maxim to test. One such
proposal suggests applying an "isolation test" to the agent's intentions as follows:
the relevant maxim includes just those descriptions of the action and circumstance
under which the agent intends the action, namely those descriptions which, if
altered, would have led the agent to act differently. Perhaps an illustration would
be helpful. Suppose I have an extra cup of coffee because I am chilly. We might
ask: would I still have had the extra cup if I were not chilly? If not, then my intention was to keep myself from being chilly, and my maxim would be roughly "to
drink a cup of coffee to stay warm."[22] Similarly, if a doctor gives me an injection
that is painful but is effective against an infection I have contracted, we might ask
if (a) she still would have given me the injection if it were not painful (presumably
she would), and (b) if she still would have given it if it were not effective against
the bacteria that are troubling me (presumably she would not). She thus intends
to cure my infection but not to cause me pain, and her maxim would be "to give
an injection to cure my bacterial infection." But since agents often "intend" their
actions on a number of different descriptions, it is unlikely that in all cases a single
relevant maxim will emerge, or if one does emerge, that maxim will often be a
complex conjunctive maxim containing multiple descriptions of the agent, act, and
circumstances, and which may therefore be unsuitable for testing via FUL's noncontradiction tests. Consider a case in which I have to choose between keeping a
promise despite failing to save a life and breaking a promise in order to save a life.
Each UC-maxim seems perfectly conceivable as a universal law of nature, and even
though I might greatly prefer (with good reason) a world in which people acted
universally on the latter, there seems to be nothing obviously contradictory about
willing either as a universal law of nature. And since FUL requires deriving a con-

tradiction, whether in conception or in the will, from the UC-maxim, FUL seems incapable of determining whether I should keep the promise (while allowing the death) or save a life (while breaking the promise), since neither maxim will fail FUL's noncontradiction tests.

Others reject the "many-to-many" view on actions and maxims, maintaining instead that we can speak of a "properly formulated maxim" for an action, one that an agent is actually acting on when acting deliberately and purposively. This maxim is linked to what the agent wills and includes a description of the action, the reasons that the agent has for performing the action, and the purpose that the agent has in acting, as in "making a false promise to secure money" and "killing someone in order to get a job."[23] But even the proponents of this view admit that it is sensitive to how "the purpose" and "the reasons" are specified, and given that agents can act on multiple reasons, and for multiple purposes, it is unclear that appealing solely to the reasons and purposes we have in acting will reveal a single "properly formulated" maxim that is appropriate for running through FUL's tests.[24] Once again, we end up with either multiple maxims to test (and the possibility of conflicting results) or a single "relevant" maxim that includes multiple conjoined descriptions of the action, circumstances, and purpose (which seems unsuitable for testing via the noncontradiction tests).

One interesting attempt to clarify the relationship between actions and maxims alleges that maxims do not refer to specific intentions, purposes or goals that we have in acting, but instead involve underlying or fundamental principles or policies that an agent has in acting. Maxims are the "highest piece of practical reasoning" and govern the choice of more specific "ancillary" principles.[25] So when an agent deliberates, the maxim reflects deep policy commitments at the level of fundamental principles. These are relatively general (although not necessarily lifelong) commitments that guide the choice of more specific principles according to which that person lives. Although applying FUL to highly general maxims produces some interesting results, one problem facing this view is that even though some of Kant's own examples of maxims do reflect general policies (the rusting talents and nonbeneficence examples, and "to increase my property by every safe means," most notably), many maxims that Kant discusses and tests by using FUL are fairly specific ("to deny that a deposit has been made when no one can prove to the contrary," "to get out of difficulty by means of a false promise") and appear not to reflect deep, general policy commitments at all. To be sure, those maxims reflect and are no doubt endorsed by the agent on the basis of deeper commitments,[26] but by no means does Kant limit either the term "maxim" or those maxims which FUL tests to maxims incorporating descriptions at that level of generality. As we shall see shortly, Kant was probably very wise not to limit FUL to testing only highly general maxims.

One final approach to the issue of maxims and FUL deserves mention. It has been argued that Kant's FUL should not be viewed as testing the actual maxims on which agents might act in some specific context, the output of which would be an actual duty (i.e., absolute, exceptionless prohibitions and requirements) for that agent to act on or refrain from acting on some specific maxim. Instead, the FUL test should be seen as working with "generic" maxims, which can apply to many different actions, and more than one of which may apply in a specific instance. The application of the FUL test to generic maxims produces "rules of moral salience," which are to be used by the agent in her moral deliberation.[27] These state moral reasons, which have the status of rebuttable presumptions, for or against some course of action.[28] That a maxim cannot be consistently willed as a universal law provides a reason for refraining from actions that would fit that maxim's description, although some other deliberative presumption might be weightier in an individual case. But whatever the merits of this approach in relegating FUL to working with generic (as opposed to agents' actual) maxims and producing rules of moral salience that serve as rebuttable presumptions (as opposed to actual duties that hold with absolute necessity), it must be viewed as a significant retreat for the role that Kant at least at times seemed to endorse for FUL.

Even if the problem of which maxim to test were solved, an analysis of how FUL is to operate would need to specify exactly what is meant by "raising one's maxim to the status of a universal law." By far the most common understanding among commentators is roughly that one should imagine a possible world in which everyone who is in the appropriate circumstances adopts and actually acts on the maxim that is being tested, whenever acting on that maxim is available to them. Testing a maxim would then involve viewing the maxim as if it operated as a casual law, not in the sense that everyone were literally *caused* to act as the maxim specifies (since agents assumedly act freely), but rather that everyone actually does act on the maxim in this possible world. The exceptionlessness and regularity of causal laws (in the actual world) would then be replicated in that possible world. Among the obvious advantages of this way of construing the FUL tests is that it coheres well with the Kantian position that what we ought to do does not depend on what others are doing, and that it will flag those maxims whose wrongness lies in what Kant identifies as the hallmark of transgressions of duty: making an exception for ourselves that we could not will to be extended to others. But it also seems to invite a series of troubling counterexamples, some of which involve maxims that could not be acted on by everyone, not for morally important reasons, but due instead to "contingent circumstances," or some logical quirk that is arguably morally insignificant.[29]

In light of these (and no doubt other) difficulties facing the position that we should view the UC-maxim on the model of a causal law (everyone does act on it), some commentators have recently suggested that the UC-maxim should be viewed as establishing a *permission* to act on the maxim, recognizing that in many cases not everyone would act on the maxim.[30] Consider the maxim of drinking a rare, fine wine on one's birthday. If the FUL test required that we try to imagine a world in which everyone did act on[31] that maxim we would have to conclude that acting on that maxim is impermissible, since a rare wine literally could not be consumed by everyone. But if the test requires only that the UC-maxim simply be universally available, then given that not everyone would choose to drink a rare wine on one's birthday, there would be no bar to conceiving or willing that maxim as a universal law.[32] Given that not everyone will want to drink a fine wine on one's birthday, the universal availability of the maxim would not undermine my ability to pursue my end by doing so. Of course this strategy requires determining with an impressive degree of reliability just what people *would* do if such a maxim *were* available to them, which in turn requires an appeal to natural laws, especially those covering human dispositions that govern how people are naturally inclined to act. Determining how *everyone* would behave if a certain maxim were made available to them would appear to be no simple task.[33] Moreover, we would need some way of determining when the availability of a maxim – presumably one that it would be immoral to act on – would result in a sufficient number of others acting on that maxim to preclude my succeeding in acting on it. Finally, this view does seem at odds with the fairly central Kantian tenets that one's duty should be independent of what others are doing, and that there is something wrong about choosing to act in ways that are available to you only because others have not chosen to act in the same way.

The Two Hegelian Objections

Hegel famously criticized Kant's Universal Law Formulas, arguing that the formulas are both under-inclusive – in failing to entail any contradiction in willing the maxims of many paradigmatically immoral actions – and over-inclusive – insofar as the maxims of many innocent actions cannot be consistently willed as universal laws.[34] Regarding under-inclusiveness, Hegel argued that that FUL is an instance of empty formalism, and used one of Kant's own examples against him, charging that in the case of denying that a deposit has been made when one has been made but no one can prove the contrary,[35] the UC-maxim would generate no contradiction unless one had already presupposed a morally justified system of deposits, which would be question-begging. Hegel also argued that if a sufficient number of people (no doubt far short of "everyone") acted on the maxim of "helping the needy," the needs of the needy would be met, then there would be no more needy persons to help; thus not everyone could act on that maxim. But this would be a startling case of over-inclusiveness, since helping the needy is not just morally neutral: Kant's fourth example identifies it as an imperfect duty.

There is a sense in which the Hegelian criticisms have set the terms for much of the discussion of Kant's Universal Law Formulas. The task for defenders of the Kantian view is to produce an understanding of the Formulas that is sufficiently "Kantian," but does not fall prey to charges of over- and under-inclusiveness. One way of looking at a large percentage of the literature on the Universal Law Formulas is as a series of proposals by defenders of the Kantian view on how to understand the formulation of the maxim, raising that maxim to the status of a UC-maxim, and spelling out conditions for which a UC-maxim can be conceived and willed as a universal law, with an eye toward answering the Hegelian charges of over- and under-inclusiveness. We should now begin our examination of some of the more important contributions to this discussion.

Contradictions in Conception

No issue raised by Kant's FUL has received more attention than the nature of the noncontradiction tests themselves. Even if the correct maxim could be identified, whether its universalization were modeled on a causal law or a law of permission, questions would remain about exactly why the maxims of all and only immoral actions cannot be consistently willed as universal laws. While it is uncontroversial that Kant claimed that some maxims cannot be conceived as universal laws and others cannot be willed as universal laws, virtually everything else about the details of the noncontradiction tests is up for grabs. We will begin with a brief look at three interpretations of the contradiction in conception test and then turn to issues regarding the contradiction in the will test.

It may be helpful to begin by pointing out that Kant's own treatment of the infamous four examples, which he rather casually referred to as "enumerating some duties," provide little guidance for applying the tests to other more complex cases. Even worse, it is not at all clear that Kant has applied his own test in a straightforward, consistent, and helpful manner to those very cases. In the suicide case, Kant claims that the contradiction emerges because committing suicide out of self-love, whose purpose it is to further life, would contradict that purpose by destroying life. But what about committing suicide for reasons other than out of self-love? And why assume that the purpose of self-love is to promote biological life? In the false promising case it is not clear why promising itself would be impossible if the maxim of getting out of difficulty by making a false promise were to become a universal law, although one might argue that if all promises were insincere that there would be no promises at all; not all promises (or even all false promises) involve trying to get out of difficulty, especially financial difficulty. And in the contradiction in the will (rusting talents and nonbeneficence) examples, Kant's analysis suggests that the contradiction emerges insofar as the pursuit of my own (presumably inclination-based) ends either requires or would be greatly assisted by employing the aid and developed talents of others, as well as my own developed talents. But it is not clear why this violates the standards of rational willing: clearly I do not always will the assistance of others, even if I need it, and there are many talents that each of us chooses not to develop for a variety of reasons, not all of which are clearly irrational (some might even be morally compelling reasons!).[36] At the very least, Kant's analysis of the examples is seriously incomplete, and numerous interpreters have undertaken the task of developing accounts of the tests and results that are more thorough and claim to be sufficiently Kantian.

Regarding the contradiction in conception test, the central question is how a maxim, which itself contains no internal inconsistency, can entail a contradiction when universalized; it would appear that if a maxim itself is internally consistent, then its counterpart UC-maxim ought to be internally consistent as well. Therefore, something beyond merely changing the individual maxim into a "universalized" maxim must be involved in determining whether the maxim could hold as a universal law of nature. But there are good Kantian reasons to proceed with caution: recall Kant's argument regarding the topic to the effect that we are permitted to appeal to nature only as regards its form, i.e., its law-like regularity, in determining whether some UC-maxim can hold as a law of nature. In numerous passages Kant warns the reader against importing too much contingent empirical information into the noncontradiction tests. It is clear that Kant intended the derivation of the Categorical Imperative itself to be *a priori* and completely independent of empirical considerations, and just as clear that Kant recognized that in the absence of very specific empirical information it would be impossible to fit our maxims to any of our actions in the actual world, and so it would also be impossible for us to figure out what our duty in any situation might be. But it is not clear exactly how much and what types of information can be included within the operation of the noncontradiction tests in order to enable the tests to yield defensible results while still avoiding what Kant condemned as "empiricism of practical reason." We should now see how various versions of the tests have tried to accomplish this difficult task.

According to the Teleological Law version of the test, a UC-maxim must be able to be conceived and willed as part of some type of teleological system of nature. Its proponents cite Kant's references to "natural purposes," especially the suicide example's reference to the purpose of self-love, in support of this contention.[37] But on this view, it is not clear that a person contemplating suicide would necessarily be committed to whatever natural purpose self-love might have, and it is difficult to see how any contradiction would emerge if self-love has some other purpose (maximal enjoyment of one's experiences) or no natural purpose at all. And whatever "natural purpose" self-love is alleged to have, if it is not *my* purpose, it is difficult to see how *my* maxim will contradict *itself* if I try to will it as a universal law. One interesting variation on this view maintains that a rational agent is necessarily committed to valuing a systematic harmony of human purposes, and that the maxims of immoral actions conflict with this systematic harmony of purposes. But then a rational being could not consistently will those maxims as universal laws.[38] Here is how it is alleged to work in the false promising case: if I rationally must will a systematic harmony of human purposes, and if that requires the institution of promising to establish trust and confidence, then insofar as false promises undermine trust and confidence, I cannot rationally will the UC-maxim of false promising. The first thing to notice is that even if all this were true, it is not just the UC-maxim of false promising that I cannot consistently will; any maxim of false promising seems to conflict with the natural purpose of promising, so that universalizing the maxim seems to play no role in generating contradictions according to this view. The view also faces additional difficulties: it is hardly clear that rational agency requires willing a systematic harmony of human purposes, or that the purpose associated with promising is one necessary for a systematic harmony of human purposes, or that any agent must be committed to the alleged natural purpose linked to promising. Indeed, an agent might make false promises for the purpose of satisfying his own ends, and nothing more.[39] Further, it is unlikely that for every immoral maxim that violates a perfect duty, there is some natural purpose that is a necessary component of the systematic harmony of human purposes that would be undermined by a universal practice of acting on that maxim (as in the "natural purpose" of promising).

The two versions of the test most commonly discussed by contemporary commentators are the Practical Contradiction Interpretation (PCI) and Logical Contradiction Interpretation (LCI) versions. PCI locates the contradiction in the agent's purpose that is included within the maxim and the UC-maxim. In its earliest incarnation (usually referred to as the "Inconsistency in Intention" view),[40] proponents of the test asked "whether I can simultaneously intend to do x and intend that everyone else to do x."[41] When I intend to act on an immoral maxim I cannot do so, because I must also intend the "normal and predictable results" of what I am doing. So if I intend to rob a bank, I must be able to will that there be a universal practice of bank robbing, but this I cannot do. Why? In willing the actual maxim of robbing a bank I obviously intend for there to be a bank for me to rob, but the normal and predictable results of everyone's robbing a bank would be the collapse of the monetary system, without which there would be no banks at all. So I could not simultaneously intend to rob a bank (which requires intending that there are banks whose money I can take) and that everyone rob a bank (this commits me to "intending" that there are no banks), and therein lies the contradiction.[42] However, critics were quick to point out that the presupposition that I must intend the normal and predictable results of what I do should be rejected: when I struggle against great odds I intend to succeed, even though the normal and predictable results of my effort might be failure.[43] And absent that provision, no inconsistency of intentions is forthcoming.[44]

More recently, proponents of PCI have identified the locus of the contradiction in the purpose within the agent's maxim. The claim is that the agent could not achieve that purpose by acting on that maxim if the UC-maxim held as a universal law of nature, that is, if everyone were acting on that maxim. Acting on the maxim would be self-defeating: the agent acts on the maxim in order to achieve some purpose, but the UC-maxim would make it impossible to achieve that purpose by acting on that maxim. To return to the false promising example, making a false promise would be ineffective as a way of securing money if everyone were to try to secure money in that way.[45] For that reason, according to PCI, acting on the maxim of obtaining money by means of a false promise would be immoral. Two important points about PCI should be noted. First, proponents of PCI see it as providing both a first-person and a third-person criterion. So in a way PCI is intended to address questions about whether FUL can generate contradictions for all and only those maxims that it would be immoral to act on whether those questions are generated from the point of view of an agent deliberating about how to act in a specific context, or in an attempt to determine the actual rightness or wrongness of some proposed course of action. And second, PCI includes a specific proposal about how to formulate the proper maxim to test when using FUL. The maxim (or at least the relevant maxim) must include the agent's purpose in acting, and each of its other components is identified through the lens of the agent's purpose. Its proponents readily admit that PCI is very sensitive to how the maxim is formulated: "a great deal depends here on what the purpose is taken to be and how it is described,"[46] and I might add, equally so for the act-description and other components of the maxim. And if I'm right in claiming that agents often act on multiple intentions and for multiple purposes, and that our actions instantiate multiple act-descriptions, PCI will likely generate either multiple maxims to test, which invites problems involving conflicts of duties, or a complex conjunctive "properly formulated" maxim containing multiple intentions/purposes and act descriptions. It is difficult to see how to test such a maxim by using PCI's criterion, namely, whether one could achieve *the* purpose in the maxim by performing *the* action as described in the maxim if that maxim were a universal law of nature.

According to its proponents, PCI reveals moral unworthiness in maxims that involve cheating, unfairness, and deception, since if everyone, for example, were cheating, no one could attain the purpose that a person has in cheating (gaining an advantage) by cheating; if everyone were cheating, it would be to no one's advantage to do so. Critics of PCI have argued that acting on any number of paradigmatically morally permissible maxims would also be self-defeating if the maxim were adopted and acted on by everyone. The two most noteworthy examples involve shopping at after-Christmas sales and playing tennis early on Sunday mornings, when the courts are not crowded. The problem is that not everyone could get bargain prices (presumably the agent's purpose) by shopping at after-Christmas sales, and if everyone played tennis early on Sundays, the courts would be packed rather than empty. But then the original maxim would be ineffective in achieving its purpose, and PCI would flag this as an immoral maxim. Thus PCI appears unable to distinguish wrongful cases of free riding (the efficacy of promising falsely depends upon any number of people promising sincerely) from cases that aren't instances of free riding at all, such as choosing to play when as a matter of fact few others are interested in playing.

One way that some proponents of PCI have tried to address counterexamples of this sort is by insisting that the UC-maxim be viewed not on the model of a causal law, according to which we imagine that everyone adopts and acts on the maxim,[47] but instead as establishing a universal permission to act on the maxim. The idea is that the maxim would be made available to everyone, and by appealing to facts about the world, most notably about the psychology of human motivation, we can determine whether people would act on the maxim if it were available to them. Presumably, a significant number of people would promise falsely to get what they want if permitted to do so, thus making false promising an ineffective means to get what one wants, but not very many people would play tennis at off-hours (that might be analytic!) or shop after Christmas, so a person could act effectively on that maxim even if it were universally available. In this way, genuine cases of free riding can be distinguished from morally neutral cases of coordinating one's actions in light of what we know others will do. Still, conjoining PCI with the maxim-as-permission view is not without difficulties, perhaps most importantly whether human motivation is so uniform and nonmalleable that we can reliably determine how people would act if a maxim were made universally available.[48] But regardless of how the UC-maxim is construed, PCI would still face the criticism that in many cases, perhaps most especially in cases of moral conflict, there will not be a single purpose that a person has in acting, and since these multiple purposes will likely be linked to different descriptions of the act, there will be neither a single maxim nor a single relevant maxim for the action, and no clear way to identify one maxim for FUL to test, which is a serious problem insofar as PCI is alleged to generate actual duties, or a single but unwieldy, complex maxim that is unsuitable for testing.

Even proponents of PCI admit that there is very little in Kant's texts to support attributing the view to Kant that there is perhaps good reason to think that Kant would have rejected the view, and that there is little doubt that much of Kant's own words cohere best with the Logical Contradiction Interpretation. According to LCI, a contradiction in conception is generated between the original maxim and the UC-maxim in the following manner: for an immoral maxim, if everyone were to act on that maxim, that would make acting on the original maxim impossible. Proponents of LCI argue that this is what Kant meant by saying that contradictions in conception involve an "inner impossibility;" the agent could literally no longer act on the original maxim in a world containing the UC-maxim. Although there is no consensus among proponents of LCI on exactly how much and what type of background information is admitted within the test, there is general agreement that teleological considerations are ruled out, and that the purpose of the agent, whether or not it is included within the maxim, is not the locus of the contradiction. By and large, LCI's proponents favor testing general rather than specific maxims, tend to specify those maxims rather minimally, and try to rely on as little background information as would be required for the test to operate successfully.[49]

Given that among the various versions, LCI has the strongest textual support, it is reasonable to ask why so many Kant scholars have been reluctant to embrace it. The answer is that many believe that few if any contradictions can be generated by FUL if the test is restricted to the logical implications of conjoining the original maxim with its UC-maxim. This lies at the heart of the Hegel's and Mill's criticism that the FUL test is empty and can generate no contradictions at all. But even some proponents of PCI have admitted that LCI can successfully generate contradictions for the maxims of immoral conventional actions, i.e., those that depend on the existence of a practice. For practices such as promising, the practice cannot exist if its rules were universally violated;[50] the possibility of making a false promise presupposes that it is possible to make promises of any kind.[51] If there are no promises at all, there can be no false promises. But then the UC-maxim of false promising would make it impossible to make a false promise, and hence the contradiction.[52] In the possible world containing the UC-maxim, it is impossible to act on the original maxim. Other critics, granting that LCI can generate contradictions for the maxims of immoral conventional actions such as falsely promising, maintain that LCI cannot generate contradictions if the immoral maxim concerns a natural as opposed to a conventional action.[53] But LCI arguably generates contradictions for the UC-maxims of enslavement, rape, deception, and coercion, each of which appears to denote a natural rather than a conventional action.[54] Yet even if LCI could handle each of these cases, there is reason to doubt that LCI can generate contradictions for *all* of the maxims that the Kantian would include within the set of perfect duties. So while fear of LCI's emptiness is no doubt overstated, its incompleteness remains a legitimate concern.

Proponents of LCI fall into two categories on the issue of how to formulate the maxim, as well as whether the test can generate actual duties. One option stipulates that maxims refer to the underlying principles on which one acts, that is, to those principles on the basis of which one chooses the more specific principles that guide one's choices in life.[55] Examples of this type of maxim include coercion, deception, and enslavement. One argument that the maxim of enslavement cannot be conceived as a universal law runs roughly as follows: if everyone were to become a slave, since slaves have no property rights, there could be no slave holders, but without slaveholders there could be no slaves either.[56] This argument contains no reference to the purposes of the slaveholder or the slave, and presupposes no teleological conception of nature; the contradiction is alleged to follow directly from the logical implications of trying to consider the maxim of enslavement as a universal law (that all agents adopt and act on the maxim). However, it appears that intentions and policies are describable at various levels of generality, and it is difficult to see how maxims such as those involving enslavement express the most fundamental principles or policies of the agent. Indeed, it is more likely that the fundamental maxim for the typical antebellum slaveholder would be something like "I will operate the plantation most efficiently," or "in such a way as to maximize my profit." Owning slaves typically served the more fundamental end of maximizing profit, and consequently would not be the agent's underlying principle. In some cases our fundamental policies and intentions are clearly morally relevant (making it a principle to refuse to render aid) whereas in other cases moral relevance seems to lie at the level of our more specific intentions (lying to spare a friend some embarrassment). Since the morally relevant maxim (assuming that there is only one) does not always lie at the level of the most basic or fundamental intentions and policies of the agent, it is difficult to see how one might specify in a non-question-begging way at precisely which level of generality of policy and intention the relevant maxim lies. I see no reason to be optimistic over the prospects of doing so. Consequently, any proposal that fixes moral relevance at some specific level of generality is likely to exclude some morally relevant maxims.

Another option is to limit the test to "generic maxims," which are minimally specified and are not claimed to be either the maxim that the agent acts on or even the maxim that should be tested by FUL as a means to determining one's actual duty in a specific case.[57] On this view the result of subjecting a generic maxim to FUL is not an actual duty to act or refrain from acting on that maxim in some specific set of circumstances, but instead a deliberative presumption for or against a certain course of action. Generic maxims represent possible willings that an agent may engage in (making a deceitful promise to get something I want), and if a generic maxim cannot be conceived as a universal law according to LCI, this would state a moral reason against acting as that maxim specifies. One's actual duty (presumably from either the first- or third-person point of view) would be determined by somehow balancing or working with the deliberative presumptions that apply in that circumstance (although it is difficult to discern appropriate grounds for assigning weights to those deliberative presumptions within the Kantian framework, and especially so within the context of FUL – it's not as if one generic maxim can be "more contradictory" when universalized than another). On this view, "actual maxims are not the input" for FUL, nor "are actual duties its output."[58] The latter is the case because a rebuttable presumption is always open to being rebutted, and just because the failure of one generic maxim to be conceivable as a universal law states a moral reason against acting in a certain way, an even stronger reason might speak in favor of acting in that same way (not only will the deceitful promise help me out, it might save an innocent life), thus effectively rebutting and overriding the presumption. But whatever might be said in favor of this approach, it remains very difficult to square with Kant's claims about the role of FUL in moral judgment and deliberation, most importantly his resistance to *prima facie* moral conclusions, and the numerous characterizations of FUL suggesting that if a maxim cannot be conceived as a universal law then it would be morally forbidden for a person to act on it. For example, FUL is claimed to generate "actual duties" and to be "the authoritative model for moral judging of action generally" (G 4:423–4). As such it is difficult not to see it as involving a retreat from some key tenets within Kantian orthodoxy.

Contradictions in the Will

The contradiction in the will test alleges to expose a volitional inconsistency that occurs when one attempts to will acting on one's maxim together with its universal counterpart. It is imperative that the test not be simply a measure of what anybody or even everybody would want or choose, and that willing can never be equated simply with wanting or wishing. I might be able to wish or want or prefer to have my cake and eat it too, but I cannot consistently *will* that I do.[59] At a minimum, willing something to be the case involves committing oneself to actually bringing something about; not simply as an idle wish, but "the summoning of every means in our power" (G 4:394). When Kant derives a contradiction in the will from the maxims of the rusting talents and nonbeneficence cases, he is not arguing that it is psychologically impossible for a person to adopt these maxims, or even that it is psychologically impossible for a person to claim or believe that he can adopt both one of these maxims and its universal counterpart. Instead, he intends to show that it would be unreasonable or irrational for a person to will the maxim and its respective UC-maxim in those cases.

There is a fairly obvious way of misconstruing the nature of the CW test, which is illustrated by the following response to Kant's argument in the nonbeneficence case. One might claim to be able to will his maxim of nonbeneficence as a universal law, since there is no problem in conceiving of or willing a world in which *he* doesn't help others, since that is consistent with his getting all the help he needs; he wills only that *he* doesn't help anyone else, and not that no one help *him*. Of course this raises issues about how to formulate the maxim and its related UC-maxim, but it also serves to illustrate an important point about how FUL's tests are supposed to operate. In both the rusting talents and nonbeneficence cases Kant relies on what commentators have referred to as a "reciprocity requirement" in constructing and testing a UC-maxim. Kant's analysis of the nonbeneficence case clearly requires that one must consider within the scope of the UC-maxim not only those cases in which one is the benefactor, but also those cases in which one is the beneficiary of someone else's beneficent action; otherwise Kant would not be able to argue that in willing universal nonbeneficence, the agent would rob *himself* of all hope of the help he wants. Just as clearly, in the rusting talents example the agent has some talents that are claimed to be useful for all sorts of purposes (presumably those of himself and others), and the contradiction is alleged to emerge insofar as the agent would not be able to achieve any of his ends that would require either his or others' developed talents.

Exactly how to spell out the remaining details of the CW test is a more complex matter. It might be tempting to argue that we must will what we want, and therefore if our UC-maxim would prevent us from having what we want, this would indicate a contradiction in the will. But this would be too quick. Just because I want or need something does not mean that I must also will it, or the necessary means for obtaining it. Suppose you were enrolled in a symbolic logic course, and were having a tough time with it. Another student in the class is a wiz at logic, with whose help you would likely get a much better grade (which you want) than you would otherwise get. One might assume that since you want to get a good grade and enlisting his help would get you a good grade that you would will his help, but that might not be so. Suppose that during your tutorial session, in the midst of clarifying issues concerning the soundness and completeness of quantification theory, the logic wiz is also likely to eat all your food, drink all your beer, and make a play for your girlfriend. You might quite reasonably conclude that it would be better to go it alone and risk or even accept getting a poorer grade in logic than to put up with his boorish behavior. It is not that you don't want the higher grade, nor is it that you don't acknowledge his help as necessary for getting a higher grade; it is simply not irrational to refuse to will the means to what you *want*. And Kant's Hypothetical Imperative would explain why this is a rational choice; you abandon (or at least put aside or override) the end of getting the higher grade in logic because the necessary means are unacceptable.

Kant's rusting talents and nonbeneficence examples clearly depend upon some standards of rational willing. The previous example illustrates how the Hypothetical Imperative might function as a normative principle of rational willing: it directs us to take some sufficient and all necessary means for procuring our end, or give up the end. Sometimes pursuing an end would require us to abandon another end that we consider more important, at other times the necessary means might be seen as too costly or even morally impermissible, in which case we rationally ought to give up or put aside the end. Insofar as the Hypothetical Imperative can be viewed as a requirement of prudential reasoning (my example is clearly about prudential reasoning), which has to do with getting what we want, and FUL relies not on what we want, but on what is reasonable or rational to will, what is involved in rational willing, although it must include adhering to the Hypothetical Imperative's demands, clearly must go further.[60]

Some have questioned whether a "rugged individualist" or "non-needy agent" might sincerely and consistently choose a policy of universal non-assistance (that might turn out to be very difficult to accomplish) even if it might conflict with some of his own ends, and thus claim that there is no contradiction in willing as a universal law the maxim in either the rusting talents or nonbeneficence case. Could this type of person claim to be able to will consistently that no one render aid to anyone else, or that no one's talents be developed, perhaps on the grounds that his commitment to rugged individualism is strong enough to override any other interests of his that might be frustrated if no one's talents were developed or no one gave assistance to anyone else? Could a person claim that when achieving any of his other ends requires a means that conflicts with the end of adhering to his rugged individualism, rugged individualism wins out? At the other end of the spectrum, questions have been raised about what some people might claim to be unable to will because of "some psychological quirk" or a "rationally indefensible bias,"[61] as in the cases of not being able to "will" eating a certain food, or even interracial marriage. Could someone claim to justify opposition to intestinal surgery or interracial marriage on the grounds of not being able to "will" its related UC-maxim?

Two complementary lines of argument might be appropriate in response. One relies on the claim that people are vulnerable and not completely self-sufficient, and often require the assistance of others in pursuit of their ends, so that even the most wealthy and powerful among us are "highly dependent and interdependent."[62] This admittedly relies on some presuppositions about human nature, but the structure of the argument in both the rusting talents and nonbeneficence examples seems to involve something of this sort: when I will a universal law of nonbeneficence I will that no one render aid to anyone else; but insofar as at least some of my own ends require the assistance of others, I will have also willed that a necessary condition for achieving my ends will be unavailable to me. So I am committed simultaneously to willing the help of others (as a necessary condition for achieving my ends) and willing that others not help me (an entailment of the UC-maxim of nonbeneficence). A similar take on the rusting talents example would have it that many of my ends involve complex actions, on the part of myself and others. But given that the UC-maxim would entail that no one develop any of his talents, this would rule out the possibility of anyone performing any complex action.[63] Once again, insofar as my ends require complex actions and the UC-maxim would prevent those actions from occurring, my willings would be contradictory. The crucial move in the argument is the claim that continuing to endorse the end of "rugged individualism" in the face of the frustration of so many of my other ends that require cooperation and assistance would demonstrate irrational willing. That requires some further argumentation, but is not patently implausible.

Similarly, one might insist that the CW test concerns what we can and cannot will *as rational beings*, not what a person might stupidly, irrationally, neurotically, or fanatically claim to want. Indeed, some have held that the CW test must draw upon some account of "rational willing," one that recognizes things such as prudent pursuit of our desire-based preferences, but goes beyond identifying what is rational in terms of fulfilling one's ends. What counts as rational willing begins but does not end with the requirements of consistency and coherence, and includes something like the Hypothetical Imperative's requirement that we adopt all necessary and some sufficient means toward our ends. One suggestion along these lines is that contradictions in the will occur when willing the UC-maxim would systematically undermine the will's capacity to will effectively, and identifies the requirements for effective willing within the conditions for rational agency itself, including being able to will that others adopt our ends as their own and act in pursuit of them.[64] Others have suggested that any successful account of the CW test must rely on at least some standards of rational willing imported from subsequent formulations of the CI, most notably the Formulas of Humanity (FH) and the Kingdom of Ends (FKE). On this view, "what we could will under Kant's universal law formula may depend on what we would will under FKE."[65] For example, given that Kant's argument for FH requires us to recognize that rational nature, wherever and in whomever it exists, is an end in itself, then insofar as willing a UC-maxim would entail treating others merely as a means or failing to treat them as ends in themselves, this would violate a standard of rational willing imported from FH. Likewise, one could argue that if my maxim could not be adopted by rational beings who are and recognize others as ends in themselves, abstracting from their personal differences and the content of their private ends, then that maxim is not rationally willable. So what we could rationally will according to FUL might turn out not to be very different from what we would rationally will (according to FKE),[66] and a maxim that violates the CW test could be seen as "undercutting ends that every rational will is assumed to have."[67] Admittedly, these are merely preliminary suggestions, and all of the important details would have to be worked out, and some might object that such a strategy amounts to smuggling in ideas about rational willing that are normatively loaded. But it is difficult to see how an account of rational willing, especially one that is capable of functioning as the CW test demands, could fail to be a highly normative one. Still, one should beware of smuggling in substantive moral principles under the guise of standards for rational willing.

Three Persistent Problems and One Very Modest Proposal

Despite the volumes of important and enlightening work that has been done on Kant's FUL, a number of difficulties raised by the formulas appear resistant to resolution. First, there seems to be no satisfactory solution to the "problem of relevant descriptions." Since our actions can be described in a number of ways, at various levels of specificity and generality, and since the content of one's maxim (whether claimed to be "the" maxim or simply the relevant maxim to test) is sensitive to descriptions of one's proposed action, intention and purpose, most proposals for how to determine what is and isn't included within the relevant maxim seem ad hoc and rely on preconceptions about how the test is supposed to come out. Nor is it likely that any proposal will identify just the right maxim to test for each and every course of action over which a person might deliberate. This is especially relevant since there are act descriptions at various levels of generality which, if included within the maxim tested by FUL, would cause difficulties insofar as they either (i) cannot be consistently willed or conceived as universal laws yet refer to paradigmatically morally neutral actions ("being first though the door," "playing tennis with a better player," "buying but not selling clockwork trains,"[68] or (ii) appear to sail through FUL's tests despite referring to clearly morally wrong actions ("telling lies to redheads," "If I give birth to a baby weighing less than six pounds I will do everything in my power to kill it").[69] Each way of construing the relevant maxim faces counterexamples of this sort.

A second related difficulty concerns the tendency of FUL to give rise to, and to be unable to resolve satisfactorily, troublesome conflicts of duties. Kant seems never to take seriously the possibility that more than one duty could apply to a single case in such a way that one duty requires embarking on a course of action that the other forbids. This is especially troubling when the conflicting duties are those that Kant at various times refers to as perfect, narrow, strict, and necessary, given that Kant seems to view these as exceptionless and not subject to being overridden. But surely it would be wishful thinking at best to hold that these duties cannot yield incompatible requirements in specific cases. Consider the classic case of conflicting duties raised in Book I of Plato's *Republic*, when Socrates asks Cephalus how his account of justice (keep your word, pay your debts) would handle the question of whether to return a borrowed knife to its owner, given that he is now foaming at the mouth and threatening to use it to kill innocent victims. Cephalus claims to be tired and decides to go home, but Kant cannot simply duck the issue. In the few passages in which Kant does address the possibility of conflicts of duty, what he says is both unenlightening and unhelpful: he maintains that there never could be a genuine conflict of duties, since only one duty (he clearly must mean *actual* duty) can apply in a single case. What might appear to be a conflict of duties is actually a case of what he calls "conflicting grounds of obligation," in which case the "stronger ground of obligation" should prevail. And this sounds eminently plausible: when grounds of obligation conflict, the weaker ground should yield to the stronger, which determines our actual duty in that case. The trouble is that nowhere does Kant provide any insight into either what a "ground of obligation" might be or how one might be recognized, let alone how to determine relative strength among conflicting grounds. FUL seems especially ill-suited to that task; other than saying that contradictions in conception always provide stronger grounds of obligation than contradictions in the will;[70] insofar as FUL relies on deriving contradictions from UC-maxims, it doesn't seem to allow room for comparative judgments. And however plausible deliberating over the merits of the universalized counterparts of complex conjunctive maxims such as "breaking a promise to save innocent lives" and "keeping a promise despite failing to prevent the deaths of innocents" might appear as a way of fixing our moral intuitions in complex cases, it is doubtful that contradictions can be generated from these UC-maxims in any straightforward way.

A third difficulty concerns the contradiction in the will test. Clearly FUL cannot test maxims according to what we would find most agreeable, or what would provide better prospects for achieving our own happiness, or even the aggregate happiness. And a very narrow criterion for rational willing in terms of coherence and consistency is unlikely to generate contradictions for all but a few of the most egregiously "unwillable" UC-maxims. The most promising approach would appear to be importing a richer account of what one can rationally will from subsequent formulations of the Categorical Imperative (especially the Formula of Humanity and the Kingdom of Ends) and using that to determine which maxims cannot be consistently willed as universal laws. This would require abandoning Kant's claims that the formulas operate independently of each other and are equivalent, but if what is at stake is the coherence of FUL itself, that concession could be viewed as relatively minor.

At this point it is tempting to throw up one's hands and join the voices of those who dismiss FUL as immature, irrelevant, and not an especially important feature of Kant's ethical thought. If that means that we must abandon the idea that FUL can succeed in yielding actual duties, and provides both a first- and third-person moral algorithm, I would agree. Although there is some bite to the argument that Kant seemed to think that FUL could do all of these, perhaps in the final analysis Kant's hope must be abandoned in favor of a more limited role for FUL. There is quite a bit of merit in using FUL to test something like generic maxims to yield not actual duties but rebuttable presumptions, which would in numerous respects resemble Rossian prima facie duties (but without the intuitionism and realism). FUL could provide a procedure for generating, justifying and unifying prima facie duties, each of which is absent from Ross' own account. One might even propose using something like Kant's FH and FKE as models for how to adjudicate conflicts between prima facie duties, thus escaping Rossian intuitionism at that level as well. What would remain to be shown is that FUL can indeed generate a defensible set of prima facie duties, and somehow solving the problem of over-inclusiveness: what to do about maxims and act descriptions that fail to denote anything of moral significance but cannot be universalized. But these appear to be more manageable and promising endeavors than solving the problem of relevant descriptions, and trying to reconcile the first- and third-person standpoints regarding the application of FUL.[71]

Notes

1 In *Groundwork* I Kant argues that the good will, which is alleged to be good in itself, not because of any consequences that might or might not flow from it, is linked to the idea of duty. This Kant parses as "acting out of pure reverence for the moral law," which is both capable of providing a sufficient motive for action and derivable from

reason alone. Further, Kant claims that there is only one only type of moral law that can determine the will such that the will can be properly called good without qualification, and that reason can regard with reverence. Next Kant illustrates how this Principle of a Good Will would entail that I ought not to make a promise with the intention not to keep it, since I cannot act on such a maxim and also will that the maxim should become a universal law.

2   The argument in *Groundwork* II differs in numerous respects from that in *Groundwork* I. After some initial, primarily methodological, claims about how moral philosophy ought to approach the most fundamental questions that it faces, the argument in *Groundwork* II contains a detailed discussion of the nature of imperatives, which Kant refers to as formulations of "commandments of reason insofar as it constrains the will." He then distinguishes hypothetical imperatives, which "command" a possible action "as a means to the attainment of something else" that an agent wants, from categorical imperatives, which "represent an action as objectively necessary, without regard to any further end." After entertaining the question of how imperatives in general are possible for beings like us in relevant ways (we are imperfectly rational and subject to the influence of our inclinations), the demonstration of how hypothetical imperatives would be possible for us involves essentially this: in willing an end, we must either will all necessary and some sufficient means toward that end, or give up the end. And since we have the capacity to set ends and to engage in means–end reasoning, there appears to be nothing problematic in claiming that hypothetical imperatives are possible for us. But next he turns to the special – and more difficult – case and asks how a categorical imperative, which he has already identified as "the imperative of morality," would be possible for us. Here one cannot simply appeal to our ability to set ends based on our susceptibility to inclination, since an imperative that commands categorically cannot do so on the grounds that an action would serve some purpose one might have. Absent some purpose that an action might serve, how can an action be recommended as one that we ought to perform? Kant is clear in admitting that at this stage in the argument he does not intend to show, nor does he claim to be able to show, that such an imperative is actually possible for us.

3   There is some controversy, which we will eventually address, about just how distinct these three formulations of the Categorical Imperative actually are. For now I will simply assert what I will argue for later: the Principle of the Good Will from *Groundwork* I is different in only subtle and ultimately unimportant ways from FUL, and FLN is not different enough in significant respects from either of those to merit independent treatment. So I will follow those scholars who group these versions of Kant's putative supreme principle of morality (PGW, FUL, and FLN) together as Kant's Universal Law Formulas.

4   I should note that Kant's four examples in *Groundwork* II appeal explicitly to FLN whereas the initial treatment of the false promising case in *Groundwork* I involves what appears to be FUL.

5   The term "Universal Counterpart" is borrowed, with minor modification, from O'Neill, 1975.

6   In chapter 1 of Mill, Utilitarianism.

7   O'Neill, 1975, chapter 2, provides an especially clear discussion of the important differences among these positions.

8   See, e.g., Kagan, 2002, and Feldman, 1986. Oddly enough neither Kagan nor Feldman present this as an objection to Kant's view; they each attribute the view to Kant.

9   See Wood, 1999, p. 80.

10 But even this leaves it open whether imagining our UC-maxim as a law of nature means that everyone acts on it, or that the maxim is made available to everyone. As we shall see, this raises interesting issues.

11 See Aune, 1979, esp. p. 52–4.

12 Other notable references occur in the *Groundwork* at G 4:434, 437 and in the *Critique of Practical Reason* at CPrR 5:28, 29, 30, 31, 34.

13 This is how we test a maxim as a possible universal law of freedom, although the only universal laws against which we might perform such a test are universal causal laws. See Galvin, 1991, p. 390, for a more detailed discussion of this point.

14 Most notably Wood, 1999.

15 The distinction in terms of criteria of action and assessment appears in O'Neill, 1975. She includes an insightful example about how these criteria may yield different judgments. Consider the case of a teacher who believes one student to be a bully, and treats that student more harshly than another student who has behaved in essentially the same way (p. 113). Although one might be tempted to associate criteria of action with evaluating one's own actions and criteria of assessment with evaluating the actions of others, O'Neill points out that one can employ criteria of assessment in evaluating one's own actions as well: for example, those performed in the past.

16 This point is clearly illustrated in O'Neill, 1975, chapter 3.

17 That a maxim passes or fails the noncontradiction test will immediately yield a judgment that acting on that maxim is permissible or prohibited, but will not immediately yield any judgments that acting on certain maxims is required. While some have argued that it is possible to arrive at the conclusion that acting on some maxims is required by employing FUL, doing so requires more than a simple application of the CC test itself. Thomas E. Hill, Jr., has argued that a positive duty might be teased from the fourth example. See Hill, 2002a, p. 121. But as Hill correctly notes, such a duty cannot simply be "read off" Kant's treatment of the case.

18 The distinction between first- and third-person criteria resembles that developed by Barbara Herman, 1996a, in arguing that the "CI-procedure" is best seen as a guide for moral deliberation as opposed to an algorithm for the derivation of duties. It is interesting to view this issue in light of the "Copernican turn" in the *Critique of Pure Reason*: adopting the first-person point of view and viewing morality "from the inside out" could be seen as the crucial move in resolving questions that arise within the third-person point of view.

19 Even O'Neill, who has often argued that Kant's view should be understood as being focused primarily on guiding agents' deliberations, also admits that that Kant "no doubt thought that it was possible to derive specific principles of justice from" FUL (1999, p. 103). And for Kant, principles of justice are concerned with actions' outward conformity with the requirements of duty.

20 Consider Kant's application of FUL to the four examples at G 4:422–4. There we find reference to "the maxim" and "his maxim."

21 See O'Neill, 1975, esp. chapter 3.

22 The example is from O'Neill, 1975, p. 40.

23 See Korsgaard, 1985, pp. 24–47. This way of formulating the maxim is characteristic of the "Practical Contradiction Interpretation" of the contradiction in conception test, which is discussed in detail below.

24 Nor does an appeal to the agent's purposes and intentions necessarily pick out a single description of the action under which the agent intends it: see O'Neill, 1975, p. 41–2.

25 O'Neill, 1990, p. 129.

26 This actually squares with the "deposit" case in the *Critique of Practical Reason*, at CPrR 5:27. Kant describes that case as follows: the agent has made it a policy to increase his wealth by every safe means, and asks whether the maxim by which he would do this in this specific case, denying that a deposit has been made when no one can prove to the contrary, could qualify as a universal law. Kant proceeds to argue that the latter, more specific, maxim would "destroy itself" and "annihilate itself."

27 For obvious reasons, that deliberation cannot take the form of subjecting prospective maxims to the CC and CW tests.

28 See Herman, 1996a. The view that I am attributing to Herman is found in this essay, which differs in numerous important respects from that found in some of her earlier essays, which are also reprinted in the same volume.

29 There also appear to be times when what we ought to do depends crucially on what others are doing. Examples include paying one's taxes (if nobody else does, it's pointless), and charging up the hill to take on a powerful enemy (again, it doesn't seem to matter that if everyone were charging, the enemy might be defeated, if no one else actually is charging up the hill with you).

30 See Pogge, 1998, pp. 189–213. Herman, 1996a, p.140, also refers to the idea of construing the UC-maxim in terms of a permission and credits the idea to Pogge and Thomas Scanlon (in note 10). Hill, 2002b, p. 71, discusses the implications of treating the maxim in a similar fashion.

31 The "drinking a fine wine" example is found in Hill, 2002b, p. 71n. Although Pogge claims to employ the "maxims as permissions" view in conjunction with the Practical Contradiction Interpretation of the CC test, there appears to be no barrier to employing that view of universalizing the maxim with other interpretations of the test, e.g., the Logical Contradiction Interpretation.

32 Pogge, 1998 develops this view in detail. There is a surprisingly impressive amount of support in Kant's texts for this view: even in the application of FUL to the four examples in Groundwork II, he considers what would happen if everyone were permitted to make a false promise.

33 Kerstein, 2002, briefly discusses Pogge's proposal, which he refers to as the "universal availability interpretation," and portrays Pogge as offering an alternative to PCI. But Pogge is clearly attempting to modify PCI in order to get around the difficulties raised by the tennis and shopping counterexamples, rather than providing an alternative to PCI.

34 Some scholars have discussed this issue under heading of false positives and false negatives, but the terminology of over- or under-inclusiveness seems less prone to ambiguity.

35 Although this example occurs in the *Critique of Practical Reason*, Kant's analysis of it follows closely his application of FUL in *Groundwork* II.

36 I may have compelling moral reasons not to develop my talents for, among other things, deception, coercion, and producing weapons of mass destruction.

37 E.g., Aune, 1979.

38 See Paton, 1948.

39 These criticisms of the Teleological Law view are discussed in detail in Korsgaard, 1985 and Galvin, 1991. I also agree with Korgaard's claim that teleological considerations really have no place in the CC test (1986, 347n).

40 See Timmons, 1984.

41 See O'Neill, 1975, esp. p. 63–81.

42 The bank robbery example is in O'Neill, 1975, 70–3. O'Neill maintains that it is a requirement of reason that we intend the normal and predictable results of what we do: this is what "commits" us to intending them. See, e.g., O'Neill, 1990, p. 92.

43 The counterexample appears in Timmons, 1984.

44 In addition, this way of understanding of the CC test is vulnerable to problems generated by agents who act on multiple intentions, which leads to multiple maxims or complex conjunctive maxims, each of which leads to either conflicts of duties or difficulties generating a contradiction for the relevant maxim. In addition, there appear to be intractable difficulties involving both over-inclusiveness and under-inclusiveness.

45 See Korsgaard, 1985. Pogge, 1998, is also committed to PCI. But whereas Korsgaard sees the maxim as operating on the model of a causal law (everyone acts on it), Pogge sees it as establishing a universal permission.

46 Korsgaard, 1985, p. 40.

47 Korsgaard clearly understands it this way.

48 This point is made by Kerstein. For a detailed criticism of PCI and Pogge's rescue attempt, see Galvin, [under review].

49 One option is to hold that the only background information included is what would be necessary to make it possible to perform actions meeting the maxim's act description. See Galvin, 1991.

50 See Korsgaard, 1985, p. 30. The classic discussion of the meaning of a "practice," and its importance for generalization tests in ethics (which obviously includes CC), is Rawls, 1955.

51 But arguably, "just as it would be impossible for every circumstance to be exceptional, it would be impossible for every promise to be made without the intention of keeping it" (Singer, 1961, p. 256).

52 Other cases are discussed in Galvin, 1991.

53 Korsgaard, 1985, p. 31.

54 For example, see the discussion of slavery and deception in O'Neill, 1990, and Galvin, 1999.

55 See O'Neill, 1990, p. 129, *inter alia*.

56 This is O'Neill's argument (1990, p 96–7). The argument in Galvin, 1999, is different, but each relies on LCI.

57 See, for example, Herman, 1996a, p. 147.

58 Herman, 1996a, at p. 148.

59 For more along these lines, see O'Neill, 1990, and Wood, 1999.

60 Herman, 1996b, 118–21 argues that the CW test requires being able to guarantee avoidance of the Hobbesian condition. But she cannot mean simply that security in achieving our ends would be doubtful or less secure, since this would not entail any contradiction in my willing. A more favorable take on the problems created by a "Hobbesian condition" would see it as creating a situation that would rule out effective agency itself, but this would result in a much narrower scope for the CW test.

61 See Hill, 2002b, p. 71.

62 See Wood, 1999, p. 95.

63 See O'Neill, 1990, p. 98.
64 See Herman, 1996b, pp. 121–2.
65 See Hill, 2002b, p. 66.
66 *Ibid.* One notable difference, however, between the two is that whereas FUL asks whether one can consistently will a maxim as a universal law in isolation, FKE invokes the idea of a systematic unity of permissible ends.
67 See Guyer, 1995, p. 355n.
68 The examples appear (respectively) in Harrison, 1969, p. 213; Galvin, 1985, pp. 79–85; and O'Neill, 1975, p. 76.
69 See, *inter alia*, Galvin, 1991, and Dietrichson, 1996.
70 Even that might not be too attractive an option either; see Herman, 1996b.
71 Special thanks go to Thomas E. Hill, Jr., for helpful comments and suggestions too numerous to mention individually.

Bibliography

Aune, B. 1979: *Kant's Theory of Morals.* Princeton: Princeton University Press.

Dietrichson, P. 1969: Kant's criteria of universalizability. In R. Wolff (ed.), *Kant's Foundations of the Metaphysics of Morals*, 163–207.

Feldman, F. 1986: Kant's ethical theory: Exposition and critique. In C. Sommers (ed.), *Right and Wrong: Basic Readings in Ethics.* San Diego: Harcourt, Brace, Jovanovich, 18–42.

Galvin, R. 1985: Tennis anyone? Problem cases for formal universalizability tests. *Southwest Philosophy Review* 2: 79–85.

Galvin, R. 1999: Slavery and universalizability. *Kant-Studien* 90: 191–203.

Galvin, R. 1991: Ethical formalism: The contradiction in conception test. *History of Philosophy Quarterly* 8, no. 4: 357–408.

Galvin, R. [Under review] The practical contradiction interpretation reconsidered. Unpublished typescript, Philosophy Department, Texas Christian University.

Guyer, P. 1995: The possibility of the Categorical Imperative. *The Philosophical Review* 104: 353–85.

Harrison, J. 1969: The Categorical Imperative. In R. Wolff (ed.), *Kant's Foundations of the Metaphysics of Morals.* Indianapolis: Bobbs-Merrill.

Herman, B. 1996a: Moral deliberation and the derivation of duties. In her *The Practice of Moral Judgment.* Cambridge, MA: Harvard University Press, 132–58.

Herman, B. 1996b: Murder and mayhem. In her *The Practice of Moral Judgment.* Cambridge, MA: Harvard University Press, 113–31.

Hill, T. 2002a: Beneficence and self-love. In his *Human Welfare and Moral Worth: Kantian Perspectives.* Oxford: Oxford University Press, 99–124.

Hill, T. 2002b: Hypothetical consent in Kantian constructivism. In his *Human Welfare and Moral Worth: Kantian Perspectives.* Oxford: Oxford University Press, 61–96.

Kagan, S. 2002: Kantianism for consequentialists. In A. Wood (ed.), *Groundwork for the Metaphysics of Morals*, New Haven: Yale University Press, 111–56.

Kerstein, S. 2002: *Kant's Search for the Supreme Principle of Morality.* Cambridge: Cambridge University Press.

Korsgaard, C. 1985: Kant's formula of universal law. *Pacific Philosophical Quarterly* 66: 24–47.

Korsgaard, C. 1986: The right to lie: Kant on dealing with evil. *Philosophy and Public Affairs,* 15 no. 4, 325–49.

O'Neill, O. 1975: *Acting on Principle.* New York: Columbia University Press.

O'Neill, O. 1990: *Constructions of Reason: Explorations of Kant's Practical Philosophy.* Cambridge: Cambridge University Press.

Paton, H. 1948: *The Categorical Imperative.* Chicago: University of Chicago Press.

Pogge, T. 1998: The Categorical Imperative. In P. Guyer (ed.), *Kant's Groundwork of the Metaphysics of Morals: Critical Essays.* New York: Rowman and Littlefield, 189–213.

Rawls, J. 1955: Two concepts of rules. *Philosophical Review,* vol. 64, 3–32.

Singer, M. 1961: *Generalization in Ethics.* New York: Knopf.

Timmons, M. 1984: Contradictions and the Categorical Imperative. *Archiv fur Geschichte der Philosophie,* vol. 66, 294–312.

Wood, A. 1999: *Kant's Ethical Thought.* Cambridge: Cambridge University Press.

3

The Formula of Humanity as an End in Itself

Richard Dean

The "humanity formulation" of the Categorical Imperative demands that every person must

> Act in such a way that you treat humanity, whether in your own person or in any other person, always at the same time as an end, never merely as a means. (G 4:429)[1]

Of the different formulations of the Categorical Imperative, or different ways of stating the fundamental principle of morality, the humanity formulation is probably the most intuitively compelling. Yet, despite its intuitive appeal, even the most basic elements of the humanity formulation – what exactly must be treated as an end in itself, what is involved in treating something as an end in itself, and why we should accept this basic moral requirement – are surprisingly unclear and even controversial. My aim in this essay is to offer a consistent account of these basic issues, while acknowledging alternative interpretations and preserving the intuitive force of Kant's principle.

Although there is significant disagreement about the details of the humanity formulation, there is at least rough consensus among commentators about some starting points.

One generally accepted interpretive idea is that Kant is not saying that exactly all and only members of the human species must be treated as ends in themselves. His use of the term "humanity" (in German, *die Menschheit*) is potentially misleading, since he also consistently says that "rational beings" are ends in themselves, in virtue of their "rational nature." Rationality is the key feature that distinguishes typical humans from all the other beings that we know of, so it is not too great a slip to say that human beings are ends in themselves. But Kant also thinks that God possesses a rational nature, more perfectly rational than our own, and he even thinks it could well be that there are races of rational beings living on other planets (A 7:332). So Kant does not mean to say that only members of our biological species can be rational or must be treated as ends in themselves. And if rational nature is what makes a being an end in herself, then being biologically human is not a sufficient condition for being an end in oneself either. Some humans – patients in permanent vegetative states, for example – lack even the most minimal sort of rationality. So there is a consensus that Kant means that rational beings are ends in themselves, not that all and only members of the species *homo sapiens* are ends in themselves.

There also is some agreement about what it means to call something an end in itself. For Kant, an end (*der Zweck*) is a reason or purpose for action. Most ends are contingent ends, based on desires or feelings that may vary from person to person. For instance, learning to speak Chinese may be an end for you but not for me, because we have different plans and desires. No person is rationally required to adopt any contingent end – there is no reason for me to adopt the end of learning Chinese if I have no desire to and if doing so does not serve any further purpose I have. But besides contingent ends, there is another kind of end that necessarily provides a compelling reason for every rational agent to act in certain ways. This is an end in itself. There are some requirements or principles built into any rational deliberation about what to do – some considerations that we can not rationally ignore – and Kant expresses this by saying that there is a necessary end that must be given weight in any agent's deliberations. This end in itself is rational nature, in oneself and in others. Because of rational nature's special status, we cannot regard it as having significance only because of what it gets us. So, we must not treat it as merely a means to the satisfaction of our own desires.

This gives an abstract idea of what the phrase "end in itself" means, but Kant of course goes further, and he specifies some of the ways in which we are required to treat rational nature because of its being an end in itself. The unique importance of rational nature, according to Kant, leads to specific duties to develop our own powers of rationality, to refrain from destroying ourselves, to give some weight to others' choices and concerns, and to treat others with respect. How exactly such duties follow from the idea of rational nature's special status is often unclear in Kant's texts and requires some speculative reconstruction of his arguments.

So, some basic points regarding the humanity formulation are clear enough. The humanity formulation requires that rational nature, and every rational being, must be given a special weight in everyone's deliberations about how to act. And Kant enumerates some particular duties that are implied by this special status. But each of these points needs further explanation. And even after Kant's view is explained, the question remains of why we ought to accept any of it. I turn now to exploring these points in more detail.

What Should We Treat as an End in Itself?

It is widely, and I think rightly, agreed that Kant thinks the end in itself is rational nature. But the term "rational nature" is ambiguous.

In part because of the influence of economic models of rationality, rationality nowadays is associated most naturally with instrumental reason, or with calculating the most effective means to satisfy one's own desires. But Kant does not use the words "reason" or "rationality" (the same German word, *die Vernunft*, is translated into either English word) or the adjective "rational" (*vernunftige*) to be associated mainly with instrumental reason. So the characteristic that makes someone an end in herself is not the ability to seek effective means to her ends. Neither does Kant mean to contrast "rational" with "emotional," so the humanity formulation is not saying that beings who suppress their emotions have a special moral status that others lack.

Kant's conception of reason or rationality should not be taken to have the same sense or connotation as these current versions of "rationality," since Kant's own account of the power of reason is perhaps the most distinctive and fundamental element of his overall philosophical system. Kant divides the power of reason into theoretical and practical aspects. In either aspect, reason is a very active faculty. In its theoretical use, reason supplies principles that guide the understanding in its task of organizing our sense impressions into coherent and understandable patterns. Theoretical reason does not just respond to passively received information, but instead spontaneously provides principles that make coherent perception and empirical scientific investigation possible. Similarly, in its practical use, reason does more than seek the best means to whatever contingent desires we passively find ourselves possessing. Practical reasoning has to do with the exercise of our will. One aspect of our will is *Willkür*, or the power to make choices about which ends we will adopt. Another aspect is *Wille*, which presents or "legislates" categorical moral principles to an agent. Every competent adult human, and any other rational being that may exist, has both *Willkür* and *Wille*, on Kant's picture. A perfectly rational agent would always exercise her power of choice, or *Willkür*, in ways that are consistent with the moral demands given by *Wille*, because her own power of reason presents these moral principles as unconditional reasons for action. But of course, actual people are imperfectly rational, and so they sometimes choose to perform actions that are contrary to self-given moral principles.

Kant's account of reason and the will presents many possible candidates for the end in itself. Perhaps it is theoretical reason that is the end in itself, or perhaps it is practical reason. Or maybe some particular aspect of practical reason, such as a being's *Willkür*, qualifies her as an end in herself. Or maybe someone is an end in herself in virtue of the power to legislate moral principles. Or, to adopt a more demanding requirement, maybe someone is an end in herself only if she not only possesses *Willkür* and *Wille*, but also is sufficiently rational to recognize and acknowledge the unconditional force of moral principles, and so regulates her particular choices in accordance with moral principles. In fact, there is no clear consensus about which of these possible readings of "rational nature" as an end in itself is correct; almost every version has received some support in recent decades. Although there has been surprisingly little attention paid to resolving the divergence in the readings of the "humanity" or "rational nature" that must be treated as an end in itself, the issue seems crucial to a proper understanding of the humanity formulation.

Some commentators have proposed that the end in itself is the power to set ends (*Willkür*), or the power to set ends plus the power to organize one's ends into a consistent package (Korsgaard, 1996, pp. 17, 110, 346; Wood, 1999, p. 118–120). The importance of the power of choice is a familiar idea to current moral philosophers steeped in political liberalism's emphasis on the foundational importance of choice. But given Kant's emphasis on the importance of choosing to obey reason's moral demands, it would be odd if the power of choice *simpliciter* were the end in itself that must be given special consideration. The power of choice is only one aspect of practical reason, and someone can possess the power of choice and yet choose to act contrary to the rationally compelling principles legislated by *Wille*, another aspect of her own power of reason. In light of this, identifying the power of choice as "rational nature" would seem peculiar.

For similar reasons, it would be even stranger if Kant took just the use of theoretical reason as the main distinguishing feature of the end in itself. While the exercise of theoretical reason does culminate in impressive theories of physical science and in some spectacular technical accomplishments, it leaves out an aspect of reason that Kant consistently emphasizes, namely the aspect related to moral reasoning. In *Groundwork*, Kant says that "Morality is the only condition under which a rational being can be an end in himself. . . Therefore morality, and humanity so far as it is capable of morality, is the only thing which has dignity" (G 4:435). In the later work *The Metaphysics of Morals* (which develops and applies the basic moral principles of *Groundwork*), Kant says the respect we should show another person is "respect for man as a moral being" (MM 6:464), and that "morality is an end in itself" (MM 6:422–3, also MM 6:436). In *Critique of Practical Reason*, Kant says that "the human being (and with him every rational being) is an end in itself" because a human being "is the subject of the moral law and so of that which is holy in itself, on account of which and in agreement with which alone anything can be called holy" (CPrR 5:131–2). In the *Critique of Judgment*, Kant says that "it is only as a moral being that man can be the final purpose [end, or *Zweck*] of creation" (CJ 5:437; CJ 5:443). The aspect of rational nature that marks a being as an end in herself, then, is the aspect related to legislating and acting on moral principles.

But this still is not a precise answer. One feature of rational nature which makes moral reasoning possible is the *Wille's* activity of legislating moral principles. Universal moral principles are built into the activity of deliberating about what to do, so every agent must take her own power of practical reason to be presenting her with unavoidable moral requirements.[2] Perhaps the power of legislating unconditional moral demands is the aspect of reason that marks a rational being as an end in herself.

But some commentators have taken the "capacity for morality" to be the distinguishing feature of beings who are ends in themselves, and this capacity involves more than just legislating moral principles. For a perfect or "holy will" like God's, the requirements of reason might be sufficient to lead to moral actions, but for beings like us, who are influenced by sensual desires and emotions, there must also be some feeling that accompanies the choice to act on the moral law. The feeling of *Achtung*, translated as "respect" or "reverence," is the key feeling that is needed. Kant distinguishes *Achtung* from the typical sort of human feeling, in that it is "not of empirical origin," instead being "produced by an intellectual ground," namely the recognition of moral principles' unconditional power to command. "Moral law strikes down self-conceit" (CPrR 5:73) by showing that there is something more important than our own inclinations, and "what in our own judgment infringes upon our self-conceit humiliates" (CPrR 5:74). But it also produces a positive feeling of *Achtung* for the moral law itself, because the "relative weightiness of the law" is made apparent by its "removal of the counterweight" (CPrR 5:76) of immoral desires. So although the moral law can produce a "feeling of displeasure" by "the lowering of pretensions to self-esteem," (CPrR 5:78–9) it also is "an elevation of the moral" and as such there is "so little displeasure in it that, once one has laid self-conceit aside . . . one can in turn never get enough of contemplating the majesty of this law" (CPrR 5:77). *Achtung*, then, is a moral feeling, a positive feeling of respect for moral principles which is inspired by the objective normative force of such principles. For beings like us, who are rational yet subject to sensual influences, the capacity for morality is most plausibly taken to be the combination of *Wille*, *Willkür*, and the moral feeling of *Achtung*, which can counteract feelings and desires that may lead us away from morality's demands. Some commentators have defended the view that this capacity for morality may be what qualifies a being as an end in herself.[3]

But to merely possess the capacity for morality is not to be rational in the fullest sense possible for human beings. Moral principles are commanded by *Wille*, an aspect of our own power of practical reason, as sufficient reasons for action. So someone who acts contrary to moral principles is acting irrationally, on Kant's picture. It may well be that by saying that rational nature is an end in itself, Kant means to say that a being is an end in herself only if she is committed to acting on the moral principles demanded by her own power of reason. This reading of the end in itself is certainly not conventional among Kant commentators, mostly because it appears to have unpalatably moralistic consequences – it appears to demand judgments of others' moral character, and differential treatment based on those judgments. But I argue elsewhere that it does not have the repugnant consequences that one might think, and that it is the most textually justified reading of the humanity formulation (Dean, 1996; 2006).

We can provisionally conclude that the end in itself is rational nature, where rational nature includes some aspect of moral reason – either the power to legislate moral principles, the overall capacity to act on moral principles, or the commitment to actually act on them. Which of these readings is most justified depends largely on which one allows the most compelling and plausible reconstructions of Kant's basic arguments related to the humanity formulation.

Value and Ends

Before turning to the argument for and applications of the humanity formulation, some explanation is needed of Kant's conception of value.

For Kant, the choices of rational agents are conceptually prior to the value of the objects chosen, so value is a matter of being an "object of practical reason" (CPrR 5:57). This no doubt sounds odd to many readers. The influence of consequentialism in moral philosophy, and the influence of rational choice theory in many disciplines, makes it seem natural to take rational choice as a matter of reacting properly to preexisting value, perhaps even by maximizing that which has value. But Kant explicitly denies this. Value does not present itself to an agent as a result of any preexisting external or internal state. In his most extended discussion of the concept of value, in *Critique of Practical Reason* 5:57–64, Kant first argues that the fact that someone wants something, or prefers some state of affairs to come about, is not sufficient to show that the state of affairs is of value. Preferences or desires by themselves are not sufficient conditions for value, they are only of value when they are consistent with one's overall happiness, because a person's "reason certainly has a commission from the side of his sensibility which it cannot refuse, to attend to its interest and to form practical maxims with a view to happiness" (CPrR 5:61). But consistency with one's overall satisfaction is only a necessary condition for value, not a sufficient condition. A rational being does not "use reason merely as a tool for the satisfaction of his needs as a sensible being." He also has a "higher purpose," of accepting a principle that is a "practical law *a priori*" – a Categorical Imperative – and making it "the determining ground of the will without regard to possible objects of the faculty of desire" (CPrR 5:62). Only choices that conform to moral law confer value, so it is "the moral law that first determines and makes possible the concept of the good" (CPrR 5:64). Value is not determined by one's desires or feelings, nor is it a property that is passively perceived. Instead value is conferred by the choices of a being who acts upon rational principles of both prudence and morality. I do not claim that the ideas just summarized provide decisive arguments against the possibility of taking value as conceptually fundamental, but just that they summarize Kant's position.[4]

In some passages in *Groundwork*, including the first of Kant's two arguments that humanity must be the end in itself, it may sound as if Kant relies on fundamental claims about value. And it is true that Kant does not explicitly and forcefully articulate his atypical concept of value until the later *Critique of Practical Reason*. But despite his occasional terminological lapses, Kant says even in *Groundwork* that value must depend on "law-making," the activity of rational willing, "which determines all worth" (G 4:436). And all the major arguments of *Groundwork*, including the arguments for humanity as an end in itself, can be cast accurately in terms that do not rely on a conceptually fundamental claim about value.

It is quite possible to take Kant's account of ends in a way that is consistent with the conceptual priority of rational choice. The most familiar type of ends are contingent or "subjective" ends, ends based on desires or feelings. It is not the case, on Kant's story, that a desire is always a reason for action in itself. It is only a reason if one chooses to makes it so. Ends, in other words, are always chosen, rather than one simply finding oneself with them. Once someone chooses to adopt an end, say the end of traveling to Egypt, Kant would then say that the end has value for that person. Kant describes the value of such contingent ends as a "relative" or "conditional" value. The value is relative, because traveling to Egypt only has value for an agent with a desire to travel to Egypt. The value is conditional in several ways. First, it is conditional in the same way it is relative – it only has value for someone on the condition of that person having the requisite desire. But it also is conditional on fitting with the overall package of an agent's ends (so the end of traveling to Egypt has no value if traveling to Egypt will thwart the satisfaction of other, more important contingent ends), and its value also is conditional on being morally permissible (so if one must act immorally in order to be able to get to Egypt, the end has no value). In these ways, claims about the value of a contingent end are conceptually dependent on the fact that the end is rationally chosen.

A necessary end differs from contingent ends in that a necessary end provides a reason for everyone to act in certain ways, regardless of her particular desires. Contingent ends are, at least typically, states of affairs to be brought about, such as the state of affairs in which I visit Egypt. But the only necessary end is rational nature, and it is not primarily a state of affairs to be brought about. It is a different kind of reason for action. Since rational nature is not something to be brought about to the maximum extent possible, we are not obligated to maximize the number of rational beings in the world, by having as many children as possible, nor are we obligated to maximize the number of rational choices that we make or maximize the extent to which we carefully ponder every choice. These consequences probably would follow from taking the value of rational nature as conceptually fundamental and then asking how to react to that value. But this is not Kant's approach. Instead, Kant's argument that rational nature is a necessary end, or end in itself, is meant to establish directly that we always, unconditionally, have a reason to treat rational nature in certain ways. That is, Kant does not at any point try to establish the conceptually prior value of rational nature and then derive duties regarding how to react to that value. Instead, he first argues that rational nature must be treated in certain ways, and any talk of the value of rational nature is just a shorthand for these requirements. Since a necessary end, or end in itself, is a reason that must carry weight for every agent in her deliberations, we can say that the value of a necessary end is absolute instead of relative, and unconditional instead of conditional on an agent's particular desires. Since no material reward can justify treating rational nature inappropriately, we can say that rational nature has an incomparably high value. But so far, this is not to specify the kinds of actions which are required by rational nature's status as an end in itself. To find these requirements, it is necessary to turn to Kant's argument for the legitimacy of the humanity formulation as a basic moral principle.

The Argument for the Humanity Formulation

A satisfactory reconstruction of Kant's argument for the humanity formulation has been elusive.

There are two general stages in Kant's overall argument. Kant first argues that if there is such a thing as a basic moral principle, then there must also be something that is an end in itself, because only an end in itself could ground a Categorical Imperative (G 4:427–8). This first stage is relatively clear. Then he tries to show that humanity or "rational nature" is the only satisfactory candidate for the position of end in itself (G 4:428–9). This second stage of the argument is remarkably cryptic, even in its most fundamental moves, so any efforts toward understanding the argument will necessarily involve significant reconstruction and filling in, rather than just interpretation. But the first, clearer, stage provides important clues for understanding the second, more difficult, argument that the end in itself must be rational nature.

Kant's arguments in the first two chapters of *Groundwork*, including the arguments regarding the end in itself, are not meant to stand independently of all everyday moral beliefs. Kant says in the preface to *Groundwork* that in the first two chapters his strategy is to "proceed analytically from common cognition [of morality] to the determination of its supreme principle," that is, to see what the content of the Categorical Imperative must be if it is to fit with basic everyday beliefs about the nature of morality (G 4:392). He says he will leave aside the project of establishing that there really are such things as moral principles – that morality is not a "mere phantom of the brain" – until chapter 3 (G 4:445). So, in arguing for the humanity formulation, Kant provisionally assumes that there are such things as basic moral principles, and points out that the only thing that could count as a moral principle or "supreme practical principle" is a Categorical Imperative, or a "universal practical law" that unconditionally demands compliance from everyone (G 4:428). Kant goes on to argue that if there is such a Categorical Imperative, then there must also be something that is an end in itself.

Contingent or relative ends cannot be the basis for a moral principle that necessarily applies to everyone, simply because such ends vary from person to person. Kant says

> [T]heir mere relation to a specially constituted faculty of desire on the part of the subject gives them their worth, which can therefore furnish no universal principles, no principles valid and necessary for all rational beings and also for every volition, that is, no practical laws. (G 4:428)

Therefore, if there are any genuine moral principles there also must be something that is an end in itself, an end that every agent must recognize as a reason for action regardless of her particular desires.[5] But to say that there must be some end that applies necessarily to everyone if there is to be a Categorical Imperative is not yet to specify what that end must be.

Kant first simply asserts that a rational being is always an end in herself, in *Groundwork* 4:428, but then he offers two arguments for the claim. The first argument is also in *Groundwork* 4:428, and appears to be an argument by elimination. Kant examines and rejects three candidates for the position of end in itself. Since the argument is not compelling, I will focus on Kant's second argument instead.

This second argument for the claim that rational nature must be the end in itself, in Groundwork 4:428–9, is intriguing, but so compressed as to be largely mysterious. Kant certainly gives some signs that he takes it to be a sound deductive argument, using the word "therefore" (in German, "*also*") to mark the conclusion, but it is difficult to see exactly what the argument is. He is talking about what the content of the Categorical Imperative or "practical law" must be like, and says

> The ground of this principle is: Rational nature exists as an end in itself. This is the way in which a human being necessarily conceives his own existence, and it is therefore so far a subjective principle of human actions. But it is also the way in which every other rational being conceives his existence, on the same rational ground which holds also for me; hence it is at the same time an objective principle, from which, since it is a supreme practical ground, it must be possible to derive all laws for the will. The practical imperative will therefore be the following: Act in such a way that you treat humanity, whether in your own person or in any other person, always at the same time as an end, never merely as a means.

Several things are puzzling here. A satisfactory reconstruction would need to explain what reason there is to suppose that every agent "necessarily" conceives of herself as an end in herself, and what is involved in conceiving of herself in this way. And once it explained why each agent must conceive of herself that way (why treating humanity as an end in itself is a "subjective" principle), it would still need to explain why she should also conceive of other agents as ends in themselves too (why it is an "objective" principle). And a satisfactory reconstruction would need to do all this without relying on claims about the value of humanity. Claims about the incomparably high value of humanity should, strictly, be used only to capture conceptually prior ideas about the humanity formulation's demands that humanity be treated as an end in itself.

The opening claim of the argument is already bewildering. Kant says that each rational agent necessarily takes her rational nature to be an end in itself, so treating her own rational nature as an end in itself is "so far a subjective principle of human action." But Kant's use of "subjective" here must be inconsistent with the definition he has just offered in 428, where he says "subjective" means something like "based on inclinations." It would not be a *necessary* principle of action if it were based on an agent's inclinations, since there could at least in theory be a rational agent who lacked the inclination that led her to act on the principle. Instead of using "subjective" here to mean "inclination-based," I think he is using it in a more common, non-technical sense, to say that the principle has to do with one particular individual. The principle has as its content only the agent's own rational nature, and applies to the agent's own actions. That is, she treats her own rational nature as an end in itself, but so far there is no mention of how she will regard others or how they will regard her. Nevertheless, the principle is still empirically false. Kant rightly acknowledges throughout his writings that it is empirically possible for an agent to fail to treat her own rational nature as an end in itself. Real human agents sometimes act immorally. So instead of being an empirical claim about how actual agents necessarily act, Kant's statement must be describing the manner in which agents are rationally required to act.

But even if I am correct so far, this is just to decipher the meaning of "subjective" in Kant's claim that treating one's own humanity as an end in itself is a necessary subjective principle. It is not yet to show what is involved in treating one's own humanity as an end in itself, nor why each rational agent should take herself as having reason to accept this requirement unconditionally.

Christine Korsgaard (1996, pp. 119–124) provides a strategy that is helpful in deciphering Kant's argument for this "subjective principle" of action, and although some details of my reconstruction diverge from Korsgaard's, I will follow her basic strategy.[6] She says "the argument is intended as a regress on the conditions" of the value of our contingent ends (Korsgaard, 1996, p. 120). So we should begin by asking what makes a contingent end worth pursuing. Following the Kantian reasoning outlined in the previous section, in the discussion of value and ends, we can see that just having a desire for something is not a sufficient condition for its value. Given the fundamental Kantian point that value depends on the rational choice of agents, an end that is contrary to rational requirements of prudence or of morality has no value. In more common language, not just everything one wants, nor even everything one chooses, has value. Since value is not prior to the rational choice of agents, it is incoherent to appeal to the supposed value of a contingent end in order to justify undermining one's own rational nature, because "if you overturn the *source* of goodness of your end, neither your end nor the action that aims at it can possibly be good, and your action will not be fully rational" (Korsgaard, 1996, p. 123). The necessary condition of the value of any contingent end is that it must be an end set by some rational nature. And the rational nature that serves as the necessary condition of the value of contingent ends is "rational nature" in a strong, Kantian sense. It is the will of a being who accepts the force of rational principles of both prudence and morality. This rational nature is the end in itself.

A properly ordered will is the end in itself that should never be sacrificed for the sake of achieving contingent ends. If this properly ordered will, or fully rational nature, is the end in itself, then there are two ways to violate the subjective principle of not destroying one's own rational nature. The most common way to give up one's rational nature is to choose to act contrary to moral requirements, and so lose the commitment to morality that marks off rational wills. Consistently with this reading of the "subjective" component of the humanity formulation, Kant makes clear later that the humanity formulation includes a duty of moral self-perfection, to strive always to make self-legislated moral principles a sufficient reason for action (MM 6:387, MM 6:392–3, MM 6:446–7). The second way to sacrifice one's own rational nature is to destroy oneself or one's minimal rational nature altogether. This kind of sacrifice – cases of suicide or of placing oneself in situations that involve great risk of losing one's life for the sake of satisfying contingent desires, or taking permanently mind-altering drugs or the like – is probably what most naturally comes to mind when one thinks of sacrificing one's rational nature, if one does not keep in mind that Kant's idea of rational nature encompasses much more than minimal rationality. And Kant of course thinks that every rational agent has duties to herself to avoid these kinds of actions, duties based on the humanity formulation (MM 6:422–3, MM 6:427–8). So, the subjective principle that is suggested by the regress argument is to avoid sacrificing one's commitment to morality for the sake of satisfying contingent desires, and also to avoid sacrificing oneself or one's minimal rational powers altogether.

But this leaves a further step in reconstructing Kant's argument for the humanity formulation, namely establishing that treating humanity as an end in itself is an "objective principle" as well as a subjective one. The support Kant offers for the objective principle is that in the same way that every agent must think of her own rational nature as an end in itself,

> it is also the way in which every other rational being conceives his own existence on the same rational ground which is valid also for me; hence it is at the same time an objective principle. (G 4:429)

In one sense, Kant's reasoning here is perfectly straightforward. The argument offered above in support of the "subjective principle" is perfectly general. It did not presuppose any particular desires, but rather showed that it is always illegitimate to appeal to the supposed value of contingent ends to justify compromising one's own rational will. So every rational agent has reason to treat her own fully rational nature as an end in itself. But Kant means the objective principle to establish more than this, namely that each of us must treat humanity as an end in itself, whether it is one's own humanity or someone else's. There is a large gap to be filled in the move from saying each agent must treat her own rational nature as an end in itself to saying that each agent must treat every rational nature as an end in itself.

Kant himself provides little clue about how to proceed, but an obvious strategy is suggested by the overall structure of *Groundwork*. Kant has supposed that if morality is to be more than a fiction, there must be a principle of morality that is binding on all rational beings. Two possible candidates for this universal principle are compatible with, and suggested by, the fact that each rational agent must treat her own rational nature as an end in itself. One possible universal principle is: Each agent must treat her own fully rational nature as an end in itself, but may treat others' rational natures as expendable means to the satisfaction of her own desires. The other possible principle is: Each agent should treat her own fully rational nature and all other fully rational natures as ends in themselves, so should not trade any rational nature for the satisfaction of her own desires. If we limit Kant to morally neutral premises, he could provide no reason for thinking that the second principle is the correct one. But he does not limit himself to morally neutral premises. In these chapters of *Groundwork*, he is analyzing what morality must be like if there is any such thing as morality. While the first principle described above does provide an imperative that is in a sense universal, it is not universal in the sense required to count as a moral principle. It would give every agent a command that verbally had the same form – "treat your own rational nature as an end in itself, so never sacrifice it for the sake of inclination" – but it would not be demanding that each agent treat exactly the same object(s) as deserving this special consideration. The common moral idea that is being analyzed demands an end that all moral beings can share, not one that will irreconcilably set them into conflict (CPrR 5:28). If morality is not an illusion, it requires an end that can be shared by all agents, and that is what justifies the move from the "subjective principle" in the argument for the humanity formulation to the "objective principle" that one must treat fully rational nature as an end in itself wherever one finds it.

But what is involved in treating humanity as an end in itself? The subjective component of the humanity formulation forbids one to sacrifice one's own rational nature by choosing to place higher priority on contingent desires than on morality, or by altogether destroying oneself and so one's will, or by permanently impairing the basic functioning of the will. The corresponding objective principle, because it must serve as a moral principle rather than a principle of strife, imposes roughly parallel requirements on the treatment of others' fully rational natures so far as possible, given the basic differences in the effects we can have on ourselves and on others. The objective principle demands that one not destroy others for the sake of satisfying one's own desires, and that one not permanently impair others' deliberative powers. Since you cannot control the choices another person makes, or the principles she chooses to adopt, you cannot strictly have an obligation to preserve others' commitments to morality. But you do have a "negative" duty not to tempt them to immorality (MM 6:394). And I think these requirements are all that Kant's argument in *Groundwork* 4:428–9 can establish.

And this is enough to reach the conclusions Kant wishes to reach in arguing for the basic humanity formulation, that humanity is an end in itself, and so should never be treated merely as a means. Humanity is an end in itself, or an objective end, because each agent is rationally required not to sacrifice her own or others' humanity, or fully rational will, for the sake of her own desires. This requirement applies to each rational agent, regardless of the desires she has. So humanity is an end that must be taken account of in action regardless of one's desires. That is what it is to be an objective end, or end in itself. The additional claim that rational nature should not be treated as a mere means emphasizes the way that one can fail to treat it as an end in itself. The way to violate the demand of treating humanity as an objective end is to undermine or destroy it for the sake of achieving desire-based ends. The language of "ends" and "means" is a little strained here, but that is not a feature unique to my reconstruction of Kant's argument. As teachers of introductory ethics classes know, it is fairly intuitive to describe some violations of the humanity formulation as cases of "using someone as a means" (deceiving someone, for example, or "using" someone in a romantic context to make another person jealous), but it is more of a stretch to make the "treating as a means" label intuitively fit cases of suicide or nonbeneficence. Kant, I think, is using the distinction between ends and means partly because it is a distinction that is readily available from the history of philosophy and seems at least roughly to capture the idea of giving the right (or wrong) kind of weight to something in one's deliberations.

But even if everything I have said about the argument for the humanity formulation is correct, it does not settle all the duties regarding humanity. Surely the humanity formulation requires more than just not destroying oneself or others, and striving to regulate one's choices with moral principles. But not all these other duties directly play a role in the argument for the humanity formulation. Instead, they are derived from the humanity formulation once it is established.

How Particular Duties Follow

It is no surprise that the argument for the humanity formulation does not itself specify all the duties entailed by the humanity formulation. Kant says, "The present *Groundwork* aims only to seek out and establish the supreme principle of morality," and he reserves for a later day the "application of that supreme principle to the whole system" of morals (G 4:392). He calls the whole system a "metaphysic of morals" (G 4:391). In the later work actually titled *The Metaphysics of Morals*, he says that

> a metaphysics of morals cannot dispense with principles of application, and we shall often have to take as our object the particular nature of man, which is known only by experience, in order to show what can be inferred from universal moral principles. (MM 6:217)

The Categorical Imperative is meant to apply necessarily to all possible rational beings. But to decide on most of the specific duties that follow from the general principle, one must take account of the circumstances and psychology of the kind of rational beings whom one is considering. To arrive at duties that apply to humans, one must consider human nature. If that strikes some readers as too contingent to be Kantian, I can only point out that it is Kant's own stated view.

Some commentators have suggested that respect or esteem for rational nature must play a key role in deriving specific duties from the humanity formulation (Wood, 1999, p. 147–9; Hill, "Editor's Introduction" to Kant, 2002, pp. 80–1). This is a sound approach, but it would be desirable to fill in more details related to this respect or esteem. It is not completely clear whether it is meant to be a feeling, an attitude, a disposition, or just a way of describing respectful actions. And if this respect is supposed to have rational nature as its object, then a more complete account would need to explain how rational nature gives rise to this feeling (or attitude, or disposition), and how particular duties are related to it. Luckily, Kant himself provides a description of a moral feeling that is well suited to play this role. It is the feeling of "*Achtung*" – of respect or reverence. As described earlier in this chapter (in defining the "capacity for morality"), the most common use Kant makes of the word "*Achtung*" is to refer to the feeling produced in finite rational beings by their recognition of the awesome force of moral law. But Kant says that people also can inspire this feeling of *Achtung*. In fact, in *Critique of Practical Reason* 5:76, which contains his most prolonged discussion of *Achtung* for moral law, he says that "[*Achtung*] is always directed to persons, never to things." *Achtung* for moral law and for persons is the same moral feeling, because the feature of a person that inspires a feeling of *Achtung* is her commitment to moral law. Only "uprightness of character" elicits *Achtung*, because the person who displays good moral character provides an example of the power to rise above material circumstances. So Kant describes the feeling of *Achtung* as arising because a finite rational being "sees the holy elevated above itself and its frail nature," and Kant is consistent throughout his writings on ethics that people who are committed to moral law inspire the feeling of *Achtung* by their example (MM 6:464, G 4:435, G 4:440). This moral feeling of *Achtung* for persons is well suited to play a theoretical role in the transition from the humanity formulation as a basic moral principle to the particular duties that follow from the principle.

The most obvious category of duty that is related to the feeling of *Achtung* is the category of duties of respect (*Achtung*) for other people. Admittedly, there can be no duty to feel respect, because one either has a feeling or not, and we can only have duties to do what is within our power (MM 6:449). But we do have duties to act in ways that embody respect, or in other words to act in the manner of someone who actually feels respect. So Kant says every person has a duty "to acknowledge, in a practical way, the dignity of humanity in every other man. Hence there rests on him a duty regarding the respect [*Achtung*] that must be shown to every other man" (MM 6:462). The feeling of *Achtung* for other rational beings would lead to a recognition that others can be as important as oneself, and so would tend to quash a feeling of arrogance. And it would lead one not to condemn or ridicule others, so as not to drag them into a position lower than they deserve. This fits with Kant's description of the vices opposed to *Achtung* for others, the vices of arrogance, defamation, and ridicule (MM 6:465–8).

Kant also describes several duties that would most naturally be described as duties of respect for oneself. Kant hesitates to say that we have a duty to respect ourselves, but again he means that we cannot properly say we have a duty to have a feeling of *Achtung*. He says, "it is not correct to say that a man has a duty of self-esteem; it must rather be said that that the law within him inevitably forces from him respect for his own being, and this feeling (which is of a special kind) is the basis of certain duties" (MM 6:402–3). So Kant means to rule out a duty to have a feeling of respect for oneself, but he does not rule out that one can have duties to perform the kinds of actions that express respect for oneself. A person's duty to avoid servility is a duty not to act contrary to "his consciousness of his dignity as a rational man, and he should not disavow the moral self-esteem of such a being" (MM 6:435). Each of us also has a duty to avoid avarice, and this avarice consists of "restricting one's own enjoyment of the means to good living so narrowly as to leave one's own true needs unsatisfied" (MM 6:432). One of the ways in which we express *Achtung* and esteem for the will of a being committed to morality is to take satisfaction in seeing such a being made happy, not because material reward is the motive for moral commitment, but because we inevitably see virtue as worthiness, and as material beings we see worthiness as worthiness to be happy.

Achtung plays a similar role in the derivation of the duty to aid others in the pursuit of their ends. The argument for the basic humanity formulation by itself does not establish that one must aid others in achieving their ends in general. It does seem to show that one ought to aid others when their survival or their powers of rationality are threatened, since one ought never to sacrifice any being's rational will for the sake of satisfying one's own desires. And sometimes Kant does speak of the duty to aid others who face great danger or hardship (G 4:423, MM 6:453). But Kant also has in mind a more general duty of "making others' happiness one's end" (MM 6:452) or "to further the ends of others" (G 4:430). The best way to account for this more general duty of aiding others in the pursuit of their ends is through the feeling of *Achtung*. The feeling of the incomparable worth of other rational beings committed to morality combats my natural tendency to arrogance and makes me aware that my own contingent ends are not uniquely important. Since another person's proper willing makes her ends worth pursuing as well, I ought to acknowledge that they are not worthless. A way to do this is to provide some aid for her in pursuing her ends, if doing so is not too great an infringement on my own pursuit of my ends.

The duties to oneself of natural self-perfection also seem best derived from the humanity formulation by employing the feeling of *Achtung*. This captures the spirit of Kant's claim that to develop one's natural abilities is to make oneself worthy of one's own humanity (MM 6:392, MM 6:387). The end-setting of a properly ordered will results in ends that are worth pursuing. Some of these ends are based on inclination, others are moral ends given unconditionally by reason. To develop one's abilities allows one to seek a wider range of contingent ends, and also allows one to seek moral ends in a wider variety of ways. One can have a good will without possessing the ability to achieve a wide variety of ends, but the feeling of *Achtung* produced by a (fully) rational will inspires us to make it possible for ourselves to set and achieve a wide range of ends. So Kant says, "there is also bound up with the end of humanity in our own person the rational will, and so the duty, to make ourselves worthy of humanity by culture in general, by procuring or promoting the capacity to realize all sorts of possible ends" (MM 6:392). This also fits with the spirit of Kant's statement in *Groundwork*, 5:430, that although failing to develop one's talents does not "conflict" with "humanity in our own person" and is consistent with the "maintenance of this end," it also does not "harmonize with this end." Failing to develop one's abilities does not literally destroy one's rational will, but it is not consistent with fully accepting and acting on the feeling of respect and worthiness to be happy that a rational will inspires.

Although these are not all the duties that Kant discusses, they are suffficient to suggest the general pattern of the derivation of particular duties from the humanity formulation, and to demonstrate the usefulness of the concept of *Achtung*.

Final Thoughts

Earlier, I set aside the issue of exactly which sort of "rational nature" is best taken as the end in itself, on the grounds that the answer would be clearer after looking at Kant's arguments. The arguments have suggested that what Kant means to identify as the end in itself is rational nature in a quite strong sense, as the entire rational nature of a being, but only on the condition that the being is committed to accepting the force of moral demands. So just the power to set ends is not an end in itself, nor is just the power to legislate moral principles, nor the (unrealized) capacity to act on moral principles.

The "regress argument" for the subjective component of the humanity formulation leads to this conclusion, since a contingent end only has value on condition of being set by a rational being who accepts principles of prudence and morality. This also fits with the claim of the opening paragraphs of *Groundwork*, that a good will is the only thing unconditionally good, and the necessary condition of all other value (G 4:393–4).

The strategy I offered for deriving particular duties from the humanity formulation provides additional support for the "good will" reading of the humanity formulation. Other commentators have suggested that a general feeling of respect or esteem for rational nature is the key in moving from the general moral principle to more specific duties, and this is plausible enough. But an account of this feeling is not strongly connected to Kant's texts, unless one takes the feeling to be the same *Achtung* that one feels for moral law. Taking the end in itself to be a good will draws a deep connection between the content of the Categorical Imperative and the effect of the Categorical Imperative on the moral agent who is subject to it. The Categorical Imperative gives rise to a feeling of *Achtung* in moral agents who are aware of its force. If the rational nature that is an end in itself is a good will then rational nature on its own accord also gives rise to the feeling of *Achtung*, because a good will is an example of the Categorical Imperative's power to outweigh contingent desires. The humanity formulation does not just command each agent to treat something as an end in itself, but more profoundly says to treat as an end in itself the kind of will that arouses the same deep moral feeling of *Achtung* as the moral law itself does.

Kant's presentation of humanity as an ideal that we ought to pursue also supports taking humanity as a good will. In many texts, Kant says that we ought to strive toward moral perfection, though it is a goal we will never fully achieve (CPR 3:384, G 4:569, R 6:61–3, R 6:183, MM 6:387, MM 6:392–3, MM 6:446). And he frequently refers to this goal or ideal as "humanity." Although we will always be imperfect, because we are subject to temptations, the striving itself is the form of moral goodness that is possible for humans. The very concept that humanity is an ideal to be pursued seems to rule out identifying the humanity that is an end in itself as something that every minimally rational agent possesses. If everyone already possesses it, it could not be something to work toward. If it seems odd to identify "humanity" as something to work toward, it may help to keep in mind some points about ordinary language. In English, the injunction to "be a man" is familiar, and so is the less sexist demand to be a little more human. In German, at least the German of roughly Kant's time, one finds the statement in Mozart's *Die Zauberflöte*, that the character Zarastro must undergo trials to learn to be a man (*ein Mensch zu sein*). The familiar Yiddish use of "Mensch" to mean not just any human being, but a decent, reliable, or upstanding human fits even more nicely.

The main obstacle to accepting good will as the end in itself is the understandable concern that this will require judgments of others' moral character, and will license mistreatment of people whom one deems immoral. But the distinction already described above, between basic moral principles and the application of those principles, provides a non – ad hoc defense against the suspicion of excessive moralism. At the level of moral theory, it is true that the end in itself is good will, or rational nature in a quite strong sense. But at the level of application to human conditions, we always (or almost always) have reason to treat other humans as ends in themselves, even if not all humans fully deserve this treatment. Kant says this himself. In the passages in *The Metaphysics of Morals* where he describes duties of respect for others (the same passages quoted above, in the previous section), Kant says that we must treat *all* other humans with respect, but he quickly adds that this is *not* because they all necessarily are worthy of respect. He is quite explicit that we should respect the vicious man "even though by his deeds he makes himself unworthy of it" (MM 6:463).

Why should we treat him with respect if he is unworthy of respect? Kant gives three reasons. The first is that to treat a human with contempt weakens her belief that she can improve herself and so discourages her from attempting to better adhere to the dictates of practical reason (MM 6:463–4, MM 6:466). A second reason for treating all humans with respect, even though only some deserve it, also depends on basic human psychological tendencies. Kant says that to treat any human with disrespect lessens our respect for all humans, "so as finally to cast a shadow of worthlessness over our race itself, making misanthropy (shying away from men) or contempt the prevalent cast of mind" (MM 6:466). Finally, the most fundamental reason for treating everyone as an end in herself, even though not everyone actually deserves such treatment, is that we are not reliable judges of others' moral character. We cannot even be sure what reasons an agent acts on in a particular case, let alone whether she embraces a higher-level principle of only acting in ways that are morally permitted. Kant maintains that it is impossible to know with certainty whether a right action has been performed because of its rightness, or from some inclination (G 4:407). He is even more explicit in *Religion* that, although we can observe an agent performimg impermissible actions, "we cannot observe maxims, we cannot do so unproblematically even within ourselves; hence the judgment that an agent is an evil human being can not reliably be based on experience" (R 6:20, also R 6:47–8, R 6:67, R 6:71). Avoiding judgments about others' overall moral character is all the more important, given the innate human tendency to elevate one's own worth in comparison to others'. Kant consistently attributes to humankind a self-love and self-conceit that leads to competition, both in the form of "an unjust desire to acquire superiority for oneself over others" and "an inclination to gain worth in the opinion of others."[7] So it is not just technically impossible to achieve absolute certainty in our judgments about character, it also is very likely that such judgments will be distorted. Kant, despite his reputation for being out of touch with human nature, provides three plausible psychological claims that provide reasons for us to treat other humans as ends in themselves, even if not everyone has earned this treatment.

The point is not trivial in Kant's moral system. He thinks that we humans must treat the obviously virtuous and the apparently immoral in mostly the same ways, but he can not mean that this is because they really deserve the same treatment. Kant maintains that we are not in a position to make judgments of others' character, but he does think that God could make such judgments (R 6:48, R 6:76–7, CPrR 5:123–4). In fact, that is the basis of Kant's arguments that one rationally can believe in a supreme being – only such a being can judge others' worthiness to be happy, and apportion their rewards to their worthiness.

If an unpalatable flavor of moralism still clings to the reading of "rational nature" I have proposed, perhaps some large-scale considerations may help. While it is both fashionable and laudable to speak of basic human rights and inalienable dignity, the point of such talk is usually to place requirements on the ways that governments or other institutions must treat people. The reading I have proposed does not undermine such demands, and in fact provides a strong philosophical basis for them. The idea that the morally worst sort of people may not really have the same moral status as the morally best is compatible with the idea that we are not in a good position to label anyone as fundamentally inferior or less deserving of respect. This duality of thought is hardly a novelty. It is familiar to billions of believers in a supreme God, and also to believers in the principle of treating a defendant in a legal case as innocent until proven guilty. If there is anything odd about the picture, the oddity should be balanced against the competing picture, that no amount of immorality can ever tarnish the inextinguishable glow that accompanies the power of choice or the capacity for morality, even if the capacity is never realized and the choices are routinely monstrous. The position that we all ought to strive toward an ideal of moral goodness is at least less peculiar than that.

Notes

1 All direct quotations from Kant's works will be from the translations cited in the bibliography, although page references will be to the standard Royal Prussian Academy edition of Kant's works.

2 Of course, I am not even pretending to summarize Kant's arguments for this claim. See Chapter 3 of *Groundwork*. A good secondary source on this is Hill, 1992, p. 97–122.

3 See Hill, 1992, p. 40–1; Herman, 1993, p. 238; O'Neill, 1989, p. 138; Paton, 1947, p. 177; Ross, 1954, p. 52–3.

4 Although the reading I give here is more or less standard, for contrary views see Herman, 1993, pp. 208–10, and Guyer, 2000, p. 2, p. 96–171.

5   Kant summarizes this argument in basically the same way in MM 6:381.

6   The main difference is that Korsgaard takes the argument to establish that the mere power to set ends is the end in itself.

7   Both quotations are from R 6:27. See also A 7:272 and MM 6:465, and various of Kant's essays of the Critical and Post-Critical period, most notably "Perpetual Peace," "Idea for a Universal History with a Cosmopolitan Purpose," and "The Contest of Faculties."

Bibliography

Dean, R. 1996: What should we treat as an end in itself? *Pacific Philosophical Quarterly* 77, no. 4: 268–88.

Dean R. 2006: *The Value of Humanity in Kant's Moral Theory*. Oxford: Clarendon Press.

Guyer, P. 2000: *Kant on Freedom, Law and Happiness*. Cambridge, New York, Melbourne, and Madrid: Cambridge University Press.

Herman, B. 1993: *The Practice of Moral Judgment*. Cambridge, Massachusetts, and London: Harvard University Press.

Hill, T.E., Jr. 1992: *Dignity and Practical Reason in Kant's Moral Theory*. Ithaca: Cornell University Press.

Kant, I. 1974: *Anthropology from a Practical Point of View*. (M. Gregor, trans.) The Hague: Martinus Nijhoff. [7:117–333].

Kant, I. 1965: *Critique of Pure Reason*. (N. Kemp Smith, trans.) New York: St. Martin's Press. [4:1–252, 3:1–594]

Kant, I. 1997: *Critique of Practical Reason*. (M. Gregor, trans.) Cambridge and New York: Cambridge University Press. [5:1–164]

Kant, I. 1987: *Critique of Judgment*. (W. S. Pluhar, trans.) Indianapolis: Hackett Publishing Company. [5:167–485]

Kant, I. 2002: *Groundwork for the Metaphysics of Morals*. (T. E. Hill, Jr. and A. Zweig, trans.) Oxford and New York: Oxford University Press. [4:387–463]

Kant, I. 1996: *The Metaphysics of Morals*, (M. Gregor, trans.) Cambridge: Cambridge University Press. [6:203–491]

Kant, I. 1998: *Religion within the Limits of Reason Alone*. (A. Wood and G. di Giovanni, trans.) Cambridge and New York: Cambridge University Press. [6:1–202]

Korsgaard, C. 1996: *Creating the Kingdom of Ends*. Cambridge, New York, Melbourne: Cambridge University Press.

O'Neill, O. 1989: *Constructions of Reason*. Cambridge, New York, Melbourne: Cambridge University Press.

Paton, H.J. 1947: *The Categorical Imperative*. Philadelphia: University of Pennsylvania Press.

Ross, W.D. 1954: *Kant's Ethical Theory*. London: Oxford University Press.

Wood, A. 1999: *Kant's Ethical Thought*. Cambridge, Melbourne, New York: Cambridge University Press.

4

Autonomy and the Kingdom of Ends

Sarah Holtman

Introduction

Whatever number we assign it among Kant's several formulations of the Categorical Imperative, the Formula of Autonomy (hereafter FA) is arguably both the richest and the most perplexing. Its richness derives from three sources: from the intimate connections Kant describes between this version of his supreme moral principle and those that have come before; from the central discussions to which it gives rise – most importantly Kant's account of a kingdom of ends and his distinction between price and dignity; and finally from the intriguing notion of autonomy itself. The puzzlement arises from the several ways in which Kant formulates this principle, from the fact that the principle may seem more explanatory than action-guiding, and from uncertainty as to whether we ultimately can make sense of laws that bind us because, and only because, we issue them to ourselves. I address each of these features of FA below. The aim is to make vivid the relationships and aspects that constitute the richness of this conception of autonomy and, if not to put puzzlement entirely to rest, at least to allay the most serious confusions and concerns associated with Kant's discussion. I close by briefly examining the implications of FA and related discussions for Kant's practical philosophy more generally.

A. The Formula of Autonomy – Initial Statements

Within a few paragraphs of commencing his discussion of FA, Kant offers us two statements of it, or more precisely of the corresponding practical principle:

> [T]he supreme condition of the will's harmony with universal practical reason is the Idea of the will of every rational being as a will that legislates universal law. (G 4:431)[1]

> Every human will is a will that enacts universal laws in all its maxims. (G 4:432)

Kant quickly offers further explication of the idea these seek to capture by comparing others' efforts to enunciate morality's first principle to his own here. These earlier, "heteronomous," views portray human beings as merely subject to moral principle. They thus require that that principle be joined with some further element, motivating compliance. Absent this, says Kant, there would be no ground or reason for acting in accord with it. Not so for morality's first principle as Kant now formulates it, which recognizes that the categoricity essential to morality can only be achieved when its dictates are ones every rational being gives himself.[2]

Kant's concern, of course, is partly that if we find our reason for complying with moral dictates, say, in our sympathetic feelings for those our actions may affect, we make our connection with those dictates subject to all manner of contingencies. Sympathetic feeling, to continue the example, varies notoriously from person to person, culture to culture, historical period to historical period. The commands of morality do not track these variations, and our duty to comply with them must have a similarly unwavering foundation.

To seek our ground for compliance in self-love, or "one's own happiness," says Kant, in his later but equally relevant discussion of heteronomy of the will, is still less appropriate. This is not merely because what yields happiness for a given actor often fails to square with moral demands, or even because virtue and prudence are, conceptually, distinct (G 4:442). It is most importantly because, were this the proper ground for moral compliance, there would be no difference between the motivations that ground virtuous action and those that ground vice. In determining whether or not to act morally, I would properly ask only whether vice or virtue best serves my interest in the case at hand. Yet this, says Kant, is to fail to appreciate the crucial difference between the reasons I have for acting rightly and those that pull in the direction of vice. The problem with self-love as a foundation for moral obligation is still partly that what will serve this interest varies among persons, times, and places. Kant's discussion here goes farther though. Morality's first principle must capture not only the categorical nature of its demands but must account for what is distinctive about the reasons I have for acting on those demands. It is not that acting morally better serves certain aims of mine than acting viciously. It is that reasons for the former are qualitatively different from reasons for the latter.

Of course, not all previously suggested grounds for moral compliance are "empirical" (as are sympathy and self-love). Philosophers and theologians have also tried to find such grounds in rationalist principles, in particular in an ontological concept of perfection or in a theological one (G 4:443). The former raises difficulties, as Allen Wood points out, if what we mean by "perfection" is either that moral compliance well serves some end we happen to have or that it is in some sense "good of its kind." Either way, my reason for such compliance will depend on an end I (or we) just happen to have and on its merely contingent relationship to moral demands. If instead the perfection in question is some objective conception of human good, Kant argues, then our problem is no longer that our reason for acting morally rests on what is contingent and shifting. It is that its basis is so "empty and indefinite" that we either cannot determine what our obligations might be and why, or we end up answering these questions by reference back to morality itself. This of course lands us in a circle, providing no explanation at all of our grounds for moral compliance.

Kant likewise objects on grounds of circularity to any attempt to found moral commitment in the perfection of a divine will. For our only way of grasping or characterizing God's perfection is by deriving it from other of our concepts, morality first and foremost. If we abandon appeal to such concepts, though, we are left with an understanding of God's will as powerful, vengeful – in general as characterized by attributes completely at odds with morality (G 4:443). Again, this last is tied not to concern for the categorical nature of moral dictates, but now to the importance of maintaining the distinction between what serves or harmonizes with morality and what is by definition opposed to it. As right and might are conceptually opposed, so are appeals to power and vengeance and those to moral grounds for our actions.

Although I will return to this question in the penultimate section, it is worth noticing now two reasons for seeing FA as less an action-guiding principle than one designed to highlight and explain key features of the supreme principle of morality. First, the statements of FA we have examined seem designed to serve such a purpose. They tell us something about the conception of a rational being that the categorical imperative presupposes but not about how such a being ought to act. Second, in teasing out or clarifying those initial statements, as well as in his later distinction between autonomy and heteronomy, Kant is centrally concerned with the nature of the reasons or grounds for right action. As we have seen, these cannot be ones that vary with person, time, or culture, nor can they be ones that end in a circular appeal to morality itself. More positively, these reasons must be qualitatively distinct from those we might see as grounds for vice. They must also offer definite substantive guidance to those attempting to act rightly, and must both sanction paradigmatically moral actions and condemn paradigm examples of wrongdoing. Kant's elaborations seem, in other words, more a meta-inquiry into the requisite features of the reasons at issue than a discussion aimed at informing actions or the decision making that precedes them. At this point in his discussion of FA, Kant has stated it only as a practical principle and not yet as an imperative directed to those who will not necessarily comply. So further examination may reveal a statement of the formulation that is more evidently designed to guide action. Nevertheless, we should keep this potential puzzle in mind as we move forward,

B. The Formula of Autonomy, the Formula of Universal Law, and the Formula of Humanity

Besides statements of what we might term the "principle" of autonomy, like those we have just considered, Kant does provide us versions in the imperative form appropriate to human agents (who are properly commanded because they will not necessarily do as they ought). These include:

> [I]f there is a categorical imperative (a law that applies to the will of every rational being), it can command us only to *act always on the maxim of its will as one which could at the same time look upon itself as giving universal laws.* (G 4:432, emphasis added)

> Never choose except in such a way that the maxims of your choice are also comprehended as universal law in the same act of will. (G 4:440)

Taken together with earlier statements of the principle, these likely will seem, at first blush, essentially to repeat the formula of universal law (hereafter FUL), which commands "act only on that maxim by which you can at the same time will that it should become a universal law" (G 4:421). There is at least one potentially important difference though. FUL restricts the set of maxims on which we rightly may act to those we also can will as universal laws. FA focuses not on the maxim at hand, but on the way in which our choice is made, or on the nature of the will that does the choosing.

That the focus of FA differs from that of FUL in this way seems further confirmed by Kant's remark that FA follows not merely from FUL, but from FUL and the formula of humanity (hereafter FHE) taken together. The latter commands "Act in such a way that you treat humanity, whether in your own person or in any other person, always at the same time as an end, never merely as a means" (G 4:429). It emphasizes that the ground for any decision regarding action-guiding rules properly lies in the notion of a rational being as an end in itself and as the "subject" of all other ends (G 4:431). It requires that, in all of our decisions about what to do, we take seriously the centrality of setting and pursuing ends to living the life of a rational agent. Further, we must make that agency, so understood, a limiting condition in all of our choices. FUL, says Kant, focuses on the form of a moral principle and on the possible form of any maxim on which one rightly may act. FHE directs our attention instead to the substance or end of such a principle and of any morally acceptable action (G 4:431). FA enunciates the implications of these prior formulations for the way in which we conceive of a moral agent's capacity to determine what action she will undertake.

We can better grasp the insight regarding moral obligation that FA seeks to capture, and that arguably flows from FUL and FHE, by considering a summary remark on autonomy near the end of Chapter 2 of the *Groundwork*: "Autonomy of the will is the property the will has of being a law to itself (independently of any property of the objects of volition)" (G 4:440). Autonomy of the will as so described has two elements. The one most closely related to our discussion so far arguably also is most closely connected to FUL. Part of what it means for the will to be autonomous, as we have seen, is that it can issue general standards of action whose basis is not contingent. Another way to put the point is to say that the autonomous will issues standards that can be laws for all because their authority does not rest on what is peculiar to some. This provides the connection to FUL. For the command that we act only on maxims that we can universalize without contradiction, Kant emphasizes, counters our frequent tendency to make an exception for ourselves, on grounds of inclination, to what we acknowledge as moral requirements for everyone else.

Of course, as we have seen, the demand for non-contingency is greatly enriched when we consider in more detail what it would be to commit oneself to such a standard, or more properly what it would be to have a will capable of issuing it. When our focus shifts from the principle (or maxim) of action to the will committed to choosing among such maxims on moral grounds, we find (again) that the non-contingent basis that moral principle requires must also have two further features. It must possess sufficient substance of its own that we can avoid assuming rather than illuminating moral requirements. It also must be one that does not merge morality with its opposite either in the reasons it provides for our compliance or in the content of its directives. It is the autonomous will itself that provides this non-contingent basis for morality's categorical demands.

We cannot fully grasp Kant's conception of autonomy, though, unless we also appreciate what it is about the will of a rational agent that allows it to provide the ground for moral law as Kant has now characterized it. This is what we are to take most directly from Kant's earlier consideration of FHE. Kant summarizes that formulation at the start of his autonomy discussion:

> [I]n this principle, we conceive humanity not as an end that one happens to have (a subjective end) – that is, as an object which people, as a matter of fact, happen to make their end. We conceive of it rather as an objective end – one that, as a law, should constitute the supreme limiting condition on all subjective ends, whatever those ends may be. (G 4:430–1)

As a rational agent, Kant claims, I am both a being who sets subjective ends and one who serves as a limit on the ends any rational being may set and pursue. The will that can give non-contingent laws of the sort Kant seeks here must then be one that can appreciate and commit itself to rational agency as such a limit on the setting and pursuit of subjective ends. In closing, we might put the point this way. To see my will "as one that enacts universal laws in all its maxims" is to see it, or more realistically to see myself, as both committed to, and capable of adhering to, a principle of respect for humanity. This principle applies to each of my decisions about what subjective ends to pursue and how to go about pursuing them.

C. The Kingdom of Ends

One way of understanding Kant's discussion of the kingdom of ends is as an effort better, or more fully, to explain the connection between the formula of autonomy and those of universal law and humanity. As such, it is not perhaps best understood as a new formulation of the Categorical Imperative. Rather, it is Kant's further attempt to capture what he intends in the formula of autonomy, which he has already expressed in at least three ways by the time he comes to discuss the "very fruitful concept" of a kingdom of ends. Whether one takes this discussion to develop a further formulation of the Categorical Imperative (the Formula of the Kingdom of Ends or FKE) or to elaborate on FA, its main import is this. In order fully to honor the demands of morality, we must conceive of ourselves and our fellow rational agents as legislators for a possible community, each member of which is an objective end (an end in itself) possessed of particular personal or subjective ends. Importantly, we must further conceive of this community as one in which we are governed by laws of our own making that reflect our mutual status as ends. Our maxims and the actions based on them should reflect this understanding of ourselves and our fellows and of the community appropriate to us. Below, I discuss the elements and implications of the kingdom of ends so conceived in some detail.

A "kingdom" Kant tells us, is "the systematic union of different rational beings under common laws" (G 4:433). As members of the kingdom of ends, he goes on to explain, rational beings are united in the first instance by the fact that "all stand under the *law* that each of them should treat himself and all others never *merely as a means* but always *at the same time as an end in himself*" (G 4:433, emphasis in original). They are, in short, united by the fact that FHE is a law, and indeed the supreme moral principle, for each of them.

As Kant has already discussed, though, FHE demands that, in determining how to act towards any rational agent, we positively acknowledge that she is not only capable of and disposed to set subjective ends, but that this capacity and disposition are central to her agency. Thus, we might say with Kant that for each member of the kingdom of ends to stand together under FHE is for each to stand together under a law that attributes supreme moral significance to rational agents as ends in themselves possessed of particular ends of their own.

This, it seems, is the insight Kant has in mind in saying that

> if we abstract from personal differences between rational beings, and also from all the content of their private ends . . . [we can] conceive of a whole of all ends systematically united . . . that is . . . of a kingdom of ends which is possible in accordance with the aforesaid principles. (G 4:433)

To leave aside what distinguishes rational agents one from another (preferences, birthplace, gender, and the like), and what distinguishes the subjective ends they set for themselves, is to see rational agents in a certain way. It is to see them, first, as a community of beings possessed of certain capacities and dispositions. Second, we must view each community member as possessed of particular ends, ends given significance by the mere fact that they are matters that rational agents value and that, in an important sense, make their lives worth living.

We do not fully grasp the fruitful concept of a kingdom of ends, though, simply by recognizing that members stand together as endsetting agents bound by and committed to FHE. For the union is, Kant emphasizes, "systematic" and the common laws that govern it are not singular but plural. By systematic, Kant seems to intend that the appropriate relationship of rational agents one to another, and of each to the subjective ends in play at any given time, is properly determined by inter-related objective standards that are applicable to each by virtue of his rationality. Although FHE is itself such a standard, Kant seems to emphasize here that the complex relationships among ends of various sorts and the means required to attain them demand standards that are more fine-grained. We can arrive at such standards, he suggests, by focusing on both the requirement "never to perform any action except one whose maxim could also be a universal law" and on the understanding, emphasized in FA, of each rational agent's will as lawgiving. More specifically yet, we enrich our understanding of this system of shared standards by exploring "the Idea of the *dignity* of a rational being who obeys no law other than one which he himself also enacts" (G 4:434).

D. Price and Dignity

Kant's distinction between price and dignity is a familiar one and one that is, especially by comparison with other of his claims and distinctions, easy to grasp. We can characterize the various ends joined under the kingdom's common laws as having either price or dignity. The values of ends having price can be compared, and those with equal price can be exchanged one for the other. Price comes in two varieties. What may serve universally shared human inclinations and needs has market price. What accords with individual tastes has attachment price. In each case, value is relative. In the first, it is relative to shared needs and inclinations and, in the second, to the tastes of particular individuals.

The term "dignity" we reserve, by contrast, for what is "the sole condition under which anything can be an end in itself" (G 4:435). This condition, in which there can exist ends universal for rational agents as such, is morality. Morality allows a rational being to be an end in itself, says Kant, because it is only through morality that one can be a "lawgiving member in the kingdom of ends" (G 4:435). He adds that humanity too has dignity, to the extent that it is capable of morality.

What this means is that, to the extent that they flow from a commitment to moral principles, and not, for example, from instinct or inclination, the values of fidelity, truth-telling, benevolence and the like have dignity. This dignity, Kant elaborates, is best understood not by appeal to some feature discernable in moral requirements or even in the external actions that fulfill them. Dignity is, rather, the value of a mental attitude. It is the value properly attributed to the commitment to doing what morality requires not from sympathy, or self-interest, or because God commands it, but because I recognize that I have objective and unbending reasons for doing so.

We can say, then, that what Kant means in claiming that morality and humanity have dignity is, first, that dignity resides in the attitude of true moral commitment and, second, that beings capable of this commitment may themselves be said to have an incomparable worth, at least as regards those of their features that are joined with this capacity. Moreover, we should emphasize again, it is this very disposition, possessed of dignity, that allows a rational being to share in giving universal laws and "renders him fit to be a member of a possible kingdom of ends" (G 4:435).

Before considering how the discussion of dignity might help us better grasp the implications of Kant's discussion of the kingdom of ends and its relationship to FA, we should pause to consider Kant's rendering of the old idea of humanity's dignity, or incomparable worth, in a bit more detail. For Kant, as we have just said, this worth resides in the capacity for genuine moral commitment. Although he does not expressly explore the question, further discussion suggests that one acts or behaves with dignity, on Kant's view, when one acts from such commitment. This remains true even if the consequences of that action are not what one would have wished. (Perhaps I keep my promise to teach you French only to find that, unbeknownst to me, you planned to use your new tongue to carry out a fraudulent land deal.) "Respect" is the name Kant gives to the esteem we properly feel for whatever possesses or expresses dignity. Thus we can say that, for Kant, dignity resides in the autonomous will and its dictates and is properly met with respect by every rational agent who encounters it.

With the discussion of price and dignity, we discover then both how it is that Kant can say that the human will "enacts universal laws in all its maxims" (G 4:432), and how we are to conceive of legislators for the kingdom of ends. One possessed of what we might term the attitude of autonomy, as any human agent properly is, limits her actions, and the maxims on which she chooses to act, first and foremost by moral commitment. In this sense, every maxim she endorses is also a fresh endorsement, a giving to herself or legislation, of moral principle. More, it is only a being possessed of such an attitude who can be a source of morally legitimate laws for a possible kingdom of ends.

What is still unclear is how we are to determine, in a more fine-grained way, what laws indeed would govern members of the kingdom of ends. Yet what we have learned about dignity surely offers some assistance here. If what makes me fit for the status of legislator for a kingdom of ends, a union of ends in themselves possessed of ends of their own, is the attitude that possesses dignity, then this is presumably the attitude that characterizes Kantian legislators, at least when taking up their lawmaking role. Residing as it does in the attitude of autonomy (or the capacity for assuming such an attitude), rather than in a fixed attribute, dignity itself resides in a way of valuing. For when I adopt the attitude of autonomy, I place moral commitment, for our purposes most importantly commitment to FUL and FHE taken together, not merely ahead of commitments to do what serves sympathy or self-interest. I make it an absolute standard against which all others are to be judged, rejected, or reshaped. But this attitude is also, as we have seen, "the sole condition under which anything can be an end in itself." Thus to treat humanity as an end in itself as FHE demands is to treat each as capable of effectively adopting the attitude of autonomy.

To develop a more fine-grained set of laws for the kingdom of ends, it then would seem, is to determine, at least in a preliminary way, what are the prerequisites for developing, maintaining and giving effect to such an attitude. For absent this, no one can realize her humanity, her status as an end in herself. Although we cannot pursue this question here in great detail, it is crucial to consider what part the capacity to set one's own subjective ends plays in this. For at least in the case of human beings, the attitude of autonomy would seem to be fully realized only when I have the prospect of developing and pursuing a reasonable number and range of ends of my own. I cannot make the moral law a supreme standard where there is nothing viable to shape or limit. Even this brief foray into the underpinnings of dignity offers some sense of the kinds of subsidiary laws that might be appropriate for the kingdom of ends.

E. Critical Remarks and Worries

(1) Autonomy

As I mentioned at the outset, a main worry (or perhaps, better, a set of worries) regarding FA springs from an uncertainty. Why do moral laws bind me only because I give them to myself? The general worry reflects at least three quite different (though not incompatible) concerns. Those expressing the first of these wonder how the lawgiver and the follower can be one and the same person. Surely this introduces an inappropriate subjectivity into the moral mix. If so, then FA fails as a moral first principle because it opens moral deliberation to the prospect of the very kind of biased and self-interested application that Kant is so keen to avoid. Those raising the second worry that we might capture under this general heading suggest a somewhat different concern. They ask how we can make sense of any basis for moral commitment other than sympathy, self-interest, or alternatively, God or some secular ideal. These seem to exhaust the comprehensible possibilities and leave us, at best, mystified and, at worst, inclined to reject moral demands as baseless and without force for beings like us. Finally, some ask why the foundations of morality will be less contingent and less likely to succumb to problems of circularity if we find them in the will of a rational agent. We can perhaps best understand this concern as a version, or offshoot, of one of the two preceding. For surely each worry arises, in part, from a sense that our grip on laws given by our own rational will quickly loosens. This potentially leaves us with an unspoken appeal to sympathy or self-interest, or with an equally unacknowledged reliance on the untutored sense of morality's demands that is necessitated by the imprecision of some objective ideal.

In a larger treatment, of course, we would want to explore interesting differences among these concerns and among Kant's potential responses to them. Here, though, I will suggest just one answer that might, at least when spelled out in detail, suffice for all three. As we have seen, the perspective of a legislator for the kingdom of ends is attained only when I am able to adopt an attitude of autonomy. It is when I am able to do this that I fully realize my status as an end that is not also a means and become capable of making laws not only for myself, but for a community of beings who share this status with me.

If we take Kant's discussion of the kingdom of ends to be a further attempt to capture what is most central to FA, then FA likewise rests on this conception of the moral agent as most centrally an agent who possesses the capacity for autonomy. This, again, is the capacity both to rein in self-interest and the like by overarching moral commitment and to comprehend, honor, and trace the implications of one's status as an autonomous agent for actions in concrete circumstances. If this is what Kant has in mind then the focus of FA, different from either FUL or FHE, is on the special capacities of the moral agent for precisely this kind of deep and overriding commitment and for tracing the concrete consequences of that commitment so as to make the demand to take up and act from the perspective of an ideal legislator contentful and un-mysterious.

Understanding Kant's discussion of the kingdom of ends as related to FA in this way also seems to provide an answer to another of our starting puzzles. For read through that discussion, FA now appears to have an action-guiding as well as a meta-ethical aspect. FA demands that the maxims on which we decide to act be ones that honor these moral capacities in myself and others. Kant's discussion of the kingdom of ends not only helps us to recognize this action-guiding aspect of FA but provides a fuller account of the perspective we must take up if we are to succeed in acting as FA requires.

(2) The kingdom of ends

Of course, this immediately raises several further concerns – now about the kingdom of ends. For we have not explored in any detail the activity of lawmaking for such a possible community, nor does Kant himself do so. What ground do we therefore have for thinking that there will be enough to guide us when we attempt to take up the perspective of moral legislators? What will save us, in the end, from succumbing to sympathy, self-interest, or circularity? Relatedly, what is the connection between the perspective of the kingdom of ends and the circumstances of morally imperfect persons in the real world? How, if at all, can the perspective of the first guide us in making moral decisions for the second?

Again, we cannot do this topic justice in a survey article. There is, though, an obvious model to which we can refer. John Rawls's original position is described for questions of basic justice rather than for morality more generally. Nevertheless, we certainly could put forward, as Thomas E. Hill, Jr. (1992, 2000) suggests, a parallel legislative perspective. Here we could attempt to capture what information ideal moral legislators would and would not possess, what criteria of generality and the like appropriate principles would have to satisfy, and what issues legislators would face and how available information and the like appropriately would change as questions of moral obligation became increasingly concrete and idealizing assumptions faded. We might too, as I have suggested elsewhere, take content for this legislative inquiry from what is arguably Kant's own recognition of the importance of insuring that certain fundamental interests, pre-requisite to realizing and maintaining rational capacities, are protected in each agent (Holtman, 1999, pp. 35–9). For these certainly would provide a basis for much more and less basic legislation for a possible kingdom of ends.

Some still may worry that, even if we could accomplish such a Rawlsian project for morality more generally, we would hardly have achieved what Kant sought. For the moral principle as he conceives it is not only categorical, but finds its basis in a kind of logical certainty that the legislative process in Rawls' original position and its relatives will hardly yield. Yet to suppose that organic argument, employing an ongoing inquiry into best grounds or reasons, is alien to Kant is to rely on a misconception of his theory. Although Kant surely had his reasons for some-times seeming to favor FUL, which appears wedded to a more rigid and logic-based conception of morality, little else in his moral theory admits, under scrutiny, of this understanding of moral argument unalloyed. Certainly the close relation-ships Kant describes among FHE, FA, and the kingdom of ends as we have traced them here do not, and we can hardly ignore these and claim to have been true to Kant.

F. The Formula's Larger Implications

Kant's related discussions of autonomy, dignity, and the kingdom of ends have implications in the realm of morality broadly construed, in a more narrow account of the just state, and in the intriguing discussion of global, or cosmopolitan, justice. These suggest further ways in which FA and its progeny are of practical and not merely meta-ethical import.

(1) Morality broadly construed

The conception of the person as one who is characterized by the capacity and disposition both to set and pursue ends and to commit herself to rational agency as a limit on such ends gives Kantian moral philosophy its distinctive flavor. For Kant, value and the norms associated with it issue from within. This is not to say, of course, that whatever the rational agent commits to has value simply by virtue of her commitment. I do not give voice to my autonomy simply by engaging in uncoerced choice and action or by choosing and acting in ways somehow most expressive of my "true self." Although setting my own personal ends free of the undue influence of others certainly is prerequisite to realizing my autonomy, the preceding discussion makes clear that I fully realize my capacity for autonomous action only by limiting my choices and actions in accord with overriding moral commitment. Likewise, Kant's own terminology and several examples make clear that one need not fully realize one's autonomy in order to be included in the ranks of moral agents possessed of dignity on his view.[3] Such an agent has the capacity to recognize and commit to a principle of respect for humanity as an overriding consideration in deliberations about how to act. It is the capacity rather than its realization that is required for autonomy as Kant describes it.

Kant's conception of persons as moral legislators thus provides us an account of the source of moral value and moral norms that contrasts sharply with any version of divine command theory. With its emphasis on persons as end-setting agents, it also differs importantly from views that deny or question the moral significance of the capacity and disposition to set ends. Its acknowledgment of the moral significance of the *capacity* for autonomy, rather than its realization, further distinguishes it from views that locate moral value solely or predominantly in moral perfection.

Kant's conception of moral agents as legislators of both individual ends and moral standards also provides him a means of explaining what is so deeply wrong with practices and institutions widely deemed to be morally abhorrent. The institution of slavery is a particularly apt example. Certainly slavery shares with many other forms of maltreatment a connection with physical suffering, with lack of opportunity for intellectual or other development, and with the psychological ills that typically accompany these. Slaves seldom flourish physically or psychologically or have realistic prospects for developing intellectual and other talents. There is no necessary connection, though, between being owned by another and being physically abused or neglected, or deprived of education, artistic training, and the like. One might be a slave and be abundantly provided for in all of these respects. A moral theory that views persons first and foremost as living things – or perhaps better as living beings possessed of intellectual or other potential – has little to say about the ills of slavery beyond noting its tendency to walk hand-in-hand with suffering and privation. For many, though, this identifies what *can* be wrong with slavery but not what makes it distinctively and inevitably wrong.

Kant's conception of persons as individual, and ultimately as moral, legislators offers a very clear account of what renders slavery, by its very nature, morally unacceptable. For if I am a slave, I am the property of another to direct and dispose of as he wishes. I technically possess the capacity to adopt personal aims and, more importantly, to recognize and commit myself to a moral principle, acknowledging each as an objective end. Yet my social or legal status denies me the ability to act on these personal and moral commitments, as it were, of my own accord. Decisions as to what I may do are made by others and in accord with their reasons. What slavery necessarily denies me, is the realization of my status as a self-legislating individual. In so doing, on the Kantian view, it denies me what is most essential to my personhood.

(2) Citizenship – national and global

Finally, we should notice the potentially fruitful connection between the moral perspective of the kingdom of ends and the accounts of citizenship and cosmopolitanism that are central to Kant's later political theory. The extent to which Kant's political theory can be said to derive from his moral theory is a matter of some controversy, and this is no place to attempt to resolve it. We can better appreciate both the nature of that controversy and the potential richness of Kant's political philosophy, though, if we briefly explore the seeming connections here.

We might say that Kant describes members of the kingdom of ends as free in the sense that they are not simply determined to act by external forces, as equal in that each possesses dignity, or incomparable worth, and as autonomous or possessed of the capacity and disposition to recognize and commit to rational principles. This last includes the capacity and disposition to recognize an overriding commitment to honor each person as an end in himself and the capacity and disposition to set personal ends consistent with that overriding commitment. In his *Rechtslehre*, or *Doctrine of Right*, Kant describes citizens of the just state in a way that echoes this account of legislators for the kingdom of ends:

> [T]he attributes of a citizen, inseparable from his essence (as a citizen), are: lawful freedom, the attribute of obeying no other law than that to which he has given his consent; civil equality, that of not recognizing among the people any superior with the moral capacity to bind the other; and third, the attribute of civil independence, of owing his existence and preservation to his own rights and powers as a member of the commonwealth, not to the choice of another among the people. From his independence follows his civil personality, his attribute of not needing to be represented by another where rights are concerned. (MM 6:314)

This passage, which describes Kant's conception of the citizen of the just state, seems to provide an interpretation of Kantian moral legislators for the peculiar circumstances that demand such a state. Freedom to choose rather than to be determined in one's actions becomes the right to participate, in some sense, in the selection of the state laws to which one is held accountable. The dignity of each person becomes the right not to be treated as a subject but always as a fellow citizen possessed of equal lawmaking authority and due equal legal concern. The autonomy of each becomes civil independence, the right to be treated as capable of exercising the capacities for judgment and commitment that are integral to being a self-determining citizen and lawmaker as opposed to one who is subject to or directed in accord with another's judgment.

In the end, the relationship between the account of legislators for a kingdom of ends and that of citizens of a just state might best be conceived either as a derivation, as an interpretation for a more concrete state of affairs, or as something far less direct. What matters for our purposes is that the implications of the kingdom of ends seem to extend beyond the realm of our individual moral obligations. At the least, they have implications for our appropriate understanding of our own status as citizens and of our relationship to those who share that status with us.

Kant's discussion of political obligations that cross national borders, those that fall within the realm of what he calls cosmopolitan justice, seems to further extend the reach of the kingdom of ends. Admittedly, the parallel between what we might term the "cosmopolitan perspective" and that of a legislator for the kingdom of ends is not as immediately evident as that between moral legislator and citizen. We nevertheless can recognize such a parallel, implicit in Kant's discussions. One example should suffice for present purposes. Consider, then, the three definitive articles of perpetual peace, set forth in Kant's essay of that title. The first of these demands that each state's civil constitution be republican; the second holds that the basis for the right of nations lies in a "federalism of free states"; and the third defines cosmopolitan right as "limited to conditions of universal hospitality" (PP 8:349, PP 8:354, PP 8:357).[4]

Kant tells us that a republican constitution is the only one that can provide a basis for just legislation. Most generally, a republican constitution separates executive and legislative powers. It thus provides a structure designed to ensure that we are ruled by the laws to which we have committed ourselves and not by the whim of an individual, or even of the many. As Kant emphasizes, when I am governed by another's whim rather than through a law backed by my own agreement, I lack freedom. We can find the parallel to this concern for individual freedom in the earlier account of the citizen's freedom as properly subject only to a law to which he has (in some sense) consented. More fundamentally, it is rooted in the characterization of members of the kingdom of ends as capable of genuine choice, not merely determined to action by prior causes. In each case, freedom requires a genuine role for individual choice and stands in contrast to the situation in which the individual is the mere plaything of external forces.

A federation of free states, or pacific federation, is at the heart of Kant's second definitive article of perpetual peace. Though the connection again is inexplicit, Kant's discussion here parallels those of civil equality and of the equal dignity of individuals. First, the federation is meant to preserve the freedom of *each* state. It does so by ensuring that no state is either ruled by a superior state or body as part of some international collaboration towards peace nor made subject to such a superior through war. Second, Kant argues that if even one member of the federal partnership is a republic, all the others likewise will tend in this direction. This means that they will tend to develop the kind of well-functioning legal institutions that would mark them as possessed of the capacity for morally legitimate self-government, and thus, as our *Groundwork* discussions reveal, of a kind of dignity.

The extent to which the state possesses dignity, or is a "moral person," is too large a topic to address at length here. Kant does emphasize, though, that states are by definition legislative entities that submit to no external legal constraint. They have, we might say, a dignity that is incompatible with any agreement to submit to external coercive rule. In one way, this marks (as Kant notes) a difference between states and individuals. For the latter can agree to submit to coercive rule. In another way, states and individuals are very similarly positioned. Individuals can submit to coercive laws only under conditions in which they properly may be said to be both legislator and subject. States must be part of a federal partnership because, absent this, there will be no authoritative moral principles to govern international relationships. They must avoid a global (or world) state because this inevitably would involve coercive rule by a superior, or so Kant argues.

The second definitive article thus advocates a pacific federation first because (in Kant's view) this is the entity capable of honoring each state as a lawmaker that is as worthy of respect as any of its fellows. Further, Kant believes, such a league can encourage the republicanism that he associates with respect for equal dignity.

This brings us to the third definitive article. Cosmopolitan right, those claims of right or justice that may be made across national boundaries, are, for Kant, "limited to conditions of universal *hospitality*" (PP 8:357, emphasis in original). For this purpose, he adds, hospitality means the "right of a foreigner not to be treated with hostility because he has arrived on the land of another" (PP 8:357–8). Hospitality does not ground a claim to the kindnesses typically accorded a guest, but rather entitles a visitor "not to be treated with hostility" provided "he behaves peaceably where he is" (PP 8:358).

Here the parallel features we should consider are the autonomy of legislators for a kingdom of ends and the independence of citizens of a just state. As with individual dignity and civil equality, the relationship of hospitality to these parallel features is twofold. First, the demand for hospitality is, for Kant, necessary if we are to acknowledge the deep interest each individual has in being self-governing and, more particularly, in engaging in work, travel, and social intercourse within the limited confines of the globe. It is required if we are fully to honor each as an autonomous agent. Second, Kant believes it is this right to travel and interact with distant others that may lead, over time, to public laws appropriate to persons as citizens of the globe, and not merely as citizens of this or that particular state. Such a body of laws, or cosmopolitan constitution, would achieve, or much more nearly approach, the realization of ourselves not only as individual agents but as members of a cosmopolitan community. For it would commit us to laws appropriate for worldly human rational agents as such and not merely for members of this or that more limited state.

Of course, our consideration of the parallels among Kant's discussions of the kingdom of ends, the just state, and cosmopolitanism do much to explain the controversy regarding the connection between his moral and his political theories. There is no clear argument or derivation to be uncovered, and for now the nature and degree of the connection must remain under-described. Nevertheless, we can see that the reach of our main topics here is extensive. The formula of autonomy and the discussion of the kingdom of ends not only comprise central elements of Kant's moral philosophy, but connect what otherwise may appear to be quite separate aspects of his practical thought.

Notes

1 Quotations from Kant's *Groundwork of the Metaphysics of Morals* use the Hill and Zweig, edition.
2 Kant claims that one of the essential features of a moral principle is that it is categorical. That is, its requirements apply regardless of the surrounding circumstances. In particular, applicability does not depend on what ends or projects one may have set or undertaken, or on what would otherwise serve individual self-interest or contribute to human happiness.

3 For example, Kant holds that a punishment may be unacceptable from the standpoint of justice because it "could make the humanity in the person suffering it into something abominable" (MM 6:333).
4 Quotations from "Perpetual Peace" use the Gregor edition.

References

English Translations of Kant

Groundwork of the Metaphysics of Morals. Thomas E. Hill, Jr., ed., and Arnulf Zweig, trans. New York: Oxford University Press, 2002. (Original work published 1785).
On Perpetual Peace. In Mary Gregor, ed. and trans., Paul Guyer and Allen Wood, series eds., *Practical Philosophy*. New York: Cambridge University Press, 1996. Original work published 1795.

Other References

Hill, Thomas E., Jr. 1992: The Kingdom of Ends. In *Dignity and Practical Reason in Kant's Moral Theory*, 55–66. Ithaca, N.Y.: Cornell University Press.
Hill, Thomas E., Jr. 2000: A Kantian Perspective on Moral Rules. In *Respect, Pluralism and Justice*, 33–55. New York: Oxford University Press.
Holtman, Sarah Williams 1999: Kant, Ideal Theory, and the Justice of Exclusionary Zoning. *Ethics*, 110:1 (October), 32–58.

Further Reading

Herman, Barbara. 1997: A Cosmopolitan Kingdom of Ends. In Andrews Reath, Christine Korsgaard, and Barbara Herman, eds., *Reclaiming the History of Ethics: Essays for John Rawls*, 187–213. New York: Cambridge University Press.
Herman, Barbara. 1998: Training to Autonomy: Kant and the Question of Moral Education. In Amelie O. Rorty, ed., *Philosophers on Education: Historical Perspectives*, 255–72. New York: Routledge.
Hill, Thomas E., Jr. 1991: Autonomy and Benevolent Lies, 25–42, and The Importance of Autonomy, 43–51. In *Autonomy and Self-Respect*, 25–42. New York: Cambridge University Press.
Hill, Thomas E., Jr. 1992: The Kantian Conception of Autonomy. In *Dignity and Practical Reason in Kant's Moral Theory*, 76–96.
O'Neill, Onora. 1989: Action, Anthropology and Autonomy. In *Constructions of Reason*, 66–77. New York: Cambridge University Press.
Rawls, John. 2000: Kant. In Barbara Herman, ed., *Lectures on the History of Moral Philosophy*, 143–322, especially 200–14. Cambridge, MA: Harvard University Press.
Wood, Allen W. 1999: *Kant's Ethical Thought*, esp. 156–190. New York: Cambridge University Press.

Part II

Argument and Critique

Part II

Argument and Critique

5

Deriving the Supreme Moral Principle from Common Moral Ideas

Samuel J. Kerstein

In the Preface to the *Groundwork of the Metaphysics of Morals*, Kant sets out his goals: to locate and to establish the supreme principle of morality (G 4:392). He devotes Section I to the first goal. Working under the assumption that there is a supreme principle of morality, he tries to locate it in the sense of specifying its content.[1] Kant strives to find the supreme principle that, on reflection, we hold to be at work in our moral practice. His attempt rests on appeals to (what he takes to be) ordinary moral reasoning. Near the end of *Groundwork* I, he proclaims success. "Thus, then, we have arrived, within the moral cognition of common human reason, at its principle, which it admittedly does not think so abstractly in a universal form, but which it actually has always before its eyes and uses as the norm for its appraisals" (G 4:403–4). This principle is the Categorical Imperative. In *Groundwork* I, Kant's main concern is to show that if there is a supreme principle of morality then it is this imperative. It is not until *Groundwork* III that Kant tries to establish the Categorical Imperative, that is, to prove that we are all rationally compelled to conform to it.

This paper focuses on Kant's attempt to locate the Categorical Imperative – an attempt which, in the idiom of contemporary Kant scholarship, is called his "derivation" of this principle. In *Groundwork* I Kant derives one particular formulation of the Categorical Imperative, namely (a version of) his famous Formula of Universal Law: *act only on that maxim through which you can at the same time will that it become a universal law* (G 4:420–1).[2] The title of *Groundwork* I is "Transition from common rational to philosophic moral cognition." Kant's starting point is "common rational moral cognition," which is a fancy term for common moral ideas. How, from this starting point, does Kant derive the Formula of Universal Law? This paper sketches an answer to this question.

In my view, Kant's *Groundwork* I derivation of the Formula of Universal Law takes place in three main steps. First, Kant tries to pinpoint criteria that we, on reflection, believe that the supreme principle of morality must fulfill. Second, Kant attempts to establish that no possible rival to the Formula of Universal Law fulfills all of these criteria. Third, at least implicitly Kant argues that the Formula of Universal Law remains as a viable candidate for a principle that fulfills all of them. With these three steps, Kant strives to prove that if there is a supreme principle of morality then it is this formula. In short, Kant argues by elimination. When we have before us a clear notion of the characteristics the supreme principle of morality must possess, Kant suggests, we are able to eliminate every candidate for this principle except the Formula of Universal Law (or equivalent principles). I call this interpretation of Kant's derivation the "criterial reading," since it emphasizes that Kant develops criteria that any viable candidate for the supreme principle of morality must fulfill.

The criterial reading of Kant's derivation is not the only one philosophers have proposed. (For alternatives, see, for example, Aune 1979, and Korsgaard 1996). Elsewhere, I have tried to demonstrate that the criterial reading compares well with other interpretations in terms of its textual plausibility and philosophical fruitfulness (Kerstein 2002). Here I limit myself to illustrating how the criterial reading helps us make sense of *Groundwork* I. In particular, I focus on how Kant appeals to "common rational moral cognition" in order to develop criteria for the supreme principle of morality.

The *Groundwork* I derivation culminates in the introduction of the Formula of Universal Law. In the sentence that immediately precedes its introduction, Kant poses a question: "But what kind of law can that be, the representation of which must determine the will, even without regard for the effect expected from it, in order for the will to be called good absolutely and without limitation?" (G 4:402). Kant is in effect asking which principle (law) can possess certain characteristics, namely ones that, according to ordinary moral thinking, the supreme principle of morality must possess. These characteristics are crystallized in the famous three "propositions" that Kant tries to establish in *Groundwork* I. The propositions encapsulate criteria for the supreme principle of morality. So by tracing how Kant arrives at his propositions, we will gain an understanding of how he develops these criteria.

The paper unfolds as follows. Parts II–III concern Kant's three propositions and the criteria for the supreme principle of morality implicit in them. The bulk of the discussion focuses on Kant's first proposition, namely that an action has moral worth just in case it is done from duty. Kant relies far more directly on ordinary moral thinking in defending this proposition than he does in defending the other two. Part IV illustrates how Kant might use criteria he develops in order to show that rivals to the Formula of Universal Law cannot be the supreme principle of morality. Unfortunately, these criteria do not enable him even to come close to eliminating all rivals. But Kant's argument gains in strength when we recognize that he suggests an additional criterion for the supreme principle of morality: it must be such that a plausible set of moral prescriptions (i.e., plausible relative to common rational moral cognition) would stem from the principle. Part V focuses on this additional criterion. According to the criterial reading, the final step of the derivation is to show that the Formula of Universal Law remains as a viable candidate for a principle that fulfills all of the criteria, including that it generate a plausible set of moral prescriptions. Determining whether the Formula of Universal Law fulfills this criterion would obviously require delving into the details of how to interpret this principle. That is a project for another occasion. The final section (VI) of this paper is devoted to a concern one might have regarding the interpretation of the derivation offered here. The interpretation emphasizes the extent to which it depends on appeals to ordinary moral thinking. But how are such appeals, which seem to be appeals to experience, to be reconciled with Kant's view that the supreme principle of morality is an a priori principle?

Before focusing on *Groundwork* I and the criteria for the supreme principle of morality that Kant there suggests, it will be helpful to consider what he means by "supreme principle of morality" in the first place.

I

According to (what I call) Kant's basic concept, the supreme principle of morality would possess four characteristics. It would be practical, absolutely necessary, binding on all rational agents, and would serve as the supreme norm for the moral evaluation of action. I call this concept of the supreme principle of morality basic because Kant suggests it in the *Groundwork*'s Preface.

To say that a principle must be the supreme norm for the moral assessment of action suggests several things. The principle would obviously distinguish between morally permissible and morally impermissible actions as well as specify which actions are morally required. In addition, whether an action was morally good would depend on how it related to this principle. Kant implies, for example, that no action that violated the principle would count as morally valuable (G 4:390). Finally, as the supreme norm for the moral assessment of action, the supreme principle of morality would be such that all genuine duties would ultimately be derived from it (see G 4:421).[3] The supreme principle would justify these duties' status as such.

Kant says that the supreme principle of morality "must hold not only for human beings but for all *rational beings as such*" (G 4:408; see also G 4:389, CPrR 5:32). The supreme principle of morality would have an extremely wide scope: one that extended not only to all rational human beings, but to any other rational beings who might exist, for example, to God, angels, and intelligent extraterrestrials.

A third feature the supreme principle of morality would have to possess is that of being absolutely necessary (G 4:389). On every agent within its scope, for Kant every rational agent, the principle would hold without exception (G 4:408). For us human agents, the supreme principle of morality would be an unconditional command (i.e., a categorical imperative in one sense of the term). That we were obligated to perform the action it specified would not be conditional on our having any particular set of desires.

Finally, for Kant the supreme principle of morality must be practical, that is, a rule on account of which agents can act. Kant implies this in the *Groundwork* Preface by specifying that morally good actions involve an agent's acting for the sake of the moral law, that is, the supreme principle of morality (G 4:390). For Kant the supreme principle must be able to figure directly in an agent's practical deliberations.

Kant claims to find in ordinary moral thinking agreement that the supreme principle of morality would have to have at least some of these features. He suggests, for example, that, according to the "common idea of duty," a moral law "must carry with it absolute necessity" (G 4:389).

II

Now that we have an idea of what, according to Kant, the supreme principle of morality would have to be like, let us focus on the details of his attempt to show that if there is such a principle then it is the Formula of Universal Law. As I indicated, Kant's attempt involves his developing three propositions, each of which implies a criterion for the supreme principle of morality. It makes sense to begin with Kant's first proposition. Although Kant does not explicitly state it, it is widely, and, I believe, correctly taken to be the following: An action has moral worth if and only if it is done from duty.

As a first step towards understanding this proposition we need to delve briefly into Kant's famous discussion of a good will. For Kant tells us that the concept of duty "contains that of a good will though under certain subjective limitations and hindrances" (G 4:397). Let us focus on Kant's discussion of the good will as it relates to us, agents who can indulge their inclinations and thereby act contrary to what morality requires. In this context, Kant seems to use the notion of a good will in two ways. According to the first usage, a good will is a particular sort of *willing* or, what for him amounts to the same thing, of acting. Kant writes of "the unqualified [*uneingeschränkten*] worth of actions" (G 4:411), presumably of actions done from duty. For he has earlier stated that actions from duty have "unconditional and moral worth" (G 4:400). Since, according to Kant, the good will is good without qualification [*ohne Einschränkung*], it appears that sometimes "good will" refers to a certain kind of action, that is, action done from duty.

According to a second usage, "good will" refers not to a particular kind of action an agent might perform but rather to a kind of character she might have. An agent has a good will in this usage, I believe, just in case she is committed to doing what duty requires, not just in this or that particular action, but overall. If an agent has this commitment, then she will presumably sometimes act from duty. (For example, she will invoke duty as her incentive to do what is morally required in cases in which she is tempted by her inclinations to act contrary to what morality demands.) In the first paragraph of *Groundwork* I, Kant intimates that having a good will amounts to having a certain kind of character. Right after suggesting that a good will is good without qualification, he tells us that certain qualities of temperament, for example, courage or resolution, "are undoubtedly good and desirable for many purposes, but they can also be extremely evil and harmful if the will that is to make use of these gifts of nature, and whose distinctive constitution is therefore called *character*, is not good" (G 4:393).[4] Sometimes Kant employs what we might (following Karl Ameriks 1989, pp. 54–9), call the "whole character" conception of a good will. This is not the place to consider in detail how these conceptions relate to one another. But I suspect that in Kant's considered view the only way an agent can have a good will in the first (particular action) sense is if he has a good will in the second (whole character) sense. In other words, Kant holds that only an agent who has an overall commitment to doing his duty can act from duty on any particular occasion.

In any case, the particular action notion of a good will is more important for our purposes. Kant suggests that a good will in the sense of good *willing* is equivalent to acting from duty. And, according to "common understanding" (G 4:394), this willing (or, equivalently, acting) has a special, moral worth. First, it is unconditionally good. In all possible circumstances in which it appears, a good will is good; moreover, the degree of its goodness does not vary according to its effects. Even if a good will "should wholly lack the capacity to carry out its purpose – if with its greatest efforts it should yet achieve nothing and only the good will were left . . . then, like a jewel, it would still shine by itself, as something that has its full worth in itself" (G 4:394). Second, according to ordinary moral thinking, the worth of a good will is especially high, Kant claims. We take a good will (good willing) to be preeminently valuable (see G 4:394 and G 4:401). That presumably implies that, in our view, no particular action that is not done from duty is as valuable as any action that is done from duty.

Let us now return to Kant's first proposition. It states that an action has moral worth if and only if it is done from duty or, equivalently, that all and only actions done from duty have moral worth. The two key concepts in this proposition are obviously those of moral worth and of acting from duty. Moral worth, as we just noted, is unconditional and preeminent worth. At this stage in his argument, Kant does not explain precisely what acting from duty amounts to. But from the *Groundwork*'s Preface, it's easy to discern the basic idea he has in mind (and takes his reader to have in mind as well). Acting from duty is doing something "for the sake of" the moral law (G 4:390). In other words, to act from duty is to do something because a valid moral principle (or at least a principle one takes to be valid) prescribes that one do it. A more rigorous account of acting from duty emerges from Kant's discussion of his third proposition.

In the *Groundwork*, Kant sets out grounds for rejecting the notion that actions from motives other than duty have moral worth. Yet he apparently finds it unnecessary to argue that all actions done from duty possess such worth. Consider, for example, his discussion of self-preservation. Kant suggests that we have a duty to preserve our life and that, the vast majority of the time, when we take steps to preserve it we are acting from an immediate inclination to stay alive. "But on this account," Kant says, "the often anxious care that most people take of [their life] still has no inner worth and their maxim has no moral content. They look after their lives *in conformity with duty* but not *from duty*" (G 4:397–8). Kant takes it to be obvious that if a person preserves his life not from inclination but from duty, "his maxim has moral content," and thus acting on it has moral worth. He assumes that "common rational moral cognition" needs no coaxing in order to see that actions done from duty possess moral worth.

In contrast, Kant does think we need a bit of help in order to discern that *only* actions from duty have moral worth. He highlights two conditions on actions with such worth, both of which he takes to be accepted by common rational moral cognition. He then intimates that no action from inclination could meet these conditions. Kant introduces the first condition in the *Groundwork* Preface:

> in the case of what is to be morally good, it is not enough that it *conform* with the moral law; but it must also be done *for the sake of the law*; without this, that conformity is only very contingent and precarious, since a ground that is not moral will indeed now and then produce actions in conformity with the law, but it will also often produce actions contrary to the law. (G 4:390)

Morally valuable action, Kant here suggests, is action done from a motive that will not produce actions contrary to duty. In the *Groundwork*, Kant maintains that acting "for the sake of the law," that is, doing something because you take it to be required by moral principle, meets this condition, while acting from inclination does not.

Kant invokes this condition in his famous discussion of the "philanthropist" (or "friend of humanity") (G 4:398). Before the discussion begins, Kant suggests a distinction between acting from a mediate inclination (self-interest) and acting from an immediate inclination (G 4:397). A mediate inclination to do something is an inclination to do it for the sake of fulfilling some further inclination. The shopkeeper in Kant's example presumably has a mediate inclination to charge his customers fairly. He wants to do it, but merely as a means to satisfying another end, for example, that of having a thriving business. An immediate inclination to do something is an inclination to do the thing itself. Since he is "sympathetically attuned," the philanthropist presumably has an immediate inclination to promote the well-being of others. His inclination to help them is not one that he strives to satisfy merely to fulfill some further desire. Kant, of course, denies that acting from this inclination has moral worth. Doing so, he says, is like acting from other inclinations, for example, the inclination to honor, "which, if it fortunately lights upon what is in fact in the common interest and in conformity with duty and hence honorable, deserves praise and encouragement but not esteem" (G 4:398; see also R 6:30–1). Here Kant underscores the possibility that in acting from an immediate inclination to help others, that is, from sympathy, an agent might do something that conflicts with duty. To echo a well-known example (Herman 1993, pp. 4–5), someone might, because of his sympathetic temperament, have an immediate inclination to help someone he sees late one night hurriedly struggling to move a sculpture out the back door of an art museum and into his waiting car. Since the philanthropist is acting from an immediate inclination, and thereby doing something that might fail to accord with duty, his action, Kant suggests, does not have moral worth.

Yet in his discussion of the philanthropist Kant points to a further condition he places on an action's having moral worth (Herman 1993, pp. 5–6). Kant says that the maxim on which the philanthropist acts "lacks moral content, namely that of doing such actions not from inclination but *from* duty" (G 4:398). Kant does not tell us explicitly what the philanthropist's maxim is. From the description Kant provides, however, we can assume that it is something like the following: "Because I want to help others, I will promote their happiness." This maxim, says Kant, lacks moral content, and it is not hard to pinpoint a reason why. The maxim reflects no commitment to the action's being morally permissible, that is, in accordance with what moral principle requires. In other words, the maxim expresses no interest in the rightness of the kind of action it specifies, namely promoting others' happiness. If we reflect on our ordinary moral understanding, suggests Kant, we find that we are willing to attribute moral worth only to actions done on maxims that (if fully specified) reflect a commitment to doing only what is morally permissible. The grounds of a morally valuable action, that is, its motive, must express an interest in the action's moral rightness. This is Kant's second condition for an action's having moral worth.

It is a necessary condition, not a sufficient one, that when an agent does some particular thing, he is committed to its being morally permissible, that it does not entail that his action has moral worth. What the agent does might be morally permissible, but not morally required. And for Kant only morally required actions can have moral worth. According to Kant, of course, actions from duty fulfill this second condition. In them, an agent's basis for acting, that is, his maxim, obviously expresses concern for his action's moral rightness, for it invokes the notion that actions of its kind are morally required.

Kant would insist that an action might fulfill the first condition for moral value without fulfilling the second (Herman 1993, p. 5). Suppose, for example, that the philanthropist's immediate inclination to help others were such that it served as the basis only for morally permissible actions. In that case, the philanthropist's beneficent actions would fulfill Kant's first condition: they would be done on a motive that always produced actions conforming to duty. Nevertheless, the philanthropist's actions would still not have moral worth, for the grounds of his actions would fail to express concern for their moral rightness, thereby running afoul of the second condition.

Kant's first proposition and his defense of it have attracted ample critical attention. Kant is perhaps too quick to conclude that, according to common rational moral cognition, an action has moral worth only if it fulfills his two conditions (and thus only if it is done from duty). He might also be precipitous in assuming widespread endorsement of the notion that all actions from duty have moral worth. My own view (Kerstein 2002, pp. 114–38) is that Kant is on much stronger ground in claiming that, according to common rational moral cognition, all actions from duty have moral worth than he is in claiming that only actions from duty have moral worth. In any case, Kant's main appeals to ordinary moral thinking occur in his discussion of the special value possessed by a good will, as well as in the closely related discussion leading up to his first proposition.

III

The arguments Kant suggests for the second and third propositions are far less directly tied to intuitive moral judgments than his arguments for the first. In his "second proposition," Kant says that "an action from duty has its moral worth *not in the purpose* to be attained by it but in the maxim in accordance with which it is decided upon, and therefore does not depend upon the realization of the object of the action but merely upon the *principle of volition* in accordance with which the action is done" (G 4:399–400). Later Kant says that "the moral worth of an action does not lie in the effect expected from it" (G 4:401; see also G 4:435).

Kant here invokes the notion of a principle of volition or maxim. We've already made use of this notion, but it makes sense to pause here to get a more precise idea of what a maxim is. The brief account of maxims that follows is certainly not the only plausible one, but it will serve to fix ideas. A maxim is a "subjective principle of acting" (G 4:421n; see also G 4:400n). It is a subjective principle in that it is held by some agent, it can be freely adopted or discarded by her, and it applies only to her own actions. An agent's maxims are principles of acting in that they play a role in the generation of her actions. An agent acts on maxims. When fully specified, a maxim includes a description of a kind of action to be performed in a kind of situation, as well as a specification of the agent's end and his incentive in performing it. An example of a maxim is the following: "From self-love, during my free time I exercise in order to stay in shape." (Self-love is the agent's incentive; staying in shape is her end.) According to Kant, whenever an agent acts, she does so on some maxim, even though she might not have it explicitly in view.

Kant's second proposition says essentially that an action done from duty derives its moral worth from its maxim rather than from its effects. The proposition relies on a distinction between an action (which is always done on some maxim) and its effects. For Kant, to act is to exercise one's will (Kerstein 2002, pp. 20–1). It is to try, based on some principle of volition, to realize a state of affairs (an object or end). This state of affairs (or whatever state of affairs actually results from the action) is an effect of the willing. Acting consists in the willing itself, not in its effects (see G 4:400). According to the second proposition, it is the maxim behind an action done from duty that gives it moral value, rather than the action's results.

Implicit in *Groundwork* I is a straightforward argument for the second proposition. Suppose that, contrary to it, the moral worth of an action from duty *did* stem from its effects. There would, then, be possible circumstances in which an action from duty did not have moral worth, namely, ones in which the action failed to produce certain effects. For Kant, however, if an action is done from duty, then it has moral worth, no matter what the circumstances may be. His first criterion incorporates this view. Moral worth is "unconditional," Kant suggests (G 4:400). Therefore, as the second proposition indicates, the moral worth of an action from duty does *not* stem from its effects. For example, suppose that an agent holds the supreme principle of morality to be: "Always do what you believe will please God." Moreover, contrary to the second proposition, the agent maintains that the moral worth of her conforming to this principle because the principle requires it, that is, the moral worth of her acting from duty stems from its effects. Whether her action has moral worth, she thinks, depends on whether it actually pleases God. Since, as a fallible being, she might be mistaken as to what would please God, there would presumably be possible circumstances in which her acting from duty would not actually please her/him. In these circumstances, the agent would be compelled to maintain, her acting from duty would be devoid of moral worth. But this acknowledgment would contradict Kant's first proposition, according to which a sufficient condition for an action's having moral worth is that it be done from duty. In short, Kant defends the second proposition by appealing to the first. That the effects of our actions can give them "no unconditional and moral worth," he says, "is clear from what has gone before" (G 4:400). What has gone before, of course, is Kant's discussion of the relations between acting from duty and moral worth: a discussion, based on common rational moral cognition, that lays the basis for his first proposition.

According to Kant's third proposition, "duty is the necessity of an action from respect for law" (G 4:400, emphasis omitted). This proposition fills in some details regarding what it means for an action to be done from duty. According to the proposition, if an action is done from duty then what determines it is "objectively the *law* and subjectively pure respect for this practical law, and so the maxim of complying with such a law even if it infringes upon all my inclinations" (G 4:400–1). By "law" here, Kant means a universally binding and absolutely necessary practical principle. When an agent acts from duty, Kant here suggests, his action stems from the notion, which is incorporated into his maxim, that a practical law requires it. Kant even says that "an action from duty is to put aside entirely the influence of inclination" (G 4:400). So, in his view, an agent who needs to rely on an inclination in order to get something done fails to act from duty. If an agent acts from duty, the notion that a law requires her action itself generates enough motivation for her to do it. It generates this motivation, Kant suggests, at least in part by producing in her a feeling of respect for the law. Kant develops his concept of respect in detail in the *Critique of Practical Reason* (CPrR 5:71–89). It is very complex, and we have no need to explore it here. But we do need to hold in view that, according to Kant's third proposition, when an agent acts from duty, her notion that her action is required by a practical law provides her with sufficient motive for doing it. In other words, this notion gives her a ground sufficient to determine her will.

But how does Kant defend this proposition? He suggests, but does not explicitly make, the following argument.[5] Suppose that in an action done from duty the notion that the action was required by a practical law did *not* give an agent sufficient motive to perform it. In that case, Kant suggests, the additional motive necessary for the agent to perform the action would have to be the agent's expectation that her action would bring about certain effects (G 4:401). But now further suppose that the action did not produce the expected effects. In that case, the agent would be rationally compelled to agree that the action had *less value* than it would have had if the expected effects had come to fruition. After all, if, in the agent's view, the action's value was not at all contingent on the effects being produced then why would she need to acquire part of her motivation for doing it from the prospect that the effects would be produced? But if an action done from duty has less value than it otherwise would have as a result of its not producing certain effects, then its value is not unconditional. And this result conflicts with Kant's first proposition, according to which all actions from duty have moral, and thus unconditional, worth. The result also conflicts with his second proposition, since according to it the moral worth of an action does not depend (at all) on the action's effects. So it makes sense for Kant to suggest, as he does (G 4:400), that his third proposition follows from the previous two.

Kant's main aim in articulating his three propositions is to derive the supreme principle of morality, that is, to show that if there is such a principle, then it is the Formula of Universal Law. Each one of the propositions implies a corresponding criterion that the supreme principle of morality must fulfill. The first proposition says that an action has moral worth if and only if it is done from duty. According to the criterion implicit in this proposition, the supreme principle of morality must be such that all and only actions conforming to it because the principle requires it, that is, all and only actions done from duty, have moral worth. The second proposition says that an action done from duty derives its moral worth from its maxim rather than from its effects. So whatever the supreme principle of morality is, goes the second criterion, the moral worth of conforming, from duty, to it must stem from the maxim of the action, not from its effects. According to the core of the third proposition, when an agent acts from duty, her notion that her action is required by a practical law provides her with sufficient grounds for acting. The criterion implicit in this proposition is the following: the supreme principle of morality must be such that an agent's notion that it is a practical law and that it requires her to do something gives her sufficient motive to do it. It's up to the agent, of course, whether she acts on this motive and does what is required rather than, say, indulging an inclination to do something else.

Let us again note that in the sentence preceding his initial presentation of the categorical imperative, Kant asks: "But what kind of law can that be, the representation of which must determine the will, even without regard for the effect expected from it, in order for the will to be called good absolutely and without limitation?" (G 4:402). He is, in effect, asking what law (principle) can fulfill each of these three criteria for the supreme principle of morality: the third criterion, which invokes an agent's representation of a law as a sufficient motive for her action; then the second criterion, which incorporates the notion that the moral worth of an action does not stem from its effects; and finally the first criterion, which specifies when an action, that is, an instance of willing, has moral and thus unconditional worth. If we can show that a particular principle is unable to fulfill any one of these criteria, then we can, Kant suggests, eliminate it as a viable candidate for the supreme principle of morality. If Kant's derivation of the categorical imperative is successful, then we should be able to see that the only principle that remains as a viable candidate for satisfying all three of these criteria (plus those criteria implicit in Kant's basic concept of the supreme principle of morality) is the Formula of Universal Law (or an equivalent principle).

IV

Unfortunately, it would be unduly optimistic to say that we are in position to see this. Kant moves extremely quickly from the criteria he develops to the conclusion that the only viable candidate for fulfilling all of them is the Formula of Universal Law. He seems to leave it to us to fill in the details regarding precisely how rivals get eliminated. Even if, employing Kant's criteria, we eliminate all rivals that come to mind, it is not clear how we can be confident that we have not overlooked some other rival.[6] Nevertheless, we are well-situated to see how we might use Kant's criteria to dismiss some well-known principles as viable candidates for the supreme principle of morality.

Kant does not explicitly argue against utilitarianism. But let us consider a utilitarian principle, U: "Always perform a right action: one that yields just as great a sum total of well-being as would any alternative action available to you." Let us suppose, as it seems reasonable to do, that the utilitarian embraces this principle largely on the grounds of her being convinced of the following. First, the amount of goodness in the world depends solely on the sum total of individual well-being in it – the higher the sum total, the more goodness. Second, the rightness of an action depends solely on the goodness of its consequences. More precisely, an action is right if that which results from it is at least as good as that which would have resulted from each of the alternative actions available to the agent.

Although U derives from these un-Kantian convictions, it would be precipitous to dismiss it as a candidate for the supreme principle of morality on the grounds of a manifest failure to conform to Kant's basic concept of this principle. U could, it seems, be a practical, absolutely necessary, universally binding, fundamental norm for moral evaluation of action.

But U runs afoul of Kant's further criteria for the supreme principle of morality. The utilitarian might insist that an agent can, from duty, comply with U. After all, what would prevent her from performing a right action just because U commands her to do so? Yet she is committed to the following view: whether an agent's conforming to U from duty has moral worth depends solely on the action's effects, specifically its effects on well-being. For she holds that the amount of goodness in the world (including the "moral worth" of actions) depends *solely* on the amount of well-being in it. So the utilitarian cannot, rationally speaking, maintain that U fulfills Kant's second criterion, namely that the supreme principle of morality be such that the moral worth of conforming to it from duty stems not at all from that action's effects.

If we think of a consequentialist principle as one according to which the good-ness of each and every action depends to some extent on the action's effects (in addition to the "effect" that the action has taken place), then it is easy to show that no consequentialist principle fulfills Kant's second criterion. For even the staunchest proponent of such a principle would have to acknowledge that she is committed to the view that the value of acting from duty depends at least in part on what that action produces.

So based ultimately on an appeal to the notion that, according to ordinary moral thinking, actions from duty have a special worth, Kant develops three criteria for the supreme principle of morality. Assuming these criteria are sound, Kant has solid grounds for dismissing some of the Categorical Imperative's rivals for status as viable candidates for the supreme principle of morality.

V

However, if, as a basis for dismissing rivals, Kant has only these three criteria, coupled with those implicit in Kant's basic concept of the supreme principle of morality, he is vulnerable to a serious criticism. Using these criteria, he would be helpless to eliminate rivals that, one would think, would have almost no chance of being the supreme principle of morality. Consider the bizarre principle, BP: "Act only on that maxim such that you *cannot*, at the same time, will that it become a universal law." Assuming that the Categorical Imperative could be a universally valid, absolutely necessary, supreme practical principle, why couldn't BP be such a principle? What argument does Kant have at his disposal that would show it to be impossible for BP to have these characteristics? Moreover, it seems that a proponent of BP would be able consistently to maintain that an action has moral worth if and only if it is done because BP requires it, that such an action's moral worth would not stem from its effects, and so forth. He would not be rationally compelled to acknowledge that BP runs afoul of the criteria implicit in Kant's three propositions.

Another, less provocative, example of a principle Kant would be unable to dismiss on the basis of his criteria is the following principle of weak universal-ization, WU: "Act only on that maxim which, when generalized, could be a universal law." WU is not equivalent to the Formula of Universal Law. And Kant himself suggests that a maxim of non-beneficence could, when generalized, constitute a universal law (G 4:423). Since a world where no one acted benefi-cently is indeed a coherent possibility, acting on a maxim of non-beneficence does not violate WU. On Kant's view, of course, acting on such a maxim does run afoul of the Formula of Universal Law. It does so, he thinks, because as a rational agent it is not possible to act on it and, *at the same time*, will that its generalization be a universal law. On the basis of the criteria discussed thus far, Kant does not appear to have the tools to eliminate WU as a contender for the supreme principle of morality. For not only is it possible that WU satisfies Kant's basic concept of the supreme principle of morality, but there seems to be no reason to think that it couldn't fulfill the criteria suggested by his three propositions.

In my view, this difficulty prompts us to see that Kant actually suggests one further criterion for the supreme principle of morality. It must be such that a plausible set of duties, that is, plausible relative to common rational moral cognition, would stem from the principle. Both BP and WU could be eliminated through an appeal to this criterion. According to ordinary moral thinking, contrary to BP and to WU, we have a duty of beneficence.

A textual basis for this criterion is not hard to discern. In *Groundwork* II, Kant offers a derivation of the Formula of Universal law that parallels his derivation in *Groundwork* I. Right after he arrives at this formula, Kant says: "Now, if all imperatives of duty can be derived from this single imperative as from their principle, then, even though we leave it undecided whether what is called duty is not as such an empty concept, we shall at least be able to show what we think by it and what the concept wants to say" (G 4:420–1). The derivation is not complete unless "all imperatives of duty" can be derived from the imperative Kant proposes as the only viable candidate for the supreme principle of morality. By "all imperatives of duty," Kant apparently means all imperatives that we, reflective rational agents, take to express our moral duties. Kant proceeds, of course, to try to show that four such imperatives, including, for example, a requirement not to make false promises for financial gain, follow from the Formula of Universal Law. He then says: "These are a few of the many actual duties, *or at least of what we take to be such*, whose derivation from the one principle cited above is clear" (G 4:424, emphasis added). If these duties' derivation from the Formula of Universal Law were not clear, for example, if it simply did not follow from the formula that we had them, then, Kant implies, we could not accept this formula as the only viable candidate for the supreme principle of morality. In the short paragraph (G 4:420–1) following his statement of the Formula of Universal Law, Kant indicates an important criterion for any viable candidate for the supreme principle of morality. We must be able to see how it follows from this candidate that, if it were established, we would indeed have moral duties that we are convinced we do have. (For further textual evidence that Kant embraces this criterion, see Kerstein 2002, pp. 87–9.)

With this additional criterion in place, Kant can advance towards eliminating rivals for status as viable candidates for the supreme principle of morality. But in order for his derivation of the Formula of Universal Law to succeed, he would need not only to show that rivals are unfit to satisfy the criteria he indicates, but also that it remains viable to think that his candidate can satisfy them. Yet this latter task poses serious challenges. Kant offers various, supposedly equivalent, formulations of the Categorical Imperative. For example, in addition to the Formula of Universal Law, he offers the Formula of Humanity: "So act that you use humanity, whether in your own person or in the person of any other, always at the same time as an end, never merely as a means" (G 4:429, emphasis omitted).

Both of these principles are difficult to interpret; it's far from obvious what either one would require us to do. In my view, it is very unlikely that the Formula of Universal Law would generate a set of duties acceptable to ordinary moral thinking (Kerstein 2002, pp. 168–174). The Formula of Humanity seems more promising on this score, but on interpretations suggested recently by Kantians, it too has implications that fail to square with common notions of morality (Kerstein 2002, pp. 177–187).

In sum, in *Groundwork* I Kant offers a derivation of the Formula of Universal Law. He tries to show that if there is a supreme principle of morality then it is this principle (or its equivalent.) He suggests a three-step process towards attaining this goal, I believe. The first step is to develop criteria for the supreme principle of morality. In order to do this, Kant appeals at key points to common rational moral cognition. He bases his notion that supreme principle must have a scope extending to all rational beings on such an appeal. The criterion implicit in his first proposition, as well as the criteria implied in his second and third propositions, stem ultimately from his notion that, according to ordinary moral thinking, an action has moral worth if and only if it is done from duty. And the last criterion we discussed appeals directly to the moral verdicts of common sense. The Formula of Universal Law is, of course, not the only principle that philosophers have sought to elevate to the status of the supreme principle of morality; Kant's principle has many rivals. The second step in the derivation is to eliminate these rivals on the basis of their manifest inability to fulfill all of the criteria. The third step is to show that the Formula of Universal Law remains as a viable candidate for fulfilling all of the criteria. Showing this involves demonstrating that this formula indeed generates a plausible set of duties relative to ordinary moral thinking.

Kant does not have to prove that the Formula of Universal Law actually does fulfill the whole set. For that would entail establishing that this principle is absolutely necessary and universally valid. And that is a project that Kant undertakes in the notoriously difficult third chapter of the *Groundwork*. Each one of these steps is controversial. But, in my view, Kant nevertheless offers a coherent, philosophically interesting argument for his conclusion that either there's no supreme principle of morality or it is the Formula of Universal Law.

VI

Let me close by considering an objection to this account of Kant's derivation. The objection is that it is not consistent with Kant's claim that the supreme principle of morality must be an a priori principle. In particular, consider the criterion according to which the supreme principle must be capable of generating duties that cohere with the moral duties we take ourselves to have. Does not whether we conclude that a given principle meets this criterion rest on experience, that is, our particular experience of morality? Already in the *Groundwork* Preface Kant says that the ground of an obligation to conform to the supreme principle of morality must be sought "a priori simply in concepts of pure reason" and that any principle that "rests in the least part on empirical grounds, perhaps only in terms of a motive, can indeed be called a practical rule but never a moral law" (G 4:389).

In order to respond to this objection, we need to understand two senses in which, according to Kant, the supreme principle must be an a priori rather than an empirical principle. It must be a priori in both (what I call) a motivational sense and an epistemological sense.[7]

Beginning with the former, the supreme principle of morality must be such that all rational agents always have available to them a sufficient motive for abiding by it. (Whether they actually act on this motive or some other one, such as an inclination, is another question.) But that means that their having sufficient motive available to them to conform to the principle must not depend on anything empirical, that is, on their particular inclinations or even on their nature, insofar as this nature is not necessarily shared with all rational agents. A principle is a priori in the motivational sense just in case any rational agent's having available to him a sufficient motive for abiding by it is not conditional on anything empirical. (In effect, a principle is a priori when it fulfills the criterion implicit in Kant's third proposition). A practical principle would be empirical, for example, when a rational agent's having sufficient motive to abide by it was conditional on his expectation that abiding by it would give him pleasure (CPrR 5:9n).

Kant's appealing to experience in his derivation of the Formula of Universal Law does not seem incompatible with all rational agents having an empirically unconditioned motive at their disposal for abiding by this formula. That we rely on our moral experience in pinpointing the supreme principle of morality does not, for example, seem to entail that our having at our disposal sufficient motive to comply with it is conditional on our expectation that doing so will get us something we want.

The second sense in which, according to Kant, the supreme principle of morality must be a priori is what I call the epistemological sense. Kant states that a practical law, and thus the supreme principle of morality, must be knowable a priori (CPrR 5:26; see also G 4:440). In the *Critique of Pure Reason*, Kant defines a priori knowledge as "knowledge absolutely independent of all experience" (CPR 3:3). If we had a priori knowledge of a judgment or proposition, this knowledge would have to be "absolutely independent" of all experience in the following sense: it would have to be *grounded* or *legitimated* without appeal to any particular set of experiences (see Allison 1983, p. 78). So, it seems, if we had a priori knowledge of the supreme principle of morality, that is, if we knew that it was necessarily binding on all rational agents, this knowledge would likewise have to be grounded or legitimated without appeal to any particular set of experiences.[8] This interpretation gains support from the *Groundwork*. After telling us that a moral law must be binding on all rational agents, Kant claims that "the ground of obligation here must not be sought in the nature of the human being or in the circumstances of the world in which he is placed, but a priori simply in concepts of pure reason" (G 4:389).

Does the account sketched above of Kant's *Groundwork* I derivation clash with the notion that the supreme principle of morality must be a priori in this sense? I do not believe so. But before explaining why, let me begin with a blunt claim. It would be a mistake to maintain that in *Groundwork* I Kant proves (or could even reasonably take himself to prove) a priori that if there is a supreme principle of morality, then it is the Formula of Universal Law. Maintaining this would be a mistake even for those who reject the notion that, according to Kant, a criterion for the supreme principle is that it generate duties in line with those that we take ourselves to have. For Kant's first proposition, which is a cornerstone of the derivation on any plausible interpretation, is based largely on an appeal to ordinary moral thinking. Kant does not establish a priori that an action has moral worth when it is done from duty. To the extent that he argues for this proposition, he does so at least in part by appealing to our reactions to a range of cases, such as those involving the philanthropist. Kant himself announces his starting point in *Groundwork* I to be "common cognition," which amounts to ordinary, every-day reflection on things moral (G 4:392). Kant appeals to particular sets of experience, not merely to concepts of pure reason, in his derivation of the Formula of Universal Law.

That is not surprising; for Kant does not assert that his *Groundwork* I derivation rests solely on a priori grounds. What he does claim is that the supreme principle of morality must be knowable a priori. It must be possible to have a certain kind of knowledge that it is valid, namely knowledge that is not based on appeals to any particular set of experiences. The derivation's being based partly on appeals to our moral experience does not itself undermine this claim. In *Groundwork* I we reflect on our judgments regarding particular sorts of cases in order to see that a certain principle is at work in our moral practice. This does not entail that we cannot know this principle a priori.

In *Groundwork* III, Kant attempts to establish the Formula of Universal Law (or at least a principle closely resembling it). He tries to show that it would be irrational for any being within its scope, that is, any rational agent, to fail to comply with it. Any argument that proved this, Kant believes, could not be based on appeals to experience. The argument of *Groundwork* III is difficult to pinpoint. But if we assume that the argument does not (even indirectly) appeal to experience, then the following point becomes evident. In establishing the Formula of Universal Law, Kant would, in effect, show that it is knowable a priori. For he would show something stronger, namely that it is known a priori, at least by those who understand the argument.

Notes

1   Kant's main task in *Groundwork* II also seems to be to derive the supreme principle of morality – in all the complexity of its various formulas.
2   Strictly speaking, the principle is a preliminary version of the Formula of Universal Law, namely: "*I ought never to act except in such a way that I could also will that my maxim should become a universal law*" (G 4:402).

3 In *Groundwork* II, Kant says that the "the categorical imperative," the principle he takes to be the supreme principle of morality, is "the canon of moral appraisal of action in general" (G 4:424). On the next page (G 4:425), Kant says: "we have . . . set forth distinctively and as determined for every use the content of the categorical imperative, which must contain the principle of all duty (if there is such a thing at all)."

4 Later Kant is discussing a man who is by temperament cold and indifferent to others, but who, from duty, acts beneficently. "It is just then," says Kant, "that the worth of character comes out, which is moral and incomparably the highest" (G 4:398–9). This passage suggests that "good will" refers not merely to a particular kind of action, but to a kind of character that can be expressed in action.

5 In my view, Kant suggests this argument at (G 4:401). However, it would also be reasonable to consider the argument to be a reconstruction rather than an interpretation of this stretch of the derivation.

6 Kant does offer a table that is supposed to give an exhaustive classification of rival moral principles. But it is questionable whether this table is complete. See Kerstein 2002, pp. 140–4.

7 For a different account of Kant's emphasis on the a priori in the development of his moral philosophy, see Hill 2002.

8 Why does Kant say that the supreme principle of morality must be knowable a priori? The supreme principle of morality would have to be unconditionally and universally valid, thus admitting of no possible exception. But in Kant's view if a principle can be justified only by appeal to particular experiences then it cannot be known that no exception to it is possible. That experience has thus far shown that there is no exception to a principle fails to entail that there will be none. To bring the point to the issue at hand, that experience has thus far shown that a given principle generates all the duties we take ourselves to have does not entail that the principle will always generate all these duties. For it to be known that there can be no exception to a principle, the principle's validity must be grounded a priori.

Bibliography

Allison, H. 1983: *Kant's Transcendental Idealism*. New Haven: Yale University Press.

Ameriks, K. 1989: Kant on the good will. In O. Höffe (ed.), *Grundlegung zur Metaphysik der Sitten; Ein kooperativer Kommentar*. Frankfurt am Main: Klostermann.

Aune, B. 1979: *Kant's Theory of Morals*. Princeton: Princeton University Press.

Herman, B. 1993: *The Practice of Moral Judgment*. Cambridge, MA: Harvard University Press.

Hill, T. E., Jr. 2002: *Human Welfare and Moral Worth*. Oxford: Oxford University Press.

Kerstein, S. 2002: *Kant's Search for the Supreme Principle of Morality*. Cambridge: Cambridge University Press.

Korsgaard, C. 1996: *Creating the Kingdom of Ends*. Cambridge: Cambridge University Press.

6

Why Kant Needs the Second-Person Standpoint

Stephen Darwall

A deep feature of Kant's ethics is the connection Kant makes between morality and rational agency. Kant holds both that the moral law is an expression of pure practical reason that is binding absolutely on any rational will and that what the moral law (and so pure practical reason) requires is treating "rational nature" as an end in itself, that every rational agent has a dignity that warrants respect. In recent years, it has become common for followers of Kant to argue that both of these central Kantian claims can be vindicated from the practical standpoint since they can be shown to be assumptions that agents are inescapably committed to in deliberating about what to do at all.[1] We can call arguments of this kind *inescapable practical presupposition arguments*, or *practical presupposition arguments* for short. Kant himself makes such an argument for the bindingness of the Categorical Imperative (CI) (the moral law) in Chapter III of the *Groundwork* when he argues that any agent must presuppose a kind of freedom that he calls "autonomy of the will" and that this entails the CI. And he gives an argument some commentators interpret similarly when, as they see it, he "derives" the Formula of Humanity interpretation of the CI (FH: "So act that you use humanity, whether in your own person or in the person of any other, always at the same time as an end, never merely as a means") (G 4:430) from the practical standpoint in *Groundwork*'s Chapter II (Korsgaard 1996a and 1996b; Wood 1999:124–32).

I am skeptical that either of these arguments can succeed in their own terms, that is, that it is possible to derive the bindingness of the moral law or the equal dignity of persons from inescapable presuppositions of intelligible deliberation. Moreover, I think there is a general explanation of why this is so. But I also believe that once we correctly diagnose the problem, we can see how the Kantian framework has other, insufficiently appreciated, resources to address it. It will take some care to present this diagnosis and describe the cure, but in a nutshell, the idea is this. There is an essentially *interpersonal* (or, as I shall call it, *second-personal*) aspect of moral obligation and our dignity as persons that may not be captured, and need not be assumed, in anything that counts as intelligible deliberation. I shall argue that moral obligation and equal dignity create distinctively *second-personal reasons* for acting. A Kantian can argue that these reasons should be registered from the practical point of view. I can deliberate about how to treat *you*, and you can deliberate about how to treat *me*. But deliberation is certainly possible outside of a *second-person standpoint*; indeed, an agent might deliberate intelligibly while denying that second-personal reasons even exist. I shall claim, however, that Kantians can nonetheless argue that second-personal reasons do exist and that, if they do, the moral law is absolutely binding and persons have equal dignity.

Here I shall suggest a practical presupposition argument of a different kind, namely, that the moral law and equal dignity are unavoidable presuppositions of the second-person perspective, that is, that we are inescapably committed to assuming them when we deliberate second-personally. And I shall argue that the ability to take a second-person point of view is an essential aspect of our practical reason overall. It is, I shall claim, the standpoint from which we grasp a distinctive freedom we have as rational agents, a version of Kant's autonomy of the will that is fundamentally different from any kind of freedom involved in theoretical reasoning about what to believe. The reasons that are grounded in the second-person standpoint are no less reasons than are any that can be grasped outside it. Indeed, once we appreciate this perspective's role in practical reason *überhaupt*, we can see how moral obligations, including those grounded in the equal dignity of persons, are invariably conclusive reasons for acting, other considerations to the contrary notwithstanding. Let me begin, then, to work toward my diagnosis.

Kantian Practical Presupposition Arguments

As proponents of practical presupposition arguments point out, the practical perspective is "first-personal." When you and I deliberate, we view things from a first-person standpoint, whether first-person singular, as when we try to work out what to do individually, or first-person plural, as when we think about what to do together. The deliberative question is "What am I to do?" or "What are we to do?"

I answer my deliberative question when I make a decision or find myself decided with an intention to do one thing rather than another. But rational agents don't make decisions *simply*. They decide to do things *for reasons*. When they act, they have *their reasons* for acting. *Agent's reasons*, as they are called, are a distinctive feature of the happenings in the world that involve agency. Suppose you drop a ball to show a child how gravity works, that is your reason for letting the ball go. There is also, of course, a reason why, once the ball has been let go of, it falls to the ground. But obviously there is nothing that is the ball's reason for dropping. A ball can't have reasons for what it does; it is not an agent. It doesn't really act at all in the sense that you do when you let go of it for some reason.

Kant marks this contrast between rational action and other natural events as follows:

Everything in nature works in accordance with laws. Only a rational being has the capacity to act *in accordance with the representation* of laws, that is, in accordance with principles, or has a *will*. (G 4:412)

To this Kant adds that since reason is "required for the derivation of actions from laws, the will is nothing other than practical reason" (G 4:412). To act at all, you must act for some reason. Moreover, agents' reasons, for example, your reason in dropping the ball, are what agents themselves take to be *normative reasons*, that is, reasons for them *to* act, considerations that weigh in favor of their action and on whose basis they act. When you drop the ball in order to illustrate gravity to a child, you treat the fact that it will provide such an illustration as a reason for you *to* drop it, as a consideration that weighs in favor of that action. And similarly for anything you do intentionally. There is always something you are treating as a normative reason to act.

Because that is so, deliberation is necessarily conducted in the currency of normative practical reasons. In determining what *to* do, you consider what there is reason for you to do. It is impossible for you to decide to do anything at all unless you can regard something as a reason to do it. And Kant believes that this latter thought commits you to something more general or universal. Whether the fact that dropping the ball would illustrate gravity to a child is a reason for you to drop it ultimately depends on what considerations are reasons for agents to act in general. Maybe, as rational egoism contends, the only facts that are genuine normative reasons are those that concern the agent's own interest. If so, then the only way the fact that it would illustrate gravity to a child can be a reason for you to drop the ball is if it is somehow in your interest to provide this illustration. Or perhaps, as instrumentalists about practical reason believe, the only facts that are normative reasons are facts about what will achieve agents' ends or the satisfaction of their desires. If so, then the only way the fact that it would help enlighten the child about gravity can be a reason to drop the ball is if that is an end or desire of yours. And so on. For you to regard any fact as a reason to do something you must be able to see it as deriving appropriately from what Kant calls "practical laws," that is, principles that say what rational agents should or have reason to do in general.

This means that the question of what there is reason for me to do (or, my question, "What do I have reason to do?") depends ultimately upon a question that can be put in third-personal terms ("What does the person currently writing this have reason to do?").[2] And, if Kant is right, that will depend ultimately on what normative reasons there are in general for agents to act or, as Kant would put it, what "practical laws" govern rational conduct. The question, "What do I have reason to do?" is ultimately the same as "What does a rational person have reason to do in the situation I face?" (Note that it is consistent with this that features of yourself, including what ends you have, might for these purposes be considered part of your situation.)

Nevertheless, it is the (first-personal) practical standpoint that makes the assumption that there actually are practical laws and normative practical reasons inescapable for us. If we were somehow able to avoid deliberation about what to do and to concern ourselves solely, say, with theoretical questions about what to believe, nothing in the conditions of rational thought would force us to assume that there are any reasons for acting at all. But this restriction seems entirely benign so far as ethics goes. For practical purposes, we simply cannot escape these assumptions.

Thus far there is nothing to which a critic of Kantian practical presupposition arguments need object. We can simply stipulate that there are normative reasons for acting and, therefore, that there are practical laws that govern the conduct of rational agents.[3] And we can also agree that anything we unavoidably presuppose in practical reasoning is, so far as ethics is concerned, true. What will remain in question is whether the CI, the moral law, and the dignity of rational persons are themselves assumptions that are inescapable in any practical reasoning. Are assumptions like these something an agent has to presuppose to count as deliberating or reasoning practically at all?

I will be arguing that they are not. Although any agent must assume that there are practical laws, he need not assume that the moral law is a practical law. For example, rational egoists suppose that there is a practical law but deny that anyone is bound by morality, at least as we normally conceive it. Of course, Kant doesn't simply assert that any rational agent must assume the moral law; he argues for that conclusion from the premise that deliberating agents must assume autonomy of the will. I will argue, however, that his argument does not go through. Although any intelligible deliberation must assume freedom of some kinds, it need not assume autonomy as Kant defines it. Similarly, Kant and some contemporary Kantians argue that any agent is inescapably committed to valuing rational nature as an end in itself and, therefore, to the equal dignity of persons. But here again, I shall argue that arguments of this form cannot prove any such conclusion. There are, to be sure, senses in which any intelligible deliberation is committed to valuing rationality (for example, the agent's own rational thinking for purposes of the deliberation at hand), but they are nothing like FH or the equal dignity of persons.

As I see it, nothing in the bare project of acting for reasons, first-personally, or attempting to discover rational principles on which to act, commits a deliberating agent to autonomy, the moral law, or equal dignity. Once, however, we appreciate this diagnosis, I believe we can see our way to an argument that has a greater prospect of success. It is, I shall claim, second-personal engagement and its role in practical reason overall, that commits rational persons to autonomy, the moral law, and equal dignity.

The Second-Personal Aspect of Moral Obligation and Equal Dignity

It will help to introduce this idea to note that even if the practical presupposition arguments we will be criticizing were to succeed in their own terms, they still wouldn't fully account for a central aspect of the *way* in which we are bound by the moral law and our equal dignity as persons, namely, that we are *responsible to* one another as equal moral persons for complying with morality and respecting our equal dignity as persons. This aspect is, in a sense I will shortly clarify, irreducibly *second-personal*; it concerns our authority to make claims and demands of one another (and to address them second-personally to each other). The most that (first-personal) practical presupposition arguments can show is that a deliberating agent must treat the moral law (and the dignity of persons) as normative reasons for compliance. But whatever the weight or priority of reasons for respecting the moral law and the dignity of persons that such an argument might establish, it would not yet have even considered whether we are responsible in the sense of accountable or answerable for such compliance. It would not yet have addressed the issue of whether any authority exists to claim or demand that we comply.

Moral obligations do not simply purport to provide supremely authoritative reasons, however. They are also what we are (morally) responsible for doing, what members of the moral community, including we ourselves, have the authority to demand that we do, by holding us accountable second-personally. Even if an argument could show that moral obligations invariably provide overriding reasons of whatever weight or priority, no such argument could establish by itself our moral responsibility for complying with them. There is simply no way to establish accountability, I believe, except within a second-personal framework. I shall argue, therefore, that the distinctive bindingness or normativity of moral obligation cannot possibly be vindicated outside a second-person point of view.

A similar point can be made about the dignity of persons. Consider what Kant says about dignity and equal respect in *The Metaphysics of Morals*.

> [A] human being regarded as a *person*, that is, as the subject of a morally practical reason, is exalted above any price . . . he possesses a *dignity* (absolute inner worth) by which he exacts *respect* for himself from all other rational beings in the world. He can measure himself with every other being of this kind and value himself on a footing of equality with them.
>
> Humanity in his own person is the object of the respect which he can demand from every other human being, but which he must also not forfeit. (MM 6:434–5)

Although it is not a theme that Kant emphasizes in the *Groundwork* or *The Critique of Practical Reason*, Kant here says that dignity includes our authority to claim or demand respect from each other.[4] The respect in question is the kind I have elsewhere called *recognition respect* (Darwall 1977). This is no form of esteem for moral merit or appraisal of how well one conducts oneself as a moral agent (*appraisal respect*), but recognition of our equal authority, standing, or "footing" as rational persons capable of moral action at all. And Kant here makes clear that that standing is an equal authority to make claims and demands of one another. Although it is rarely explicit, this second-personal aspect is also central to the ethical and political thought that derives from Kant. Rawls gives expression to it when he says that persons are "self-originating source[s] of valid claims" (Rawls 1980). And Joel Feinberg gets at the same thing when he emphasizes the second-personal aspect of the "nature and value of rights":

> [I]t is claiming that gives rights their special moral significance . . . [h]aving rights enables us to 'stand up like men,' to look others in the eye, and to feel in some fundamental way the equal of anyone. (Feinberg 1980)

The very idea of a right involves that of an authority to claim or demand something, a place to stand in asserting the claim or addressing a valid demand. Kant invokes the same metaphor when he says that dignity enables a person to "value himself on a footing of equality" (MM 6:435).

If we read this theme from *The Metaphysics of Morals* back into Kant's earlier ethical works we get a picture of the moral community, the "kingdom of ends" (G 4:433–4), as *mutually accountable* rational agents.[5] And we get a view of the moral law as what we are responsible for doing, again, *to* one another and to ourselves, as what members of the moral community have the authority to demand and hold one another to as equal moral persons.

But what, exactly, is this second-personal aspect that I am claiming is central to our concept of moral obligation and to the dignity of persons? Suppose that someone is standing on your foot, and consider three different kinds of reasons there might be for him to get off it.[6] One might simply be the badness of your being in pain and the fact that he could bring about a better state of the world by moving his foot. But suppose, second, that you and he hold a norm of conduct according to which one should not step on others' feet and should remove one's foot promptly should one find it on top of someone else's. This would be a different reason than the first. The first would be an *agent-neutral* reason for moving his foot.[7] The reason would not be essentially *for him* as the agent causing another person pain. It would exist, most fundamentally, for anyone who is in a position to effect your relief and *therefore* for him, since he is well placed to do so. Since, however, the second reason derives from an *agent-relative* norm (that is, a norm that is reflexive and where the reason description makes ineliminable back reference to the agent), it is an agent-relative reason, unlike the first. Despite the fact that violations of the norm are all equally criticizable, or bad, the norm counsels that one not do what would violate it *oneself*. If, for example, the person on your foot could prevent two comparable foot-mashings by the shocking spectacle of keeping his foot firmly planted on yours, the norm would not counsel him to do so.

Consider now the idea, not just that there is this agent-relative reason not to step on others' feet, but also that persons have the *authority to demand* that they not step on one another's feet. This adds a new reason of a fundamentally different kind. We might think, for example, that all individuals have the authority to demand that others not step on their feet without their consent, that we all have the right not to have our feet stepped on. We might also think that not stepping on people's feet is something we have the authority to demand, as equal members of the moral community (the realm of ends), that persons not do to one another, and, therefore, that we are answerable or accountable for not doing so to one another.

This third kind of reason not to step on others' feet is agent-relative also, but it is an additional reason. I might accept an agent-relative norm of whatever stringency, generating reasons for acting of whatever weight or priority, that proscribes stepping on others' feet without accepting that this is something they (or anyone, even God) have the authority to claim or demand. What is distinctive about reasons of this third kind is their essential connection to second-personal address. Someone can sensibly accept this third reason for moving his foot, one embodied in a claim or demand, only if he also accepts the authority *to* demand this of him (second-personally). That is just what it is to accept something *as a valid claim or demand*. And if he accepts that you can demand that he move his foot, he must also accept that you will have grounds for complaint or some other form of accountability-seeking response if he doesn't. Unlike the first and second reasons, this third reason is second-personal in the sense that, although the first and second are conceptually independent of the second-personal address involved in making claims and holding persons responsible, the third is not.

Second-personal reasons are invariably tied to a distinctively second-personal kind of *practical authority*: the authority to make a demand or claim. Making a claim or a demand as valid always presupposes the authority to make it and that the duly authorized claim creates a distinctive reason for compliance (a second-personal reason). Moreover, these notions all also involve the idea of responsibility or accountability. The authority to demand implies, not just a reason for the addressee to comply, but also his being responsible to the addresser (at least) for doing so. Conversely, accountability implies the authority to hold accountable, which implies the authority to claim or demand, which is the standing to address second-personal reasons. These notions – second-personal authority, valid claim or demand, second-personal reason, and responsibility to a person – comprise an interdefinable circle; each implies all the rest. Moreover, I contend that there is no way to break into this circle from outside it. Propositions formulated only with normative and evaluative concepts that are not already implicitly second-personal cannot adequately ground propositions formulated with concepts within the circle. So any argument that establishes that the moral law entails normative reasons of whatever weight or priority will not yet establish this second-personal aspect of the moral law and the equal dignity of persons.

Kant's Argument for the Moral Law in *Groundwork* III

We are now in a position to consider whether Kantian practical presupposition arguments do succeed in their own terms and show that any rational agent has (conclusive) normative reasons to comply with the moral law and respect the equal dignity of persons. Kant's argument for the former comes in Chapter III of the

Groundwork just following a remarkable passage at the end of Chapter II in which he notes that it is consistent with his arguments to that point that morality might be nothing but a "figment of the mind" (G 4:445).[8] He believes that he has already shown in Chapters I and II that morality is "grounded on . . . autonomy of the will," which he defines as "the property of the will by which it is a law to itself independently of any property of the objects of volition" (G 4:445, G 4:440). Morality's fundamental principle, he has argued, is the CI, and that holds only if the will can be subject to a law solely by virtue of its form and independently of any properties of its objects (or matter).[9]

But so far his argument has been entirely analytic. Kant has analyzed the "generally accepted" concept of morality and argued that it presupposes autonomy of the will (G 4:445). And conversely, he has argued that the very idea of a will bound only by its form entails the CI (G 4:402, G 4:420–1). All this shows, however, is that *if* there is such a thing as morality, then the will must have autonomy *and if* there is such a thing as autonomy, then the CI (the moral law) must be the will's law. It is consistent with all of Kant's arguments in Chapters I and II of the *Groundwork* that the moral law, the dignity of persons, the CI, and autonomy of the will are all "chimerical idea[s]" (G 4:445). Autonomy and the CI both require, Kant says, "a possible synthetic use of practical reason," so neither can be established without a critique of practical reason (G 4:445). This is what Kant embarks on in *Groundwork* III.

Kant begins Chapter III with interrelated definitions of will and freedom, respectively: "*Will* is a kind of causality of living beings insofar as they are rational," and freedom is "that property of such causality that it can be efficient independently of alien causes *determining* it" (G 4:446). Kant points out, however, that since this defines freedom only negatively, it must be inadequate. A random "choice"-generating device might operate independently of external causes, but it would not be a free *will*. The will is, or includes, practical reason, so it must involve guidance by "practical laws" ("laws of freedom")[10] (G 4:448). An adequate definition of the will must therefore include both a negative and a positive concept of freedom. A will determines itself independently of alien causes (negative freedom) and in accordance with rational norms (positive freedom).

Kant realizes that it doesn't follow from these reflections that we actually are free in either a negative or a positive sense. What we have so far is actually just another equivalence thesis, this time between the will, on the one hand, and negative and positive freedom, on the other. If the will exists as Kant defines it, then so do negative and positive freedom, and vice versa. It is consistent with that being the case, however, that the will and negative and positive freedom are all "chimerical ideas."

What gets us inside this circle of concepts, according to *Groundwork* III, is the idea that freedom is an inescapable presupposition of the deliberative standpoint:

> I say now: every being that cannot act otherwise than *under the idea of freedom* is just because of that really free in a practical respect, that is, all laws that are inseparably

bound up with freedom hold for him just as if his will had been validly pronounced free also in itself and in theoretical philosophy. (G 4:448)

Kant's strategy is as follows. We assume it is already established that autonomy entails the moral law. And we attempt to show that any deliberating agent must presuppose autonomy. It will then follow that any deliberating agent must also presuppose that she is bound by the moral law. And if so, then for practical purposes she *is* so bound.

Now it seems quite plausible that presupposing negative and positive freedom in at least some senses is necessary to deliberate intelligibly. Take negative freedom. A deliberating agent must assume she can deliberate "independently of alien causes determining" her if "alien causes" include causal factors that might interfere with her reasoning. (Kant apparently also thinks that we have to assume that we can deliberate free of *any* causes, but we can ignore that for our purposes.) Similarly, if positive freedom is the capacity to deliberate in accordance with and act on rational norms, then a deliberating agent must suppose, for purposes of her deliberation, that she can.

So far, it is important to see, the relevant presuppositions of negative and positive freedom are in no way unique to or distinctive of *practical* reasoning. Whether one is deliberating about what to believe, what to feel, *or* what to do, one must assume that one can think free of *alien* causes and in accordance with rational norms. And Kant says as much: "One cannot possibly think of a reason that would consciously receive direction from any other quarter with respect to its judgments, since the subject would then attribute the determination of his judgment not to his reason but to an impulse" (G 4:448). Whenever we make normative judgments concerning what there is reason to believe, feel, *or* do, we must presuppose negative and positive freedom *in the sense that* we can think free of alien causes and in accordance with rational norms.

So far, so good. But Kant also claims that the positive freedom deliberators inescapably presuppose is identical with autonomy of the will. "What, then, can freedom of the will be other than autonomy?" (G 4:447). Autonomy requires that the will be "a law to itself independently of any property of the objects of volition" (G 4:445, G 4:440). This means that fundamental practical laws must be *formal*. That, after all, is why it was plausible for Kant in Chapters I and II to maintain the equivalence of autonomy and the CI, at least in its Universal Law formulation (FUL: "Act only in accordance with that maxim through which you can at the same will that it become a universal law") (G 4:421). It follows that for autonomy of the will to hold, fundamental practical laws and practical reasons cannot come from the will's *matter*, that is, either from the intrinsic nature of *actions* (as deontological intuitionists like H. A. Prichard, W. D. Ross, and, more classically, Richard Price believe) or from intrinsically valuable features of possible *states of the world* that actions can bring about (as consequentialist intuitionists like G. E. Moore believe) (Moore 1993 [1903]; Price 1974; Prichard 2002; Ross 1930). But why should that be so? What has been said to rule out these intuitionist alternatives?

I should make it clear that I am not defending either alternative. Both face significant metaphysical and epistemological problems, although both have also found vigorous defenders in recent years (e.g., Audi 2004; Parfit 1997). My point is simply that it is unclear what inescapable practical assumptions rule them out. Why is an agent committed to rejecting them if she is to count as deliberating intelligibly at all?

Consider what we might call a naïve agent who deliberates from the perspective of her beliefs and desires. In desiring various states of the world (and, as well, in taking pleasure in various outcomes), it will seem to such an agent that these states are intrinsically good, that they are outcomes there is some normative reason, and, in that sense, that she ought, to bring about (other things being equal). The point is not that she takes herself to have reason to bring about such states on account of her desires. Her desires are "backgrounded"; they are not in the deliberative foreground (Darwall 1983; Pettit and Smith 1990; Scanlon 1998:41–55). Rather, *in* desiring some possible state it seems to her as if there is reason to bring about that state.

To such an agent, reasons seem to come from properties of the objects of her desires (and so her volitions). In deciding to bring about p for the reason that p would be good, or for reasons embodied in features that make p good, it is to her as if reasons for acting come from properties of her desire's object. The primitive deliberative phenomenon is taking some fact about the world as a reason to do something. Wondering how to spend a free evening, I scan the newspaper to find an attractive possibility, say, a film. What I take as reasons for desiring to go and actually going are aspects of the possible state of seeing the film, or, if I cannot articulate these, the fact that, as it seems to me, seeing the film would be desirable or good, a possible state or outcome that there is some reason to bring about.[11] Evidently enough, if I decide on either basis to go to the film, my reasons for going will derive from properties of the object of my volition; I apparently would not have had to assume anything like autonomy of the will.

But do we yet have genuine agency and a will? For Kant, rational action must involve, not just beliefs and desires, but, as we saw, some norm or principle that I accept and implicitly make my own in acting on it (G 4:412). For intelligent pursuit of an outcome I desire to involve my will, I must deliberate on the basis of some norm that I take to apply to any possible rational agent. And I must presuppose that I am bound by such norms as a condition of the intelligibility of my deliberation. What norm might I accept in deciding to go to the film on the grounds that that will bring about an intrinsically valuable state? A natural answer is G. E. Moore's in *Principia Ethica*. I might accept the norm of doing whatever promotes good or desirable states or outcomes, and think, in accepting that, that any rational agent should do so likewise (Moore 1993:§17, 77). In so doing, however, I would steadfastly believe, with Moore, that the features that make outcomes intrinsically worth bringing about are features that are intrinsic to them, that is, features of the "object of volition."

But do we have an agent even yet? Obviously, a being who deliberates simply from the perspective of her current desires and beliefs, and who is incapable of stepping back and critically revising these, is not an agent in any sense we should be interested in here. A deliberating agent must, as Korsgaard says, both be, and be able to see herself as, "something over and above" her desires who "chooses which desire to act on" (Korsgaard 1996b:100). It seems quite possible for a naïve agent to do that, however, without assuming autonomy in Kant's sense. She could, while denying autonomy, step back from her current desires and reevaluate their objects, getting a better conception of which outcomes are really worth bringing about. Just as a theoretical reasoner can bring experience and reflection to bear on the dispositions to belief that are involved in his current experiences, overriding or defeating any tendency to believe that an apparently bent stick in water before him is really bent, so also can a naïve practical reasoner analogously critically revise her desires. A naïve deliberating jogger encountering a charging dog, for example, might draw on past experience and reflection to override a strong tendency of fight or flight and form a desire to continue at his leisurely pace while keeping his palms down and feigning indifference. The capacity for bringing critical reflection to bear on current deliberation obviously involves a kind of positive freedom, one, indeed, that is frequently called "autonomy" (e.g., Dworkin 1988). But it is also obvious that this is not autonomy in Kant's sense. I shall take it, therefore, that nothing in the deliberative standpoint alone forces the assumption that fundamental practical laws are formal in the sense that autonomy requires and hence that Kant's *Groundwork* III argument for autonomy and the bindingness of the moral law fails.

Let us turn, then, to the interpretation that Christine Korsgaard and Allen Wood have defended of Kant's "derivation" of rational nature as an end-in-itself, and therefore of FH, in *Groundwork* II (G 4:430; Korsgaard 1996a; Wood 1999:124–32). Although Kant explicitly notes that his argument there for FH depends on assumptions that he will only later attempt to prove in Chapter III (in the argument just canvassed) (G 4:429n), these writers put it forward as a free-standing argument.

Korsgaard and Wood present Kant's argument as a "regress of conditions."[12] The argument takes two somewhat different forms. One proceeds from a premise about the kind of valuing of ends in general that any practical reasoning necessarily involves (the *value of ends* argument). And a second proceeds from the kind of value that any deliberating agent must attribute specifically to her own rational agency (the *value of rational agency* argument).

The *value of ends* argument begins with the premise that when an agent acts for a reason, she must act for some end that she regards as objectively valuable (Korsgaard 1996b; Wood 1999:129; see also Gewirth 1978). It then claims that an end can have objective value only if something is the source of its value or if the "conditions" of its having objective value are realized.[13] In one way this claim is uncontroversial. If there are conditions on some end's being valuable, and if whether there is reason to do something depends on the value of that end, then in acting for that reason, the agent must presuppose that the relevant conditions hold.

The argument then shifts to what an agent must presuppose to be the condition or source of the value of her ends and what follows from this. Korsgaard puts Kant's argument as follows.

He asked what it is that makes these objects good, and, rejecting one form of realism, he decided that the goodness was not in the objects themselves. . . . Kant saw that we take things to be important because they are important to us – and he concluded that we must therefore take ourselves to be important. (Korsgaard 1996b:122)

Wood puts a similar formulation by saying that "we can regard this goodness [i.e., the objective goodness that we must see our ends as having] as originating only in the fact that we have set [the] en[d] according to reason." "Rational choice of ends is the act through which *objective* goodness enters the world." Wood concludes on Kant's behalf that "the source of all such value is nothing but the value of rational willing itself, which can confer objective value on other things only if it is presupposed that it has objective value" (Wood 1999:129–30).

Now in one sense it is uncontroversial that an end an agent sets for herself has objective value only if choosing the end accords with reason. Consequentialist realists like Moore can agree, since they will take it that a valuing fails to accord with reason when it fails to accord with independent facts about the value of possible states of the world that provide reasons for choice. What they are bound to reject is that laws of practical reason are formal (have their source in the form of the will) and hence that the desirability of outcomes and the choiceworthiness of actions depends on whether they can be desired or willed in accordance with such formal laws. What they assert is that the laws of practical reason are given by the independent value of outcomes or possible states of the world, to which desires and evaluations of states apparently respond.

It is clear, however, from Korsgaard's opposing the premise to a form of realism that Kant meant to reject ("substantive realism" of the sort Moore is generally thought to represent), that the premise of her argument *already* assumes autonomy of the will. But if, as Kant believes, nothing can warrant that assumption other than a critique of practical reason of the sort he undertakes in *Groundwork* III, then, so far as the materials of the *Groundwork* go, the resulting argument for FH must ultimately depend on the argument for autonomy in *Groundwork* III, which we have already found wanting.

It follows that without an argument for autonomy already on hand the *value of ends* argument cannot establish FH. What, then, about the *value of rational agency* argument? This version finds better support within Kant's own text.

The human being necessarily represents his own existence [as a rational agent] in this way [as an end in itself]; so far it is thus a *subjective* principle of human actions. But every other rational being also represents his existence in this way consequent on just the same rational ground that also holds for me; thus it is at the same time an *objective* principle from which, as a supreme practical ground, it must be possible to derive all laws of the will. (G 4:429)

This passage directly precedes Kant's statement of FH, so it can reasonably be interpreted as intended to support it.

Now there are uncontroversial senses in which a deliberating agent must treat her own rational agency as an end in itself. For purposes of her deliberation, she has no rational alternative but to value thinking and acting rationally, at least implicitly. If this has no value, then there is something else she should be doing besides deliberating. And she must also assume the value of reasoning *well*. Deliberation is something one can do at all only by trying to do it properly. In these senses, a presupposition of the value of rational practical thinking is simply built into deliberation. Moreover, serious deliberation, by its very nature, attempts not just to answer, as it were, an advisor's question: "What is the best advice to give myself about what to do?" It attempts also to direct the will rationally. In all these senses, a presupposition of the value of rational agency is simply part of serious deliberation.

But that seems as far as the presuppositions that are necessary for first-personal reasoning go (Regan 2003). I could quite intelligibly deliberate under the assumption that, although my rational thought has great value now, it might not some time from now. It is not obvious, of course, how I could justify such an assumption. But there is nothing incoherent in it, and assuming it would be perfectly compatible with intelligible deliberation. And I could certainly think that the value of my thinking and acting rationally in the future is overridden by other values if, for example, I were given a Hobson's choice in which I could continue as a well-functioning rational agent only at the cost, say, of my children's lives.

Moreover, in none of these senses, it is important to see, does valuing my own rational agency commit me to valuing others'. For example, when I deliberate, I authorize my own rational thought and agency, in the sense of presupposing that I am competent to judge reasons and to act on them.[14] But nothing in that authorization commits me either to thinking it present in others, or even to thinking that it will continue through time in me. I am, of course, bound to recognize that others are committed to their own rational authority insofar as they deliberate, but that doesn't mean that I must authorize them, or even that they are committed to authorizing themselves in the future. I might think that I or they, or that both of us, are simply not to be trusted as practical reasoners in the future. Neither is it the case that to deliberate intelligibly now, I must think that I have reason to promote or respect their, or even my own future, rational agency. Again, I am not saying for a moment that there is any justification for thinking any of these things. I am just saying that they seem not to be ruled out by any norms that are constitutive of the activity of rational deliberation. Someone would certainly still count as deliberating if she accepted them, though she wouldn't, for example, if she didn't seek normative reasons for acting or assume that she could think rationally for purposes of her own deliberation.

These possibilities can all be made vivid by considering the Moorean picture that I have been suggesting as the natural way of seeing things from a naïve first-person deliberative standpoint. From this perspective, rational authority is fundamentally *epistemic*: anyone's title, one's own or anyone else's, ultimately depends on how reliably she reflects an independent order of facts about the intrinsic value of outcomes. So viewed, rational authority must be earned just as epistemic authority is in theoretical reasoning (although one will, of course, have to assume that one deliberates sensibly in either area). Clearly enough, taking one's own powers of inquiry to warrant trust in the present moment does not commit one now to trusting one's past or future judgment or to trusting now the judgment of any other would-be inquirer.

It is significant, therefore, that when Kant says that every "rational being also represents his existence on just the same rational ground that holds for me," he remarks in a footnote that he "here put[s] forward this proposition as a postulate" and that "the grounds for it will be found in the last Section" (G 4:429n). This shows a recognition on Kant's part that in order for a rational agent's claim of the value of her own rational existence to entail the Formula of Humanity, it must itself be grounded in autonomy of the will. But if that is so, any such claim that does not already presuppose autonomy will be insufficiently strong to entail the moral law, and, as we have already seen, Kant doesn't think that anything he has said in Chapters I and II proves autonomy.[15] He believes that the arguments he provides before Section III are consistent with the moral law and autonomy of the will both being chimerical ideas. Consequently, the *Groundwork*'s case for the vindication of dignity and the moral law hangs on the argument of *Groundwork* III, and, as we have seen, that argument does not work.

By the time he wrote *The Critique of Practical Reason*, Kant had apparently given up on the strategy of *Groundwork* III. In the second *Critique* he holds that there is no access to the concept of freedom except through awareness of the moral law:

> [W]hereas freedom is indeed the *ratio essendi* of the moral law, the moral law is the *ratio cognoscendi* of freedom. For, had not the moral law been distinctly thought in our reason, we should never consider ourselves justified in *assuming* such a thing as freedom (even though it is not self-contradictory). But were there no freedom, the moral law would *not be encountered* at all in ourselves. (CPrR 5:4n)

Were the deliberative standpoint not to involve an "encounter" with the moral law, it would require no presupposition of autonomy. When, however, we become conscious of being morally bound, we acknowledge "a determining ground" that cannot "be outweighed by any sensible conditions" and that is "quite independent of them." And this "leads directly to the concept of freedom" (CPrR 5:29–30).

Kant makes his point by asking us to imagine someone whose prince demands "on pain of . . . immediate execution, that he give false testimony against an honorable man whom the prince would like to destroy on a plausible pretext" (CPrR 5:30). Whether this person would refuse to do such a thing, Kant writes, "he would perhaps not venture to assert." But whether he would or he wouldn't, he "must admit without hesitation that it would be possible for him."

> He judges, therefore, that he can do something because he is aware that he ought to do it and cognizes freedom within him, which, without the moral law, would have remained unknown to him. (1996:30)

Once he acknowledges that he should refuse to comply with his prince's demand even on pain of execution, he cannot coherently think it impossible for him to refuse owing to an irresistible desire for self-preservation. The point seems to follow from the nature of a deliberative (normative) practical judgment. Were he to suppose his desire for self-preservation to be literally irresistible, he would be forced, in reasoning practically in light of that, to conclude that he should do something else – after all, he can't do that. But Kant evidently thinks that nobody really believes there is anything else he should do in this case other than refuse to betray an honorable man. When we're being honest with ourselves, we acknowledge that we shouldn't give in to a corrupt tyrant to destroy an honest person, perhaps even at the pain of our own death. And if we acknowledge that, then we are also forced to assume that that is something we can refuse to do.

Kant is here simply drawing out the logical consequences of what he takes to be already involved in accepting the bindingness of the moral law. The consciousness of the moral law is, he says, a "fact of reason,"

> [b]ecause one cannot reason it out from antecedent data of reason, for example, from consciousness of freedom (since this is not antecedently given to us) and because it instead forces itself upon us of itself as a synthetic a priori proposition. (CPrR 5:31)

Kant clearly believes that his readers will agree with his moral phenomenology if they will just be honest with themselves, and we can read the example as being offered in that spirit. We put ourselves into the shoes of the person in the example, simulate practical thought from that perspective, and agree that in those circumstances the thing to do is to refuse the corrupt tyrant's offer and not have an honest person's death on our hands. Do we think we would do that? We may not know, but we must accept at least that we could.

Just after this passage we have been discussing, Kant presents what he calls the Fundamental Law of Pure Practical Reason (FPP): "So act that the maxim of your will could always hold at the same time as a principle in a giving of universal law" (CPrR 5:30). This is, in essentials, the same as the more formal versions of the CI from the *Groundwork*, for example, FUL "Act only in accordance with that maxim through which you can at the same time will that it become a universal law" (G 4:421). But why, we should ask, does Kant think that the fact of reason supports a formal principle like FPP? The reasoning in the Remark that follows FPP appeals essentially to autonomy of the will: "The will is thought as independent of empirical conditions and hence, as a pure will, as determined by the mere form of law" (CPrR 5:31). Then Kant says, again, "Consciousness of this fundamental law may be called a fact of reason . . . because it forces itself upon us of itself as a synthetic a priori proposition" (CPrR 5:31).

But what exactly is the connection between the claim that, since one should do what the moral law requires and refuse the prince's demand, one can so refuse, on the one hand, and autonomy of the will as Kant understands it, or FPP, on the other? The connection between autonomy and FPP seems clear enough. But what does the "fact of reason" example have to do with either autonomy or FPP? A deontological intuitionist like Prichard, Ross, or Price could easily grant what Kant says about the example, and generalize from it that whatever a person morally ought to do must be something she can do. But why should she conclude FPP from that? Couldn't she deny that any principle like FPP underlies the list of duties he accepts or that such a formal principle is required to explain why it would be wrong to give in to the prince? Couldn't she even deny FPP?

If he agrees with Kant about the example and about "ought" implies "can", why should he be led from that to autonomy of the will? Deontological intuitionists deny autonomy, as we noted earlier, since they hold that actions (objects of volition) can be intrinsically right or wrong and that the law derives from that. Nothing in what Kant says about the example should lead them to abandon this position. And if Kant adds that we are directly conscious of the CI as a synthetic a priori principle, then it seems he is simply fighting deontological intuitionists on their own turf and just disagreeing about whether moral duties can be summed into a single principle. In any case, there seems no obvious route from the "fact of reason" to autonomy of the will like FPP.[16]

Now I believe that there actually *is* an argument for FPP and the CI that can be made from intuitive examples like the one Kant presents. However, such an argument would rely on the second-personal aspect of moral obligation I mentioned before: its conceptual tie to accountability. Recall, first, that the sense of "can" that is in play in Kant's own discussion is simply that of an open deliberative alternative, that is, something such that one's abilities and opportunities with respect to it do not preclude intelligible deliberation on whether to do it. But now note that the fact that someone can do something in this sense is entirely consistent with her not knowing that she ought to do it, with her not being able to know it, and with her lacking any formal process of practical reasoning (involving a formal principle of the will like FPP) through which she could determine that this is what she should do and determine herself to act accordingly. A Rossian intuitionist, for example, can hold that someone (call her "Citizen") ought to refuse the prince's demand even if she doesn't know she should do so, couldn't know she should, and had no process of reasoning, like FPP or the CI through which she could discover this or determine herself to do so. Even so, the Rossian can agree with Kant that, since Citizen ought to refuse the prince's demand, she can do so. But, again, that doesn't entail anything about the CI or autonomy.

It is common ground that Citizen is morally obligated to refuse the prince's demand, that it would be wrong for her not to do so, and that that is therefore what she should do and, consequently, what she can do. But if moral obligation is conceptually connected to moral responsibility, then if this is what Citizen is morally obligated to do, then it is also what she is accountable or responsible for doing; it is what the moral community (and she as a member) has the authority to demand that she do. Now if we, as members of the moral community, accept second-personal norms that support these demands, and, on this basis, address this proposition to Citizen,[17] we are not simply informing her of how things are "in the moral community," as an anthropologist might inform someone of mores he does not himself accept. We implicitly address the demands to Citizen and put them forward as authoritative, as, indeed, does Citizen herself when she acknowledges the moral obligation.

We relate to Citizen through what Gary Watson calls "moral address" (Watson 1987:263–4). And in so doing, we are subject to what Watson terms "constraints of moral address," that is, conditions that must be satisfied for the addressing of demands, holding responsible, blaming, and so on, to be intelligible in their own terms (Watson 1987). Thus, although there is no conceptual pressure to hold that the mere existence of good and sufficient reasons for someone to do something entails that she knows or even can know this (would that it were so!), it does seem to be a conceptual requirement of blaming and holding Citizen responsible for not refusing the prince's demand (if she fails to) that we presuppose that she must have been in a position to know that she should have refused and that she could have determined herself to refuse by the relevant reasons.

When we hold people responsible, we imply that they had it within them to act as they should have, not just in the sense that the alternatives were open to them or that they weren't physically prevented, but that there was a process of reasoning they could have engaged in by which they could have held themselves responsible and determined themselves to act as they should have. We imply that they could have decided to do it by, in Bernard Williams's words, a "sound deliberative route"[18] (Williams 1981). But what reasoning process can we assume that those subject to moral obligations must have available to them? Kant's idea is that it would have to be a procedure that is itself tied to what it is that makes us subject to moral obligation in the first place, our being rational wills, and therefore that it must be tied somehow to the "form" of the will. The CI and the FPP are Kant's proposals for the requisite reasoning process, in effect, *the form that moral reasoning would have to take if it is to lead us to conclusions that we can intelligibly be held responsible for reaching*. And autonomy of the will follows as a corollary. But my point is that it takes a focus on the second-personal aspect of moral obligation to appreciate the connection between thinking that Citizen is morally obligated (responsible for refusing), and thinking that there must be a process of reasoning (the CI or FPP) through which she could have determined her obligation and determined herself to refuse. A second-personal interpretation of this Kantian claim is that (something like) CI reasoning is part of second-personal competence.

What is fundamental in this way of thinking is the second-personal authority that I have been claiming is an essential aspect of the dignity of persons: the (equal) authority that persons have, as such, to make claims on and demands of one another at all. Autonomy of the will and the necessity of a formal deliberative process derive from this more fundamental idea – as necessary conditions for the possibility of second-personal authority, and as necessary to mediate second-personal relations – rather than *vice versa*. There can be second-personal authority only if there is second-personal competence. And persons can be assumed to have second-personal competence only if we can assume autonomy and some form of moral reasoning like the CI. People can sensibly be held accountable for complying with norms only if they can themselves accept and determine themselves by them (Pufendorf's Point). But that can be guaranteed to be so only if what makes the demand-warranting norms valid is their issuing from a process that people can, at least in principle, go through in their own reasoning and thereby make the relevant demands of themselves.

Notes

1 Here I have in mind especially the pioneering work of Christine Korsgaard, for example, "Two Distinctions in Goodness" and "Kant's Formula of Humanity," in Korsgaard 1996a, and Korsgaard 1996b. See also Hill 1985 and Wood 1999. For arguments in this broad Kantian tradition, see Darwall 1983, Gewirth 1978, and Nagel 1970.

2 A delicate point: maybe "currently writing this" is first-personal too, since to fix "currently" you have to refer to the time that *you* are reading it. And similarly for "this." Both are "indexicals" whose reference is fixed by the (first-person) perspective of the writer or the reader. But never mind. We can fix the reference in some other third-personal way: "What does the person writing Why Kant Needs the Second-Person Standpoint, at time X have reason to do?"

3 Particularists might object that normative reasons don't require universal practical laws, but, since the issues we shall be concerned with lie elsewhere, let us simply grant this Kantian thesis.

4 I discuss the complexities in Kant's view in Darwall 2008.

5 For an excellent discussion of this aspect, see Christine Korsgaard's "Creating the Kingdom of Ends," in Korsgaard 1996a.

6 I discuss these matters at much greater length in Darwall 2008, on which I here draw.

7 Agent-neutral reasons contrast with agent-relative reasons, whose formulation includes an ineliminable reference to the agent for whom they are reasons (like "that it will keep a promise I made," "that it will avoid harm to others (i.e., people other than me," and so on). Agent-neutral reasons can be stated without such a reference: "that it would prevent some pain from occurring to someone (or some being)." On the distinction between agent-relative (also called "subjective" or "agent-centered") and agent-neutral (also called "objective") reasons, principles, values, etc., see Nagel 1970; Parfit 1984; Scheffler 1982. For a discussion that raises a question about the value of this distinction, see Korsgaard 1996a.

8 This is Allen Wood's translation of this passage, which seems superior to Mary Gregor's.

9 The plausibility of this thesis is most apparent in the "Universal Law" formulation (FUL) of the CI: ("Act only in accordance with that maxim through which you can at the same will that it become a universal law (or 'universal law of nature')") (G 4:421).

10 Of course, Kant cannot simply assume that norms of practical reason involve autonomy (and so are "laws of freedom" in that sense) without begging the question.

11 Of course, these might include facts about myself, my expected mood, how I would expect to enjoy the film, and so on, that I take as reasons for going, and for wanting to go. But these are still facts about the objects of my desire most properly understood, not the fact of my desire itself.

12 Korsgaard gives a streamlined version of her interpretation of Kant's argument for FH in Korsgaard, 1996b:122.

13 Korsgaard favors the latter formulation in Korsgaard 1996a and the former in Korsgaard 1996b.

14 Wood makes an argument that is relevant here. See Wood 1999:130. The kind of authority under discussion here differs from other forms of valuing in play in the preceding paragraphs.

15 In Korsgaard 19996b, Korsgaard puts forward a different argument for the Formula of Humanity that is rooted in the self-reflective character of the deliberative standpoint. Korsgaard notes that agency requires some degree of self-reflection, that the agent must see himself as "something over and above all [his] desires" who "*chooses* which desire to act on" (Korsgaard 1996b:100). This commits the agent to a "practical identity," a normative conception of himself, which he draws on in deliberation. She argues that there is one practical identity I cannot question as a deliberating rational agent, namely, my identity *as* a deliberating rational agent. I am committed from within the deliberative standpoint to my "identity simply as *a human being*, a reflective animal who needs reasons to act and to live" (1996b:121). This means, she argues, that I must treat my own humanity or rational agency as somehow a source of normative reasons for me. To vindicate the bindingness of the moral law, however, we need to be able to conclude that I am committed to treating rational agency in others as normative for me also. Korsgaard's argument from here is complex, drawing primarily on Wittgensteinian themes about the impossibility of a private language (1996b:131–6). The basic idea is that the claim that rational nature is a source of *agent-relative* reasons – that is, that the agent's rational nature gives reasons distinctively to *him* – treats these reasons as the kind of essentially private phenomenon that Wittgenstein showed to be incoherent. The moral of the private language argument for practical philosophy, Korsgaard argues, is that all reasons must be "public and shareable" (1996b:136). Consequently, whatever reasons an agent's normative identity as rational gives him must be public and shareable too. Therefore, the rational nature of others is no less normative for him than is his own.

The problem with this strategy is that any lesson that can be drawn from Wittgenstein's private language argument is quite general and applies in theoretical reasoning no less than in practical reasoning. Moreover, theoretical inquiry is no less self-reflexive than is practical deliberation. A rational believer, like a rational agent, must be able to see herself as "something over and above" her inclinations (in this case, to beliefs as these are given in experience). And, as we have seen, she must also see her reasoning as free of determination by alien causes and guided by rational norms. Finally, in inquiry we are guided by a rational conception of ourselves as theoretical reasoners no less than we are by a practical identity in deliberation. We must give ourselves a kind of authority in our own reasoning about what to believe no less than we must in deliberation. It follows that these considerations, taken by themselves, are insufficient to establish autonomy or anything that is equivalent to it, since they are consistent with the sort of heteronomy that characterizes theoretical reasoning. For example, they are consistent with the Moorean realism of the naïve deliberative standpoint. Of course, Korsgaard would reject realism of this form, as would I. But the point is that nothing in the argument from practical identity or the impossibility of a private language itself rules Moorean realism out. So the argument cannot establish autonomy or the moral law.

16 Of course, if the "fact of reason" itself includes awareness of the CI, then there is no step to take.

17 Or, indeed, if Citizen addresses it to herself.

18 Williams himself argues that blame presupposes this (he think illicitly) (Williams 1995).

Bibliography

Audi, R. 2004: *The Good in the Right: A Theory of Intuition and Intrinsic Value*. Princeton, NJ: Princeton University Press.

Darwall, S. 1977: Two kinds of respect. *Ethics* 88: 36–49.

Darwall, S. 1983: *Impartial Reason*. Ithaca, NY: Cornell University Press.

Darwall, S. 2006: *The Second-Person Standpoint: Morality, Respect, and Accountability*. Cambridge, MA: Harvard University Press.

Darwall, S. 2008: Kant on respect, dignity, and the duty of respect. In M. Betzler (ed.), *Kant's Ethics of Virtue*. Berlin: Walter de Gruyter.

Dworkin, G. 1988: *The Theory and Practice of Autonomy*. Cambridge: Cambridge University Press.

Feinberg, J. 1980: The nature and value of rights. In *Rights, Justice, and the Bounds of Liberty*. Princeton, NJ: Princeton University Press.

Gewirth, A. 1978: *Reason and Morality*. Chicago, IL: Chicago University Press.

Hill, T. E., Jr. 1985: Kant's argument for the rationality of moral conduct. *Pacific Philosophical Quarterly* 66: 3–23.

Kant, I. 1996: *Practical Philosophy*, M. Gregor (ed. and trans.). Cambridge: Cambridge University Press. References to this work are to *Preussische Akademie* volume and page numbers.

Korsgaard, C. 1996a: *Creating the Kingdom of Ends*. Cambridge: Cambridge University Press.

Korsgaard, C. 1996b: *The Sources of Normativity*. Cambridge: Cambridge University Press.

Moore, G. E. 1993 [1903]: *Principia Ethica*, revised edition with the preface to the (projected) second edition and other papers, ed., with an introduction by T. Baldwin. Cambridge: Cambridge University Press.

Nagel, T. 1970: *The Possibility of Altruism*. Oxford: Clarendon Press.

Parfit, D. 1984: *Reasons and Persons*. Oxford: Clarendon Press.

Parfit, D. 1997: Reasons and motivation. *Proceedings of the Aristotelian Society*, supp. vol. 71: 98–146.

Pettit, P., and Smith, M. 1990: Backgrounding desire. *The Philosophical Review* 99: 565–92.

Price, R. 1974: *A Review of the Principle Questions in Morals*. D. D. Raphael (ed.), Oxford: Clarendon Press.

Prichard. H. A. 2002: *Moral Writings*, J. McAdam (ed.). Oxford: Oxford University Press.

Rawls, J. 1980: Kantian constructivism in moral theory. *The Journal of Philosophy* 77: 546.

Regan, D. H. 2003: The value of rational nature. *Ethics* 112: 267–91.

Ross, W. D. 1930: *The Right and the Good*. Oxford: Clarendon Press.

Scanlon, T. M. 1998: *What We Owe to Each Other*. Cambridge, MA: Harvard University Press.

Scheffler, S. 1982: *The Rejection of Consequentialism*. Oxford: Clarendon Press.

Watson, G. 1987: Responsibility and the limits of evil: variations on a Strawsonian theme. In F. D. Schoeman (ed.), *Responsibility, Character, and the Emotions: New Essays in Moral Psychology*. Cambridge: Cambridge University Press.

Williams, B. 1981: Internal and external reasons. In *Moral Luck*. Cambridge: Cambridge University Press.

Williams, B. 1995: Internal reasons and the obscurity of blame. In *Making Sense of Humanity*. Cambridge: Cambridge University Press.

Wood, A. 1999: *Kant's Ethical Thought*. Cambridge: Cambridge University Press.

Part III

Justice: Private, Public, and International Right

7

Kant on Law and Justice

Arthur Ripstein

olitical philosophy is sometimes thought of as a branch of applied moral philosophy.* For John Stuart Mill, for example, questions about the legitimate use of state power are answered by reference to the same utilitarian considerations that govern ordinary moral life. A reader whose familiarity with Kant's practical philosophy was limited to the *Groundwork* could be forgiven for expecting Kant to adopt a parallel strategy, seeking to apply the categorical imperative to questions of political legitimacy, state power, punishment, or taxation, or perhaps viewing the state as a coordinating device that would enable people to carry out their moral obligations more effectively. Alternatively, such a reader might expect Kant to stand back from such questions, and recommend a stoic indifference to matters of politics. Kant is often taken to understand morality in terms of the principles upon which a person acts. As such, it would seem to depend contingently or not at all on the kind of society in which the agent found herself.

The reader who approaches the *Doctrine of Right* armed with either set of expectations is in for a surprise. Not only does Kant offer detailed analyses of things that seem irrelevant from the point of view of individual virtue – property, contract, taxation, and punishment – but he does so without reference to the principles upon which people are supposed to act. He barely mentions the categorical imperative. More puzzling still for any "applied ethics" reading, he appears to argue that might makes right outside of a state, when he contends that persons are under no obligation to refrain from interfering with the goods of others unless they have an assurance that others will do the same.[1]

The *Doctrine of Right* is also likely to surprise readers familiar with the modes of argument prominent in contemporary political philosophy. Kant insists on a

* I am grateful to Andrew Botterell, Tom Hill, and Ernest Weinrib for comments on an earlier draft of this chapter. I am also grateful to the members of the law and philosophy discussion group at the University of Toronto for joining me in weekly discussions of the *Doctrine of Right* over the past several years, and to Ron Daniels, the Dean of the Law Faculty, both for providing a weekly lunch for a group of Kant scholars and for recognizing the importance of philosophy for legal education.

sharp divide between the *metaphysics* of morals he will provide and an *anthropology* of morals that focuses on human nature (MM 6:217). He argues that law and justice are morally required "no matter how well-disposed and law abiding men might be" (MM 6:312), explicitly denying that either is a response to unfortunate features of the human situation. He denies that needs generate any direct obligations of mutual aid, dismissively treating it as no different from "mere wish" (MM 6:230). Yet he formulates many of his arguments in terms of coercion, which most recent philosophers assign a secondary role in law and politics. Most striking of all from the perspective of contemporary readers, he denies that justice is concerned with the fair distribution of benefits and burdens.

Instead of pursuing any of these familiar paths, Kant seeks to explain justice and law in terms of a distinctive conception of freedom as independence. In what follows, I will first explain the central idea of independence. I will then trace the three stages of his development of this idea, explaining how it leads first to private right, which governs the interactions of free persons, and then to public right, which requires the creation of a constitutional state. (The reference to "three stages" may lead to a disappointed expectation when we get "first to private right" and then (presumably second) "to public right" but not mention a "third.") The idea of independence carries the justificatory burden of the entire argument, from the prohibition of personal injury, through the minutiae of property and contract law, on to the details of the constitutional division of powers. Kant argues that these norms and institutions do more than enhance the prospects for independence: they provide the only possible way in which a plurality of persons can interact on a ground of equal freedom. Kant's concern is not with how people should interact, as a matter of ethics, but with how they can be forced to interact, as a matter of right.[2]

The core idea of independence is an articulation of the distinction between persons and things. A person is a being capable of setting his or her own purposes, while a thing is something that can be used in pursuit of purposes. Kant follows Aristotle in distinguishing choice from mere wish on the grounds that to choose something a person must take himself to have means available to achieve it.[3] You can wish that you could fly, but you cannot choose to fly unless you have or acquire means that enable you to. In this sense, having means with which to pursue purposes is conceptually prior to setting those purposes. In the first instance, the means that you have, just as a matter of what Kant calls "the innate right of humanity" in your own person, are your own bodily abilities. You are independent if you are the one who decides the purposes your means will be used to pursue. You are dependent on someone else's choice if that person gets to decide what purposes your means will be sued to pursue.

This recasting of the familiar Kantian distinction between means and ends provides a distinctive understanding of the ways in which one person can interfere with the independence of another, either by drawing that person into purposes that she has not chosen, or by depriving her of her means. Fraud is a familiar example of the first type of interference, bodily injury a familiar example of the second. In doing either, the wrongdoer fails to respect the other person's capacity to set her own purposes, treating her instead either as a means to be used in pursuit of another person's purposes, or as a mere obstacle to be gotten around.

Interference with another person's freedom creates a form of dependence; *independence* requires that one person not be subject to another person's choice. Kant's account of independence contrasts with the more robust conceptions of autonomy prominent in contemporary political philosophy, which usually focus on some mix of the ability to identify with your own choices, and having an adequate range of choices so as to make that identification meaningful. Autonomy is usually represented as a feature of a particular agent. On this conception, if there were only one person in the world, it would make sense to ask whether and to what extent that person was autonomous.[4] Kantian independence is not a feature of the individual person considered in isolation, but of relations between persons. Personal autonomy contrasts with dependence on circumstance. Independence contrasts with dependence on another person, being subject to that person's choice. Independence is relational, and so cannot be predicated of a particular person considered in isolation. The difference is important: in principle a slave with a benevolent master and favourable circumstances could be autonomous in the contemporary technical sense. A slave could never be independent, because what he is permitted to do is always dependent on his master's choice or grace. Independence is an entitlement that provides the normative measure of legitimate institutions.

Independence is the basic principle of right. It guarantees equal freedom, and so requires that no person be subject to the choice of another. The idea is again similar to one that has been the target of many objections. The basic form of almost all of these focuses on the fact that *any* set of rules stops people from doing what they would otherwise do, so that, for example, laws prohibiting personal injury and property damage put limits on the ability of people to do as they wish. Not everyone can be allowed to do as they please, because different people have incompatible wants, and to let one person do what he wants will typically require preventing others from doing what they want. Thus, it has been contended, freedom cannot even be articulated as a political value, because freedoms must always be traded off against other goods.[5] This objection has some force against freedom understood as the ability to do whatever you wish, but fails to engage Kant's conception of independence. Limits on independence generate a set of restrictions that are by their nature equally applicable to all. Their generality reflects the extent to which they abstract from what Kant calls the "matter" of choice and focus instead on the capacity to set purposes without having them set by others. What you can accomplish depends on what others are doing – someone else can frustrate your plans by getting the last quart of milk in the store. If they do so, they don't interfere with your independence, because they impose no limits on your ability to use your powers to set and pursue your own purposes. They just change the world in ways that make your means useless for the particular purpose you would have set.

Kant aims to show that independence, understood in this way, comprises a self-contained domain of reciprocal limits on freedom. Setting the problem in this way both poses the problem and gives him the resources to provide a principled account of the most puzzling features of political life. Those who imagine that political powers can be used whenever doing so will bring about beneficial consequences see no need to draw a principled line around them. The Kantian commitment to freedom requires a principled account, because both the power to displace individual judgment, by having institutions and officials empowered to make decisions binding on everyone, and the power to enforce those decisions, appear to be in tension with the idea that individuals are free to set their own purposes according to their own judgment. Kant aims to do no less than show that the existence of such powers is not only consistent with, but in fact required by individual freedom.

Kant develops the idea of independence in three stages. He first articulates the relation of independence in its simplest form as a constraint on interactions between persons. He calls this "the innate right of humanity" in one's own person, because it does not require any act to establish it. Instead, people have it simply because they are persons capable of setting their own purposes. This form of independence is incomplete, and needs to be extended to take account of the possibility that people could have entitlements to things other than their own bodily powers. Those entitlements fall under private right, and cover the traditional categories of Roman private law, relations of property, contract, and status, which govern rights to things, to performances by other persons, and, in special cases, rights *to* other persons. These categories provide a complete specification of independence between interacting persons, but need to be further extended to take account of the possibility of disputes about them. The possibility of dispute about rights gives rise to public right, which requires the creation of a state with legislative, executive, and judicial branches.

Innate Right

Kant formulates the innate right of humanity from two directions. First, each person has the right to independence from others, and so also a right to equality with all others, innately, prior to any affirmative act to establish it (MM 6:237). My right to my own person guarantees that I am free to use my own powers as I see fit, consistent with the freedom of others to do the same. Innate right also includes the right to be "beyond reproach" (MM 6:238), the right to have only your own deeds imputed to you, and to be assumed innocent unless you have committed a wrong. From the other direction, innate right carries with it the imperative of rightful honor. Kant interprets the Roman jurist Ulpian's precept *honestas vive* ("live honorably") as the requirement not to allow yourself to be a mere means for others (MM 6:236). Where other philosophers, including Hobbes, Locke, and Hume, have drawn attention to the *tendency* of people to be unwilling to benefit others because of observed features of human behaviour, Kant focuses on the *entitlement* to be unwilling to benefit others as a consequence of the entitlement to be the one who decides what purposes you will pursue. His claim is not that people should be selfish, but only that in dealing with a person, no *other* private person could ever be entitled to assume that you are acting for anyone's purposes but your own. I can accept the gift that you offer me, but I cannot use force against you to extract it from you if you dispute my claim to it.

Innate right governs interactions between free persons, but does so in a way that is incomplete. Each extension of the idea of a right of humanity in one's own person is required because of the human capacity for choice. Although rights to external things and the possibility of disputes both seem particularly pressing in what David Hume called the "circumstances of justice," they do not enter Kant's account as responses to empirical circumstances. Instead, they enter because the only way that independence can be systematically consistent is if it is subject to all and only those limits required by freedom. Rights to external things are required by independence; both the possibility of disputes about rights and the need for public right to resolve them follow from rightful honour's entitlement to refuse to be a mere means for other people's purposes. The extensions also show how the two striking inequalities of political life are consistent with the equal freedom required by innate right. *Private right* – the areas of law governing property, contract, and other legal relationships between private parties – explains how inequalities in material wealth, including holdings of property, contractual obligations and employment, and familial relationships can be consistent with the equality of innate right. *Public right* – the areas of law governing the lawmaking powers of the state, including constitutional law, criminal law and the traditional "police powers" – explains how differentiated offices are both consistent with and required by innate right.

Private Right

Innate right is an incomplete account of independence, because it regulates only a person's entitlement to his or her own person and reputation. This opens the possibility that there could be other means available that a person might use in setting and pursuing purposes. This possibility requires a further "postulate," an extension consistent with, but not contained in innate right.[6] Kant argues that it would be inconsistent with innate right if usable things could not be rightfully used. The ability to use things for your purposes could be satisfied through a system of *usufruct,* in which things are borrowed from a common pool for particular uses. However, because of the way that Kant conceives of the relation between having means and setting ends, using things is not enough to extend your freedom; it would merely enable you to succeed at some particular purpose or other. To enhance your freedom, you must be able to have usable things at your disposal, to use as you see fit, and so to decide which purposes to use them for. Any other arrangement would subject your ability to set your own ends to the choice of others, since they would be entitled to veto any particular use you wished to make of anything. The innate equality of all persons entails that nobody could have standing to limit the freedom of another person, except to protect his or her own independence. To allow others to have a veto on your use of things would be inconsistent with independence, because your ability to set your own purposes would depend on their choice, but not in a way that was required to protect their freedom. Nobody else is deprived of *their* means simply because you have external things as *yours*. At most, it deprives them of things that they might wish for, but frustrating the wishes of others is not inconsistent with their freedom, because nobody is entitled to have others organize their pursuits around his or her wishes. So it must be possible to have them as your own. All persons are symmetrically situated with respect to innate right; private right introduces the space for an asymmetry, because it allows different people to have different claims. You and I can own different things, and we can stand in different contractual and status relations.

Kant presents private right through an analysis of the categories of Property, Contract, and Status, which form the backbone of all Western legal systems. He introduces them as corresponding to the Categories of Substance, Causality, and Mutual Determination from the *Critique of Pure Reason*. They provide an exhaustive specification of the possible types of interaction consistent with freedom. Property concerns rights to things; contract rights against persons, and status contains rights to persons "akin to" rights to things.[7] Kant remarks that the person/thing dichotomy makes room for only these possibilities. The intuitive idea is that free persons can only interact in three basic ways. They can interact independently, each pursuing his or her separate purposes. This is the structure of innate right. Property has a corresponding structure, because as a proprietor, what is mine is subject to my purposes and nobody else's. I can be wronged with respect to property in the same two ways that I can be wronged with respect to my person: by having my property used on behalf of another, or by being prevented from using my property on my own behalf. I have both possession and use of my property. If you use my house without my permission, you use it on your behalf, not mine; if you damage it, you prevent me from using it on my own behalf. Contract covers the case in which parties interact interdependently and consensually. If I invite you into my home, you do not wrong me; if I agree to do something for you, my powers to do so are now at your disposal, and you are entitled to use them as specified in our agreement. If I fail to do what I have agreed to do, I wrong you, by depriving you of means that you were entitled to.

For Kant, a contract is not understood as a narrow special case of the more general moral obligation of promise keeping,[8] but as a specifically legal institution governing the transfer of rights (MM 6:271). I transfer my powers to you, for my powers include both my ability to do certain tasks, such as cutting your lawn, or paying you a sum of money, and my legal powers to do things, such as transferring a piece of property to you. If I fail to perform as required, I wrong you in pretty much the same way as I would have wronged you had I given you something, either as a gift or in exchange for something else, and then taken it back. In a contract, I have given you that thing, as a matter of right, and so if I fail to deliver, I wrong you in the way I would if I took it back. In cases of contract, one person has the use of the other's powers, as specified by their agreement, without having possession of the other person.

Relations of status are the mirror image of contractual relations, because in relations of status one person has possession of but *not* the use of another person. Such relationships are possible when people interact interdependently, but non-consensually. The structure of this relationship parallels the situation in which one person is in possession of another's property: if I am repairing your car, I am allowed to take it for a drive to see if it is working properly, but not to take it to visit friends. To do so would be to use what is yours in pursuit of my purposes, rather than your own. Kant recognizes that there is a limited class of cases in which a person can be in possession of another person, in a way that the latter is not in a position to consent to the ways in which his or her affairs are managed. Of the examples that Kant considers, the most familiar is the relationship between parents and children. Kant notes that parents bring children into the world "without the consent of the children and on [our] own initiative," (MM 6:280) and takes this to entail that parents have both a duty to act on behalf of their children, and a right to "manage and develop" (MM 6:281) the children.[9] In such circumstances, the only way their interaction can be rendered rightful is if the parents act on behalf of their children. Once again, the intuitive idea is familiar in a wide variety of contexts. Teachers are not allowed to take advantage of their students, because their asymmetrical relationship undermines the ability of the students to give genuine consent. Because teachers are precluded from acting for their own purposes, the relationship can only be rightful if they act on behalf of their students.

This analysis of the basic types of rightful interaction makes no use of any conception of harm. It is possible for one person to harm another without wronging her – as when I open a competing business that lures away your customers, or use my property so that you no longer have the pleasant view you once did. It is also possible to wrong someone in each of the three ways without doing that person any harm. If I touch you without your consent while you sleep, or use your property without your consent while you are absent, I draw you into my purposes, and wrong you even if, as it turns out, you never learn of my action, and your body or property suffers no identifiable harm. If I breach a contract with you, I wrong you even if, as it turns out, you had not done anything in reliance on the contract, and the expectation I deprived you of was purely prospective. The person in possession of another in a status relation who takes advantage of the relationship does wrong even if the ward of the relationship suffers no loss. This is not to say that the Kant's analysis has no explanation of why harm is significant – it is significant when it diminishes a person's powers, and so her freedom. But it is not significant merely because it diminishes either welfare or wealth.

The relations of right that Kant focuses on are initially introduced as ways in which free persons can interact consistent with each being independent of all the others. Kant devotes a separate discussion to the question of how a person can come to have a right to a particular thing, whether a piece of property, another person's performance, or to have another person act on his or her behalf. Where recent political philosophers have considered property at all, they have tended to follow John Locke in assuming that the starting point for understanding property is an explanation of how acquisition of property differentiates the owner from all others in relation to a thing. Kant sees that this strategy cannot work. He mocks it as the "guardian spirit" theory of property, noting that property is a relation between persons, not a relation between a person and a thing (MM 6:260). Kant's theory of property explains the nature of that relationship, before explaining how persons can come to stand in that relationship with respect to a specific previously unowned thing. Instead of focusing on the expenditure of toil in appropriating the thing, Kant focuses instead on the result of acquisition, the sense in which the owner has the right to use it for his or her own purposes, to the exclusion of all others. Toil or effort as such is neither necessary nor sufficient for acquisition. It is not sufficient because you can fritter away your efforts without acquiring a thing, as you do if you chase a wild animal that escapes. It is not necessary because you can take possession of a piece of land without working on it or using it for any specific purpose. What is acquired is the right to decide how the thing will be used. Using something, even using it legitimately, is not sufficient to generate a right to decide future uses of a thing, or limit other people's access to it. Nor can that right depend on having somehow acquired it for rightful use already, on pain of regress. Instead, taking possession of a thing subjects it to the owner's choice, so that anyone who subsequently uses the thing deprives the owner of means that are for his choice.

Coercion

These forms of rightful interaction are at the same time the outer limits of rightful interaction. Anything done in violation of them will be wrongful, and so, for Kant, coercive. If I interfere with your property, either by using it for my purposes, or damaging it so that you cannot use it for your purposes, I coerce you, in that I deprive you of your capacity to use what is yours to set your own purposes. If I breach a contract with you, I deprive you of particular means you were entitled to – in this case, the use of my powers in the specified way. And if I take advantage of a relationship the terms of which you cannot consent to, either because you are ill or a child, or because you are not in a position to supervise the particulars of my use of it – I coerce you in the sense that I draw you into my purposes. In each of these disparate ways, I interfere with your freedom, either by compromising the means against which you choose your own purposes, or, alternatively, by using you or your means to pursue purposes you have not made your own. In each case, I wrong you if I make you subject to my choice, because I violate the reciprocal limits on freedom that protect each of us from the choice of others. Because any such coercion is inconsistent with reciprocal limits on freedom, Kant argues that *hindering* such coercion is consistent with reciprocal limits on freedom (MM 6:230). Kant characterizes rightful coercion as the "hindrance of a hindrance," and surprises his readers by claiming further that the relation between limits on freedom and the use of coercion to protect them is "analytic." The claim is surprising if the justification of coercion is understood in terms of its efficacy, in the way that punishment is often rationalized in terms of its effects in reducing future crime. No such effects could follow analytically from any principle. Kant means something quite different: he says that "external constraint" can "coexist with ends as such."[10] The prospect of redress for the violation of universal laws of external freedom does not interfere with the capacity of persons to set their own purposes in conformity with such laws. Instead, the limits on the ways in which one person can use force against another are equivalent to the limits on the ways that people can forcibly prevent others from wronging them. It does not set up the one who has been wronged as master over the wrongdoer, but simply stops one person from being subject to the choice of another.

A proper coercive response to a private wrong gives the wronged party what he was entitled to all along. Your goods are to be used only for your purposes. Any use I make of them for my purposes does not change your entitlement to have them be used for yours alone, so any benefits I gain by using them properly belong to you. If I deprive you of means by injuring you or damaging your goods, making me restore your means guarantees that you have what you were entitled to all along. Again, my failure to perform a contract with you deprives you of my performance, but not of your right to my performance, so that forcing me to perform, or to give you the equivalent of what you would have received had I performed, is consistent with our interacting on terms of equal freedom. In each case, the use of force does not serve to restore everyone to the situation he or she was in prior to the wrong, but to restore the independence of the one who was wronged, by making it as though he had never been subject to the choice of the other.[11]

From Private Right to Public Right

Kant's focus on the right to exclude generates a puzzle for his theory of property. Any *act* of acquisition will be merely unilateral: as I wrap my hand around a previously unowned apple, you are not party to my deed. If I am to come to own the apple in a way that entitles me to coercively exclude all others, even after I have put it down, there must be a sense in which *everyone* is party to my act of acquisition, despite the fact that almost none of them will even be aware of it. The problem here is not that my appropriation of an unowned thing narrows their range of opportunities, since others are no longer free to use or acquire it. That may be true, but that relates to their wishes, not their rights, because it does not make them subject to my choice, or deprive them of means to which they already had a right. At most, it deprives them of an opportunity to which they had no right, in something like the way that you deprive me of an opportunity to which I have no right by buying the last carton of eggs in the store before I have a chance to, or by declining my invitation to go into business with you.

The real difficulty is that my unilateral act carries with it the right to exclude. Prior to my act, you did no wrong by happening to be wherever you were. Once I have appropriated a piece of land, you are no longer allowed to be there, and I am allowed to use force to keep you out. If I have appropriated an apple, the problem is not that you are not allowed to appropriate it, but that you now need to take care not to damage it, and must seek my consent before using it. My right to exclude makes it legitimate for me to use force to prevent you from doing things that you could have done rightfully before. So equal freedom requires that it be possible for people to have external things as their own, and so to acquire them, but any act of acquisition appears to be a case in which one person unilaterally changes his relations with others, in a way that seems inconsistent with the idea of equal freedom.

How can your rights change through the acts of others to which you are not a party? Kant's answer is that, because equal freedom requires that such acts do bind you, there must be a sense in which you *are* a party to them, so that my unilateral act binds you because it takes place against the background of everyone authorizing acts of appropriation by others. Nobody could object to such acts on grounds of freedom, because they don't deprive anyone of any powers, they merely change the context in which each person is free to exercise his or her powers.

Kant's point isn't that you just need to think of others as authorizing your deed in order for it to bind them. The idea of a united choice that is presupposed by acquisition doesn't determine the respects in which others are bound by your (implicitly omnilateral) deed. That is a matter that is by its nature open to dispute. Your claim is only provisional, because your judgment about the significance of your unilateral act for the freedom of others is from their standpoint nothing more than your unilateral judgment, even if we both think of ourselves as upholding a system of equal freedom. We can, and should, strive to do what is right in a state of nature; every duty of right is also indirectly a duty of virtue, which "commands us to hold the right of human beings sacred" (MM 6:395). But the most anyone can do is "what seems good and right to him," that is, to enforce his own unilateral will. The unilateral aspects of your deed are reproduced in your judgment about its significance.

Kant's point about disputes is not just a reiteration of Locke's familiar claim that people often disagree about the application of principles to particular situations, especially when their interests are at stake. Unilateral judgment is a problem because of the two dimensions of the innate right of humanity. The innate right to freedom demands that people be able to acquire things as their means without the explicit leave of others. Rightful honor entitles people to stand up for their rights, so that no person is required to defer to any other private person's judgment in cases of dispute about what either is permitted to do. If you think that you have performed an act establishing a right, you are entitled to stand by your claim in the face of all who contest it, but those who contest it are no less entitled to stand by *their* claims. Rightful honor requires that each party accept no standard other than "what seems right and good" to him" (MM 6:312), because any other standard would cede to another person's choice the right to decide what means you have, and so which ends you can pursue. The only reason to defer is because you can't win. Might makes right, regardless of how "good and law-abiding" you or the person who disputes your claim might be.

The solution to disputes about rights is to make the omnilateral will institutional. Disputes can be resolved in a way that is consistent with rightful honor if the parties to it are subject to the authority of an impartial judge, and an enforcer who can carry out the decision. The state is a generalized version of this structure. It is a common authority, charged with making, applying, and enforcing law. It is legitimate because it makes it possible for people to resolve disputes about rights in a way that is consistent with the rightful honor of all. Legitimacy flows from what the state does, and so does not require an explicit act of instituting it.

Kant's argument for the moral need for a state does not depend upon factual assumptions about scarcity, selfishness, or the likelihood of bias if someone is judge in his or her own case. It is not that we are likely to disagree about whether my act binds you because of different desires or perspectives, but that we must already be in the right kind of relationship for my act to have any significance for you. That requirement reflects the normative requirements of right. People must be able to acquire means through their deeds, and stand up for their rights. The two requirements are only compatible in a rightful condition.

Because these problems are formal features of the contrast between unilateral acts and reciprocal limits, they are not limited to the special case of property. They apply also to relations of contract and status. There must be a way of making them give rise to enforceable obligations consistent with the freedom of all.

Kant's solution to these problems takes a form superficially similar to the familiar modern idea of a social contract. There must be a way of understanding an act of acquisition as implicitly authorized by the "united will of all" (MM 6:314). Kant explains how wills can be united in his discussion of contract, noting that agreement must be something the two people do together, not a pair of separate acts by the two of them, or even the pairing of interlocking acts. If I promise to do something for you, and you promise to do something in return, two *other* people who made a parallel pair of promises would not, without more (much more) be entitled to discharge their obligations to each other by giving each of *us* what we were respectively entitled to through *our* contract. A contract does not confer an entitlement to have something happen; it confers an entitlement on someone in particular to have somebody else in particular make that thing happen. That relation can only be understood if their separate acts are taken to be expressions of what Kant calls a "united will." Kant models the possibility of a united will in the law of contract through the idea of *lex continua*, familiar from his discussion of causation in the *Critique of Pure Reason*. Just as an idea of continuity must be imposed in order to distinguish between a succession of appearances and an appearance of succession, the same idea of continuity is presupposed by the distinction between unrelated acts of separate persons and the transfer of powers inherent in a contract.

More generally, one person's unilateral act can only be relevant to the rights of others if all share a more general united will. The right to exclude presupposes the background of a united will, competent to adjudicate disputes, and in whose name the results of those adjudications can be enforced. Otherwise, appropriation and enforcement are merely unilateral, and so inconsistent with the rightful honor of others.

The problem of appropriation is introduced through the category of property (*factum*); the idea of people doing things together is introduced through the category of contract (*pactum*); the idea that people can be bound through their deeds without intending to enter into an arrangement is introduced through the category of status (*lege*). Both property and contract are acquired through affirmative acts. Relationships *lege* are deemed to apply in order to make forms of interaction rightful. If actual consent is impossible, rightful relations must be deemed to hold anyway, as in the case of parents and their children. In the case of the state, someone sympathetic to Locke's political philosophy might contend that it is possible to have actual consent, suitably construed. Kant's point is that the actual consent of all, understood as a particular affirmative act, is the wrong standard for a rightful condition. In order for actual consent to bind everyone, it would need to be unanimous: a contract requires the actual choice of the parties to it. The problem is not that unanimity is unlikely to be secured, but that as a matter of contract doctrine, private parties are entitled to refuse a contract if they do not *take* it to be to their advantage, even if it really *is* to their advantage. Nobody can be forced to enter into a private transaction, even one that benefits him. As it is sometimes put, freedom *of* contract requires freedom *from* contract. To carry the right to refuse over into the context of public right would subject each person's ability to live in a rightful condition to the choice of indefinitely many other actual persons. Thus everyone would be subject to the choice of everyone else, because each person would hold a veto on the ability of others to be in a rightful condition. As a result, the postulate of public right requires that everyone enter into a rightful condition, and so licences others to use force to bring the unwilling into such condition. To allow an outsider to exercise such a veto would leave everyone in the condition in which everyone is subject to the choice of whomever they are immediately interacting with, which would be inconsistent with rightful honor.

To sum up, independence requires both enforceable reciprocal limits on freedom and the ability to acquire things without the consent of all. The two requirements can only be reconciled in a rightful condition. That there are differences in the powers of officials and private citizens is consistent with the equality of all, because some official powers are required to preserve equal freedom. The arguments of Public Right go on to show the types of power, and the limits on them, that are required. Kant's claim is not that citizens are more likely to be independent if officials make, apply, and enforce laws: they cannot be independent without them.

Public Right

The innate right of humanity in your own person explains both the structure of right as a system of reciprocal limits on coercion and the basis for rightful relations with respect to external things. The other aspect of innate right, rightful honor, generates the need for a united will: the refusal to submit to a united will leaves you vulnerable to the choice of others, in a way that is inconsistent with rightful honor. Rightful honor plays a further role in Public Right, by providing the rationale for the various powers that Kant supposes a state must have, as well as the relation between the various powers in the state.

Kant defends the modern view of the division of powers between executive, legislative, and judicial branches of government. The legislative branch is charged with making law, the executive with carrying out and enforcing law, and the judiciary with applying it to particulars in cases of dispute.[12] The functions are distinct because only the legislature has the power to make law. It does so as the voice of the people, so that they rule themselves. The executive branch does not make general rules, but takes up means to give effect to them. The judiciary resolves particular disputes and calls upon the executive to "render to each what is his" (MM 6:317). Together the divided powers preserve independence by putting people under common rules governing their interactions, and common procedures enforcing them so that no person is subject to the power or judgment of others.

Rightful honor also sets out the powers that the state must have. To the modern reader, Kant's list of the consequences that follow from the social contract looks like a sort of grab-bag of eighteenth century powers: the role of "supreme proprietor of the land," including the power to tax and overturn perpetuities in land ownership (MM 6:233); a separate duty to impose taxes in support of the poor; the right to distribute offices; the right to punish and grant clemency. Underlying this apparent miscellany is the requirement that the state not allow one person to be subject to the choice of another. Prohibiting and punishing crime is a clear example of this: the state cannot allow one person to make the wronging of another the means through which he pursues his purposes. The duty to support the poor protects independence in a different way. As a matter of private right, nobody has a right to means that are not already his or her own, and, as Kant coldly puts it, "need or wish" are irrelevant. The duty to support the poor is not a way of coordinating efforts to discharge prior obligations to support those in need. There are no enforceable private obligations to do so. The only private obligation to support the needy is an obligation of charity, which does not dictate specific actions, but requires only that each person make the needs of (some) others one of her ends (MM 6:390). The state's duty to support the poor sustains independence in the face of the possibility that through a series of otherwise rightful private transactions, some people might come to have no assets, personal or external, with which to support themselves, and so be dependent on the charity of others. To be dependent on the generosity or grace of others is to be subject to their choice, which is inconsistent with rightful honor (MM 6:326). In a parallel way, perpetual estates in land subject future generations to the choice of past ones, by requiring them to use and bequeath it in a particular way. As a result, it would not be subject to their choice, but would amount to a sort of serfdom (MM 6:324, MM 6:368). Each of these restrictions can be cast in terms of the idea of a social contract, because each serves to preempt or repair a type of dependence that is made possible by the existence of enforceable obligations. Free persons concerned to preserve their independence could only enter a rightful condition provided that it was secure against these further types of dependence. Of course, there was no point at which they all agreed to enter the condition. That actually strengthens Kant's point. The appropriation of unowned things, or the transfer of rights, can only be rightful against the background of a régime of equal freedom, and such a régime must contain more than the apparatus of property and contract through which individual transactions are conducted.

Kant also argues that the Idea of a social contract precludes a right of revolution (MM 6:320). Reaction to this claim has been has been less puzzlement than outrage. Kant offers a number of arguments for a number of distinct but related claims. One argument is about the ability of institutions to deal with a right of revolution. Kant argues that no one can sit in judgment of the sovereign, on the grounds that the person who could do so would be the sovereign, and so, either the real sovereign, or subject to having still *others* sit in judgment, generating a regress. This argument strikes many readers as too legalistic to be of much interest, but it is worth noting that it is a generalization from Kant's earlier discussion of the traditional legal problem of recovery of a stolen object. Suppose somebody steals my horse, and you, in good faith and in a public market "regulated by police ordinances," purchase it from the thief.[13] I then see you with the horse, and accuse you of theft. You show me all the paperwork. We have both been cheated by a single rogue, who has dropped out of sight. Who gets to keep the horse? Kant notes that as a matter of natural right, it seems clear that I do, because a right in property is not extinguished just because the owner is no longer in physical possession of the thing. Nonetheless, he argues that a court can make no such decision and must instead allow the purchaser to keep it. His reasoning is instructive: the original owner's title is only as good as the rightful condition that initially secured it. It is impossible to trace the history back to ensure no wrong had occurred in all of the transactions relevant to my title in the horse (including the transaction through which various people acquired things they used in those transactions). Going back to my earlier acquisition faces exactly the same problem as your more recent one: the most I could ever show is that I acquired it in a legitimate and publicly rightful way. My claim to the horse is on all fours with yours, but you have a more recent, and so superior, ratification of your title (MM 6:299).

Kant's point about the impossibility of judging the sovereign has exactly the same structure: the only thing that *qualifies* the sovereign to rule is the Constitution that *empowers* the sovereign to rule. There is no rightful claim to property outside of a rightful condition, only a series of potentially competing provisional claims, none of which generate a coercive right in relation to any other. There is also no rightful claim to rule outside of a rightful condition, only potentially competing provisional claims. Those provisional claims may be better or worse on the basis of moral argument, but nobody has standing to adjudicate between them or enforce any of them, because they are merely unilateral.

The problem of revolution illustrates the sense in which a rightful Constitution is what Kant calls an "Idea of Reason" (MM 6:371). It provides the normative basis against which constitutions can be judged, and so provides the standard to which they should aspire. If that idea is to apply to particulars, however, there must be procedures for applying it, including procedures that determine who will apply it. Those procedures must take priority over any abstract formulations of the idea of a rightful Constitution, because the most basic tenet of a rightful Constitution is the idea of procedures to make it binding on all, and so consistent with the innate right of humanity of each person.

On this understanding, Kant's argument is anything but banal. It is also much less reactionary than Kant's critics have usually taken it to be. Kant is often saddled with the view that it would have been wrong to rebel against Nazis or for blacks in South Africa to take up arms against the apartheid régime. It does not commit Kant to the claim that every organization that holds a near monopoly of force in the geographic area is entitled to allegiance from the residents of that area, or that they do wrong if they rise up against it. The analogy with reclaiming stolen goods makes this clear. The purchaser only gets to keep the horse if the purchase takes place in a public market with police ordinances, but the purchaser gets to keep it even if those ordinances are imperfect in any number of ways. It does not follow from this that every transfer of stolen property, or even every transfer under the supervision of the local warlord, gives the new possessor good title. Your title to your property is only as good as the procedures that affirm it. If such procedures are in place, your title is also superior to that of the person who receives stolen goods in secret. Nor does it mean that you have no coercive right against the person. In the same way, a constitutional system of government takes priority over the claims of natural right, even if the Constitution and the positive law passed under it are flawed in any number of ways. It does not follow from this that every organized use of power and violence is a legitimately constituted state. Nor does it follow that those who find themselves oppressed by a powerful oppressor have no right to use force, either to protect themselves, or, if possible, to bring that person into a rightful condition with them. A state of nature is an Idea of Reason just as a rightful condition is, and Kant's argument leaves open the possibility that the rogue régimes of the world are in a state of nature, so that those to whom they do violence are not only *entitled* but *required* to use force to bring them in to a rightful condition.

Kant also claims that the existence of a rightful condition makes it wrong to look to the history of that condition "with practical intent." His claim is not only that we will never discover the appropriate founding moment, but the more striking claim that history must ultimately be irrelevant. No doubt every existing political régime exists as a result of wrongdoing in the past. But just as the unwillingness of some "independent" to enter into a rightful condition cannot deprive others of their entitlement to live on grounds of equal freedom, so the existence of past wrongs by others cannot forever preclude entry into a rightful condition (MM 6:318).

Crime and the Right to Punish

Public right also contains Kant's discussion of the criminal law and the right of the sovereign to punish and grant clemency. That discussion has received a disproportionate amount of attention from commentators, despite the fact that Kant makes it clear that punishment is the prerogative of the sovereign, and not the case of coercion that is central to right. Nonetheless, his discussion of punishment is striking, because he introduces, seemingly out of nowhere, the retributive principle that a wrong should be visited back upon a wrongdoer. This is not the place to develop Kant's account of punishment in the detail it deserves. I will remark only that it, too, is said to "follow" from the idea of a social contract. Crimes must have a different remedy than civil wrongs do, in order to preclude the possibility that someone could claim an entitlement to wrong another person and simply pay damages. The criminal law does not make such behavior empirically impossible, but it does make it impossible for someone to do so as a matter of right. Punishment takes the form of retribution because the state must preclude such wrongs, and the only means at its disposal are coercive ones, since it can shape only external conduct. The insufficiency of civil damages is part of the problem, so the further coercive response takes the form of making and carrying out threats. The state must be prepared to punish any crime if it occurs, and the quantum of punishment for any particular crime must not be out of proportion to the punishments for other crimes. Kant concludes that the wrong itself provides the appropriate measure of punishment: the state must threaten to use the same type of force against the criminal that the criminal has used for his own purposes. Crime is not prohibited because of the ends the criminal sets, but because of the means he uses to get them. Kant argues that the illicit means that the criminal uses in pursuit of his purposes provide the measure of his penalty. A greater or lesser punishment would treat the criminal as a mere means in pursuit of social purposes, whether protective or philanthropic. Threatening to visit the crime back on the criminal is consistent with his independence. He is treated as he chooses to treat others (MM 6:332).

Kant appears to back away from his commitment to retribution when he insists that paradigmatic crimes of honor cannot be given the punishment they deserve. He focuses on the eighteenth-century examples of the mother who kills her illegitimate child, and the soldier who kills another when challenged to a duel (MM 6:336). After parenthetically noting the standard contemporary analyses of these as examples in which the murder victim lacks or forfeits rights against murder (an analysis that Kant must reject on the same grounds that he rejects slave contracts: the innate right of humanity cannot be alienated through a deed or act of consent), Kant explains the cases in terms of the idea of honor. Kant elsewhere remarks that the sense of honor and shame provides the basis for morality, because it creates the possibility of acting on the basis of a conception. His concern here, however, is internal to the idea of right, and does not depend on the relation between honor and virtue. Instead, what is at stake in each of these examples is rightful honor. On Kant's understanding of sexuality, the mother of an illegitimate child has allowed herself to be treated as a mere thing (MM 6:278), and the child exists as proof that she has done so; the soldier challenged to a duel has had his right to be beyond reproach (MM 6:238) called into question. The problem with punishing in either case is that to do so would be to "declare by law that the concept of honor counts for nothing." The difficulty here is that honor is the model for right. Throughout private right, Kant introduces concepts of right through a development of empirical examples that serve as models. Physical possession is the model for rightful possession; a present transfer is the model for contract; two people taking sexual possession of each other is the model for relations *lege*. In the same way, empirical honor is the model for rightful honor, and where "legislation itself . . . remains barbarous and undeveloped" the subjective and objective incentives of honor come apart. But the law cannot deny its own model. So it must adopt the barbarous and undeveloped conception of honor as its own.

Conclusion

Kant's legal and political philosophy starts with a simple but powerful conception of freedom as independence from another person's choice. The idea of freedom provides him with a systematic answer to the most basic questions of political philosophy. It explains how inequalities in wealth and power are consistent with the innate equality of all persons. It also shows that giving special powers to officials is consistent with equal freedom for all. It shows why some people must be given the power to tell everyone (including themselves) what to do, and why others must be empowered to force people to do as they are told. The answer is distinctively Kantian: political power is legitimate and enforceable because freedom requires it.

Notes

1　All references are to Immanuel Kant, *The Doctrine of Right*, Part I of *The Metaphysics of Morals*. Because the work exists in so many different editions, all references are to the Prussian Academy pagination appearing in the margins (MM 6:256).

2　The German word *recht* and its cognates have no exact English equivalent. It covers both law and the more general idea of a legitimate power. Recent translators have used the word "right," which has the merit of preserving some of this ambiguity in a way that neither "law" nor "justice" usually does. In Kant's usage, right refers to the domain of enforceable obligations.

3　MM 6:213; Aristotle, *Nicomachean Ethics* 1111a: 25.

4　Here as elsewhere, the work of John Rawls is more Kantian. For Rawls, "full autonomy" is a distinctively political value that is "realized in public life by affirming the political principles of justice and enjoying the protections of basic rights and liberties." Full autonomy is distinct from "the ethical values of autonomy and individuality, which may be applied to the whole of life" (Rawls, 1993, 78).

5　H. L. A. Hart, G. A. Cohen, Charles Taylor, and Ronald Dworkin have been recent advocates of the objection.

6　MM 6:246. (Because of the recent discovery of a printing error in earlier German editions, the Postulate appears *after* MM 6:250 in recent editions, but still has its academy pagination.)

7　Kant explicitly excludes the fourth possibility, rights to things akin to rights to persons – on the grounds that a thing could not owe a contract-like obligation (MM 6:338). The same point could be made by saying that category must be empty because such rights would involve neither possession nor use.

8　Most enforceable contracts involve promises because they concern future arrangements. On Kant's analysis, the transfer of rights is fundamental to a contract, whether it is a present transfer or a future one expressed through a promise.

9　The sense of "possession" here is formal: parents are in a position to decide things about what their children will do, and so to determine which ends the children will pursue in a way that the children do not (and until they reach maturity could not) consent to.

10　MM 6:396. Strikingly, he contrasts it with the basic principle of virtue, which is synthetic.

11　In each of these examples, one of us ends up with more or less than we would have had the wrong never occurred: I may end up with a "windfall" because you use my goods in a profitable way that I could not have done on my own, or I may end up with a loss because I must use my means to make up the loss I wrongfully inflicted on you. Such changes are irrelevant from the standpoint of right; a régime of equal freedom must treat them no differently than it treats other fluctuations in the size of people's holdings.

12　Kant compares this to a practical syllogism: the legislature formulates a law (major premise) the executive takes up means (minor premise), and the judiciary makes the binding determination (conclusion) (MM 6:313). Like Aristotle, Kant understands the practical syllogism as the taking up of means, with an action as its conclusion, rather than as a series of inferences between propositions that happens to have action as its subject matter. For Aristotle's view of the practical syllogism, see *Nicomachean Ethics* 1147 a27, and John Cooper, 1975.

13　Had I branded the horse, I would have made it much harder for the thief to sell it in a regulated market. Procedures for regulating transfers make the brand relevant; the marking, simply as such, does not.

Bibliography

Aristotle, *Nicomachean Ethics*.

Cooper, J. 1975: *Reason and Human Good in Aristotle*. Cambridge, MA: Harvard University Press.

Herman, B. 1994: Could it be worth thinking about Kant on sex and marriage? In L. Antony and C. Witt (eds.), *A Mind of One's Own*. Boulder: Westview.

Kant, I. 1996: *Metaphysical First Principles of the Doctrine of Right*. In *The Metaphysics of Morals*. References are to page numbers of the Preussische Akademie edition.

Rawls, J. 1993: *Political Liberalism*. New York: Columbia University Press.

8

Kant on Punishment

Nelson Potter

Persons living in a civil society that has the institutions of law, courts, and police, are subject to punishment if they violate the criminal law. Such imposition of punishment calls for justification because it involves inflicting pain or deprivation on the person punished, and such harms, in the absence of special justification, would understandably be objected to. Sometimes punishment is justified by alleged beneficial consequences that result, such as deterring others and also the very person punished from future such violations: a teleological, consequentialist, or utilitarian rationale. Sometimes punishment is justified by a rationale that looks only to the past, to the crime, and that thinks of the punishment as an appropriate response to this past wrongful action, the taking of retribution.

Immanuel Kant is well-known for taking a retributivist position on the justification of punishment under the criminal law. That is, he thinks that the harm, loss, or deprivation that is inflicted on the person being punished is to be justified as a response to some wrongful action the person is responsible for. In fact, Kant subscribes to a particularly strong version of retributivism, the *lex talionis*, which in its best-known Biblical version urges "an eye for an eye, a tooth for a tooth, a life for a life." But this fact of Kant's retributivism is only a part of his theory. When we reach a fuller view of Kant's views on punishment, we find that he was not a pure retributivist: there are significant non-retributive elements in Kant's views.

The most important text where Kant gives us a sustained discussion of his views on this topic is in the *Rechtslehre (Doctrine of Law/Right)* portion of his late work, *The Metaphysics of Morals* (MM 6:331–7).[1] The broader subject under discussion therein is Kant's theory of the state. A state, by definition, publishes and enforces laws. The citizens of a state, who live under its laws, are protected against various sorts of harm from others by its criminal laws. The criminal law forbids theft, assault, murder, fraud, and other such harms. All such laws provide that persons who violate them shall have appropriate punishments imposed upon them.

In an opening discussion in *The Metaphysics of Morals*, in a general introduction to the two main divisions of the work, the *Rechtslehre (Doctrine of Right or Law)* and the *Tugendlehre (Doctrine of Virtue)*, Kant tells us that any prescriptive lawgiving must involve two elements:

> first, a law, which represents an action that is to be done as *objectively* necessary, that is, which makes the action a duty; and second, an incentive, which connects a ground for determining choice to this action *subjectively* with the representation of the law. (MM 6:218)

An action that is objectively necessary is simply one that *ought* to be done; if that action is subjectively connected to our choice, then we have an incentive or motive to do it. That is, a law will tell us what to do and give us a motive for doing it. Punishments are externally imposed motives. In the *Rechtslehre* the topic will be externally imposed laws, particularly those imposed by the state. In the *Tugendlehre*, the topic will be internally self-imposed ethical laws, that is, inner moral commandments to ourselves that we obey regardless of whether anyone may be externally coercing us to perform those actions. Here I follow Kant in using "ethical" to mean having to do with morality internal to the self, "right" or "law" as having to do with externally imposed rules, and "moral" as a broader term to specify any practical commandment, whether internal or external.

Hence the main contrast between the two major parts of Kant's moral theory is that between externally imposed laws (*Recht*) and internally self-imposed ethical laws (*Tugend*). And although there may be some differences in the content of the requirements, the defining distinction between the two realms of moral or practical law is in terms of the types of *incentives* (motives) that accompany each demand. For example, our laws may require us to file an annual income tax return by April 15; such a rule does not codify any pre-existing moral duty, and hence exists only as a rule of *Recht*. (Any ethical duty to file one's income tax return by this deadline would be merely a consequence of the legal rule.) In contrast, the law against murder does codify a preexisting moral duty, that is, a moral duty that we have prior to any such law being in force. In this instance we might say that the laws of the state reinforce certain moral duties. And then there are certain ethical duties of generosity or charity, and duties aimed towards the development of good inner dispositions and habits of mind (e.g., in the directions of kindness and conscientiousness) that could never be externally imposed.

Within the *Rechtslehre*, then, we are not assuming any actual inner moral motivation within agents. The incentives under discussion are going to be entirely external, coercive motivations, and the institution of punishment will be the main if not the only such incentive-providing institution. It is a further implication of the above quotation from Kant that such an account of incentives must be provided. That is, it is an essential and indispensable part of any account of law, for a law without incentives is scarcely a law at all. As an example of this "not quite a law" situation I would mention something that happened in my home state of Nebraska some years ago: the legislature passed a law forbidding riding a motorcycle without wearing a protective helmet. The law was duly passed by the legislature and signed by the Governor, thus meeting all the constitutional requirements for being a law. However, the text of the law as thus passed failed to include any provision of a penalty for the violation of this law. Two years later the legislature remedied this deficiency by adding penalties. During this initial two year period did Nebraska have a (valid?) law against riding a motorcycle without a helmet? I would say No, not quite, and more importantly, so would Kant.

In a similar vein, Kant discusses a well-known example from the history of legal theory: after a shipwreck one man in the sea takes over a piece of wood another man was holding on to, allowing the first to survive and causing the second to drown. The first has committed an act of murder, but, according to the tradition, should not be punished. The threat of a later death penalty for murder could not have been adequate to deter him, since if he had not seized the wood, he would have drowned. When a law cannot provide an adequate incentive against the crime, it ceases to be a proper law, and thus the punishment specified may not be imposed (MM 6:392).

Now let us consider how punishment would function as an incentive. As already mentioned, punishment inflicts pain, loss, or deprivation on those subject to it, and all such inflictions are of a sort that people strongly wish to avoid. The strong wish to avoid is the incentive. People keep close to the posted speed limit, when they do, even if they have no concern for the safety of others or for not violating the laws of the state, because they wish to avoid paying the penalties for speeding. Some people are deterred from robbing banks for the same sorts of reasons. Sometimes, any motivational deterrence will fail to be adequate, and hence people sometimes speed, rob banks, or (contrary to their own internal moral commitments) fail to act kindly, even in the face of a strong incentive. But unless a deterrence-imposing system is present, we don't yet have a system of law at all.

In the Kantian framework our motives for avoiding the various miseries imposed by punishment are what he would call non-moral incentives. The moral incentive of seeking to do one's duty just because it is one's duty is, of course, an incentive entirely internal. When Kant is talking about the state, and its external system of law, then he is entirely leaving aside any mention of a properly moral incentive. Such inner incentives are entirely outside the topic of the *Rechtslehre*. So in the latter work we are interested in a system of laws that is governed only by non-moral incentives, those providing punishment.

The discussion of such a system of laws may seem odd in a Kantian context, and may seem to be something less than a fully Kantian system of duties. That is certainly true for those who think of Kant's ethical theory primarily through their reading of the *Groundwork of the Metaphysics of Morals*. For there is in the *Rechtslehre* no mention of virtue or moral goodness, little is said directly about the categorical imperative, and in general the inner character of duty as described in the *Groundwork* is entirely absent.

When we wield the state weapon of punishment, we are dealing in non-moral motives, those related to the agent's personal happiness and his feelings of pleasure and pain, which are the source of his desire to avoid punishment. This means that punishment will inevitably have significant teleological (forward looking, purposive) elements to it, elements of a sort that in most instances would seem to be quite foreign to Kant's moral philosophy. State laws *aim* to deter their violation through the provision of punishment, and agents *aim* to avoid punishment by conforming their actions to law.

The laws of the *Rechtslehre*, as practical laws, are applicable only to those individuals who possess moral freedom, and it is Kant's doctrine that moral freedom is possessed only by those capable of acting from purely moral motives. So we take it that laws are applicable to and only to human persons. Kant has little to say about exceptions to such applications: the mentally ill, the very young, the person guilty merely of negligence rather than criminal intent, the developmentally disabled, and other such exceptions. When we hold a person responsible for a violation of criminal law, and hence we hold him to be a proper subject of punishment, we do so in the belief that that person possesses inner moral freedom. Nevertheless the (external) systems of criminal law and punishment operate entirely without any direct reference to this terribly important inner fact of moral freedom or responsibility, at least so far as Kant discusses these issues. Some two hundred years later, we are more aware than Kant's era was of the inner complexities of mental illness and disability that may result in a person not being criminally responsible for what are usually taken to be criminal acts.

Kant, as a retributivist in relation to punishment, is a deontologist in moral theory. The distinction between deontology and teleology in ethical theory is hard to state in a clear and uncontroversial way, but let us briefly draw the distinction, without finally wanting to put much weight on it. The deontologist takes as basic in his moral theory words and concepts such as duty, ought, obligation, permitted/forbidden. As such she judges acts as right or wrong in virtue of their inherent character, as, for example, lies or acts of kindness. The teleologist in contrast takes as basic such terms/concepts as those of the good and the desirable. He therefore judges actions in relation to their beneficial or harmful consequences. The classic utilitarian, who assesses actions depending on their total consequences for pleasure and pain for all those affected by the action, is a teleologist. The tendency is for the deontologist to be against an action of lying because of its inherent moral wrongness, and in spite of good consequences supposed in some cases to result from it. The teleologist may favor an action like lying, but only in those situations where it can be well argued that good consequences on the whole will be the result, and in spite of (deontological) condemnations of lying because of the inherent nature of the act. Within the theory of the justification of punishment, the utilitarian theory of punishment, which seeks to justify punishment based on its good consequences of deterrence, reform, and such, is a teleological theory, and retributivist theories of punishment, including the Kantian, are deontological theories, because they have no regard for such beneficial or harmful consequences, and rather determine appropriate punishment by looking backward "to make the punishment fit the crime." The connection that some suggest between retributive punishment and the human impulse to revenge wrongdoing is never mentioned by Kant.

From the above we have already seen that the arch-retributivist Kant introduces into the very heart of his theory of punishment teleological considerations relating to deterrence in the state. Does this amount to an inconsistency or an incoherency in Kant's theory? As we shall see further below, the answer is No. The deontological *lex talionis* determines the degree and nature of the punishment. The teleological result of criminal deterrence is a sort of side-effect of imposing such punishments, though it is an indispensable such effect, because it provides the incentive for obeying the law that is necessary for its functioning as a law.

How does the criminal law function in Kant's theory of the state? Kant, following in the social contract tradition of Hobbes, Locke, and Rousseau (and with differences from each), claims that we have an obligation to leave the state of nature, and enter into a political commonwealth. The purpose of this transition is so that the state can protect the rights to property and person that we already possess in the state of nature, but that are "provisional" and undefended so long as we remain in that state. That is, we are obliged to seek to create a commonwealth so that our rights and those of all others can be protected. The basic mechanism by which the state will protect these rights is the institution of criminal law, which forbids the broad range of acts that are violations of external rights, and which provides negative incentives through criminal punishment for violating those laws.

Now we might think that if this is the rationale for the state, then corrupt states which fail to protect such rights, and which in fact grossly infringe them are not proper or valid states at all, and that in fact we should have a right to revolt against the power of such states, in order, again, to assure that the rights of all are protected. However, Kant's view is that there is no right of revolution. This in spite of the fact that he admired the political ideals of the French revolution as close to his own republicanism. Why he took this view, and whether it is compatible with his other views about the importance of individual rights and freedom are issues that have generated considerable discussion, but that we are not able to explore more deeply here. It appears that Kant, perhaps incorrectly, believes that a right of revolution contradicts the proper, complete, and absolute idea of sovereignty, as developed and argued by Hobbes, and that it also violates the very idea of law. Here we can say only that, whether he is right or wrong, it is Kant's position that although the sovereign has duties to his citizens to protect their rights, the citizens have no rights against the sovereign, and hence that the worst imaginable kleptocratic or murderous government may not be revolted against. On the other hand, Kant does favor conscientious refusal, that is, the refusal to do wrongful acts even when they are required by the law or the sovereign (CPrR 5:30).

Kant sometimes contrasts the lawless freedom that we possess prior to entering a commonwealth with the lawful freedom that is given back to us by the commonwealth. And it may be that he believes that the disordered anarchy of stateless freedom is one in which individuals can make no advance toward a morally ordered life. The state and its laws, even when defective, provide the first major advance towards assuring moral progress.

The incentive that accompanies external law cannot be the inner moral incentive of moral goodness. This latter motivation comes from within ourselves and can be imposed only by ourselves on ourselves. The only possible incentive for law is external coercion. However, moral individuals can decide to obey the law, for example, not to steal, based on purely ethical motivation, but the point is that we want more assurance than this, by in addition providing a state with institutions of criminal law that will create enough social order to make inner moral development socially and psychologically possible.

External coercion takes place in the phenomenal world, according to Kant, where the law of cause and effect holds sway. This means in Kant's view that, psychologically speaking, the motivational forces working on individuals will be limited to the desire-belief model that he spells out in his account of hypothetical imperatives: a person has a desire, he has a belief about how he may assuage this desire, and, moved by that desire, which preexisted his deliberation, he takes the relevant means to his end. In the case of punishment, someone may greatly desire a beautiful piece of jewelry that lays before him in the store, but he reflects that if he were to walk out with the jewelry without paying for it (and he does not have enough money to buy it), he would be detained and charged with theft, and ultimately punished. So his action is constrained by the thought of (possible) punishment. The effectiveness of such constraint provides no evidence of moral worth within the character of the agent, even when it prevents him from performing what would be an act of theft.

Here then in the state we have a moral system, like, but distinct from, the system of inner morality expounded by Kant in his earlier *Groundwork*, and in the *Tugendlehre* of *The Metaphysics of Morals*. This inner morality is found in the individual, with incentives provided by the metaphysical (extra-phenomenal) power to act purely from the motive of duty, a capability that Kant believes human beings, as rational beings, possess. In the moral system of the state the incentives are provided by the state system of criminal law and punishment. Hence deterrence is an essential and basic purpose of the institution of punishment, and Kant's theory of punishment is not and cannot be a system of pure retributivism. In a footnote Kant later explains that only a system of external incentives based on concepts of right (and hence on retribution) can be called "punitive justice" and that "punitive justice" can be distinguished from "punitive prudence," which "is based on experience of what is effective in eliminating crime." Prudence tells us about what is useful, justice about what is moral (MM 6:363n).

Yet his theory is in important ways retributive. Let us discuss this side of the theory. Kant notably says, "The law of punishment is a categorical imperative, and woe to him who crawls through the windings of eudaemonism" in order to justify releasing the wrongdoer from some portion of his punishment (MM 6:331). The categorical imperative in this context is a deontological (and hence anti-teleological) principle that determines the appropriate sort of punishment, without reference to any standard of utility or *eudaimonia*. How does this work?

We are told that the measure for such punishment is a "principle of equality" that brings back on the wrongdoer whatever he has done to another:

> Accordingly, whatever undeserved evil you inflict upon another within the people, that you inflict upon yourself. If you insult him, you insult yourself; if you steal from

him, you steal from yourself; if you strike him, you strike yourself; if you kill him, you kill yourself. But only the *law of retribution (ius talionis)* – it being understood of course, that this is applied by a court (not by your private judgment) – can specify the quality and quantity of punishment; all other principles are fluctuating and unsuited for a sentence of pure and strict justice because extraneous considerations are mixed into them. (MM 6:332; also see MM 6:233, where Kant compares the principle of right to the Newtonian law by which bodies move freely "under the law of the *equality of action and reaction*")

One of the classic objections against the *lex talionis* is that it cannot work for certain crimes. You cannot or should not rape the rapist, or defraud the defrauder. This objection is an issue that Kant struggles with, for which he presents a range of examples, and to which he returns in an Appendix added to a later edition (MM 6:362–3). Another limitation, if that is what we want to call it, would be that it does not readily cover victimless crimes, such as prostitution or public drunkenness. (Some would ague that this shows that such "crimes" should not be regarded as criminal violations at all.) One sort of example for which Kant does a reasonable job is theft:

> Whoever steals makes the property of everyone else insecure and therefore deprives himself (by the principle of retribution) of security in any possible property. He has nothing and can also acquire nothing; but he still wants to live, and this is now possible only if others provide for him. But since the state will not provide for him free of charge, he must let it have his powers for any kind of work it pleases (in convict or prison labor) and is reduced to the status of a slave for a certain time. (MM 6:333)

This approximates the institution of imprisonment as it is familiar to us 200 years later, although with these differences: (1) Today punishment through imprisonment is not limited to versions of theft, which would include robbery, burglary, tax evasion, and fraud, but not assault or murder. (2) The function of imprisonment in incapacitating the person punished is not mentioned by Kant. Today such incapacitation (rendering the criminal incapable of further victimizing the general population by his acts, at least for a period of time) is commonly thought to be an important function of imprisonment. (3) Kant considers imprisonment as primarily an economic punishment, leaving aside those deprivations of freedom that are not directly economic, such as loss of opportunities for most sexual activity, lack of choices in personal association, and general regimentation of one's life. And it has often proved difficult to arrange for the prisoner to engage in economically beneficial activity; in such situations he may be detained without being required to work.

Kant's main discussion of punishment is full of examples. The last of these we will discuss at greater length below, because of its continuing interest: capital punishment. The *lex talionis* idea specifies both the kind and the amount of punishment, as Kant indicated in the passage quoted above: "if you insult him, you insult yourself." (MM 6:332).

Some of Kant's examples deal with complexities introduced by differences in social rank. For example, someone wealthy might willingly pay a fine for insulting someone of a lower class; so it would be better to punish the insulter by likewise injuring his pride: the upper-class person must publicly apologize and kiss the hand of the person of lower class (MM 6:332). This example may not have much resonance with us since we seldom punish verbal insults, and since the class distinctions involved in the kissing of someone's hand are not familiar to us. In the same spirit, Kant adds that a violence-prone upper-crust person who strikes an innocent person of lower class might be sentenced to solitary confinement with hardship: "in addition to the discomfort he undergoes, the offender's vanity would be painfully affected, so that through his shame like would be fittingly repaid for like" (MM 6:432–3). I take it that Kant is here seeking after effective punishment, and his thought is that upper-class people can be most effectively punished by being shamed. For us today, imprisonment as such carries shame, and this perhaps explains why we often insist that guilty corporate CEOs should receive some prison time. In addition, these comments also point to an aspect of Kant's theory of punishment that Joel Feinberg has called attention to: criminal punishment expresses society's condemnation of the agent and denunciation of his act, and this, apart from any more material aspect of punishment (such as a fine or deprivation of liberty), serves to punish and to provide a deterrent effect, and also serves to distinguish punishments from mere penalties (Feinberg, 1965). Feinberg did not note, as he might have, the difference that social class could make in such condemnation, which we can generalize as follows: the higher the social class the greater the loss, shame, and inner personal cost attached to the mere fact of criminal punishment. Feinberg also emphasizes what might seem to be a Kantian point, that punishment attempts to make clear that the one punished is the one responsible, while the victim and others are quite innocent. Kant explicitly discusses this expressive aspect of punishment that Feinberg finds in Kant:

> In every punishment there is something that (rightly) offends the accused's feeling of honor, since it involves coercion that is unilateral only, so that his dignity as a citizen is suspended, at least in this particular case; for he is subjected to an external duty to which he, for his own part, may offer no resistance. A man of nobility or wealth who has to pay a fine feels the loss of his money less than the humiliation of having to submit to the will of an inferior. (MM 6:363)

Kant briefly mentions some other examples in a later comment where it might seem difficult to come up with a punishment in kind under the idea of the *lex talionis*.

(1) "The punishment for rape and pederasty is castration" (MM 6: 363). We may refuse, according to today's sensibilities, to consider a punishment that involves mutilation (compare cutting off the thief's hand). I do not wish to defend this Kantian proposal. It is proposed as a retaliation in the spirit of the *lex talionis*, since we cannot rape the rapist. Is the thought that castration is an appropriate

retaliatory abuse of the rapist's sexual faculties in return for his abuse of his victim's? If so, the punishment is proposed without reference to the teleological fact that it also leaves the offender incapacitated for future rape. Both rape and pederasty (sex with children) have victims; the victim of rape is raped against her will, the child is not competent to consent to sexual activity, and, whether the child "consents" or not, he or she is arguably harmed by it.

(2) "[T]he punishment for bestiality, permanent expulsion from civil society, since the criminal has made himself unworthy of human society" (MM 6:363). The idea seems to be that the wrongdoer by his choice of sex with a non-human animal has entered into commerce with non-human society and has thereby excluded himself from human society, and this is what makes the proposed punishment appropriate as a payback. This is hard to defend in a straightforward way. Kant seems to be reacting to the *perverse* character of this sort of sex, and is hence regarding it as a purely animalistic act that defeats the purposiveness of human sexual faculties. Some might wish to consider such behavior guilty of the wrong of cruelty to animals (if it is painful to the animals involved), but we will not pursue this line of thought here, except to say that if such cruelty is avoided, that is unlikely to answer the objections of those who disapprove of such activity. Notice that bestiality would, according to Kant's own views, approximate a victimless crime, since only another human being could be a proper victim. If we think of such sexual acts as perversions, we might consider bestiality as a violation of a duty to *oneself*. But as such, it would not fall in the area of law or *Recht* at all, but with the rest of duties to oneself, in the *Tugendlehre*.

Kant comments of all three of these sorts of crimes, that they "are called unnatural because they are perpetrated against humanity itself" (MM 6:363). Any sort of sex that we consider illicit we also tend to regard as animalistic, sub-human, and perverted. The humanity of the victim is violated by any crime against him and her. If there is no such victim in any other person, then the discussion here of bestiality in particular might remind us of Kant's discussion of masturbation as a violation of a perfect duty to oneself.

Capital Punishment

We need to discuss Kant's views favoring capital punishment for murder in some detail, both because they are famous, and because the topic raises interesting issues about Kant's views on punishment generally. It may seem that the execution of the murderer is a particularly clear example of the *lex talionis*, and so it appeared to Kant. To many he has seemed excessive in his devotion to this form of punishment when he writes:

> Even if a civil society were to be dissolved by the consent of all its members (e.g., if
> a people inhabiting an island decided to separate and disperse throughout the world),

the last murderer remaining in prison would first have to be executed, so that each has done to him what his deeds deserve and blood guilt does not cling to the people for not having insisted upon this punishment; for otherwise the people can be regarded as collaborators in this public violation of justice. (MM 6:333)

Though this statement is arguably rhetorically excessive and seems to partake of an unseemly enthusiasm for executions, it is at root simply a reaffirmation of Kant's retributivism, and a reminder that retributive punishments are to be carried out as morally appropriate, and hence without reference to beneficial consequences. There would be none in the case Kant describes, because in the absence of a continuing society there could be no deterrent effects.

Kant's enthusiasm for executions is stimulated again a little later when he attempts to respond to one of the earliest principled arguments against capital punishment, proposed by Marchese Beccaria in his now classic "Of Crimes and Punishments." We might compare this aroused response to Beccaria to Kant's soon to be written response to Benjamin Constant in "On a Supposed Right to Lie from Philanthropy" (8:425–30). In both cases Kant seems to have been stimulated by his opposition to an adversary's teleological views into what some regard as an extreme statement of his own position.

But there is more to say. In Kant's day many crimes in addition to murder and treason called for the death penalty, and yet Kant never proposes it for any crime other than those two (he seems to think of treason as a kind of attempted murder of the state). So his view can be regarded as a transitional view (whether Kant so regarded it or not) away from excessively broad use of capital punishment.

Further, Kant's discussion of capital punishment in particular makes clear the centrality within his theory of punishment of the theme of moral respect for persons even in relation to the punished criminal.

(1) Kant several times emphasizes that we should be able to justify the punishment even to the person who is punished. When we punish, we are not acting in disregard of him or his views, as we might be thought to act in disregard of the views of any sort of vermin we wish to exterminate as a nuisance or worse. (Of course, this does not mean that we should expect the subject of punishment finally to accede and agree to her own punishment.) When Kant sums up his views on punishment in remarks added to a 1798 edition of the *Rechtslehre*, he writes,

[T]he only time a criminal cannot complain that a wrong is done him is when he brings his misdeed back upon himself, and what is done to him in accordance with penal law is what he has perpetrated on others, if not in terms of its letter at least in terms of its spirit. (MM, 6:363)

He adds (MM 6:334) that the murderer sentenced to death can never complain that he is being punished too severely, and therefore wronged: "Everyone would laugh in his face if he said this." It seems Kant proposes the *lex talionis*, among other reasons, because the punishments it entails are transparent in their justification, as well as being easily anticipated by the person to be punished.

(2) The other point here is even more significant. Kant, while insisting on capital punishment for murder adds that this punishment "must be freed from any mistreatment that could make the humanity in the person suffering it into something abominable" (MM 6:333). Kant thus rejects torture executions, such as drawing and quartering, which were sometimes still practiced in his time. He comments at greater length:

> Nevertheless, I cannot deny all respect to even a vicious person as a person; I cannot withdraw at least the respect that belongs to him in his quality as a person, even though by his deeds he makes himself unworthy of it. So there can be disgraceful punishments that dishonor humanity itself, such as quartering someone, having him torn by dogs, cutting off his nose and ears. Not only are such punishments more painful than loss of possessions and life to those who love honor, who claim the respect of others, as everyone must; they also make a spectator blush with shame at belonging to a species that can be treated in that way (MM 6:463).

Kant soon adds a more general comment:

> [T]he censure of vice . . . must never break out into complete contempt and denial of any moral worth to a vicious human being; for on this supposition he could never be improved, and this is not consistent with the idea of a *human being*, who as such (as a moral being) can never lose entirely his predisposition to the good (MM 6:463–4).

Kant is here resisting the tendency to see vicious murderers or one's enemies in war as non-persons, as sub-human, as vermin. Such attitudes have encouraged massacres by Hutus of Tutsis, by Europeans of Native Americans, or by Nazis of Jews and Gypsies. They have also been used to encourage individual state killings of such despised persons as Ted Bundy, or John Gacey, or more generally any fully guilty person sentenced to death for murder in the United States in the last 25 years.

We will return to this idea of respect for humanity in Kant's theory later, but now let us note some specific comments and examples mentioned in his continuing discussion of capital punishment.

(1) He says, somewhat surprisingly, that only by imposing a sentence of death upon the murderer can we pronounce a sentence proportional to the criminal's "*inner wickedness*" (MM 6:333). But punishment is not for inner wickedness, which, it might be thought, only God could judge; it is rather for external wrongdoing. This seems to be a slip on Kant's part, though it can be said that sometimes there is a reliable inference from certain external actions to such inner wickedness. For example, when A kills B, attempting to conceal his role in B's death, when he knows he will inherit a large sum of money from B's death, then, failing other countervailing considerations,

there is arguably a reliable inductive inference to the wicked motivation for the action.

(2) Next, Kant introduces some specific problem cases involving the death penalty. When men of honor and scoundrels are given a choice between death or convict labor as punishment, Kant tells us that men of honor will choose death, scoundrels convict labor, because (only) "the scoundrel considers it better to live in shame than not to live at all," while the man of honor saves his honor by choosing death (MM 6:333–4). Kant adds that if both sorts were sentenced to convict labor, such a sentence would be too hard on the man of honor, and too easy on the scoundrel, whereas a death sentence for both would result in a proper equalization of penalty between the two. Thomas Hill suggests to me that for such honorable men, Kant's position would have then been a rather straightforward application of *lex talionis*, because the "worse" man would be matched with the "worse" punishment (a life of disgrace at hard labor) and the "better" man would be matched with the "better" penalty (execution) (see Hill 1999).

(3) Kant considers another case, which may be beyond my powers of interpretation. "If the number of accomplices [to murder] is so great that the state, in order to have no such criminals in it, could soon find itself without subjects" (MM 6:334), and the state does not wish to terminate itself, then the sovereign should remedy this situation by executive clemency. This clemency would provide, for example, for "deportation" (MM 6:334; cf. the discussion of this penalty at MM 6:338). But of course deportations would deplete the society of its members as much as executions. Apart from this objection, we can comment that this case shows that Kant is willing to modify otherwise proper executions when not doing so would be harmful to the continuation of the civil society, and this is a reminder that the function of punishment is the defense and preservation of civil society. Thomas Hill suggests to me that this case presents us with a specific example of a circumstance in which Kant suggests a sovereign prudentially should exercise his power to grant clemency, though the case does not accord very well with Kant's drawing of moral limits on the appropriate use by the sovereign of that power.

(4) Then follows a discussion of the views of Marchese Beccaria, who argued that those participating in the original social contract would not consent to lose their own lives through this penalty being imposed on them; without such advance consent the death penalty could not be a valid part of law. In response Kant says that punishment is always imposed contrary to the will of the one punished, and "it is impossible *to will* to be punished" (MM 6:335). He then distinguishes between (a) pure reason in me that legislates rights (that is, as one of those creating the original social contract), and (b) myself as a subject who may be punished. The former is *homo noumenon*, and the latter *homo phenomenon* (MM 6:335). The point that we can never consent to our own punishment, even if not quite correct, emphasizes the idea that punishment is generally against the will of the person punished. Thomas Hill also suggests to me that the response to Beccaria also accords

with Kant's view that the relevant "original contract" to which we may appeal in political philosophy is a hypothetical idea of agreement by idealized decision makers, rather than an actual, might we say Hobbesian, consent by individuals who might have been consenting out of ignorance, partisanship, or selfishness.

(5) Kant presents two applications of the idea that murder entails the punishment of death, two difficult cases: the mother's killing of her child born out of wedlock, and a killing in a duel. The motive of both such killings is one of (admirable and true) honor. Discussing these cases Kant distinguishes between the objective demand of the ideal law (for the execution of such killers) and the subjective feelings of the people who would regard such executions as an injustice. The law of a given state may be based on the latter rather than the former, and thus depart from the ideal (MM 6:336–7). This does not quite answer the question as to whether such killers in Kant's view should be executed, for Kant seems to wish this question to remain open.

There is a certain train of thought coming in the historical wake of Kant's concern for the humanity of the person punished: there is all the work on punishment of Herbert Morris, perhaps especially "Persons and Punishment," and "A Paternalistic Theory of Punishment." Compare also the remarkable "The Hegelian Theory of Punishment" by J. McTaggart. There are views like those of "The Moral Education Theory of Punishment" by Jean Hampton. So although Kant's theory of punishment, based on what he himself actually wrote about it, might seem excessively harsh, and, may I say, Prussian, the tradition that emerged took what was a point very basic and central to Kant's view, the personhood of the punished, and made it quite basic, a sort of guiding thread for the development of our moral ideas about punishment.

In his discussion of punishment as in other cases in the *Rechtslehre* Kant is proposing what is required by the moral law. It is apparent that actual systems of law may fail to accord with such ideals, just as individuals may act contrary to inner morality in violating duties to oneself or imperfect duties to others. To mention another such example of a proposed ideal, Kant argues that maintaining a hereditary aristocracy (as most European societies did in his day) is unjust. In such a case, as in the case of punishment, we can use the moral/legal ideal to guide our actions as we critique or reform and improve our society's legal structure (see MM 6:329, and TP 8:297, for discussions of hereditary aristocracy). So Kant's statements in his discussions of punishment are statements about what an ideal system of law on this subject would be like, and how such an ideal system might attempt to deal with certain problematic examples (which would be applications of the general moral law).

Kant's rejection of torture executions because they cause the humanity of the person punished to be held in contempt presents a limitation upon the *lex talionis*. It may be that some murderers have tortured their victims before or as they killed them, and a response in kind might therefore seem appropriate. But Kant claims a moral limit to such responses, and so a quick (and therefore minimally painful) execution of a torture murderer would be a punishment that incompletely mirrored the crime. This limit is imposed in respect for the humanity of the person punished; such respect must be universally applied, even to the criminal, who has failed to act as if he were a person worthy of such respect. The idea of respect for persons is absolutely central to Kant's theory of punishment, and the main person respect for whom is in question is the person being punished. We might also urge that respect for the humanity of the crime victim is implicit in the requirement that such wrongful treatment be punished. Kant does not explicitly make this point, but it perhaps lies behind his insistence that it is wrong for the degree of punishment to fall short of the gravity of the crime. When a punishment is too light, it arguably fails adequately to respect the personhood of the victim by its underestimation of the seriousness of a certain crime against such a person, and hence an underestimation of his full status as a person.

The Kantian tradition of making the personhood of the one punished central to theory has also been contributed to by Supreme Court Justice William Brennan, when he argued in his opinion in the decision of *Furman v. Georgia* (408 U.S. 238, 1972) that the Eighth Amendment to the U. S. Constitution, which forbids "cruel and unusual punishment" thereby forbids all capital punishment. Brennan's view was finally a minority view on the U.S. Supreme Court, and thus jurisdictions in the United States remain free to impose the death penalty (with certain restrictions) in cases of aggravated murder. Brennan with four other justices in *Furman* formed a majority overturning death penalty laws as they then existed in the U.S. in 1972, but in 1976 a majority of the Supreme Court in *Gregg v. Georgia* accepted some reforms of death penalty laws that made them a constitutionally acceptable option again, and Brennan (with Thurgood Marshall) found himself in minority opposition. But Brennan's opinion remains one of the best statements of that position, and the heart of it presents a Kantian rationale against the death penalty:

> Death is a truly awesome punishment. The calculated killing of a human being by the State involves, by its very nature, a denial of the executed person's humanity. An individual in prison does not lose "the right to have rights." . . . A prisoner remains a member of the human family. Moreover, he retains the right of access to the courts. His punishment is not irrevocable. . . . As one nineteenth-century proponent of punishing criminals by death declared, "When a man is hung, there is an end of our relations with him. His execution is a way of saying, 'You are not fit for this world, take your chance elsewhere.'" (Ibid.)

The notable difference between Kant and Brennan is where they draw the line of acceptable punishment. Kant rules out torture executions, and Brennan all executions. But apart from this difference, their rationales for drawing such a line are similar: We must maintain respect for the humanity of the person being punished. We might add that for Brennan (and not him alone) the U.S. Constitution at least at some points serves to state a moral ideal to which reference can be made in determining what actual law *ought* to be. Brennan writes as a judge, whose views in proper circumstances may have the force of law (the main circumstance being here that enough of the other judges on his court agree with his conclusions, as they did in *Furman v. Georgia*, though not always with his reasons), whereas Kant was writing merely as a moral philosopher making proposals to be considered by anyone as to their correctness.

Retributivism also has had many defenders among philosophers and lawyers in the later twentieth century. The central ideas in punishment that only the guilty may be punished, and that the punishment should fit the crime, are by many taken to be insights primarily gained from retributivism, and more difficult to defend from the perspective of a teleological, including a utilitarian, justification of punishment (see Rawls, 1955). And such ideas are certainly also central to the retributive elements of Kant's theory of punishment.

In Kant's views on punishment there is a theme of equality of respect for all before the law; punishment is taken to restore that equality, when it has been breached by the criminal act. Though Kant thinks punishment is to deter, there is no adjustment of the amount of punishment in order to secure maximum benefit for each unit of punishing. Compare the utilitarian Jeremy Bentham, who proposes additional punishment for each additional blow in an assault. Such microadjustment to maximize the deterrent efficiency of punishment is fundamentally a teleological way of looking at punishment. It might be thought that without such adjustments the *lex talionis* may in particular cases produce excessive punishment or not enough. Punishment would be excessive when the same or nearly the same amount of deterrence might be brought about by less punishment; the excess punishment would then be purely retributive. Punishment would be not enough when it would fail adequately to deter. However, any punishment will fail to deter in some cases, so we cannot maintain a standard requiring complete deterrence. It seems unlikely that a retributively adequate punishment would be inadequate in its deterrent effect. Arguably, most, perhaps all, cases of alleged inadequate punishments, so called wrist-slaps, will also be retributively inadequate.

So in sum, according to Kant the deterrent effect is essential to the idea of punishment, but the quantity and quality of punishment are to be determined on purely retributive grounds. Is there a contradiction here? It might seem an odd theory, but not a contradiction. It attempts to determine appropriate punishment based on the idea of respect for persons (the second formulation of the categorical imperative, respect for persons) and on equality before the law (arguably related to the first formulation, requiring that policies be universal laws). And it attempts to have punishment provide an indispensable social function, deterrence that protects the rights of all in civil society.

Conclusion

Kant never more than briefly sketches his ideas on punishment in a few pages. Those ideas clearly reflect important central ideas in his moral philosophy: the categorical imperative, respect for persons, practical laws as universal, and the moral necessity of the state as guarantor of external rights to person and property.

Such a sketch leaves questions unanswered. The apparent harshness of Kant's views seems to flow from his deontological approach, which will sometimes argue for punishment in excess of what could be justified by utilitarian considerations. On the other hand, Kant does indicate "*punitive prudence*" (MM 6:363n) as a distinct area of study (distinct from punitive justice); perhaps it would be on the basis of such societal prudence, for example, that prisons undertake to educate and provide job skills at least for those inmates who are to be released after their terms are completed. Kant writes, "He must previously have been found punishable before any thought can be given to drawing from his punishment something of use for himself or his fellow citizens" (MM 6:363n). This points to the possibility of arranging punishment so as to benefit the prisoner and society. Some of the peculiarities of Kant's discussion flow from his use of examples more apposite in the eighteenth century, such as issues concerning killing in duels and by mothers of children born out of wedlock.

Almost completely omitted from Kant's discussion are the complexities concerning imputation of responsibility for crimes that are added by the countervailing claims of social causation, mental illness, or mental inadequacy, and the changes in our institutions of punishment that such claims would require. These complexities have been added to our social and psychological thinking since the time Kant wrote, though even in Kant's day they might have been more filled out in Kant's writing if he had written more than a sketch of his views. For instance, it was as obvious in Kant's day as it is in our own that children should be regarded as bearing responsibility for criminal behavior in a different way and to a different degree than those who are fully competent adults, and hence should be punished differently, if at all, but Kant did not address this issue.

Note

1 All references to Kant's works refer to the Prussian Academy pagination appearing in the margins of most translations.

Bibliography

Beccaria, C. 1963. *Cesare Bonesana, Marchese di Beccaria, On Crimes and Punishments*. New York: Bobbs-Merrill, 1963.

Feinberg, Joel, 1965: The expressive function of punishment. *The Monist* 49: 397–423.

Hampton, Jean, 1984: The moral education theory of punishment. *Philosophy and Public Affairs* 13: 208–38.

Hill, T. 1999: Kant on wrong doing, desert and punishment. *Law and Philosophy* 18, no. 1: 407–41.

Kant, I. 1785: *Grundlegung zur Metaphysik der Sitten*. AK 4. Foundations of the Metaphysics of Morals.

Kant, I. 1793: *Über den Gemeinspruch: Das mag in der Theorie richtig sein, taugt aber nicht für die Praxis.* AK 8 (275–313). On the Old Saw: "That May Be Right in Theory, But It Won't Work in Practice."

Kant, I. Über ein vermintes Recht aus Menschliebe zu lügen. AK 8 (425–30). On a Supposed Right to Lie from Altruistic Motives.

Kant, I. 1798: *Metaphysik der Sitten.* AK 6. Doctrine of Law, in Metaphysics of Morals. trans. Mary Gregor. Cambridge: Cambridge University Press, 1996.

McTaggart, J. 1896: Hegel's theory of punishment. *International Journal of Ethics* 6: 479–502.

Morris, H. 1968: Persons and punishment. *The Monist* 52: 475–501.

Morris, H. 1981: A paternalistic theory of punishment. *American Philosophical Quarterly* 18, no. 4.

Rawls, J. 1955: Two concepts of rules. *The Philosophical Review* 64: 3–13.

9

Kant's Vision of a Just World Order

Thomas Pogge

I

Fundamental to Kant's political philosophy is an apparently sharp, binary distinction between two kinds of social condition, a state of nature and a juridical state. A juridical state is characterized by the fact that its participants have precise and secure domains of external freedom. This in turn has five presuppositions. First and foremost, there must be *recognized clear laws* laying down what each participant is entitled, permitted, forbidden, and required to do. It is crucial for Kant's notion of a juridical state that it requires not merely the existence of political power but also its exercise through and under laws. Without laws, persons can subject others to their will and thus create a kind of social order. But such subjection without legal rights and duties, rule without rules, still counts for Kant as a state of nature.

Moreover, there must be a recognized way of producing *authoritative interpretations* of these laws in situations where their meaning or practical implications are controversial. The laws as authoritatively interpreted must be *complete*, so that persons do not have conduct options whose deontic status (entitled, permitted, forbidden, required) is left indeterminate. The laws as authoritatively interpreted must be *consistent*, so that whatever any one participant is entitled or required to do no other participant is permitted to prevent her from doing. And the laws as authoritatively interpreted must be *effectively enforced* through recognized procedures and agencies, so that the domains of external freedom defined by these laws are truly secure.[1]

Kant held that a juridical state requires an absolute sovereign conceived in the traditional way prevalent also in Hobbes and Rousseau: a person or group of persons with ultimate – (almost) unlimited, undivided, and unsupervised – political authority over the promulgation/recognition, interpretation/adjudication, and enforcement of laws. Kant's reasoning in support of this requirement is also conventional: If such political authority were limited or divided in any way, then disputes over the exact location of the limit or division would remain without an authoritative path of legal resolution. Disputes could arise about whether some political agency has overstepped its limits or about which political agency has jurisdiction over some particular matter. And the possibility of such disputes would render domains of external freedom insecure.[2]

Endorsing absolute sovereignty as a presupposition of a juridical state, Kant also requires a separation of governmental powers into legislative, executive, and judicial. He sees this separation of powers, conceived by Montesquieu, as compatible with absolute sovereignty provided one of these branches has ultimate authority over the others. Kant envisions the legislative branch as sovereign. It decides how to institute executive and judicial agencies, and it retains ultimate control over them: "[T]he governor, as administrator, should stand under the authority of the law, and is bound by it under the supreme control of the legislator. The legislative authority may therefore divest the governor of his power, depose him, or reform his administration" (MM 6:317:9–13).[3] The executive ("governor") as well as the courts thus exercise authority at the discretion of the sovereign whom they cannot legally constrain. And Kant's requirement of a separation of governmental powers is then an extra-legal demand on the sovereign that it should confine itself to general legislation while delegating administrative and judicial decisions about particular cases to executive and judicial officers and agencies.

Kant presents such a separation of powers as one of two requirements of a *republican* – as opposed to a *despotic* – juridical state. The second requirement is that sovereignty, importantly including the authority to decide about war and peace,[4] should be vested in the people to be exercised through their elected representatives. In contemporary language, we may call this latter a requirement of democracy. But "democracy" is, traditionally and more literally, also used to signify a regime in which the people exercise executive and/or judicial powers. Understood in this sense, democracy is incompatible with republicanism or, as Kant puts it, "democracy, in the proper sense of the word, is necessarily a despotism" (PP 8:352:19–20). The reason is that, when the people exercise executive or judicial powers, then one of the two requirements for republicanism necessarily remains unfulfilled. For the people's exercising legislative authority as well is then *forbidden* by the requirement of the separation of powers even while it is also *prescribed* by the requirement of popular sovereignty.

With these preliminaries, let us examine how Kant conceived the ideal of a just global order in which all human beings enjoy secure domains of external freedom under republican institutions. He considers two ideas for overcoming the state of war among states. The first is a league of free states (*Föderalism freier Staaten* – PP 8:354:2) or pacific league (*Friedensbund, foedus pacificum* – PP 8:356:7), which is not based on coercive laws. The second is a universal (*allgemeiner* – PP 8:379:9) or international state (*Völkerstaat, civitas gentium* – PP 8:357:10) or, more specifically, a world republic (PP 8:357:14). For Kant, these two ideals are sharply distinct: With a league, each member state continues to have its own sovereign, while in an international state there is only a single, global sovereign.

Which of these ideals does Kant endorse? His Second Definitive Article of Perpetual Peace demands that international law be founded upon a league of sovereign states. But his discussion of this article nonetheless ends with a ringing endorsement of a world republic:

> For states in their relation to one another, there cannot be any reasonable way out of their lawless condition which entails only war except that they, like individual human beings, should give up their savage (lawless) freedom, adjust themselves to public coercive laws, and thus establish a continuously growing international state (civitas gentium), which will ultimately include all the nations of the world. But under their idea of the law of nations they absolutely do not wish to do this, and so reject in practice what is correct in theory. If all is not to be lost, there can be, then, in place of the positive idea of a world republic, only the negative surrogate of an alliance which averts war, endures, spreads, and checks the force of that hostile inclination away from law, though such an alliance is in constant peril of its breaking loose again. (PP 8:357:5–17)

The tension in Kant's text can be explained. His highest ideal is that of a world republic, because only through a world state with one global sovereign can humankind achieve that which alone can make peace truly secure: a *fully juridical condition*. This is a condition in which each person's domain of external freedom is legally delimited against that of every other person (with whom she might come into contact) and in which there are common adjudication mechanisms through which disputes about the precise limits of legal rights and their alleged violation can be authoritatively settled as well as common enforcement mechanisms through which these domains (formulated in terms of legal rights) are protected. A league of sovereign states falls short of achieving a fully juridical condition. It may feature, to be sure, recognized clear terms of association, such as a body of international law. But such a league cannot fulfill the second presupposition for a juridical condition: authoritative interpretation. The reason is that, however the terms of such a league may delimit the powers of the various states against one another (in terms of geography or citizenship or whatever), disputes are possible over the exact location of these delimitations.

Instituting a central international court to adjudicate such disputes about international law is no solution because there may then still be disputes over whether some particular dispute falls under the jurisdiction of this international court or under that of some national political authority. A fully juridical condition could be achieved, if the international court were decisive in such meta-disputes. But this court could then overrule any (contested) decision by any national political authority. In virtue of having this competence, such a court would annihilate the sovereignty of states and thereby negate the idea of a league. Such a league of sovereign states requires that national authorities be decisive in meta-disputes over jurisdiction, which means that the international court can settle disputes only insofar as the relevant national authorities in all of the states involved recognize its competence and jurisdiction. The instituting of an international court thus provides no authoritative path of legal resolution for any international disputes that involve one party denying that the court has jurisdiction in the matter.

This dilemma cannot be solved through an even higher court authorized to decide which disputes fall under the jurisdiction of the international court and which under the jurisdiction of this or that national authority. Such a higher court would merely repeat the dilemma on a higher level: To fulfill its role, it would have to have the authority to overrule any (contested) national claim to jurisdiction, and this authority would annihilate national sovereignty as Kant understood it. Without this authority, it would not provide an authoritative path of legal resolution for any dispute involving a contested claim to national jurisdiction.

While a league of sovereign states necessarily leaves some possible disputes without an authoritative path of legal resolution, it is nonetheless far superior to a pure state of nature in which *all* relations among persons are of this kind. I have called it a *semi-juridical condition*: a condition that is juridical insofar as many, or even all, persons are subject to some sovereign or other, thereby standing in law-governed relations with the other subjects of this same sovereign, and non-juridical insofar as each person stands in non-law-governed relations to some others.[5]

If Kant considers a fully juridical condition to be superior to a semi-juridical one, then why does he not endorse the former clearly and unambiguously? One possible reason is indicated in the quoted passage: States "absolutely do not wish" to "give up their savage (lawless) freedom [and] adjust themselves to public coercive laws." With the road to a world republic blocked for the foreseeable future, Kant thought it important to develop the inferior but far more realistic ideal of the best possible semi-juridical condition: the ideal of a pacific league of sovereign states. He may well have thought that such a pacific league would make a world republic more achievable, and also that dwelling too much on the best but, for now, unrealistic ideal of a world republic would make it too easy to dismiss his rejection of the status quo as a philosopher's pipe dream.[6] On this reading, Kant's emphasis on a league of sovereign states rather than a world republic is strategic: Kant hints in the quoted passage that he is really committed to a world republic as the highest ideal. But he also understands that a pacific league is more easily reachable from the status quo, and that a world republic is more easily reachable from a pacific league than from the status quo. In an essay primarily addressed to present and future politicians, Kant therefore marginalizes his true commitment while emphasizing the intermediate aim of a league of sovereign states – or so the strategic reading conjectures.

While the quoted passage fits nicely with the strategic reading, there are other passages that are frequently and gleefully cited by opponents of global political institutions and authorities. To be sure, these passages could be read as Kant's strategic attempts to gain credibility with his readers by distancing himself from his highest ideal. But, to read them in this way, we must suppose that the champion of the Categorical Imperative was prepared to mislead some of his readers into believing that he was convinced by arguments that he did not actually find conclusive. The credibility of this supposition largely depends on the quality of the arguments Kant endorses.

There are basically two such arguments. One challenges the path to a world state: "While natural law allows us to say of human beings living in a lawless condition that they ought to abandon it, international law does not allow us to say the same of states. For as states, they already have a juridical constitution, and have thus outgrown the coercive right of others to subject them to a wider legal constitution" (PP 8:355:33–356:1).

The premise of this argument, stated in the second sentence, asserts an important disanalogy between a state of nature among states and a state of nature among individuals. This premise has been vigorously disputed and ably defended.[7] It is significant that Kant himself seems to dispute it two years later, writing that states must not remain in "the condition of natural freedom" but have the "right to compel [*nöthigen*] one another to abandon this state of war and thus must seek a constitution that will establish an enduring peace" (MM 6:343:21–4). It is at least uncertain, then, whether Kant was committed to the view that states must not use force to establish a world state.

More importantly, the assumption that Kant was so committed does not refute the belief that he was committed to a world republic which, after all, may be achievable without the use of force. Kant may well have held that states ought to abandon their lawless condition but must not coerce one another to do so. This compatibility is illustrated by Kant's position on lying: He asserts a duty not to lie and also opposes a right to coerce compliance with this duty through criminal-law penalties.[8]

However interpreted, Kant's first argument is thus rather obviously inconclusive and therefore no serious threat to the strategic reading.

The second argument commonly adduced contends that a plurality of independent states "is still to be preferred to their amalgamation under a single power which has overruled the rest and created a universal monarchy. For the laws progressively lose their impact as the government increases its range, and a soulless despotism, after crushing the germs of goodness, will finally lapse into anarchy" (PP 8:367:12–17).[9]

On its face, the forward-looking objection expressed in this passage addresses and opposes not a world state as such, but a "universal monarchy," that is, a specific *despotic* (non-republican) world state in which sovereign power would be exercised by a single person. One might have thought that Kant considers such a universal monarchy superior to the status quo – for he repeatedly insists that even a highly imperfect (despotic) juridical condition is still to be preferred over a state of nature and thus presumably also over what I have dubbed a semi-juridical condition.[10] Kant dispels this thought by asserting that a universal monarchy would not in fact uphold a juridical condition. It would degenerate into a worse form of despotism, a condition in which a great deal of political power would be concentrated in a single person (or group) but would not be exercised in accordance with the presuppositions of juridicality. Such power would be used arbitrarily, for example, without recognized laws that clearly instruct persons in advance about what they are legally required, entitled, permitted, or forbidden to do. On Kant's understanding, such a ("soulless") despotism, just like the anarchy he predicts will follow it, counts as a state of nature and thus as clearly inferior to a world of sovereign states.

Such a world of sovereign states, as it existed in the eighteenth century and would continue to exist in a pacific league, is thus for Kant intermediate between two other possible human worlds: a world state that, satisfying the five presuppositions of juridicality, sustains a fully juridical condition and a global state of nature featuring more concentrated (monarchical) or dispersed (anarchic) exercises of lawless power. Because of the gain in juridicality it represents, a world state is lexically superior to a world of sovereign states which in turn, and for the same reason, is lexically superior to a global state of nature.

We can now push one step further our question whether Kant's emphasis on a league of sovereign states rather than a world republic is merely strategic. The answer depends on whether Kant believed that *no* fully juridical condition is sustainable. On the straightforward reading I have given, the cited passage does not settle the matter because the universal monarchy Kant rejects is quite distinct from other forms of world state, notably a world republic. Eager readers insist that Kant's worry extends to any kind of world state.[11] They can say that "the laws progressively lose their impact as the government increases its range" and that, with global range, the laws' impact would be insufficient to maintain secure domains of external freedom (MM 6:350:12–17). And their opponents can shoot back that Kant would not have written that "the state of nature among nations, just like that among individuals, is a condition that should be abandoned in favor of entering a juridical state" (MM 6:350:6–8) if he had thought such a global juridical state to be impracticable.

Kant was deeply committed to the view that we should never assume that something so far unachieved is therefore unachievable, nor shrink from fulfilling a duty unless this is "demonstrably impossible" (TP 8:310:3; cf. MM 6:354–5). I find it hard to believe that Kant took his remarks about the impact of laws diminishing as their range increases as a conclusive demonstration of the impossibility of a world state. I am more inclined to ascribe to him the view that a fully juridical condition – specifically a world republic – may be possible and that we therefore ought to work toward its realization.[12] If this is right, then Kant endorsed a pacific league of sovereign states strategically: as an improvement over the status quo that might also make it easier to realize a world republic. This is my best judgment on the basis of the evidence. I am not sure it is correct, and I strongly doubt we will ever know for certain.

More fundamentally, I believe we should not care. We should not care, because the last 200-plus years have greatly expanded our historical experience relevant to this question, have vastly improved our social theorizing, especially in economics and political science, and have brought new technologies (such as computers) that critically enhance our capacity for the uniform administration of large areas and populations under the rule of law. Against the background of all the knowledge, understanding, and technology that was lacking when Kant wrote, whatever he may have believed about the sustainability of a fully juridical condition can only qualify as a wild guess. This is not to say, of course, that precise judgments about the sustainability of various kinds of world state are possible today. It is to say only that it is useless, as so many writers are doing, to appeal to Kant's authority in this matter – and downright silly to rest one's whole case against a world state on such an exegetical appeal without so much as a cursory look at how well states of different sizes have actually done in upholding an effective rule of law.

II

Thinking about Kant's discussion now, over 200 years later, we can see its most serious flaw: his assumption of a sharp binary distinction between a juridical condition and a state of nature, based on the presence or absence of a consistent and complete body of law that is formulated, adjudicated, and enforced under a single ultimate political authority (the sovereign). This false assumption blinded Kant to options intermediate between a world state and a world of sovereign states.

Kant was aware, of course, of the intermediate possibility of a semi-juridical condition as exemplified by the social world in which he lived as well as by the pacific league he envisioned. He may not have fully understood, though, the ways in which such worlds, featuring "bubbles" of juridicality within a larger state of nature, can be more or less distant from the two ideal types of a fully juridical condition and a thoroughgoing state of nature: Such worlds differ, for instance, with respect to what proportion of the human population live within juridical states and with respect to the size of these bubbles. Thus, closest to a fully juridical condition, there is the possibility of a social world consisting of two juridical bubbles that together contain the entire human population. From there, we can move away from a fully juridical condition by dividing and subdividing the bubbles (creating an ever larger number of ever less-populous states) and by dissolving such bubbles so as to increase the proportion of humankind living outside any juridical state. Moving along both these dimensions, we reach worlds in which only minute fractions of humanity live in tiny mini-states meeting the presuppositions of juridicality and finally arrive at a thoroughgoing state of nature.

Even when all these intermediate possibilities are recognized, Kant's conceptual structure remains fundamentally binary. Each person either does or does not have a precise and secure domain of external freedom by belonging to a state that fulfills the presuppositions of juridicality: recognized clear laws, authoritative interpretation, completeness, consistency, and effective enforcement. As Kant did not sufficiently acknowledge, these presuppositions can be fulfilled to a greater or lesser degree.

Such gradations are evident with respect to the fifth presupposition of effective enforcement, as is reflected in Kant's cited passages about laws progressively losing their impact (PP 8:367:14–15 and MM 6:350:12–15). By and among human beings, laws cannot be enforced so perfectly that every participant's domain of external freedom is absolutely secure. Kant clearly assumed that most European states of his day had internally attained a juridical condition even while they fell short, in various degrees, of effective law enforcement.

Analogous points hold for the first, third, and fourth presuppositions of juridicality: The laws of eighteenth century Prussia or France were more or less successful in avoiding vagueness and ambiguity, none perfectly so. They were known and recognized to a greater or lesser extent within their respective jurisdictions. And each state's body of law was probably incomplete, perhaps even inconsistent, in various minor ways. Yet, despite all that, Kant was willing to say that these were juridical states – a predicate he would have denied them if they had fallen short in these ways to a much larger extent.

The most prominent presupposition of juridicality in Kant's texts is the second, that there must be a recognized way of producing authoritative interpretations and adjudications of the laws. Using conventional reasoning, Kant takes this presupposition to require that, for any possible dispute about external freedom, there must be an authoritative path of legal resolution. And he infers that this rules out any limit or genuine separation of governmental powers as these would leave disputes about who is in charge of some particular matter without an authoritative path of legal resolution.

But a complete political decision-making mechanism of the kind Kant envisions is a mirage. Even the most concentrated and absolute form of sovereignty leaves disputes over who is the sovereign without an authoritative path of legal resolution. A dispute over who the rightful sovereign is cannot be resolved by any candidate sovereign because his/her/its authority to resolve such disputes is precisely what the dispute is about. If a juridical condition presupposes a complete political decision-making mechanism that can authoritatively resolve all possible practical disputes, then such a condition has never existed anywhere and could never possibly exist. If, on the other hand, juridical states did and do exist, as Kant evidently assumed, then the second presupposition of juridicality, too, must be construed in a more relaxed way: A juridical condition requires that all – or nearly all the more important – practical disputes that actually arise among the participants are resolved in a way that all – or nearly all – participants actually accept. When the political authorities do well, participants' domains of external freedom will tend to be secure, although the possibility of a break-down of the political system can never be completely banished. As political authorities do less well in this regard, participants' domains of external freedom tend to be less secure and then it becomes ever less appropriate to speak of a juridical state.

I conclude that Kant was willing to accept as juridical existing states in which the five presuppositions are met well enough, but in which none is met fully. With respect to all five presuppositions, he thus implicitly accepted gradations in regard to how precisely delimited and secure a person's domain of external freedom is. Yet, Kant does not explicitly acknowledge these gradations, but presents juridicality in stark binary terms. One main reason for this is, presumably, that he wanted to support a widespread willingness to obey the laws, without which effective enforcement and hence a juridical condition is altogether impossible. His arguments for an unconditional duty of obedience most clearly require the binary presentation. Here is one notorious example:

> Even if [the supreme legislative] power or its agent, the chief of state, has violated the original contract [...] the subject is still not permitted to offer counter-resistance.

The reason for this is that the people, under an existing civil constitution, has no longer any right to determine how the constitution should be administered. For suppose it did have this right, and that it disagreed with the judgment of the actual chief of state, who is to decide which side is right? Neither can act as judge of its own cause. Thus there would have to be another chief above the chief of state to decide between the latter and the people, which is self-contradictory." (TP 8:299:26–300:7)[13]

Kant's conclusion – that no right to judge any practical matter can be conceded to the people – follows only if the very possibility of a practical dispute between sovereign and people (for which there could then be no authoritative path of legal resolution) must be ruled out as destructive of a juridical state. But then, as we have seen, this possibility *cannot* be ruled out: In the question who the sovereign is, the people cannot defer to the actual political authorities because who these are is precisely the question. Therefore, if a juridical condition is to be possible at all, then it cannot require that there be an authoritative path of legal resolution for all possible practical disputes, but only that such authoritative resolutions are available for sufficiently many of the practical disputes that actually arise to ensure that participants' domains of external freedom are reasonably precisely delimited and reasonably secure.

If we think of juridicality along these lines – as a non-binary property of social states that depends on how precisely delimited and how secure their participants' domains of external freedom are – then the question whether a right to resistance is compatible with a commitment to juridicality is a complex empirical one, rather than a simple question of logic as Kant suggests. Such a right may, on the one hand, diminish juridicality by encouraging groups of citizens to transgress the laws. Yet it may also, on the other hand, encourage existing political authorities to govern more juridically: to formulate a clearer, more consistent and complete body of law, to ensure its wider publicity, and to apply and enforce it more effectively, predictably, and even-handedly.

As the non-binary understanding subverts the view that juridicality requires a sovereign with *unlimited* authority, so it also undermines the conviction that juridicality requires the powers of sovereignty to be undivided and their exercise to be unsupervised. Perfect juridicality is not to be had in any case. And a very high degree of juridicality can evidently be achieved in modern states featuring a genuine separation of powers. These states are, to be sure, subject to *ultimate* conflicts: to disputes in regard to which even the legally correct method of resolution is contested. To see this, one need only imagine how a constitutional democracy's three branches of government might engage in an all-out power struggle, each going to the very brink of what, on its self-serving interpretation, it is constitutionally authorized to do: The President might order the arrest of all opposition members of Congress, the Congress might vote the Supreme Court out of existence, or the Supreme Court might depose the President and declare itself constitutionally authorized to do so. But such scenarios may never (or very rarely) arise. And even when they do arise, they need not lead to a breakdown of the juridical condition: One of the authorities involved in the dispute may eventually retreat, impelled perhaps by what Habermas has aptly dubbed the forceless force of the better argument, by moral suasion, by widespread condemnation, by the desire to avert a crisis for the benefit of the whole society, or by a sober calculation that it would lose if the dispute were to be decided by the force of arms. There are some examples of such retreats in the American experience: *Marbury v. Madison* (where the U.S. Supreme Court successfully claimed for itself the authority to interpret the U.S. Constitution), the 1937 constitutional crisis concerning the New Deal (where Franklin D. Roosevelt abandoned his attempt to "pack" the U.S. Supreme Court with six additional judges and the Court abandoned its practice of invalidating Roosevelt's New Deal legislation), and the 1973–4 crisis surrounding the Watergate tapes, which ended with Richard Nixon's capitulation and subsequent resignation. The experience of the last 200 years shows conclusively that what does not work in (Kant's) theory may work quite well in practice. In fact, states with a genuine separation of powers, like the United States, have proven *more* enduring and more protective of precise domains of external freedom than states governed by an absolute sovereign (which also fall short of Kant's impossible ideal on account of the who-is-the-sovereign problem).

The same experience also shows that a genuine *vertical* (federalist) separation of powers is compatible with a high degree of juridicality, even though such a separation must leave some possible conflicts over the precise allocation of powers without a legal path of authoritative resolution. This practical workability of a genuine vertical separation of powers shows that Kant – quite understandably, of course, in light of the more limited historical experience available to him – is operating with a false dichotomy. We need not choose between an international state, in which ultimate political authority is concentrated in a single world government, and a loose association of sovereign states, each of which is ruled by a government that retains full ultimate political authority over the state's people and territory. We can avoid both the danger of a "soulless despotism" (PP 8:367:16; TP 8:311:3), which Kant associates with world government, and the danger of hostility breaking out again, which he associates with a voluntary association of sovereign states (PP 8:357:16–17). There is an intermediate paradigm that Kant did not consider possible: a multi-layered scheme in which ultimate political authority is vertically dispersed. In such a scheme, there would indeed be a world government with central agencies that fulfill certain legislative, executive, and judicial functions.[14] But there would also be smaller political units – such as the European Union, Great Britain, Scotland, and the City of Edinburgh – whose governmental agencies would also have some ultimate political authority over the unit's internal affairs and over its relations with other units of all kinds. The existence of many independent political units on several levels greatly reduces the danger of (both forms of) despotism by affording plenty of checks and balances, which ensure that, even when some political units turn tyrannical and oppressive, there will always be other, already fully organized political units (above, below, or on the same level) that can render aid and protection to the oppressed, publicize the abuses and, if necessary, fight the oppressors.[15]

Kant would surely have envisioned a world republic as containing smaller political units. But his commitment to the doctrine of absolute sovereignty prevented him from thinking of these units as having any *ultimate* political authority. In several of his political writings, however, Kant seems at times to be on the verge of overcoming this constraint upon his thinking. Thus he once suggests (MM 6:311:22–5) that public law (*Staatsrecht*) and international law (*Völkerrecht*) might together lead to the idea of a public law of peoples (*Völkerstaatsrecht*). He writes that a civil society "would require – if only human beings were smart enough to discover it and wise enough willingly to submit to its coercive power – a *cosmopolitan* whole [*weltbürgerliches Ganze*], that is, a system of all states that are in danger of affecting one another detrimentally" (CJ 5:432:33–7). He envisions (*Idea for a Universal History* 8:26:9–15) as the final step of human progress a unification of states (*Staatenverbindung*), which involves a united power (*vereinigte Gewalt*) that enforces a law of equilibrium among states and thereby introduces a cosmopolitan condition of public security of states (*einen weltbürgerlichen Zustand der öffentlichen Staatssicherheit*). And he asserts that "there exists no other remedy against this [oppressive burden of military expenditure] except an international law (in analogy to the civil or public law of individual men), which is founded upon public and enforcable laws to which each state would have to subject itself" (TP 8:312:25–9). The last three passages seem especially suggestive, because they clearly juxtapose the continued existence of states with the existence of a central coercive mechanism of law enforcement. They show that Kant at least caught a glimpse of the kind of multi-layered political structure that is emerging in the European Union and that – globalized – may well be the best chance for achieving what Kant so ardently sought: lasting peace for humankind.[16]

Notes

1 My term *participant* may be thought of as covering not only natural persons, but also artificial persons such as firms, associations (universities, churches, foundations, clubs, etc.), and public agents and agencies. Still, the claims, liberties, immunities and powers of such artificial persons are generally reducible to those of natural persons. A firm's freedom to sell a certain piece of corporate property, for instance, can be cashed out in terms of a complex set of claims, liberties, immunities, and powers held by corporate officers, shareholders, and possibly other individuals.

2 This line of thought was reigning dogma for nearly a millennium, stated and restated by (among many others) Aquinas, Dante, Marsilius, Bodin, Hobbes, and Rousseau all the way to John Austin in the last century. Its most sophisticated statements can be found in Hobbes' Leviathan (Hobbes, 1981), Chapters 14, 26, and 29. Rousseau endorses it in *On the Social Contract*, Book 1, Chapter 6 (Rousseau, 1762). And Kant states it most clearly at TP 8:291:21–33 and 299–300, and at MM 6:320:21–34. For a detailed history of the idea, see Marshall, 1957, Part 1; Benn and Peters, 1959, Chapters 3 and 12; and Hart, 1961.

3 References to Kant's works give either an acronym (see volume bibliography) or an abbreviated title, followed by the volume, page, and line numbers in the Academy Edition of Kant's works.

4 "The consent of the citizens is required to decide whether or not war is to be declared" (PP 8:351:4–6); cp. TP 8:311:19–23; MM 6:345–6.

5 Pogge, 1988, pp. 428 and 430.

6 As, he realized, had been the fate of the similar proposals formulated by St. Pierre and Rousseau (*Idea for a Universal History* 8:24:29; and TP 8:312–13).

7 Kleingeld (2004) offers a detailed account of the debate as well as an able defense of Kant's premise, providing not merely textual support but a philosophical rationale for it as well.

8 It is possible to reply that Kant here uses "ought" in a special sense that involves enforceability. If this is true, then Kant's premise does entail the desired conclusion. But then this conclusion does not show the path to a world state to be blocked: Even if states have no *enforceable* duty to unite into a world state, it may still be the case that they (or rather their various sovereigns) should to do just that, without coercion. Such moral or religious duties, which no one else is authorized to adjudicate or to enforce, are quite consistent with absolute sovereignty as (*pace* Kant – TP 8:303–4). Hobbes well realized under the title of obligations *in foro interno*. Insisting that, *in foro externo*, in the public realm of legal determination, every act of the sovereign must count as right and lawful, Hobbes acknowledges that laws promulgated by the sovereign – though *just* by definition – are not always *good* (Hobbes, 1981, Chapter 30, esp. the twentieth paragraph). See Lloyd, forthcoming, Chapter 1.

9 I disregard the path-related objection suggested in the first sentence, which has already been disposed of: Kant's opposition to a single state overpowering the others does not stand in the way of sovereigns voluntarily (without any coercion) merging their states into one.

10 See, e.g., PP 8:373n. This thought plays an important role in Kant's argument against any citizen right to resist – let alone rebel against – the existing sovereign.

11 One prominent example is John Rawls, who writes: "Here I follow Kant's lead in *Perpetual Peace* (1795) in thinking that a world government – by which I mean a unified political regime with the legal powers normally exercised by central governments – would either be a global despotism or else would rule over a fragile empire torn by frequent civil strife as various regions and peoples tried to gain their political freedom and autonomy" (Rawls, 1999, p. 36). Rawls's appeal to Kant is marred by a faulty translation. What Kant rejects is *not* "the amalgamation of states under one superior power, as this would end in one universal monarchy" (Ibid., note 40), but, in a literal translation, "their amalgamation by means of a power that overgrows the other and develops into a universal monarchy [*die Zusammenschmelzung derselben durch eine die andere überwachsende und in eine Universalmonarchie übergehende Macht*]" (PP 8:367:12–14).

12 In fact, Kant says as much himself: "I trust to a theory which is based upon the principle of Right as determining what the relations between men and States, *ought to be*; and which lays down to these earthly gods [holders of political power] the maxim that they ought so to proceed in their disputes that such a universal International State may be introduced thereby, and to assume it therefore as not only possible in practice but such as may yet be presented in reality" (TP 8:313:7–12).

13 See also PP 8:382–3 and MM 6:318–20. Once again, the argument is not original with Kant, who knew it from Rousseau's account of why the general will, though it is not always enlightened, must always be obeyed (Rousseau, 1762, Book IV, Chapter 2, in conjunction with Book II, Chapter 6). Kant was apparently not fully convinced

by this argument, however. He occasionally suggests that there may be situations in which citizens exceptionally do not have an absolute duty of obedience. There are three passages: "When human beings command anything that in itself is evil (directly opposed to the law of morality) they must not, nor ought they to, be obeyed" (R 6:99n; cp. R 6:154n; *Reflexionen* 19:569, Reflexion 7975). "It is a categorical imperative: Obey the authorities (in all matters not contradicting inner morality) which have power over you" (MM 6:371:21–2). The people "must not resist/disobey except in those cases that fall outside the civic union, e.g., forced worship, coercion to commit unnatural sins: assassination etc." (*Reflexionen* 19:594–5, Reflexion 8051).

14 Such agencies might well grow out of ones that already exist today – the UN General Assembly and Security Council and the International Court of Justice – if their powers became less dependent on national governments which, as things stand now, are free to quit the UN and to exit the jurisdiction of the International Court at their discretion.

15 I present a detailed case for the desirability of such a scheme in Pogge, 2008, Chapter 7.

16 I am much indebted to Andreas Follesdal, Tom Hill, Thomas Mertens, and especially Pauline Kleingeld for instructive comments and criticisms.

Bibliography

Benn, S.I., and Peters, R.S. 1959: *Social Principles and the Democratic State*. London: Allen and Unwin.

Hart, H.L.A. 1961: *The Concept of Law*. Oxford: Oxford University Press.

Hobbes, T. 1981: *Leviathan*. Harmondsworth: Penguin.

Kant, I. 1784: *Idee zu einer allgemeinen Geschichte in weltbürgerlicher Absicht*. Ak 8. Idea for a Universal History from a Cosmopolitan Point of View.

Kant, I. 1925–34: *Reflexionen*, Ak 14–19. Reflections.

Kleingeld, P. 2004: Approaching perpetual peace: Kant's defence of a league of states and his ideal of a world federation. *European Journal of Philosophy* 12, no. 3: 304–25.

Lloyd, S. [Forthcoming]: *Cases in the Law of Nature: The Moral Philosophy of Thomas Hobbes*. Cambridge: Cambridge University Press.

Marshall, G. 1957: *Parliamentary Sovereignty and the Commonwealth*. Oxford: Oxford University Press.

Pogge, T. 1988: Kant's theory of justice. *Kant Studien* 4/79 (Winter): 407–33.

Pogge, T. 2008: *World Poverty and Human Rights: Cosmopolitan Responsibilities and Reforms*, second ed. Cambridge: Polity Press.

Rawls, J. 1999: *The Law of Peoples*. Cambridge, MA: Harvard University Press.

Rousseau, J. 1762: *On the Social Contract*.

Part IV

Virtue: Love, Respect, and Duties to Oneself

10

Beneficence and Other Duties of Love in *The Metaphysics of Morals*

Marcia Baron and Melissa Seymour Fahmy

Important though Kant's *Groundwork of the Metaphysics of Morals* is, the work for which it serves as the groundwork, the *Metaphysics of Morals*, surely deserves at least as much attention as the *Groundwork* itself.[1] "Intending some day to publish a metaphysics of morals, I issue this groundwork in advance," Kant writes in the Preface to *Groundwork* (G 4:391). Mysteriously, Kant's readers often neglect the *Metaphysics of Morals*.

Why it is not nearly as well known as the *Groundwork* is beyond the scope of our essay. Fortunately, it is now beginning to receive its due. We say "fortunately" not only because it is a major work of Kant's and is the culmination of his ethical writings, but also (and relatedly) because most of the widespread myths about Kant's ethics – e.g., that it concerns actions, not character or how to live; that it is all about applying a rule to generate a clear decision about how we should act; that it is rigid, leaving no room for hard cases; that it is not sensitive to the particulars of the situation and to the nuanced character of moral life; that it does not take into account any feature of persons other than their rationality; that the Categorical Imperative not only is not based on anything empirical but is supposed to be applied in such a way as to ignore empirical facts – lose whatever semblance of plausibility they might otherwise have once one reads the *Metaphysics of Morals* (in particular, Part II).

The *Metaphysics of Morals* divides into two parts, the *Rechtslehre*, or *Doctrine of Right* (also translated as "*Metaphysical Principles of Right*"), and the *Tugendlehre*, or *Doctrine of Virtue* (also translated as "*Metaphysical Principles of Virtue*"). Our focus will be on the latter, and specifically on the duties of love. Duties to self and duties of respect for others are discussed in Allen Wood's contribution to this volume.

Duties of love are ethical duties (as opposed to juridical duties) and therefore they do not entail corresponding rights to exercise compulsion (MM 6:382).[2]

Moreover, as "duties of virtue," duties of love have as their objects ends. Indeed, as Kant states it, the duties of virtue *are* the ends: "Only *an end that is also a duty* can be called a duty of virtue" (MM 6:383). Duties of virtue are first and foremost duties to have certain ends and to adopt, correspondingly, certain maxims.

Just what does this mean? First, duties that have as their objects ends are not primarily duties to perform certain kinds of actions. More generally, "Ethics does not give laws for actions . . . but only for maxims of actions" (MM 6:388; see also MM 6:390). Ethics (as opposed to *Jus* – Law or Right) requires us to adopt certain policies or ways of conducting ourselves (maxims of actions), for example, treating others with respect, and developing our natural talents, but it does not give us "laws for actions." Although there are some implications for the permissibility of particular actions – for example, killing oneself is almost always impermissible[3] – it is a mistake to expect Kant's ethics to tell us (and is a mistake to think that it purports to tell us) with respect to every action we might consider performing whether the action is required, permissible, or impermissible. What it tells us is that a particular maxim is, or is not, permissible (or that it is, or is not, required). It thus speaks more to our way of conducting ourselves than to isolated actions. Second, and more positively: Kant's ethics tells us that certain ends are obligatory, and that we must act accordingly. But, as noted above, just what it is to act accordingly is (intentionally) left somewhat open. Some of our duties are narrow (such as, duties of respect for others); others are "wide" (e.g., the duty of beneficence to others), meaning that they allow us greater latitude. Just how much latitude is an issue to which we will turn later.

The Obligatory Ends

The two obligatory ends are one's own perfection and the happiness of others (MM 6:385). Since the focus of this essay is the duties of love, the end of particular interest to us is the happiness of others. Some attention to the other obligatory end is in order, however, because we need to understand the obligatory ends in relation to each other. Of foremost importance is that the obligatory ends of perfection and happiness "cannot be interchanged" (MM 6:385).[4] Others' happiness is an obligatory end for me but my own is not; my own perfection is an obligatory end for me but the perfection of other people is not. The asymmetry is especially prominent in the original German. In response to his question, "What are the ends that are also duties?" (a question that appears as the heading), Kant replies in an uncharacteristically short, simple (and partially rhyming) sentence: "*Sie sind: Eigene Vollkommenheit–fremde Glückseligkeit*" ("They are *one's own perfection* and *the happiness of others*") (MM 6:385).

Kant's explanation of why one's own happiness is not a duty is as follows:

> [One's] *own happiness* is an end that every human being has (by virtue of the impulses of his nature), but this end can never without self-contradiction be regarded as a duty. What everyone already wants unavoidably, of his own accord, does not come under the concept of *duty*. (MM 6:385–6)

He explains why the perfection of others is not an obligatory end for the agent as follows:

> [I]t is a contradiction for me to make another's perfection my end and consider myself under obligation to promote this. For the perfection of another human being, as a person, consists just in this: that he himself is able to set his end in accordance with his own concepts of duty; and it is self-contradictory to require that I do (make it my duty to do) something that only the other himself can do. (MM 6:386; see also MM 6:381)

Anti-paternalism and the Duty of Beneficence

Kant's denial of a duty to perfect others is a reflection of the emphasis he places on self-government: we are to perfect ourselves; others are not to do it for us. Indeed, the end of one's own perfection might more aptly be termed "self-perfection"; this brings out the idea that it is not just a goal to be attained by one means or another, but involves the agent perfecting herself. (The idea in holding that one cannot be perfected by others presumably is not that one could not get some help from one's friends, but that one must initiate the process and take charge. Friends can help but only by helping the agent attain her ends.) We see in his insistence that we have no duty to perfect others – or put differently, in the end being self-perfection rather than perfection – his rejection of moralistic paternalism. While a good parent will employ various tactics in order to shape and direct the conduct and character of a child, to treat an adult in this manner – even from strictly altruistic motives – shows a lack of respect for her as a rational being.

Opposition to paternalism is also evident in Kant's clarification of the duty to promote others' happiness. The duty of beneficence is nicely summarized in the following statement: "To be beneficent, that is, to promote according to one's means the happiness of others in need, without hoping for something in return, is everyone's duty" (MM 6:453). This prompts at least two questions: Happiness understood how? And how narrowly should we understand "in need"? Our focus in this section is on the first question.

Although Kant does not spell out fully just how happiness is to be understood, one thing is clear: happiness is not to be understood paternalistically:

> I cannot do good to anyone in accordance with *my* concepts of happiness (except to young children and the insane), thinking to benefit him by forcing a gift upon him; rather, I can benefit him only in accordance with *his* concepts of happiness. (MM 6:454)

In seeking to promote others' happiness – the happiness of (sane) adults, that is – we are not to impose on them our conception of what their happiness consists in. "It is for them to decide what they count as belonging to their happiness." (MM 6:388)[5]

So far, this sounds straightforward and unequivocal. But in fact the story is somewhat complicated. Kant immediately adds this qualification:

> [I]t is open to me to refuse them many things that they think will make them happy but that I do not, as long as they have no right to demand them from me as what is theirs. (MM 6:388)

He also urges a different, and more moralistic, sort of caution; he mentions that the "happiness of others also includes their moral well-being . . . and we have a duty, but only a negative one, to promote this." To this end,

> it is my duty to refrain from doing anything that, considering the nature of a human being, could tempt him to do something for which his conscience could afterwards pain him. (MM 6:394)

A related qualification is that we are not to promote any impermissible ends. "The duty of love for one's neighbor can . . . also be expressed as the duty to make others' ends my own (provided only that these are not immoral)" (MM 6:450). (See also MM 6:388 and, for a slightly different qualification, MM 6:480–1.)

These qualifications notwithstanding, the starting point for understanding what it is to promote another's happiness is to conceive of it as constituted by those ends that the person in question regards as constituting it. The point of beneficence is thus decidedly not to try to improve others by promoting what we think they should – but at present do not – have as their ends. We may choose which of their ends to promote by taking into account which ones *we* think will make them happy (though Kant does not say that we have a duty to choose in this way).

A quotation three paragraphs above has a parenthetical qualifier that needs to be borne in mind: "I cannot do good to anyone in accordance with *my* concepts of happiness (except to young children and the insane)" (MM 6:454). On Kant's account of beneficence, paternalism towards the (severely) mentally ill and towards (young) children often is permissible. An important way of promoting the happiness of children is to help them be able as adults to set ends for themselves and promote their ends. To that end, we may need to further their (future) happiness by promoting for them ends (such as to be able to have a satisfying career) that they may not at present endorse.[6]

Beneficence: The Finer Points

Kant's discussion of beneficence offers some additional indications of how we are to go about promoting others' happiness. The discussion is noteworthy for its sensitivity to the many ways in which kindhearted intentions to benefit another may fail to benefit her, as well as ways in which desires to aid may be tainted by superciliousness, wishes to feel superior to another, or wishes to put another in one's debt. The following passage is one of many that reflect such sensitivity (sensitivity that belies those textbook depictions of Kant's ethics as concerned just with mechanically applying a principle, as contrasted with Aristotle's ethics, so rich with attention to the particulars). Kant writes:

> Someone who is rich (has abundant means for the happiness of others, i.e., means in excess of his own needs) should hardly even regard beneficence as a meritorious duty on his part, even though he also puts others under obligation by it. The satisfaction he derives from his beneficence, which costs him no sacrifice, is a way of reveling in moral feelings. He must also carefully avoid any appearance of intending to bind the other by it; for if he showed that he wanted to put the other under an obligation (which always humbles the other in his own eyes), it would not be a true benefit that he rendered him. Instead, he must show that he is himself put under obligation by the other's acceptance or honored by it, hence that the duty is merely something that he owes, unless (as is better) he can practice his beneficence in complete secrecy. (MM 6:453)

This passage brings to mind the Aristotelian idea that acting well involves not just doing a virtuous action, but doing it in the right way, and with the right tone and gesture. It is not enough that we render aid; we need to do it well. Depending on the nature of the aid, we may do more harm than good if we humiliate the person we are (supposedly) trying to aid. (See Baron, 2001, pp. 608–12.)

Kant also suggests that beneficence on the part of the rich towards the poor may not even deserve to be called beneficence at all, since the uneven distribution of wealth is "for the most part" due to social and political injustice.

> Having the resources to practice such beneficence as depends on the goods of fortune is, for the most part, a result of certain human beings being favored through the injustice of the government, which introduces an inequality of wealth that makes others need their beneficence. Under such circumstances, does a rich man's help to the needy, on which he so readily prides himself as something meritorious, really deserve to be called beneficence at all? (MM 6:454)

We can see that in promoting others' happiness we need (a) to avoid being paternalistic, (b) to avoid leaving those we aid with a sense of being beholden or inferior to us, and (c) to bear in mind (particularly if we are wealthy, and are giving to the needy) that what we think of as beneficence may really be a case of giving them something they are owed. After all, as the saying goes, "There, but for fortune, go you, or I" . . . or more aptly for our purposes, "There, but for injustice that happens to benefit me, go I." The hint seems to be that much of what the affluent do for those who are not affluent should be viewed by the "benefactors" as a matter of justice, not as a matter of beneficence. (As we'll see later, Kant does not recommend that the *recipients* so view it.)

In addition, (d) thanks to the duty to perfect ourselves, it would not be permissible for us to judge that we cannot really do much to help others because we are impatient, insensitive, self-centered, arrogant, or lazy. It might be tempting to think, "Well, beyond giving some money to charity, I can't really be of any help"; but regarding one's character as fixed, beyond our capacity to improve, would be at odds with the duty to perfect ourselves morally.[7]

Although this tells us something about the duty of beneficence, it leaves some questions unanswered, or only partially answered. We can see that (with some qualifications) we are to promote others' happiness as they see it, rather than superimpose our conception of happiness – and what we think they should regard as their happiness – on theirs; but questions remain about just how Kant understands beneficence. Let's return to a statement that we quoted earlier: "To be beneficent, that is, to promote according to one's means the happiness of others in need, without hoping for something in return, is everyone's duty" (MM 6:453). What is the import of "in need"? Is the idea that the duty of beneficence is simply a duty to meet fundamental needs? Or is the duty broader than that, namely, to help another even when help is desired but not desperately needed, and is desired for aims that are expendable?

It may be tempting to read "in need" as restricting the scope of the duty, as if Kant holds that our duty to promote the happiness of others entails helping only when they are very much "in need" of our help (and perhaps also when the need is for something vital, not something expendable). But that reading is not supported by the various passages that explain the duty. The following sentence could, if read in isolation from the context, be regarded as supporting the narrow reading, according to which the duty of beneficence is only a duty to help those in distress:

> But beyond *benevolence* in our wishes for others (which costs us nothing) how can it be required as a duty that this should also be practical, that is, that everyone who has the means to do so should be *beneficent* to those in need? (MM 6:452; see also MM 6:453)[8]

The very next sentence discloses, however, that "in need" in the previous sentence should be understood more loosely, and the duty thus understood more broadly:

> [B]eneficence is the maxim of making others' happiness one's end, and the duty to it consists in the subject's being constrained by his reason to adopt this maxim as a universal law.

It is noteworthy that there is no qualification here, nothing to suggest that the duty of beneficence is a duty only to adopt the maxim of helping when the person is in distress (or in dire need). Equally important is the fact that Kant often speaks of the duty of beneficence as a duty to make others' ends one's own, a phrasing that strongly suggests that the duty of beneficence should be understood broadly. (See, e.g., MM 6:388 and MM 6:450, both quoted above.)

It is best, therefore, not to take "in need" as restricting the scope of the duty, and to understand "need" in the passages cited above as covering not only dire need or basic aid, but also need of assistance with personal projects – assistance with pursuing ends one has set for oneself. That Kant is likely to have had in mind assistance with personal projects is also supported by the fact that happiness is, on his view, highly subjective (entirely different from the conception of *eudaimonia* in ancient ethics).

Exactly what Kant thinks happiness consists in is, admittedly, obscure. He sometimes defines happiness as the satisfaction of one's inclinations (G 4:405; CPrR 5:73) yet at other times speaks of it as "satisfaction with one's state, so long as it is assured of lasting" (MM 6:387). What is clear, however, is that he means by "happiness" the happiness of a particular individual, and that it reflects an agent's particular preferences and choices of ends, including professional aspirations, personal commitments, as well as recreational interests. These personal ends are expressions of the agent's capacity to freely set ends, though due to the limitation of human agency, achieving most of these ends will require some form of assistance from others. Kant's decision to frame the duty of beneficence in terms of the *happiness* of others is a clear indication that he intended the duty to extend to assistance in achieving these ends.

The Question of Latitude

An additional question that needs to be addressed is just how much latitude the duty of beneficence entails. As noted earlier, the duty of beneficence is "wide" or "broad," leaving agents more latitude than is afforded them by perfect or juridical duties. Just how much latitude the duty permits, however, is unclear. It is very common to look to the *Groundwork* for an answer to this question, given the close connection between a duty's breadth and its status as perfect or imperfect. In the *Groundwork* Kant distinguishes perfect from imperfect duties, classifying the duty of beneficence and the duty to develop one's talents as imperfect, and explaining the distinction as follows: "I understand here by a perfect duty one that admits no exception in favor of inclination" (G 4:422n). This suggests that imperfect duties *do* admit exceptions in favor of inclination, though Kant does not state this explicitly. What Kant does state explicitly is that his method for distinguishing types of duties in the *Groundwork* is merely provisional, and will be taken up with more care in a future *Metaphysics of Morals*. Although some scholars have read the *Metaphysics of Morals* with the expectation that the *Groundwork* statement of the distinction would be likely to carry over into the later work, we prefer not to do so, for two reasons. First, Kant says that he reserves the division of duties entirely for that future work, and draws the distinction between perfect and imperfect duties in the *Groundwork* only "for the sake of arranging my examples." Second, the natural way of reading G 4:422n is at odds with the example of beneficence as it is developed at G 4:430. There the duty is explained as requiring that everyone try, "as far as he can, to further the ends of others." Given the tension between saying that one is to try as far as he can to further the ends of others and implying that perfect duties differ from imperfect duties in admitting no exceptions in favor of inclinations, it seems wise to take Kant at his word when he says that he is adopting the division only for the sake of arranging his examples and will work it out later. We opt therefore to ignore all remarks in the *Groundwork* regarding how to differentiate imperfect from perfect duties as we address the question of how much latitude the duty of beneficence allows.

Returning, then, to the *Metaphysics of Morals*, let us examine the following passage:

> [I]f the law can prescribe only the maxim of actions themselves, this is a sign that it leaves a playroom (*latitudo*) for free choice in following (complying with) the law, that is, that the law cannot specify precisely in what way one is to act and how much one is to do by the action for an end that is also a duty. (MM 6:390)

In this passage Kant identifies two kinds of latitude, the latter of which is unique to duties of virtue. First, because the law *cannot specify precisely in what way one is to act*, much is left to the discretion of the agent; she must decide *how* she will promote the obligatory end. Certain restrictions naturally apply; for instance, one cannot violate a perfect or narrow duty for the sake of a wide duty. I cannot treat others as mere means in order to perfect my talents, or even to promote their happiness. Maxims of actions, Kant tells us, must "qualify for giving universal law" (MM 6:389). They must be universalizable: I must be able to will, consistently with having and acting on my maxim, that others act on the same maxim (see Korsgaard, 1996, ch. 3). But even when we acknowledge these restrictions, we may still find that agents enjoy a significant degree of latitude with respect to *how* they go about promoting an end that is also a duty.

Kant also stipulates that the law cannot specify precisely *how much* one is to do for an end that is also a duty. This is a second kind of latitude, and on one natural reading, the presence of this kind of latitude rules out the possibility that we could be required to do *as much as possible* to promote obligatory ends. It should be noted that the passage can be read differently: if emphasis is placed on the word "precisely", it is not clear that that possibility is ruled out. One might argue that Kant is saying that the law can indicate how much one is to do and how one is to act, but cannot specify this with precision. This reading would be consistent with an interpretation according to which the latitude is very restricted.

However, it does seem that the duty of beneficence allows considerable latitude – indeed, considerable latitude of both types just described, though we focus on the second type of latitude. The evidence for this comes from such passages as the following, together with what Kant does not say.

> I ought to sacrifice a part of my welfare to others without hope of return, because this is a duty, and it is impossible to assign determinate limits to the extent of this sacrifice. How far it should extend depends, in large part, on what each person's true needs are in view of his sensibilities, and it must be left to each to decide this for himself. For, a maxim of promoting others' happiness at the sacrifice of one's own happiness, one's true needs, would conflict with itself if it were made a universal law. Hence this duty is only a *wide* one; the duty has in it a latitude for doing

more or doing less, and no specific limits can be assigned to what should be done. (MM 6:393)

This passage does not decisively rule out the possibility that Kant thinks that we must do all we can to help others; after all, he could hold that we cannot assign determinate limits to the extent of this sacrifice because it depends on the agent's needs, but that everyone has a duty to do all that they can (constrained only by lack of resources or by their own true needs) to promote others' happiness. But this reading is implausible (though not as clearly ruled out as a reading that holds that we are to optimize – that we must always pursue the course of action that will maximize happiness). For one thing, Kant says (at the end of the passage quoted above) that the duty "has in it a latitude for doing more or doing less," and this is hard to interpret as meaning only that how much the agent is morally required to do depends on his or her needs (and resources). The natural reading is surely that we do not have to do as much as we possibly can. Furthermore, if we thought Kant's view was that we have to do as much as we possibly can, we would expect him to say so, yet he does not.

By contrast, Kant does speak in stronger terms of the duty to increase one's moral perfection. The law requires that one "*strive with all of one's might* that the thought of duty for its own sake is the sufficient incentive of every action conforming to duty" (MM 6: 393; emphasis ours). Kant's claim that we must strive *with all of our might* to bring it about that the thought of duty is always a sufficient incentive suggests that with respect to the duty of moral self-perfection we are required to do as much as we can to further this end. The fact that he does not speak similarly in the *Metaphysics of Morals* of the duty to promote others' happiness or the duty to develop our natural talents suggests that he considers these duties to allow more latitude than does the duty to perfect oneself morally. Moreover, he describes the duty to increase one's moral perfection as *narrow* with regard to its object (perfection), but *wide* with respect to its subject (MM 6:446); yet he makes no such distinction with respect to the duties of beneficence or developing one's talents.

It seems, then, that Kant is allowing for a fair amount of latitude in the duty of beneficence and the duty to develop one's talents. There are of course still constraints; I cannot really be said to have embraced the end of others' happiness if I only help when it is very easy, or when I feel confident that helping will ultimately promote my own interests. But it is reasonably clear that his position is not that we have to help others as much as possible, or develop our talents as much as possible.

The question remains, though, of what sorts of reasons for not helping are acceptable. A passage in the *Metaphysics of Morals* suggests that the acceptable reasons are quite limited. But the passage is obscure, and interpreters differ on just how it should be read. In the course of describing the latitude inherent in wide duties of virtue, Kant cautions:

But a wide duty is not to be taken as permission to make exceptions to the maxim of actions but only as permission to limit one maxim of duty by another (e.g., love of one's neighbor in general by love of one's parents), by which in fact the field for the practice of virtue is widened. (MM 6:390)

This passage invites what is often called a "rigorist" or "rigoristic" interpretation of the latitude permitted by wide duties of virtue, such as beneficence. According to the rigorist interpretation, one may permissibly decline to perform an act that promotes an obligatory end only for the sake of performing another action that is also commended (or required) by a maxim of duty. For instance, as Kant's example suggests, one may decline to contribute to a particular charitable organization in order to be able to properly care for one's aging parents. In this sense, one limits the maxim of promoting the happiness of others in general by the maxim of caring for one's parents. Alternatively, one may decline an opportunity to promote the happiness of others for the sake of pursuing some activity that will allow her to further develop some talent. These alternative activities need not be comparable in any significant sense, and to legitimately forego doing an action commended by a (wide) duty of virtue, it is not necessary that one do at least as much as one would have done by that action to promote others' happiness or to develop one's talents.

It is important to be clear on what the rigorist interpretation does not entail. Like its non-rigorist counterpart, the rigorist interpretation does not entail a requirement to maximally promote either others' happiness or one's own perfection (nor does it entail a requirement that one maximally promote the two ends, taken together).[9] Agents remain free to promote these ends as they see fit and as they prefer. Still, it is impermissible on the rigorist interpretation to decline to perform an action that promotes an obligatory end for any reason other than to perform another action that falls under a maxim of duty.

Many of Kant's commentators have found the rigorist interpretation excessively restrictive and moralistic, and, thinking it uncharitable to attribute it to Kant, some have proposed an alternative reading of Kant's statement that "a wide duty is not to be taken as permission to make exceptions to the maxim of actions but only as permission to limit one maxim of duty by another." It has been suggested, for instance, that "the 'exceptions' may mean a relinquishing of the maxims of promoting obligatory ends, rather than a mere refusal to act, here and now, in pursuit of such an end" (Gregor, 1963, p. 105; see also Hill, 1992, p. 152). Kant's admonition would then amount to saying that we may not give up the maxim to promote the happiness of other human beings generally, even when a special obligation to our parents overshadows the more general requirement.

This alternative reading is not very plausible. Kant's stipulation that "a wide duty is not to be taken as permission to make exceptions to the maxim of actions" is given by way of explaining and qualifying what he means by saying that duties of virtue leave a "playroom (*latitudo*) for free choice in following (complying with) the law" (MM 6:390). Thus Kant has already indicated that the latitude permitted by wide duties applies to how one goes about applying the maxims of action prescribed by duty once these maxims have been adopted. Furthermore, it is more natural to read the term "exceptions" (*Ausnahme*) as indicating merely provisional deviations from a rule that remains in existence rather than a wholesale abandonment of the maxim.

But perhaps there is a more plausible reading of Kant's warning that "a wide duty is not to be taken as permission to make exceptions to the maxim of actions" that also resists the rigorist interpretation. Kant may be intending to caution his readers against thinking that latitude in adopting different instantiations of the maxim of beneficence goes further than it does. On this reading, Kant is saying that although we may limit somewhat our aid to strangers if we are taking care of our elderly parents, we are permitted only to limit it somewhat, not to confine our beneficence entirely to just a few people. Thus we may limit our maxim of beneficence towards people we do not know by our maxim of beneficence towards our parents, but we may not excuse ourselves altogether from aiding those not closely related to us. Permission to limit one maxim of duty by another ought not be confused with permission to limit ourselves entirely to one or two particular instantiations of the obligatory end (particularly when the end in question is others' happiness).

While this interpretation is certainly plausible,[10] it depends on viewing "love of one's neighbor" and "love of one's parents" as different instantiations of the same duty of beneficence. However, if we consider the possibility that we may have special (narrow) obligations and responsibilities to particular persons (obligations which are owed) it may be more natural to read "love of one's neighbor" and "love of one's parents" as indicating two distinct duties. If this is the case, then it will be much more difficult to read "exception" as referring to a particular instantiation of the duty of beneficence.

It should also be noted that the rigorist interpretation can be understood in more than one way, and the motivation for avoiding it may rely on assumptions that it has to be more extreme than in fact is necessary. The rigorist interpretation claims that the only legitimate reason for declining to perform an action that promotes an obligatory end is to perform another action that falls under a maxim of duty. This is usually taken to mean perfect duties and wide duties, but another possibility is to include *indirect* duties as well, and in particular the duty to promote one's own happiness (G 4:399; MM 6:388). Exactly when indirect duties could weigh in would have to be worked out; the matter is complex, because if promoting one's happiness even in a minute way were allowed to be a reason for foregoing to help another, the rigorism of the rigorist interpretation would disappear altogether. We will not try to work out the details of such a revised rigorism here. But assuming that a rigorist interpretation that recognizes indirect duties is possible, it could allow that while we may not omit to perform an action that falls under a principle of wide duty just because we generally have been "doing our share" and simply do not feel like performing the action now, we may omit to do so for reasons having to do with our own happiness, if the effect on our happiness is weighty. A rigorist interpretation that includes indirect duties in the scope of acceptable reasons for declining to promote an obligatory end will thus limit an agent's freedom to pursue her own happiness less severely and better reflect Kant's views on the value of personal happiness (see Seymour, 2007).

Even if upon reflection we decide that such reasons in fact are not adequate, on the rigorist interpretation, for declining to perform an act that falls under a principle of wide duty, the rigorist interpretation may still be less restrictive than is often assumed. It needs to be borne in mind that there will likely be considerable overlap between activities that promote obligatory ends and activities that promote an agent's happiness. Clearly, these categories are not mutually exclusive. Organizing a group of friends to participate in a race that benefits cancer research will promote one's own perfection, the happiness of others, and most likely one's own happiness as well. Many other activities that we consider pleasurable will also promote obligatory ends, such as reading or engaging in conversation with friends.[11] Acting on a maxim of duty need not entail foregoing one's own happiness. Consequently, while the rigorist interpretation may restrict an agent's freedom to pursue her own happiness, it may turn out that this restriction is only slightly greater than what we would find given a non-rigorist interpretation.

The rigorist interpretation may still strike some as undesirably moralistic insofar as it seems to moralize all of life, treating our happiness as valuable largely insofar as happy people are, *caeteris paribus*, more able to resist temptations to act immorally than are unhappy people, and asking us to justify our use of our time and energy entirely in moral terms. We do not have the space here to address that objection beyond pointing out that because "moral" is used quite broadly in Kantian ethics, the "moralization" is not as leaden as it might seem.

That said, we also want to acknowledge that the rigorist interpretation is by no means the only plausible reading. Those who find it unpalatable can take comfort in the fact that the passage at MM 6:390 from which the rigorist interpretation is derived is undeniably obscure, leaving room for challenging the rigorist account of wide duties. (See Hill, 2002, ch. 7.)

Latitude and (Im)partiality

A further question about latitude deserves mention. So far we have discussed latitude mainly in connection with how hard we should have to work, or how much personal sacrifice we should be willing to make, to promote others' happiness. We have seen that although it is clear that Kant does not hold that we have a duty to do as much as we can to promote others' happiness, it is less clear what sorts of reasons are permissible reasons for omitting, in a particular instance, to help another. Related to this is the question of what reasons are permissible for opting to help one person rather than another. It is occasionally assumed (hopefully exclusively by those who know Kant's writings only slightly, or only secondhand) that Kant holds that we must choose impartially among the possible recipients of our beneficence. There is no evidence for this position. Indeed, Kant makes it plain that the idea is not to be equally beneficent to everyone. "I can, without violating the universality of the maxim, vary the degree greatly in accordance with the different objects of my love" (MM 6:452).

Those looking for explicit indications from Kant as to how much one must do for strangers compared to how much one should do for acquaintances, and how much for those one loves, will be disappointed. In general, Kant offers little by way of guidelines for deciding whom to help and how. We take it that this is not an oversight, but simply something on which he does not believe that people need him, or other ethicists, to provide advice or direction. It is clear from his discussion of beneficence, together with his more general discussion of obligatory ends, that we are to exercise good deliberative judgment in our promotion of the obligatory ends. Thus, rather than randomly selecting beneficiaries, we ought to consider thoughtfully the needs of others, our own capabilities, and the impact our beneficence will have on the recipient's well-being.[12]

Attention to such details may have the effect of encouraging somewhat more aid to those to whom we are close than to strangers, depending on the nature of the aid. It will not entail that aid should always be only to those near and dear to us. (Indeed, since it is much easier today than it was in Kant's time to render aid to people who live thousands of miles from us, there is less of a basis now for the view that beneficence should be exclusively or primarily to those close to us.) (See Herman, 2002.)

Beyond these points, we can summarize what Kant's ethics tells us regarding whom to aid – and more specifically, whether we may favor those close to us simply because of the personal tie (rather than because of the impact our beneficence will have, and similar considerations) – as follows. It is clear that the happiness of persons in general makes a claim on us, and so it would be wrong to neglect altogether to help everyone other than our close friends. At the same time, it is permissible, as he says in MM 6:452, to vary greatly the degree of our aid depending on the closeness of the tie we have to the person in question. In addition, as Allen Wood notes in his contribution to this collection, we do have special duties to others, including duties of friendship. Thus in addition to duties to aid people in general, we have (depending on their content) more stringent duties to help those who stand in particular relationships to us. (Of course the stringency may vary depending on the nature of the relationship and on the needs of each party. We have more stringent duties to care for our children than to promote the happiness of our able-bodied, adult siblings.) That Kant offers no further guidelines is not, in our view, a shortcoming; it is part of Kantian ethics that the moral agent is not following a set of rules that tell one precisely how to act, but rather, must think for herself, working out reflectively how to live.[13]

Gratitude

As we noted above, the rich man is supposed, in aiding the poor, to avoid giving the recipient the feeling that he wants to put her under an obligation. Nonetheless, recipients have a duty of gratitude to their benefactors. This duty is given some salience inasmuch as Kant differentiates duties of love from duties of respect as follows: duties of love put others under obligation (specifically, an obligation of gratitude), while duties of respect do not. Performing the first, Kant says, "is *meritorious* (in relation to others)"; while "performing the second is fulfilling a duty *that is owed*" (MM 6:448).

Gratitude is one of three duties of love, the others being beneficence and sympathy (MM 6:452).[14] It is a "sacred duty . . . the violation of which (as a scandalous example) can destroy the moral incentive to beneficence in its very principle" (MM 6:455). Its sacredness consists in this: "the obligation with regard to it cannot be discharged completely by any act in keeping with it (so that one who is under obligation always remains under obligation)." The idea is not to perform some action that will discharge one's debt, or "even things out"; gratitude consists in "*honoring* a person because of a benefit he has rendered us." It has both an attitudinal and an actional component: one is to be appreciative and to express that appreciativeness. (An additional actional component, implicit in the attitudinal component, is that one is to cultivate appreciativeness in oneself.) The appreciativeness extends not only to people we know, or other contemporaries who have benefited us, but also to our predecessors, "even to those one cannot identify with certainty." Thus it is wrong to treat the ancients with disdain, though Kant adds that:

> [I]t is a foolish mistake to attribute preeminence in talents and good will to the ancients in preference to the moderns just because of their antiquity, as if the world were steadily declining. (MM 6:455)

Gratitude involves

> not regarding a kindness received as a burden one would gladly be rid of . . . but taking even the occasion for gratitude as a moral kindness, that is, as an opportunity given one to unite the virtue of gratitude with love of man, to combine the *cordiality* [*Innigkeit*] of a benevolent disposition with *sensitivity* [*Zärtlichkeit*][15] to benevolence . . . and so to cultivate one's love of human beings. (MM 6:456)

Sympathy

One of the most intriguing discussions in the *Doctrine of Virtue* is the section entitled "Sympathetic feeling is generally a duty."[16] Kant already explained (MM 6:399) that there are certain moral endowments that are "natural predispositions of the mind" for being "affected by concepts of duty, antecedent predispositions on the side of *feeling*." It is by virtue of these that we "can be put under obligation." Among these moral endowments is "love of one's neighbor" (*die Liebe des Nächsten*) (MM 6:399) or "love of human beings" (*Menschenliebe*) (MM 6:401). The idea that we are endowed with morally vital feelings, or receptivity to feeling, comes up again in "Sympathetic Feeling is Generally a Duty," where Kant says that nature "has implanted in human beings receptivity" to sympathetic joy and sadness, and that we have a duty to use this receptivity "as means to promoting active and rational benevolence" (MM 6:457). We have a duty to cultivate our compassionate feelings, and this involves putting ourselves in situations that will elicit them. It is "a duty not to avoid the places where the poor who lack the most basic necessities are to be found but rather to seek them out, and not to shun sickrooms or debtors' prisons and so forth in order to avoid sharing painful feelings one may not be able to resist" (MM 6:457). But although we should not harden ourselves against such feelings or avoid situations that are likely to elicit them, the idea is not simply to let the feelings wash over us. We are to cultivate them, not just let them happen. We are to moderate them and utilize them properly, preventing them from overwhelming us without endeavoring to extinguish them. We need to keep them in check lest they become passions or, more likely, affects [emotions] so intense that they eclipse reason. (In *Anthropology* Kant explains the difference between affects and passions: "In an affect we are taken unawares by feeling, so that the mind's . . . self-control is suspended. So an affect is rash: . . . it rises swiftly to a degree of feeling that makes reflection impossible." Passion works more slowly but roots itself more deeply and tenaciously. "We should think of an affect as a drunken fit that we sleep off: of a passion, as a madness that broods over an idea which settles in ever more deeply" (A 7:253).)

Exactly to what purpose, or how, we are to utilize these feelings is not clear. Kant says, just after the quote above from MM 6:457, "For this is still one of the impulses that nature has implanted in us to do what the representation of duty alone might not accomplish."[17] This is a little surprising, given his emphasis throughout his ethical writings on our ability to act from duty alone, and his claim that we should not look for other incentives to sweeten the task of doing our duty; we should rather "adopt the law *alone* as [our] *sufficient* incentive" (R 6:30). If duty alone is a sufficient incentive, and if it is "impure" to try to mix other incentives with duty, why is Kant encouraging us to utilize our sympathetic feelings "to do what the representation of duty alone might not accomplish"? It is beyond the scope of this essay to answer this question, a question that parallels the question of what motivational role a belief in God and an afterlife can legitimately play for the Kantian agent. One possible explanation, in each case, is this: even though duty should be a sufficient motive, the counterweights stemming from inclinations that are contrary to duty are such that many agents will find it hard to resist them unless they have cultivated their sympathetic feelings or believe that virtue is eventually rewarded (or better yet, both). (For doubts about this explanation, see Baron, 1995, ch. 7.) In addition (though Kant does not mention this), our sympathetic joy and sadness will attune us to what is going on with others, so that we will be engaged, noticing ways in which we can contribute positively to their lives. Relatedly, as our sympathetic impulses are cultivated, we become more sensitive to the needs of others and to ways in which we might help, and more broadly, we are better able to understand others, and, indeed, human nature (in particular, human joys and human pains, in their manifold diversity).

While it is not as clear as one would like exactly why Kant thinks that sympathetic feelings should be cultivated, it is clear is that he thinks they should be. And it is clear that at the heart of what we are to do is to get them under our control so that they aid us morally rather than, say, paralyze us or disable us from helping others (as when someone is so upset about a friend's loss that she avoids her friend so as to lessen her own pain).

Nonetheless, one might wonder if Kant does justice to the value of sympathy, for while clearly it is important to keep it in check, there also seems to be value in the sympathetic feelings beyond their usefulness "as a means to promoting active and rational benevolence." There seems to be something missing in someone who lacks such feelings, or has them only slightly . . . and perhaps there is even something missing in someone who is as able to shut off such feelings as Kant seems to favor. On this there is certainly room for debate. (See Baron, 1995; for a defense of Kant, replying to Baron, see Denis, 2000. See also Sherman, 1997.)

Conclusion

In this essay we have examined the three duties of love that Kant enumerates in the *Metaphysics of Morals*. First and foremost is the duty of beneficence – our duty to make the happiness of others our end and to promote this end accordingly. We have emphasized the importance of Kant's stipulation that we must promote the happiness of others *as they understand it* (with some qualification) and have noted some other constraints on how we are to aid; in addition, we argued that the duty of beneficence is not reducible to a duty to aid only those in desperate need, but rather should be understood more broadly to include assisting others with personal projects and endeavors. We then turned our attention to a thorny interpretive issue: just how much latitude does the wide duty of beneficence permit, and how much are we expected to sacrifice for the happiness of others? Finally, we have explored the less prominent duties of love, gratitude, and sympathy, and the role they play in Kant's ethical theory. These duties reveal Kant's (often overlooked) interest in the cultivation of dispositions, attitudes, and even feelings, and show that it is a mistake to hold that Kant considered rationality to be the *only* morally important feature of persons. While duties of love may be less fundamental than duties of respect, it is clear that Kant considered duties of love to be a vital component of a moral life.[18]

Notes

1 This is emphasized in Wood, 2002.
2 This bears emphasis, because in twentieth century ethics we often find it asserted that it is part of the concept of a duty that it entails a corresponding right to compel one to act accordingly. See, e.g., Urmson, 1969. That Kant denies this, holding that juridical duties entail such a right but ethical duties do not, underscores the difference between his concept of duty and that of many contemporary or recent ethicists. For further discussion, see Baron, 1995, chs. 2–3.
3 Possible exceptions include killing oneself to prevent oneself from harming others after having been bitten by a rabid dog, knowing that there is no cure and that one is already

beginning to go mad; and a leader's using a fast-acting poison to take his own life after being captured by the enemy, so that he cannot be forced to agree to "conditions of ransom harmful to his state" (MM 6:423–4).

4   Also of importance is something we note below: the duty to perfect oneself removes what might otherwise be acceptable excuses for not aiding others in various ways, e.g., "I'm not a good listener; I'm no good at comforting the bereaved; I don't have the patience for children/sick people/tedious tasks."

5   See also MM 6:454.

6   For discussion of paternalism and children in connection with Kantian ethics, see Shapiro, 1999.

7   It is true that in spelling out the content of the duty to perfect ourselves morally, Kant stresses the duty to "strive with all one's might that the thought of duty for its own sake is the sufficient incentive of every action conforming to duty" (MM 6:393), and one might for that reason think that self-perfection, on his view, has nothing to do with being patient, sensitive, and so on. Nonetheless, his detailed discussion of various virtues and vices makes it clear that we are to strive to be more virtuous and less vicious in these respects, as well. The duty to cultivate certain impulses likewise reflects a general duty to cultivate our characters, and in this way, too, to perfect ourselves morally.

8   It is worth noting that the term that Gregor translates here as "in need" is "*Bedürtifigen*" ("*Bedürtifige*" in the nominative), whereas the term in the passage from 454 that we cited earlier and that she also translates as "in need" is "*in Nöten*." We thank Dieter Schönecker for bringing this to our attention. The difference between the German terms is that "*Bedürtifige*" refers to those in need in virtue of poverty, whereas "*in Nöten*" applies to a wider range of neediness. We do not think this is a serious translation flaw, however, because although the terms have different meanings, Kant appears, judging from his argument at 453, to regard the differences as insignificant for his purposes. He uses "*in Not*" in his premises and "*Bedürtifige*" in his conclusion.

9   Some commentators understand the rigorist interpretation as entailing a requirement to do as much as possible toward an obligatory end. (See Gregor, 1963, p. 107.) We think it is important to distinguish these logically separable claims – that one may permissibly decline to perform an action that promotes an obligatory end only for the sake of performing another action that is also commended (or required) by a maxim of duty, and that one must do as much as possible towards an obligatory end (or to the two ends taken together). On our view, rigorism entails only the former claim.

10 And endorsed by one of us: Baron.

11 It is relevant here that Kant holds that "human beings have a duty of friendship" (MM 6:469).

12 Recall his attention to how beneficence can humiliate. No doubt the issues that we are to take into account in thinking about *how* to aid are among those that we should take into account in thinking about *whom* to aid.

13 In "What is Enlightenment?" Kant emphasizes how tempting it is not to think for oneself: "If I have a book that understands for me, a spiritual advisor who has a conscience for me, a doctor who decides upon a regimen for me, and so forth, I need not trouble myself at all." Enlightenment, Kant says, is the emergence from a self-incurred inability to think for oneself (8:35).

14 The term that Gregor translates as "sympathy" is "*Teilnehmung*," perhaps better translated as "participation." See Fahmy, "Active Sympathetic Participation: Reconsidering Kant's Duty of Sympathy."

15 "*Zärtlichkeit*" could also be translated as "tenderness" or "affection"; indeed, it is a stretch to translate it as "sensitivity."

16 This is Gregor's translation of "*Teilnehmende Empfindung ist überhaupt Pflicht.*" See note 12 above.

17 A note on translations is in order here. The previous editions of Gregor's translation of the *Tugendlehre* translate "*würden*" as "would" rather than "might." Native speakers of German whom we have consulted confirm our hunch that "might," though not ruled out, is a bit of a stretch, though it does make the passage a little less puzzling than it is if "*würden*" is read as "would."

18 We are grateful to Dieter Schönecker and Thomas E. Hill., Jr., for their helpful comments on an earlier draft of our paper, to Elizabeth Tropman for her editorial assistance, and to Georg Theiner for his help with some translation questions. In addition, Melissa wishes to thank the Dolores Zohrab Liebmann Foundation for fellowship support, and Marcia wishes to thank Dartmouth College for providing a supportive environment in which to work on this paper June–July, 2005.

Bibliography

Baron, M. 1995: *Kantian Ethics Almost without Apology*. Ithaca: Cornell University Press.

Baron, M. 2001: The moral significance of how things seem. *Maryland Law Review* 60: 607–41.

Denis, L. 2000: Kant's cold sage and the sublimity of apathy. *Kantian Review* 4: 48–73.

Fahmy, M. S. 2009: Active sympathetic participation: Reconsidering Kant's duty of sympathy. *Kantian Review* (forthcoming).

Gregor, M. 1963: *Laws of Freedom: A Study of Kant's Method of Applying the Categorical Imperative in the* Metaphysik der Sitten. New York: Barnes & Noble.

Herman, B. 1993: *The Practice of Moral Judgment*. Cambridge, MA: Harvard University Press.

Herman, B. 2002: The scope of moral requirement. *Philosophy and Public Affairs* 30: 227–56.

Hill, T. E., Jr. 1992: *Dignity and Practical Reason in Kant's Moral Theory*. Ithaca: Cornell University Press.

Hill, T. E., Jr. 2002: *Human Welfare and Moral Worth: Kantian Perspectives*. Oxford: Clarendon Press.

Korsgaard, C. 1996: *Creating the Kingdom of Ends*. Cambridge: Cambridge University Press.

Seymour (Fahmy), M. 2007: Duties of love and Kant's doctrine of obligatory ends. Ph.D. diss., Indiana University.

Shapiro, T. 1999: What is a child? *Ethics* 109 (July): 715–38.

Sherman, N. 1997: *Making a Necessity of Virtue: Aristotle and Kant on Virtue*. Cambridge: Cambridge University Press.

Urmson, J. O. 1969: Saints and heroes. In J. Feinberg (ed.), *Moral Concepts*, 60–73. London: London University Press.

Wood, A. 2002: The final form of Kant's practical philosophy. In M. Timmons (ed.), *Kant's Metaphysics of Morals: Interpretive Essays*, 1–21. Oxford: Oxford University Press.

11

Duties to Oneself, Duties of Respect to Others

Allen Wood

1. Kant's Division of Duties

One of the principal aims of Kant's *Metaphysics of Morals*, especially of the Doctrine of Virtue, is to present a taxonomy of our duties as human beings. The basic division of duties is between juridical duties and ethical duties, which determines the division of the *Metaphysics of Morals* into the Doctrine of Right and the Doctrine of Virtue. Juridical duties are duties that may be coercively enforced from outside the agent, as by the civil or criminal laws, or other social pressures. Ethical duties must not be externally enforced (to do so violates the right of the person coerced). Instead, the subject herself, through her own reason and the feelings and motives arising a priori from her rational capacities – the feelings of respect, conscience, moral feeling and love of other human beings, must constrain herself to follow them (MS 6:399–404).[1] Among ethical duties, the fundamental division is between duties to oneself and duties to others.

Within each of these two main divisions of ethical duty, there is a further division between duties that are strictly owed, requiring specific actions or omissions and whose violation incurs moral blame, and duties that are wide or meritorious, the specific actions not strictly owed, but deserving of moral credit or merit. Kant treats these latter as "duties" (eschewing any category such as "supererogation") because the actions in question are conceived as fit objects of self-constraint – things we can make ourselves do through the exercise of reason and the moral feelings arising from the application of practical reason to our faculty of desire. Regarding duties to oneself, this division is between "perfect" and "imperfect" duty; regarding duties to others, the strict or narrow duties are called "duties of respect" while the wide or meritorious ones are called "duties of love."

We may represent the major divisions of Kant's system of duties in the following diagram:

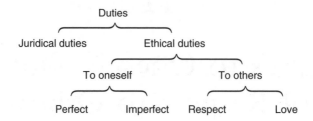

Figure 11.1

The aim of this essay is to discuss the three classifications of duties that appear leftmost on the bottom line of this figure: Ethical duties to oneself (both perfect and imperfect) and duties of respect to others. Juridical duties and duties of love to others are not part of our topic here.

It is important to recognize, however, that Kant's *Metaphysics of Morals* does not attempt to cover all the ethical duties that we have. This is because Kant confines the "metaphysics" of morals only to those duties that are generated by applying the principle of morality to human nature in general. But many of our duties, as Kant recognizes, arise from the special circumstances of others, or our relations to them, and especially from the contingent social institutions defining these relations.

In Kant's German idealist followers, Fichte and especially Hegel, the system of ethical duties came to be defined, or even superseded, by an account of the social structure. (Fichte spoke here of "particular" duties, Hegel of the "rational system of ethical life" that is supposed to replace a "doctrine of duties" in his system of objective spirit.) Perhaps some people, who might call themselves "cultural relativists," could even think that all ethical duties arise solely out of such social institutions and relations. More cosmopolitan and universalistic, Kant holds that there are universal duties that we have, both to ourselves and to others, simply as human beings, and he regards these as in some sense the foundations of all our duties, within which we also acquire duties in consequence of social customs, institutions, and relationships. Some of these duties might be to ourselves, though most will no doubt be to others; some will no doubt be narrow and others wide; and some may in effect convert wide duties into narrow duties, as when responsibilities to others convert our wide duty of beneficence into a narrow duty to contribute in determinate ways to the welfare of our family or friends or clients in some professional relationship. Kant holds that we have duties based on social institutions and relations, and that they are important; but they fall outside the scope of what he intends to cover in the *Metaphysics of Morals*.

2. Kant's Theory of Duties is his Theory of Moral Reasoning

For some reason, reading Kant's *Groundwork for the Metaphysics of Morals* tends to create in you a kind of reflex reaction. To the stimulus "Kantian ethics," you tend to emit the response "universalize your maxims." Some Kantians have even thought that the very essence of Kantian ethics is the use of a "CI-procedure" (involving the testing of maxims for universalizability) to decide what to do, or even to "construct" all ethical truth.[2] All who would understand Kant's actual theory of moral reasoning, however, ought to begin by performing a bit of minor surgery on themselves, severing the nerve that connects the stimulus with this reflexive response. In place of this reaction, we should think of Kant's theory of moral reasoning as a theory about the way our different duties bear not only on our individual actions, but on our maxims and on the choices through which we, as self-governing rational beings, shape our lives and give meaning to them.

It may be true that for Kant every action conforming to duty involves a maxim that can be willed to be a universal law; it is certainly true for Kant that the fundamental principle of duty is a law given universally for all rational beings by the idea of the will of every rational being. But because they are propositions about the philosophical foundations of morality, Kant does not think that either of these propositions tells us very much about the structure of everyday moral reasoning. Instead, as Kant presents things in his final work on moral philosophy, the *Metaphysics of Morals* itself, the normal procedure of moral reasoning depends on the constraints of duty, on the wide variety of duties we have, and on the different kinds of duties that ought to determine our choices in various ways.

This point about the need to supplement the formula of universal law with a theory of duties, based on a different formulation of the principle of morality, is clearly stated early in the Doctrine of Virtue:

> [In] the formal principle of duty, in the categorical imperative "So act that the maxim of your action could become a universal law," . . . maxims are regarded as subjective principles which merely qualify for a giving of universal law, and the requirement that they so qualify is only a negative principle (not to come into conflict with law as such). – How can there be beyond, this principle, a law for the maxims of actions?
>
> For maxims of actions can be arbitrary [*willkürlich*], and are subject only to the limiting condition of being fit for a giving of universal law, which is the formal principle of actions. A *law*, however, takes away the arbitrariness of actions. (MS 6:389)

The law that goes beyond the merely formal principle of duty has to do with the "matter of choice," namely with its ends.

> Only the concept of an *end* that is also a duty, a concept that belongs exclusively to ethics, establishes a law for maxims of actions by subordinating the subjective end that everyone has to the objective end. (MS 6:389)
>
> The supreme principle of the doctrine of virtue is: act in accordance with a maxim of *ends* that it can be a universal law for everyone to have. – In accordance with this principle a human being is an end for himself as well as for others, and it is not enough that he is not authorized to use either himself or others merely as means; . . . it is in itself his duty to make the human being as such his end. (MS 6:395)

Here it is clear that the "supreme principle of the doctrine of virtue" is more closely allied to the formula of humanity as end in itself than to the formula of universal law. It is also clear that this principle will establish duties via establishing that there are certain ends which it is our duty to have – to which ends Kant gives the name "duties of virtue" (MS 6:394–5).

The ends that are duties to have in accordance with this principle are of two kinds: Our own perfection, and the happiness of others. Regarding the former, Kant says:

> The capacity to set oneself an end – any end whatsoever – is what characterizes humanity (as distinguished from animality). Hence there is also bound up with the end of humanity in our own person the rational will, and so the duty, to make ourselves worthy of humanity by culture in general, by procuring or promoting the capacity to realize all sorts of possible ends. (MS 6:392)

This argument rests our duty to make our own perfection into an end firmly on the formula of humanity as end in itself. Regarding our duty to make the happiness of others our end, the argument is different:

> The reason it is a duty to be beneficent is this: since our self-love cannot be separated from our need to be loved (helped in case of need) by others as well, we therefore make ourselves an end for others; and the only way this maxim can be made binding is through its qualification as a universal law, hence through our will to make others our ends as well. (MS 6:393)

This argument, while clearly alluding to the idea that humanity is an end in itself, also has evident parallels with the argument used in the fourth illustration of the formula of universal law in the *Groundwork*, where appeal is also made to the fact of human interdependence, that our self-love cannot be rationally separated from our need to be helped by others (G 4:423).

A closer look, however, reveals that the two arguments are decisively different, and that the formula of universal law could not serve as the basis in this case. For there the question is only whether the maxim of refusing (on principle) to make the welfare of others our end can be willed without contradiction to be a universal law (or a law of nature). Since it can't, it is impermissible to adopt it. But as Kant has noted, the formula of universal law (as a merely formal principle of duty) is only a *negative* test for maxims, and cannot give rise to any moral *laws*. Even if the maxim of principled non-assistance is impermissible, it might still be the case that helping or not helping others is an equally permissible policy in general, that it should be possible to adopt no maxim making the happiness of others an end. But that is precisely what the present argument is supposed to rule out.

It does so by asking not whether the maxim of principled non-assistance can be thought without volitional conflict to be a universal law, but instead what *we necessarily will to be an actual universal law* consequent on our rationally necessary volition that we be an end for others. This question is the one posed not by the formula of universal law, but by the formula of autonomy, in those formulations that require us to act only on maxims that include at the same time the volition that they actually be universal laws (G 4:437–8, 440, 447). For it is only through such maxims that we can regard ourselves as legislating universally for all rational beings, in accordance with "the idea of the will of every rational being as universally legislative" (G 4:431).

None of this need come as a surprise to an attentive reader of the *Groundwork*. For Kant tells us that his search for the supreme principle of morality, which proceeds from the formula of universal law (and of the law of nature) through the formula of humanity as end in itself, to the formula of autonomy (and of the realm of ends) constitutes a progression – a progression in which one of the formulas combines the other two in itself (MS 6:436). This evidently refers to the fact that the formula of autonomy was derived by combining the formal principle of duty (the formula of universal law) with the principle specifying the matter of duty (the end in itself) (MS 6:431, 436). So we might have known that the formula of universal law, as the earliest stage of the progression, would also be the most provisional, least adequate, and (as a merely formal principle) the poorest in content of the three formulas, while the formula of humanity would be the one from which insight into the matter of duty (the ends that are duties) could be had most easily, and the formula of autonomy would be the purest and hence the "universal formula," which is the final touchstone of moral judgment, as Kant says it is, and as he also makes it in the *Critique of Practical Reason* and the *Metaphysics of Morals* (KpV 5:30; MS 6:225). But this is not the place to try to explain why readers of the *Groundwork* have so often and so mistakenly given priority to the formula of universal law in interpreting Kant's ethics.[3]

3. Obligatory Ends (Duties of Virtue) as the Ground of Ethical Duties

In general, the easiest way to make out the distinctions needed for Kant's taxonomy of ethical duties is through the use of the formula of humanity as end in itself. A duty *d* is a duty toward (*gegen*) *S* if and only if *S* is a finite rational being and the requirement to comply with *d* is grounded on the requirement to respect humanity in the person of *S*. A duty is wide or imperfect (or, if toward others, a duty of love) if the action promotes a duty of virtue (that is, an end it is a duty to set); an act is required by a strict, narrow or perfect duty (or a duty of respect to others) if the failure to perform it would amount to a failure to set this obligatory end at all, or a failure to respect humanity as an end in someone's person. An act violates a perfect duty (or duty of respect) if it sets an end contrary to one of the ends it is our duty to set, or if it shows disrespect toward humanity in someone's person (as by using the person as a mere means). No corresponding account of these matters seems derivable from the formula of universal law; that is a further reason for regarding it as a merely provisional formula, poorer in consequences than the formulas of the same moral law that Kant derives later in the progression.

This also shows how there might be narrow or perfect ethical duties, even though all ethical duties, as duties of virtue, are fundamentally wide duties. For the duty to promote an end involves not only a duty to refrain from adopting the maxim of refusing in principle to promote it, but also a duty to refrain from setting all ends that are opposed to the obligatory end – specifically any end of *decreasing* one's own perfection (or doing anything that makes you less worthy of humanity), or making the unhappiness of any person your end (as happens in the "vices of hatred": envy, ingratitude, and malice) (MS 6:458–61). We thus have a perfect duty to avoid any action that involves these forbidden ends, and also a narrow or perfect duty to perform any action whose nonperformance would amount to the principled renunciation of the obligatory end.

In grounding duties of virtue on the ends of our own perfection and the happiness of others, Kant does not mean to say that we have a duty to *maximize* our own perfection or the happiness of others. Rather, these duties, he argues, are *wide* duties, duties that determine us to make something our end, but leave us with latitude (or "play-room") regarding how far we promote the obligatory ends, and which actions we take toward them (MS 6:390–4). All such actions are meritorious, but their omission is not blameworthy, unless it proceeds from a principled refusal to adopt the end in question (MS 6:390).

Kant's theory regards the active pursuit of any end of these descriptions (the development of any talent or gift or capacity in ourselves, the contribution to anyone's happiness, or any component of their happiness) as in general meritorious (unless, of course, it proceeds by way of the violation of a strict, narrow, or perfect duty). It is up to us to decide which such ends to include in our plan of life. Our relation to others in determinate social institutions (the aspect of morality Kant deliberately leaves out of a "metaphysics" of morals) may render some of these imperfect duties perfect. (Caring for our children, or parents, or friends in determinate ways may be perfect duties, for the neglect of which we might be blamed.)

Moreover, it is apparently also up to us, to some extent, to decide how wide or narrow to make a duty of this kind: "The wider the duty, therefore, the more imperfect is a human being's obligation to action; as he nevertheless brings closer to narrow duty (duties of right) the maxim of complying with wide duty (in his disposition), so much the more perfect is his virtuous action" (MS 6:390). Thus if I commit myself to perfect myself in certain determinate ways, this can create something approaching a perfect duty to perform actions that promote this perfection. (Thus a devoted musician or athlete might be blamable for failing to practice or keep in condition, in ways that a casual amateur at these pursuits would not be.) But one might have expected that an ethics of autonomy would leave a lot to individuals in determining their lives, including determining the content of their duties.

Regarding most narrow duties, including perfect duties to ourselves and duties of respect to others, however, Kant seldom appeals to the ends of our own perfection and the happiness of others. He more often goes behind the back of these obligatory ends, so to speak, appealing to something even more fundamental – to the worth of humanity as end in itself, and the requirement that we show respect for it in our actions.

Humanity as end in itself is not an "end" in the sense of a future state of affairs to be brought about, but rather a value whose worth we are required to acknowledge expressively in our actions – an "end" only in a somewhat broader sense: that for the sake of which we act. This kind of end creates obligations to avoid acting in any way that shows a lack of respect for the worth or dignity of humanity. We could describe this by speaking about the value of ends, as by saying that conduct contrary to duty treats humanity as if it had value "only as a means" to some end to be produced, or treats the dignity of humanity as having lesser value than something whose value is mere price. But in order to be guilty of this conduct, it is not sufficient that you treat humanity as a means or use humanity in seeking something whose value is mere price. For doing all that might still be compatible with also treating humanity as an end in itself and as having dignity, if your conduct also expressed that valuation of humanity. However you use humanity in relation to other ends, the crucial question always comes down to whether your conduct expresses respect for the dignity of humanity or, on the contrary, betrays a lesser valuation of humanity than its dignity demands.[4]

A few of the perfect duties to oneself that we will be discussing appear to be based on the thought that their violation would be incompatible with making one's own perfection an end, but even there, the deeper reason why failing to set that end is contrary to duty is that this failure shows disrespect for the dignity of humanity as an end in itself.

4. Duties to Oneself

In the Anglophone tradition of moral philosophy, the concept of a duty to oneself is commonly applied to alleged duties to promote one's own welfare. But this is not what the concept means in Kant's ethical theory.[5] Kant does not regard one's own happiness as a fundamental duty of virtue at all, because in general our own happiness is something we inevitably pursue without the constraint of duty (MS 6:386). But he does think that I have a duty to promote my happiness whenever failing to do so might tempt me to violate other duties (G 4:399), and also insofar as my happiness falls under the heading of my perfection (MS 6:387). Further, though duty may sometimes require us to sacrifice our happiness, Kant thinks it cannot be lawful to adopt the general maxim of sacrificing one's own happiness for the sake of others, since this maxim would destroy itself (frustrate the happiness of all) if made a universal law (MS 6:393). But none of these points has anything at all to do with "duties to oneself" as Kant understands that notion. Duties to oneself are not about self-interest but about self-perfection and being worthy of one's humanity.[6]

Kant begins by facing squarely the question whether the concept of a duty to oneself is contradictory, since it seems to make a constraining person (or *auctor obligationis*) the same as the person constrained (the *subjectum obligationis*), permitting the latter (in his person as the former) always to release himself from the obligation, thus making it fundamentally null and void (MS 6:417). The response is to deny that the author of the obligation is identical to its subject. Rather, what is distinctive about the concept of an imperfectly rational and self-governing being (a being with "personality" in the Kantian sense) is that this concept involves that of a relation between two persons who are combined in one and the same being. I contain in myself both the person of the rational legislator, whose law is necessary, objective, and binding on all rational beings, and the person of the finite, imperfect being who has the capacity to obey this law, but also the possibility of failing to obey it.

Kant employs here his distinction between the sensible and the intelligible (MS 6:418), but it is doubtful whether that distinction, with its metaphysical baggage, makes any sense at all in this context. The point is rather that the Kantian conception of self-legislation is misunderstood when it is interpreted as the subjectivizing of moral value, as by those who present it as the metaethical thesis that it is *we humans* who "construct" the moral law or "confer value" on things through our choices. The moral legislator for Kant is rather (as he puts it in the *Groundwork*) the "idea" (or pure rational concept, to which no experience can be adequate) of every rational being as giving universal law (G 4:431), while the subject of these laws is a finite and fallible being whose volitions are subject to this law, and have objective value only through conformity to it. The welfare and the choices of such a being do have value, but only because the moral law makes this being an end in itself.

Perfect duties arising from our animal nature

The basic division within duties to oneself, as noted already in our diagram in Section 1, is between perfect and imperfect duties. Kant describes the former as "limiting (negative) duties" that "forbid a human being to act contrary to the end of his nature and so have to do merely with his moral *self-preservation*" (MS 6:419). These duties are in turn divided into those arising from our animality and those arising from our moral nature (MS 6:420). Under the duties to ourselves regarding our animality, Kant includes the duty to preserve our lives (and forbidding killing oneself), the duty forbidding "defiling oneself by lust" and the duty forbidding "self-stupefaction through food and drink" (MS 6:422–7). Some of Kant's views about these matters seem quaint (or worse) to us today, but this may pose an obstacle to our recognition that his categories, and even his general approach, may still make a lot of sense, even if we come to very different conclusions from his on the moral issues themselves.

Suicide. Kant approaches issues regarding our animality through the idea that our animal predispositions have natural purposes, and respecting ourselves requires treating this purposiveness with respect, rather than simply making everything serve our inclinations. His views proceed from the proposition that the fundamental natural purpose of self-love is the preservation of the life of the individual

(G 4:422). We are unlikely to accept this judgment today, and may even be skeptical about the whole idea of natural teleology. But we should, and probably do, have views about the value of our lives and of the role of sexuality in human life, views that might support the thought that we show disrespect for ourselves when we act in disregard of that value, and we should therefore also be susceptible to Kant's argument that suicide is at least sometimes an act that shows blamable self-contempt (MS 6:422–3).

In some places, Kant seems to be aware of (though never wholly to accept) the idea that suicide might be compatible with, or even a necessary expression of, the preservation of our own dignity – when we face the prospect of a life deprived (by disease or by the mistreatment by others) of the conditions under which our human dignity can be maintained (MS 6:423; VA 7:258; VE 27:374). In light of this idea, it seems one-sided for Kant to suggest that any act of suicide constitutes a denigration of one's person and a case of treating it as a mere means (G 4:422; MS 6:422–3).

Sexuality. Kant's abhorrence of sexual activity for pleasure, which he regards as inherently degrading to human beings, is likely to excite only amusement or indignation among us (MS 6:277–80; 424–6). Yet we ought to think a little more deeply about the matter. The thought that sex is only "for pleasure" is not directly false, but it is shallow. Hedonism, the general doctrine that pleasure is good, is likewise not false but shallow in a way that makes it profoundly misleading about the nature of value and the relation of pleasure to value. Hedonism at least neglects the truth (insisted on even by a hedonist such as Mill) that pleasures differ in quality, and thereby also directly denies the deeper truth behind this (which Aristotle recognized) that the value of pleasure is not fundamental, but derivative, based on the value we place on the functions and activities with which a given pleasure is associated, and on the value of their proper ends. To say that we engage in sex "for pleasure" is misleading because it simply elides the crucial distinctions here, and thereby fails to acknowledge the importance of the manifold, sometimes ambiguous, connections of sexual pleasure with human life, and the qualitatively different values, even among pleasures, that these involve.

Kant's discussion of the duty against sexual "self-defilement" in the Doctrine of Virtue is premised on the claim, which few nowadays are likely to accept, that the sole natural purpose of sexual desire is reproduction of the species (MS 6:424–6). In another context, however, Kant observed that sexuality has a role in human life different from, and more important than, the role it has in any other animal species, because it is precisely not confined to its periodic reproductive function, and because it involves both the operation of the imagination, the attempt to excite and control desire of another, and also the attempt to make oneself the object of another's desire while at the same time retaining the other's respect. In the desire excited by sexual refusal Kant finds the origins of all morality (MA 8:113; cf. VA 7:152).[7]

Thus it is sad that Kant did not apply these acute and adventurous observations to his thinking about the morality of sex. (Perhaps he did not know how to do so without entering on paths of thought that he could not comfortably follow as far as we would be willing to today. But we should at least credit him with catching a glimpse of where they might lead.) The nature of sexual pleasure often has little or nothing to do with the "natural purpose" of reproduction and everything to do with the expression of distinctively human meanings, such as self-concealment, self-revelation, self-withholding, and self-bestowal, both in the flesh and in the imagination, and the possibilities of intimacy that arise out of the ambiguities and transitions between offering and refusing oneself, giving and taking, possessing in reality and in the imagination.

Yet it is also precisely for these reasons – and not at all because of any animal reproductive function – that some forms of sexual activity can indeed involve the degradation of one person by another, and also self-degradation. Kant had to be aware of this, since so many of his pronouncements about sex are admirably (if also often misguidedly) sensitive to just these terrible possibilities (MS 6:277–8, 425).[8] Issues about the ways that sexual activity might involve a violation of duties to ourselves as well as others are obviously more subtle than Kant ever acknowledged, but he was not mistaken in viewing these issues as turning on duties of self-respect based on the purposiveness (albeit individual and social as well as natural purposes) of sexual desire and sexual self-expression. The noise in our heads provoked by Kant's wrongheadedness on the surface too easily prevents us from listening for the ways he gets things right at a deeper level.

Gluttony and drunkenness. It should be less controversial that we show disrespect for our humanity when we show contempt for our capacities, as by harming or depriving ourselves of them. This is the way Kant understands the violation of duty to ourselves involved in drunkenness or gluttony (MS 6:427). Kant is aware, of course, that what counts as a loss of capacity in one respect or in one context may not in another, or it may even count as an enhancement. In his "casuistical questions" he suggests that the slight intoxication afforded by the consumption of wine may even promote our healthy sociability at a dinner party, for example, by enlivening conversation, making it less reserved and more candid (MS 6:428).

Perfect duties regarding our moral nature

Kant regularly recognizes three objects of human desire in society affecting our use of others as means to our ends: power, wealth and honor. This triad may be the principle ordering the three negative duties to ourselves regarding our moral nature: against lying, miserly avarice, and false humility (servility).

Lying. Some of Kant's conclusions on this topic are infamously extreme, which tend to conceal from view the fact that the principles from which he derives them are conspicuously sensible and plausible. Lying is a violation of a duty to oneself when, and because, it is a violation of a rational being's self-respect (MS 6:429). This seems right, even if it is not plausible to trace this back to the supposed natural purposiveness of our capacity for communication (MS 6:429) or to think that it forbids all intentional telling of untruth to others. Kant apparently sees no lack of self-respect in untruths told out of mere politeness or in accordance with social conventions (MS 6:431; VA 7:151–3). It should have occurred to him that there might be other cases in which, for quite different reasons, intentional untruthfulness might even be a direct expression of self-respect (as when it defies the disrespectful intrusiveness of those who are prying into one's private affairs).

This is not the proper place to discuss Kant's brief, late, and notorious essay on the right to lie, in which he claims that lying to a would-be murderer about the whereabouts of his victim is a violation of the right of humanity (RML 8:425–30). For this is not only not about a duty to oneself, but is even about a duty of right rather than ethics. But so prurient is people's curiosity about this essay, that it would probably seem a dereliction of my present responsibilities not to say a few words about it. What is puzzling and shocking about Kant's discussion of this example is once again not the principles from which he was arguing but rather the way he chose to relate it to them. Kant clearly recognizes cases in which a person is not wronged by being told an untruth because the context is such that he has no ground to rely on what is said. Thus he acknowledges that we are sometimes "authorized" (*befugt*) to communicate our thoughts to others "telling or promising them something, whether what [we say] is true and sincere or untrue and insincere (*veriloquium aut falsiloquium*); for it is entirely up to them whether they want to believe [us] or not" (MS 6:238). Why did not Kant regard the case of the murderer at the door in this light? In the essay on the right to lie itself, Kant's basic principle is that it is a wrong to humanity in general, regardless of the consequences, to tell an untruth under conditions where to permit people to do so would undermine the foundations of a rightful order in society (RML 8:426). And this seems right, if applied, for instance, to knowingly false declarations made under oath in a legitimate court of law, or by a public official (such as a U.S. President or executive appointee) who, under the pretext of "executive privilege" or "national security," lies under oath to a congressional inquiry. What is perplexing is not this principle, but rather Kant's apparent belief that this applies to every case in which I make an untruthful statement, even including my declaration to the would-be murderer at the door. I think the proper understanding of this perplexity must depend on a correct account of how Kant saw the issue between himself and Benjamin Constant about the requirement of truthfulness in political life, which is the real topic of the essay.

Kant distinguishes the "outer lie" (to others) from the "inner lie" – what we would now call "self-deception" (MS 6:430–1).[9] Here, in the case of inner lies, I think he quite plausibly regards lying as *always* an expression of disrespect for oneself, hence always violation of a duty to oneself. Kant is also quite perceptive in bringing some religious beliefs under this heading, especially those that rationalize such beliefs as incitements to good conduct when they are nothing of the kind:

> Someone tells an inner lie, for example, if he professes belief in a future judge of the world, although he really finds no such belief within himself but persuades himself that it could do no harm and might even be useful to profess in his thoughts to one

who scrutinizes hearts a belief in such a judge, in order to win his favor in case he should exist. Someone also lies if, having no doubt about the existence of this future judge, he still flatters himself that he inwardly reveres the law, though the only incentive he feels is fear of punishment. (MS 6:430)

Kant's view seems to be that what is most reprehensible, as well as dangerous, about the inner lie is that it is also the commonest source of the outer lies that corrupt people's relations with one another: "Such an insincerity . . . deserves the strongest censure, since it is from such a rotten spot (falsity, which seems to be rooted in human nature itself) that the ill of untruthfulness spreads into his relations with other human beings as well, once this highest principle of truthfulness has been violated" (MS 6:430–1). Kant's principled objections to all religious creeds and catechisms derives from his conviction that their principal effect on people is to teach such hypocrisy and even to promote the superstitious idea that it is the most sacred of all duties (MVT 8:269; R 6:102, 108, 137, 180, 185–90).

Avarice. Kant distinguishes "miserly avarice" (*karger Geiz*) from "greedy avarice" (*habsüchtiger Geiz*) (MS 6:432). The latter, which is a desire to have more possessions than others, is a violation of a duty of beneficence to them (MS 6:432). Miserly avarice, however, is a propensity to hoard one's possessions with no intention of using or enjoying them. This is a violation of a duty to oneself, because it involves a failure to respect one's rational capacities to employ the means of one's own happiness to their proper end.

In his lectures, Kant makes some perceptive remarks about the psychology of this brand of self-contempt, which exhibits its close alliance to a kind of self-deception. Misers "go poorly clad; they have no regard for clothes, in that they think: I might always have such clothes, since I have the money for it. . . . Possession of the wherewithal serves them in place of the real possession of all pleasures, by merely having the means thereto, they can enjoy these pleasures and also forego them" (VE 27:400). "The invention of money is the source of avarice, for prior to that it cannot have been widely prevalent" (VE 27:402). For money gives the illusion of material substance to our imaginary power over the goods of life that we forego in order to possess and retain it. The imagination of what we might enjoy serves as the substitute for what we do not enjoy, and even multiplies our imaginary power of enjoyment in direct proportion to our deprivation in reality: "While still in possession of the money, we would have to expend it disjunctively, in that we could use it for this or that. But we think of it collectively, and fancy we could have everything in return" (VE 27:403).

In the same way, misers have the illusion of power over others, even of their admiration, since they possess the means to influence others and to be the objects of their envy: "Miserly people are scorned and detested by others, and they cannot understand why" (VE 27:401). "The miser is thus a stranger to himself; he does not know his own nature," and this makes avarice a vice that is especially difficult to correct (VE 27:402). Misers, Kant says, are fearful and anxious, because their riches are so important to them; they also tend to be superstitious, and religiously devout, because they regard the fetishism of religious observances as a substitute for the good conduct pleasing to God in the same way that they regard money as a substitute for the goods of life: "In their anxieties, they wish to have comfort and support; and this they obtain from God, by means of their pieties, which after all cost nothing. . . . [The miser] pays no heed to the moral worth of his actions, but thinks that if only he prays earnestly, which costs him nothing, he will already be on his way to heaven" (VE 27:401). Kant's discussion of miserly avarice, both in its psychology and in the social analysis surrounding it, contains much that anticipates Marx's critique of the fetishism of commodities.

Servility. The proper measure of our self-worth is the fundamental issue for Kantian ethics. Kant's conception of human nature also makes this measure deeply ambiguous. As sensible beings, we seem to have little worth or importance; but as moral beings, we have a dignity beyond all price (MS 6:434–5; cf. KpV 5:161–3). All human beings share alike and equally in this incomparable worth, yet we have a powerful natural tendency to self-conceit, to value ourselves, our welfare, and inclinations above those of others, and to treat other human beings as mere means to our own ends. This makes the moral feeling of respect – especially, self-respect – profoundly ambiguous (MS 6:437; KpV 5:72–5). Hence we must value ourselves simultaneously by a low and by a high standard (MS 6:435). Comparing ourselves with the moral law results in humility, or even humiliation (MS 6:435–6); but recognizing ourselves as both authors and subject of that law, and as having the capacity for a good will, exalts our value beyond every other we can even conceive (MS 6:436; G 4:393). In relation to others, therefore, our duty is twofold: to avoid the arrogance of rating our worth above anyone else's, and also the servile disposition that tempts us to subordinate ourselves to others, either for our own advantage or because of the self-contempt that may result from our failure to achieve competitive priority over them.

The complexity of the duty to avoid false humility (or servility) may be briefly indicated by the variety of different requirements Kant regards as falling under it: (1) "Be no man's lackey. – Do not let others tread with impunity on your rights." (2) Avoid excessive indebtedness to others, which makes you dependent on and inferior to them. (3) Do not be a flatterer or a parasite. (4) Do not complain or whine, even in response to bodily pain. (5) Do not kneel down or prostrate yourself even to show your veneration for heavenly objects – for Kant, this is the true meaning of idolatry (MS 6:436–7).[10]

The fundamental duty to oneself: conscience

Kant concludes the discussion of perfect duties to oneself by describing a duty he regards as the most fundamental of all duties whatever. This is the duty to serve as inner judge of one's own actions, before a (metaphorical) court, which is Kant's favored depiction of *conscience*.[11] It cannot be our duty to have a conscience, since unless we do, we are not moral beings at all and cannot be held responsible for our actions (MS 6:400). But it is our duty to act as prosecutor and as judge of ourselves, as before a court of justice, and then attend to the verdict of this court (MS 6:438). Kant's conception of conscience shows (what he also makes explicit in this context) the way in which an imperfect rational being, in being self-legislating and self-governing, involves a "dual personality": on the one hand, in turn as rational legislator, prosecutor, and judge, on the other as moral agent who acts subject to the law and must stand before the bar of this inner moral court (MS 6:438n).

Conscience plays two roles in our actions: as warning us (before we act) and as pronouncing a verdict (of guilt or acquittal) over the actions we have performed (MS 6:440). This metaphor might make us think that Kant might view us also as having the duty to punish ourselves for our misdeeds (as by depriving ourselves of happiness of which we judge ourselves unworthy). But this would be a fundamental misunderstanding of his ethical theory. If we represent ourselves as unworthy of some happiness that we either enjoy or hope for, it is never our duty to deprive ourselves of it, as long as no direct violation of duty is involved in acquiring or enjoying it (such self-deprivation is simply irrational), but rather only to strive to make ourselves worthy of it by improving our conduct. Kant regards self-inflicted punishment as an impossibility (MS 6:335), and scorns the whole idea of religious penance, for example, as both "slavish" and "hypocritical" (R 6:24n). Punishment is a kind of external coercion, and ethical duties are never the proper object of external constraint but only of the inner constraint of our own reason. The inner court sentences us to no punishment except the painful feeling, a moral feeling (not an empirical one) that arises necessarily from the influence of reason on sensibility, attendant on the recognition that we have violated the moral law. This is why Kant also discusses conscience under the heading of those moral feelings that we can have no duty to have because susceptibility to them is a presupposition of being morally accountable at all (MS 6:400–1).

The first command of duty regarding conscience, Kant says, is to "know (scrutinize, fathom) yourself" regarding your own maxims and the incentives on which you act (MS 6:441). This is a duty Kant regards as impossible to fulfill completely, and whose fulfillment is attended with some serious dangers. One danger is "enthusiastic contempt" for oneself (or for the entire human species), which we avoid through becoming aware of the moral predisposition in us (the absence of which would not signify evil but simply a lack of moral personality altogether) (MS 6:441). Here Kant's target is the morose self-scrutiny of certain religious self-examiners (such as Haller and Pascal), which leads sooner to madness than to truth (VA 7:133). This is closely allied in Kant's mind to the pietistic religiosity in which Kant himself was raised, which "reduces [the moral agent] to a state of groaning passivity, where nothing great and good is undertaken but instead everything is expected from wishing for it" (R 6:184; cf. SF 7:55–7). The opposed danger – which in the end even bears a strong resemblance to its opposite – is the "egotistical self-esteem that takes mere wishes – wishes that, however ardent, always remain empty of deeds – for proof of a good heart" (MS 6:441). The self-knowledge Kant insists is a duty is rather the sober resolve, as far as we are able, not to deceive ourselves about our deeds or about their sources within us, a knowledge whose sole aim is constructive moral improvement.

Imperfect duties to oneself

These duties are ends that we are required to have regarding our own perfection, whose promotion in action is meritorious, but the failure to promote them is never blamable (unless it proceeds from a principled refusal of the obligatory end). Kant divides these duties into those regarding our *natural* perfection and our *moral* perfection.

Natural perfection is further divided into "powers of spirit" (or reason), powers of soul (or understanding, including memory, imagination, and taste) and "powers of the body" (MS 6:445). These include the cultivation of our theoretical reason, the talents of mind falling under the various departments ranked along with understanding, and our bodily strengths and skills, including its general health and vitality. The Kantian theory is that it is not up to morality to determine in general what our priorities regarding these perfections should be:

> Which of these natural perfections should take precedence, and in what proportion one against the other it may be a human being's duty to himself to make these natural perfections his end, are matters left for him to choose in accordance with rational reflection about what sort of life he would like to lead and whether he has the powers necessary for it. (MS 6:445)

The only constraint here is that each of us should try to make ourselves into useful members of the world, as a way of showing respect for the worth of our humanity (our rational capacity in general to set and actualize ends of all sorts) (MS 6:446).

Moral perfection includes our power to conform our actions to the requirements of morality. This includes both our ability to do our duties from duty, as well as our moral virtue – that is, our power, which insofar as the ends of morality are multiple, consists in a plurality of distinct virtues – to conform our volitions to the maxims of the good will (MS 6:446–7; cf. 6:405–9). This includes not only the inner strength that makes us immune to affects but also the cultivation of inclinations which add to the strength of our good maxims (MS 6:408–9).[12]

What may surprise us is Kant's position that even these duties of moral self-perfection are *imperfect* duties – that is, duties to *strive* for moral perfection, but not duties to achieve it. Of course, our strict or narrow duties themselves remain what they were – the imperfect character of our duty to improve ourselves constitutes no excuse for our failure to *act* so as to avoid blame. But apart from that, we are not blamable for remaining morally imperfect, and our efforts to improve ourselves morally are meritorious rather than strictly required. Thus a person who does his narrow duties from some motive other than duty, and whose striving to improve himself on this point is only minimal and even unsuccessful, is not blamable.[13] Nor is a person blamable simply because he has not made himself better able to withstand temptation than he has been in the past. His efforts in these regards are, however, meritorious.

5. Duties to Oneself that Appear to be Duties to Other Beings

Above we characterized a duty *to* (*gegen*) *S* as one where *S* is a finite rational being and the requirement to comply with *d* is grounded on the requirement to respect humanity in the person of *S*. It follows, and Kant accepts the conclusion, that we have duties only *to* human beings – ourselves or others. Properly speaking, there can be no duties whatever *to* non-human living things, or to the natural world, or to God (or other non-human spirits). Strictly speaking, all beings for Kant fall either into the category of persons (rational beings) or things (non-rational beings). Persons are ends in themselves, while things have value only as means (G 4:428). But Kant realizes that we do seem to have duties to animals. He thinks we ought not to treat them as mere tools to be disposed of for our convenience, and does not intend his theory to slight these duties or release us from them.

Kant's solution is to claim that although there appear to be duties to (*gegen*) non-human beings, all duties in regard to (*in Ansehung auf*) non-human or super-human beings are really duties to oneself. In regard to non-human animals, for example, our duties to treat them with kindness, not to overwork them, to treat with gratitude those that have served us with devotion or affection, are really duties to respect our own humanity, which would be dishonored by cruelty or indifference to the sufferings of animals, or duties to perfect our moral character by cultivating virtuous qualities through our treatment of non-human beings (MS 6:442–3). Analogously, Kant argues that we have duties to preserve, and not destroy, what is beautiful in inanimate nature, and to respect the system of natural ends that we find in the natural world. This too, however, is really a duty to ourselves (MS 6:443).

Elsewhere I have argued that Kant's arguments on these points are unconvincing – they either beg the question or fail to establish that we have the duties Kant claims we have; but I have argued that Kant's ethical theory has the resources to do better than he in fact does, and to ground our duties regarding animals and inanimate nature on the dignity of rational nature without having to interpret these duties as duties to ourselves and without having to treat animals or other non-rational beings as mere things whose only value is that of means. I won't repeat those arguments here, but only refer the reader to them.[14]

What seem to be duties to God, according to Kant, are also in fact duties to ourselves. We have, according to Kant, a "*duty of religion*, the duty of 'recognizing all our duties as (*instar*) divine commands'" (MS 6:443; cf. R 6:153–7). However, this is really a duty of the human being to himself (MS 6:444); the duties we owe under it contain no special duties to God, but only our duties to human beings. The notion that we can serve God in any other way, as by praying, or churchgoing, or the reciting of creeds, or the performance of rituals, or placing ourselves in otherwise morally indifferent emotional states of belief or penitence or devotion, Kant condemns as "religious delusion" and "counterfeit service of the Deity" (R 6:167–75). I have also discussed elsewhere the reasons why Kant thinks we have a duty of religion; once again, I refer the reader to those discussions.[15]

6. Duties of Respect to Others

Humanity in the person of every rational being has *dignity* – that is, a worth that is above all price, a worth that must always be respected and cannot rationally be sacrificed in exchange for any other value (even the value of something else that has dignity) (MS 6:462).[16] *Respect* is the proper rational attitude toward something that has objective value.[17] *Contempt* is treating something as without value, or else as having lesser worth than it in fact has. So treating any human being as if they lacked dignity is to treat them with contempt (MS 6:462–3).

Kant thinks that people can act in such a way as to make themselves unworthy of their human dignity, but he does not think that when they do so, they actually forfeit it or deprive themselves of it. Thus the duty of respect for others entails that "I cannot deny all respect to even a vicious man as a human being; I cannot withdraw at least the respect that belongs to him in his quality as a human being, even though by his deeds he makes himself unworthy of it" (MS 6:463). This means, for example, that there must be no "disgraceful punishments that dishonor humanity itself (such as quartering a man, having him torn by dogs, cutting off his nose and ears)" (MS 6:463) – or, one might add, seeking to extract information even from "bad guys" by photographing them in sexually degrading positions and threatening to show the photos to their families.

Kant thinks we must show respect for others even in the logical or theoretical use of their reason, and even in pointing out their mistakes. We thus have

> a duty not to censure [a human being's] errors by calling them "absurdities", "poor judgment" and so forth, but must rather suppose that his judgment may yet contain some truth and we must try to seek this out, uncovering, at the same time, the deceptive illusions [that misled him], so as to preserve his respect for his own understanding. (MS 6:463)

We also have a duty not to "give scandal" – by which Kant means tempting others, through example or through inducements, to do things that will later cause them to be ashamed of themselves (MS 6:464; cf. 6:394). In other words, what is most fundamental for Kant to our duty to respect others is actually the duty to preserve their *self*-respect, and this involves a narrow or perfect duty to avoid doing anything that would cause them to lose respect for themselves as rational beings with dignity.

Under the heading of duties of respect to others, Kant specifically lists three vices that violate these duties: arrogance, defamation, and ridicule.

Arrogance. If the violation of perfect duties to oneself fundamentally involves treating humanity in one's own person with contempt, the violation of duties of respect to others involves treating someone else with contempt. Kant calls the violation of such duties "self-conceit" or "arrogance" because its typical form is that of thinking of *oneself* as of greater value than another – which, however, is impossible, since the worth of all persons is incomparable and absolute, hence equal. From this standpoint, self-conceit or arrogance cannot consist in rating your own existence too high, but rather in rating the existence of another too low. But as soon as we think of the worth of persons as something that can be comparative, or competed for (with winners and losers), we are already treating *all* persons with contempt, since their true worth is beyond anything that could be competed for with winners and losers. In that sense, arrogant people (who think they have won such a competition, and are entitled to treat others as having lesser value than themselves) directly treat these others with contempt, but they also indirectly treat themselves with contempt as well.[18]

"*Arrogance* (*Hochmut*) (*superbia* and, as this word expresses it, the inclination to be always *on top* (*oben zu schwimmen*)) is a kind of *ambition* (*Ehrbegierde*) (*ambitio*) in which we demand that others think little of themselves in comparison with us" (MS 6:465). Arrogance is closely allied to our natural human desire for *honor* (*Ehre*) – for the good opinion of others, which – along with power and wealth – is one of the basic goods for which people compete, and which Kant even regards as the psychological foundation of morality itself (MA 8:112–3). But he realizes there is something paradoxical in this, since competing for honor implies that people might be unequal in their worth, whereas the basic principle of morality, in the formula of humanity as end in itself, declares all rational beings to be of equal worth as ends in themselves. The point, however, is that what is basic to morality is establishing the correct rational standard for self-valuation, which involves valuing oneself for one's humanity and not for anything in which one might even possibly be regarded as superior to others.

Defamation. This could be regarded as the characteristic vice of moralists, the desire to blame others and expose them to blame. By "defamation", Kant does not mean *slander* (or spreading false and malicious reports about others) but rather the spreading, simply for its own sake, or because we take pleasure in it, of *true* information that detracts from the honor of another (MS 6:466). It is wrong – a violation of a strict duty, and a proper object of blame – to gossip about others, to expose their faults to public censure, when this is done not for the purpose of guarding others against their misdeeds but simply in order to bring them (or even human nature in general) into disrepute. Kant includes under the vice of defamation "a mania for spying on the customs or morals (*Sitten*) of others (*allotrio-episcopia*) – an offensive inquisitiveness on the part of anthropology, which everyone may resist with right as a violation of the respect due him" (MS 6:466). In other words, respect for others means what we might rather call "respecting their *privacy*," or simply "minding your own business."

Ridicule. If defamation involves taking pleasure in what is discreditable in the conduct of others, ridicule involves finding amusement in what makes them objects of mockery or derision. Kant distinguishes this from "banter" or "joking" (*Scherz*), "the familiarity among friends which makes fun of their peculiarities that only seem to be faults but are really marks of their pluck in sometimes departing from the rule of fashion (which is not a form of *derision*)" (MS 6:467). It is also different from the use of humor as a way of brushing aside a malicious attack on oneself (for that is really nothing but a way of defending one's dignity against the attack of another without descending to maliciousness). The crucial question is whether you take pleasure for its own sake in making the other into a laughing stock.

For Kant, the vices of disrespect for others display something very fundamental about human nature, which is closely allied to our radical propensity for evil. We know that all rational beings are of absolute, hence equal, worth, and yet we seek superiority over others, whether by making ourselves exceptions to what we ourselves will to be universal laws, or using other rational beings as mere means to our ends, or by adopting ends that systematically conflict with theirs (and therefore violate the laws of a realm of ends). Kant realizes that as moral beings we are entangled in social relations that involve competitiveness and a false sense of human worth at their foundations.

This creates an ambiguity regarding duties of respect. Kant already acknowledges this when he speaks of showing to a vicious man "at least the respect that belongs to him as a human being" – as though (self-contradictorily) there might possibly be a *greater* respect shown to something than that to which it is entitled as a being with *dignity* or absolute *and incomparable worth*. Yet because our social customs are often grounded on this self-contradictory assumption, it is sometimes necessary, in social life, to treat people according to the rank that our corrupt customs assign them. Kant places beyond the scope of a *Metaphysics of Morals*, which is supposed to apply pure rational principles only to human nature in general, to set forth "all the different forms of respect to be shown to others in accordance with differences in their qualities or contingent relations" (MS 6:468). Yet he clearly thinks that it would be arrogant and disrespectful to the humanity of others simply to ignore all this in our dealings with them. At the same time, Kant clearly disapproves of – and regards as itself an affront to the dignity of humanity – the social customs enshrining various forms of inequality whenever they are not expressions of the obedience to civil authority needed to preserve right:

> Preferential tributes of respect in words and manners even to those who have no civil authority – reverences, obeisances (compliments) and courtly phrases marking with the utmost precision every distinction in rank, is something altogether different from courtesy (which is necessary even for those who respect each other equally) – the *Du, Er, Ihr and Sie, or Ew. Wohledeln, Hochedeln, Hochedelgeborenen, Wohlgeborenen (ohe, iam satis est!)*[19] as forms of address, a pedantry in which the Germans seem to outdo any other people in the world (except possibly the Indian castes). (MS 6:437)

Kant's discussion of duties in the *Metaphysics of Morals* often seems to us too bound to the prejudices and conventions of his time (and perhaps also to some of his own perverse or unenlightened crotchets). But we should not forget that even the latter are sometimes his ways of trying to deal with the inherently conflicting demands of expressing appropriate valuation for humanity as an end in itself in a social world grounded on principles of mutual hostility and inequality between human beings. And we should not use our critical reactions to Kant on this or that issue as an excuse for perpetrating on ourselves the illusion that the dilemmas of upholding rational moral values in a fundamentally irrational human world are any easier for us to negotiate than they were for him.

Notes

1 Kant's writings will be cited according to the abbreviations listed in the Bibliography.
2 See Rawls, 1980, pp. 167–175, 235–252; Korsgaard, 1996; O'Neill, 1989, pp. 206–19.
3 For more on this see Wood, 1999, ch. 3.
4 See Wood, 1999, ch. 4.
5 See, e.g., Sidgwick, 1981, p. 7.
6 On this topic, see Denis, 2001; and Reath, 2002, pp. 349–70.
7 See Wood, 1999, pp. 238–43.
8 Regarding the institution of marriage, Kant departs from the traditional view that its purpose is the procreation and upbringing of children. Instead, marriage is a matter of right, an arrangement that permits human beings to engage in sexual activity (which Kant regards as inherently a threat to the dignity of their humanity) without violating the rights of humanity in the person of the sexual partners (especially of the woman, for whom the unequal status involved in physical weakness and economic dependence makes her especially vulnerable to being dominated and used as a mere means to the man's pleasure) (MS 6:277–80). While Kant's view that sex is inherently degrading will seem unhealthy or even monstrous to many of us today, we should not fail to acknowledge the justice of his claim, which feminists still rightly insist on, that sexual activity can pose a threat to the rights of humanity (especially in the case of women), and that the juridical order of society needs to make provision for their protection. On the other hand, it is far from evident that monogamous marriage is adequate for this purpose. Kant seems to think that the dignity of sexual partners is protected if they are granted the exclusive right to have access to their partner's sexual capacities (MS 6:278). But there seems to be no protection against what might seem to us some of the worst violations of right threatened by sexual activity. In the course of arguing that it might be excessive "purism" to condemn sex when its aim is pleasure apart from any reproductive aim, Kant lists among the circumstances in which sexual activity might be permitted the case where the wife "feels no desire for intercourse" (MS 6:426). It is not difficult to imagine that marriages in Kant's day, or even in our own, sometimes involve intercourse under those conditions, where the wife is a more or less unwilling participant in her husband's pleasure. But one might have thought that this would be something from which Kant would want juridical institutions to protect her. Sexual exclusivity – the fact that she is the only woman from whom her husband can get

sexual pleasure unwillingly – does not seem much protection against the violation of human dignity involved here. No doubt sexual fidelity serves most people as an indispensable part of the understanding through which they can maintain intimacy and mutual trust as life-partners. But there seems no good argument, based on either the dignity or the rights of humanity, why partnerships might not involve some different kind of understanding. The best means for protecting the dignity of women in sexual relations would seem to be economic independence, combined with more permissive and egalitarian sexual mores, that do not intrude on the privacy of human beings or penalize women disproportionately for their sexual choices. When it comes to sex, the biggest threat today to both the rights of humanity and human dignity are unenlightened attempts to impose the regimen of "family values": no sex outside monogamous heterosexual marriage – in other words, to enforce the very rules regarding sexuality that Kant favors on the (now totally implausible) pretext that they protect human rights and human dignity.

9   See Potter, 2002, pp. 371–90.

10 For further treatment of this theme, see Hill, 1991; and Grenberg, 2005.

11 For a good account of this topic, which, however, is on some points at odds with what is said here, see Hill, 2002, chs. 9 and 11.

12 On this last point, see Engstrom, 2002, pp. 289–316.

13 See Dietrichson, 1967.

14 Wood, 1998, pp. 189–210.

15 Wood, 1999, ch. 9; and Wood, 2002, pp. 498–511.

16 No doubt the dignity of humanity in human beings entails that their lives are of great value, since not to care about the survival of a human being is surely to treat them with contempt. But this does not necessarily entail that the life of a human being cannot be sacrificed for the sake of the lives of others, if this happens in such a way that the value of the human being is still respected (as, perhaps, when the person rationally consents, or the sacrifice occurs only of necessity and according to a plan to which all involved do rationally consent, or should rationally consent). To think otherwise may result from confusing an existing or "self-sufficient" end – that is, something existing whose value requires that it be shown due respect – with an end to be produced – a possible future state of affairs to be brought about. This might lead us to infer invalidly from "X is an existing end whose value cannot be sacrificed" to "X's continued existence, as a future state of affairs, must be brought about, no matter what the cost."

17 For this reason, metaethical antirealists behave inconsistently if they ever show respect for anything at all. (Antirealists will no doubt hasten to show that they can reconstruct in antirealist terms some psychological facsimile of respect for objective value, without actually being committed to objective values. This shows, however, only that they might be capable of mustering some false facsimile of respect for the things to which they direct this artificially constructed attitude, not that they are capable of honestly respecting anything. Perhaps they do honestly respect some things; but in so doing they act in a manner that is inconsistent with their metaethical convictions.) Since respect is a fundamental attitude in Kantian ethics, Kantian principles can be properly interpreted in metaethical terms only as some kind of metaethical realism. Kant himself, however, did not directly address twentieth century metaethical issues, and no direct warrant for ascribing any metaethical view at all to him can be found in his writings.

18 See Wood, 1999, pp. 132–9, 250–65, 283–91.

19 "Thou, He [the honorific use of the third person in addressing someone], Ye [the honorific use of the plural familiar in addressing an individual], and You [the polite form of address still used in German], or Your most noble, high noble, high nobly born, well born (oh, that is enough!)" Kant's Latin exclamation of disgust is a quotation from Horace, *Satires* 1.5.12.

Bibliography

Kant's cited works

Anthropologie in pragmatischer Hinsicht, Ak 7, 1798. Anthropology from a Pragmatic Standpoint. (VA)

Cambridge Edition of the Writings of Immanuel Kant, 1992. New York: Cambridge University Press. (Ca; This edition provides marginal Ak volume:page citations.)

Grundlegung zur Metaphysik der Sitten, Ak 4, 2002. Groundwork of the Metaphysics of Morals. (A. Wood, trans.). New Haven: Yale University Press. (Original work published 1785.) (G)

Immanuel Kant's Schriften, 1902–. Ausgabe der königlich preussischen Akademie der Wissenschaften. Berlin: W. de Gruyter. (Ak; Unless otherwise noted, writings of Immanuel Kant will be cited by volume:page number in this edition.)

Kritik der praktischen Vernunft, Ak 5, 1788. Critique of Practical Reason. (KpV)

Metaphysik der Sitten, Ak 6, 1797–8. Metaphysics of Morals. (MS)

Religion innerhalb der Grenzen der bloßen Vernunft, Ak 6, 1793. Religion within the Boundaries of Mere Reason. (R)

Streit der Fakultäten, Ak 7, 1798. Conflict of the Faculties. (SF)

Über das Misslingen aller philosophischen Versuche in der Theodicee, Ak 8, 1791. On the Miscarriage of All Philosophical Trials in Theodicy. (MVT)

Über ein vermeintes Recht aus Menschenliebe zu lügen, Ak 8, 1797. On a Supposed Right to Lie from Philanthropy. (RML)

Vorlesungen über Ethik, Ak 27, 29. Lectures on Ethics. (VE)

Other works cited

Denis, L. 2001: *Moral Self-Regard: Duties to Oneself in Kant's Moral Theory*. New York: Garland.

Dietrichson P. 1967: What does Kant mean by acting from duty? In R. P. Wolff (ed.), *Kant: A Collection of Critical Essays*, 314–36. Garden City, NJ: Anchor.

Engstrom, S. 2002: The inner freedom of virtue. In M. Timmons (ed.), *Kant's Metaphysics of Morals*, 289–316. Oxford: Oxford University Press.

Grenberg, J. 2005: *Kant and the Ethics of Humility: A Story of Dependence, Corruption and Virtue*. Cambridge: Cambridge University Press.

Hill, T. E., Jr. 1991: Servility and self-respect. In *Autonomy and Self-Respect*. New York: Cambridge University Press, 1991.

Hill, T. E., Jr. 2002. *Human Welfare and Moral Worth*. Oxford: Clarendon Press, 2002.

Korsgaard, C. 1996: *The Sources of Normativity*. Cambridge: Cambridge University Press.

O'Neill, O. 1989: *Constructions of Reason*. Cambridge: Cambridge University Press.

Potter, P. 2002: Duties to oneself, motivational internalism and self-deception in Kant's ethics. In M. Timmons (ed.), *Kant's Metaphysics of Morals*, 371–90. New York: Oxford University Press.

Rawls, J. 1980: Kantian constructivism in moral theory: the Dewey lectures. *Journal of Philosophy* 77, no. 9: 515–72.

Rawls, J. 2000: *Lectures on the History of Moral Philosophy*. Cambridge: MA: Harvard University Press.

Reath, A. 2002: Self-legislation and duties to oneself. In M. Timmons (ed.), *Kant's Metaphysics of Morals: Interpretive Essays*. Oxford: Oxford University Press.

Sidgwick, H. 1981: *The Methods of Ethics*. Indianapolis: Hackett.

Wood, A. 2000: Religion, ethical community and the struggle against evil. *Faith and Philosophy* 17, no. 4 (October): 498–511.

Wood, A. 1998: Kant on duties regarding non-rational nature. *Proceedings of the Aristotelian Society*, suppl. vol. 72: 189–210.

Wood, A. 1999: *Kant's Ethical Thought*. New York: Cambridge University Press.

Part V

Retrospective

12

Reflections on the Enduring Value of Kant's Ethics

Arnulf Zweig

When I try to think seriously about the enduring value of Kant's ethics, I find myself facing a number of problems. Philosophers are not prophets, so the empirical question of the endurance of this or that theory or value is inevitably a matter of speculation. (When asked what he thought of the French Revolution, China's former prime minister Zhou En-lai responded, "It's too early to tell.") The question should rather be, what *deserves* to endure? But that is not easy to say either, for I cannot overlook the diversity of issues Kant addresses and the variety of interpretations and responses to his arguments. My judgment is thus inevitably personal, reflecting my own values, something that Kant's disciple Fichte once claimed to be true of all philosophical theories. There seem to be many Kants. The Kant I admire and whose ideas I would want to see endure is the Enlightenment critic of irrationalism, mysticism, and sanctimonious religiosity, the Kant who challenges prejudice and bigotry, feudal injustices, despotism, and at least some forms of inequality. But there is also a Kant whose parochial attitudes and conventional moral judgments reveal him to be a child of his times and background. Given this diversity in his doctrines and convictions, it is not surprising that his disciples and critics have also been diverse. In the political sphere, there have been Libertarian Kantians, Marxist Kantians, and Social Democrat Kantians, and even – one hates to admit – Nazi Kantians, or at least Nazis who supposed themselves to be Kantians. While some reactions to Kant's ethics seem to me to involve misunderstandings and distortions, these diverse responses can each find at least a suggestion of support in some aspect of his arguments. In the religious sphere, where some see only the secular Kant, who defends a morality independent of divine instruction or divine decrees, others can point to passages that show a deeply spiritual thinker who never doubts, though he cannot prove, the existence of God and the intelligent design of man and nature. Both of these perspectives capture an important aspect of Kant's thinking. The "intelligent design" view, for example, is clearly expressed in Kant's suggestions for a "moral catechism," in his *Metaphysics of Morals*:

TEACHER: Does reason in fact have its own grounds for assuming the reality of a power that distributes happiness according to the merit and guilt of human beings, a power that reigns over the whole of nature and that rules the world with supreme wisdom, i.e., grounds for believing in God?

PUPIL: Yes; for we see such extensive and profound wisdom, in the works of nature that we are capable of judging, that we can explain it to ourselves in no other way than through the inexpressibly great art of a creator of the world." (*Metaphysics of Morals*, Ak. 6:482, "Fragment of a Moral Catechism")

Given this diversity of readings of Kant, disagreement as to what is most important in Kant's ethics is unavoidable, and one will have to choose which Kant to applaud and which to reject.

Kant is hard to read and even grasping his meaning can be a problem. His sentences are long, his arguments subtle and complex, his explanations often abstract and opaque. Kant's vocabulary can be troublesome for a modern reader, for even when Kant uses ordinary words – *die Menschheit* (humanity), *ein guter Wille* (a good will), *Glückseligkeit* (happiness) – some of those words are archaic or had religious overtones that they no longer possess in today's German let alone in translation. Our modern word "happiness," for example, does not carry with it the old theological idea of "beatitude" the way "*Glückseligkeit*" does. Though, as I have suggested, a salient feature of Kant's ethical theory is its secular character – Kant explicitly rejects grounding moral claims on the will of God or the authority of Scripture – his religious background nevertheless colors his thinking about good and evil, duty, accountability, and guilt. He sometimes assumes without much argument that his reader shares this moral outlook, an orientation to life that is stoical and tough, an outlook that many people and especially students nowadays may find off-putting. The worldview he takes for granted includes a veneration of Duty (*Pflicht*) and what sometimes comes across as a puritanical distrust of normal human inclinations and feelings. It is a severe morality and may sound excessively demanding to modern ears. Sometimes Kant writes as though there could never be any excuse for human weaknesses or even for some harmless misdeed. Of course that is not the whole story. There is Kant the moralist and Kant the anti-moralist, Kant who accepts no excuses, and Kant who reminds us of the opacity of the human heart and the fallibility of our judgments of others and even of our own motivations.

The chapters in this volume provide exegeses and defense – as well as criticism – of Kant's arguments and should help to remedy some ostensible difficulties and to correct misunderstandings of his position. Such well-known phrases as "humanity," "persons," "end in itself," "the moral law," and "respect," and such issues as what the Categorical Imperative in its various formulations means and how it might be applied to specific moral issues such as punishment, international justice, and duties to ourselves, are examined and illuminated. Kant's writings on moral and political philosophy have turned out to be almost inexhaustible subjects for scholarly debate and analysis, and one might argue facetiously that his provision of material for the employment of Kant scholars is one of the enduring values of his work.

Appraising Kant's moral philosophy is made difficult also by the complexity and range of his writings, and by the way his ethical theory is connected to the rest of his philosophy. As Kant scholars stress, there is much more to his moral philosophy than one finds in the *Groundwork for the Metaphysics of Morals*, more than the famous Categorical Imperative, and Kant's claims about duty-doing and freedom and the good will. But even the *Groundwork* requires some familiarity with his views concerning such things as the nature and limits of a priori knowledge. In his metaphysics and epistemology, Kant is famous for maintaining that a number of non-analytic principles and judgments are known a priori – necessary and universal truths that do not depend on variable human experience and neither can nor need to be validated by empirical evidence. Some of these "a priori synthetic" judgments are found in "rational sciences" like mathematics; others constitute the unconditional foundations and limits of scientific knowledge. Although such principles are not derived from experience, they make experience possible. In ethics too, Kant defends a priori principles and methods. Rejecting the possibility of empirical foundations for morality, he claims that the fundamental principles of moral conduct and moral deliberation must be unconditional and a priori. Empirical judgments, he maintains, are at best contingently true, and a merely empirical foundation, whether for science or ethics, undermines the "necessity" of the principles in those domains, rendering them vulnerable to exceptions. An ethical theory that relies on empirical facts, Kant argues, one such as "eudaimonism," which makes the pursuit of happiness the basis of morality, could not support the idea of *inescapable* duties, the unconditional moral "must." This belief in the absolute bindingness of moral laws constitutes one of the background conditions and cornerstones for his moral system. The supreme principle of ethics, which he calls the Categorical Imperative, does not tell us in any detailed way *what* exactly is unconditionally required of us as moral agents. But it sets forth an inviolable set of considerations for evaluating more specific rules or maxims.

In his own time, Kant could refer without argument to "the common knowledge of morality," and appeal to it in introducing his basic concepts and distinctions. So the special value of a "good will," a commitment to doing what's right because it is right, and not for the sake of personal profit or the satisfying of some interest one happens to have, needs no special argument for Kant's intended audience. Like Aristotle, Kant could refer to the distinction between what is prized and what is praised, and expect his reader to concur. On the substantive questions of ethics and human life too, he could count on shared attitudes and general agreement, for example, the wrongness of suicide to shorten pain, or the right of a husband or wife to compel a runaway spouse to be returned. While Kant recognizes the diversity of practices and temperaments in what he calls anthropology, his examples of rectitude and transgressions assume a community of shared values. For better or worse, no such consensus exists today, and, given the divisions we observe in our own society and the world, one may wonder how likely it is for such unanimity to emerge in the foreseeable future. Debate over issues such as suicide, assisted suicide, marriage, abortion, the rules of warfare, even the justification of murder when done in the name of some supposedly sacred cause, is passionate and often shrill. Disagreement exists on many levels, particular cases, and general principles. When Kant defends a moral position that today sounds uncompromising, his students and readers, accustomed to the idea of divinely sanctioned moral commandments, might well have felt no discomfort with his stance, just as readers with such a background today might find his defense of certain absolute prohibitions perfectly congenial. While, as mentioned, Kant rejects a religious grounding for ethics, he thinks we should look at moral imperatives *as if* they were divine laws. And so he does. To readers committed to unchanging traditions and taboos, Kant's most important legacy might be his defense of such rules as the prohibition of suicide, extramarital sex, and all "unnatural" sexual practices. To readers who do not share his confidence in conventional norms, the enduring value of Kantian ethics must be sought elsewhere.

But there is another side to Kant. His unbending commitment to morality includes a defense of human rights, cosmopolitanism, and political liberalism that should make his ethical theory attractive to anyone troubled by nationalism, religious zealotry, warfare, and the claimed superior virtues of the powerful. To such readers, Kant's diagnoses of the evils of colonialism and his advocacy of world citizenship and a league of nations to secure perpetual peace seem prescient and worthier of attention than his opinions about sex and suicide. Here, for example, is his powerful criticism of European conquests and the mistreatment of indigenous peoples. Kant speaks of

> the inhospitable actions of civilized and especially commercial states of our part of the world. The injustice they show to lands and peoples they visit (which is equivalent to conquering them) is carried out to horrifying lengths. When America, the lands inhabited by the Negro, the Spice island, the Cape, etc., were discovered, they were considered by their civilized intruders to be lands belonging to no one, for they counted the inhabitants as nothing. In the East Indies (Hindustan), they brought in foreign soldiers under the pretext of merely proposing to set up trading posts, but used them to oppress the natives, incite the various Indian states to widespread wars, spread famine, rebellion, treachery, and the whole litany of evils which afflict mankind. (*Toward Perpetual Peace*, Third Definitive Article for Perpetual Peace, 8:358f.)

Kant calls attention to "the most refined and cruel slavery" imposed on the natives. "This service is rendered to powers which make a great show of their piety, and while they drink injustice like water (Kant is quoting Job, 15) they regard themselves as the elect in orthodoxy."

As we see from this expression of moral outrage, Kant is not indifferent to empirical facts. Though the foundation of his moral theory is a priori, he is very much "in the world." Nor is he rigid in his moralizing, as his defense of the "necessity" of moral commandments, in the *Groundwork*, and a few of his examples of duty might suggest. He acknowledges the open character of many ethical questions, the need for wisdom and judgment in deciding how abstract moral truisms, principles of justice, and broad "duties of virtue" are to be applied to actual cases. Though he sometimes comes across as an unforgiving preacher, he cautions us to admit our fallibility in judging others, and he offers telling objections to accepted pieties and prejudices. In politics, he provides a forceful defense of freedom of thought and expression, as of progressive, anti-authoritarian ideals and republican forms of government.

Some of the values Kant defends – rationality, impartiality, moral egalitarianism, autonomy – have inspired generations of readers, and it is clear that Kant regards them as universally valid. While I fervently hope he is right about this, in fact those ideals are not universally acknowledged even today, and I cannot help wondering whether people born into a very different world and culture will be able to make sense of his thinking them universal, or will consign some of those concepts to a no longer relevant European past. That Kant is now or will be out of date may seem a ridiculous possibility to philosophers devoted to unraveling his arguments. For don't we see the Categorical Imperative – the phrase, at least – referred to even in the popular press, in newspaper editorials, and op-ed articles? Yet it is not absurd to wonder whether the moral outlook he explicates and defends, with its Enlightenment faith in the competence and authority of "reason" and in the rights of individual moral agents, may seem to coming generations as moral relics of a bygone time, as now they are dismissed by some as merely western liberal or secular thinking. Opposition to that Enlightenment faith is thriving in many quarters today, and who can say that some form of it may not be triumphant in a coming dark age?

Nor is it only inspired zealots and religious fundamentalists whose moral, or amoral, outlook is at variance with Kant's. Though Heinrich Heine famously portrayed him as a revolutionary thinker with "world-destroying" thoughts, there is also a side to Kant's ethics that is not modern at all. Consider the rejection of "cost/benefit analysis" implicit in this extraordinary rhetorical address to Duty and the Moral Law, in Kant's *Critique of Practical Reason*:

> Duty! Sublime and mighty name that embraces nothing charming or ingratiating but requires submission, and yet does not seek to move the will by threatening anything that would arouse natural aversion or terror in the mind but only holds forth a law that of itself finds entry into the mind and yet gains reluctant reverence (though not always obedience), a law before which all inclinations are speechless, even though they secretly work against it; what origin is there worthy of you, and where is to be found the root of your noble descent which proudly rejects all kinship with the inclinations, descent from which is the indispensable condition of that worth which human beings alone can give themselves? (*Critique of Practical Reason*, 5:86)

For better or worse, Kant's writing is usually less ecstatic and "inspirational" than this famous encomium to Duty, here personified and virtually deified, and his analysis of human strengths and virtues, though stern, is elsewhere not as totally dismissive of "inclinations" as it is here.[1] In fact, in the *Metaphysics of Morals* he condemns the fanatically moralistic person whose "fantastic" devotion to virtue and goodness degenerates "into a passion that allows nothing to be morally indifferent." Kant's reverence for duty and the cultivation of virtues does not make him insensitive to such deplorable moral "enthusiasm" or *Schwärmerei* – always a bad word in Kant's vocabulary – "that would turn the government of virtue into tyranny" (*Metaphysics of Morals*, 6:409). Kant's discussions of specific duties, virtues and vices, and his excursions into what he calls "casuistry," the application of moral principles to concrete situations, show a surprising degree of flexibility and pragmatism. He is cognizant of the nuances of human perversity, self-deception, laxity, insincerity, but he does in fact recognize the difference between trivial and serious transgressions, and he is often sensitive to the existence of marginal cases. With these qualifications in mind, respect for duty seems not an unworthy habit to try to teach one's children.

Kant's worshipful attitude toward the idea of duty, however, has misled some readers to see him in a frightening light. In a paper entitled "Kant in Auschwitz," one philosopher holds Kant's teachings about duty partly responsible for the sort of unquestioning obedience to authority exhibited by various Nazis and war criminals.[2] How such an interpretation of Kant can be squared with Kant's insistence on impartiality, justice, and respect for the humanity in every person is difficult to see.[3] The "Duty" Kant praises here and the "duties of virtue" and "duties of right" examined in his *Metaphysics of Morals*, are not duties in the sense in which people have job-related functions or obligations, duties one could get rid of or wriggle out of. Kant's reverence for Duty expresses a tenacious commitment to justice and personal integrity, not to the blind carrying out of orders. As another recent philosopher[4] has observed:

> In the case of duties towards others, Kant writes instructively regarding meanness and sycophancy on the one hand, and also regarding beneficence, gratitude, sympathy, respect, friendship, fidelity, and the avoidance of pride, scorn, and slander on the other hand. In all these cases he uses the criterion of respect for persons much more than the more abstract criterion of universality. Kant appears, in fact, to be no mean moral counselor, and the fact that his discussions say much even to our own contemporary susceptibilities bears witness to the timeless validity of his moral theory.

It must be granted, however, that some of Kant's discussions of virtues and vices, in the *Metaphysics of Morals*, while helpful in illustrating how he applies abstract principles, would not make his moral judgments more attractive to a reader who does not already share his intuitions and attitudes.[5] In fact, some examples such as his notorious prohibition of lying even to a murderer, may hinder rather than help to persuade his reader. These examples seem clearly intended for an eighteenth century audience both more priggish and less cynical than many of today's students, an audience of well-brought-up gentlemen who agree with (or at least pay lip-service to) Kant's attitudes on such matters as sex, truthfulness, honor, chastity, and how to treat servants and animals.[6] Kant's intended reader may need to be talked out of "eudaimonism" but not out of moral nihilism of the sort that tempts some people today – the sort of view expressed by Casey, in John Steinbeck's *The Grapes of Wrath*: "Maybe there ain't no sin and there ain't no virtue, they's just what people does. Some things folks do is nice and some ain't so nice, and that's all any man's got a right to say."

Kant is cognizant of the possibility that morality (specifically the ideas of accountability and the unconditional bindingness of moral imperatives) might be an illusion. At least he says he is, though I think he views this only as a theoretical possibility, defeated by his transcendental idealism,[7] not as a serious option. The Moral Law is, after all, one of those two things – the other being the starry heavens above me – that "continually fill the mind with ever new and increasing reverence and awe, the more steadily they are contemplated" (Conclusion of the *Critique of Practical Reason*, 5:161f.). He assumes that his reader shares this belief in the sanctity of "the moral law within," which finds expression as duty, virtue, the good will, and in his specific prohibitions and ideals, as well as the moral emotions of guilt, remorse, and self-chastisement that accompany our moral transgressions. His arguments are more concerned with showing how this cluster of moral attitudes must be grounded than with answering a moral skeptic who thinks them unfounded.

I have noted the variety of interpretations of Kant. Even in his own day Kant was read in different ways. Many welcomed his opposition to religious orthodoxy, political authoritarianism, feudal distinctions of rank, and so on, and saw these political stands as growing out of his moral philosophy. That was the Kant celebrated by his sympathetic Enlightenment contemporaries. But there were critics as well: Romantics, *Schwärmer*, "enthusiasts," men like J. G. Hamann and J. G. Herder who saw Kant as short-changing human feelings, sentiments, pleasure, love. Disciples such as Fichte applauded Kant's theory but transformed it into forms Kant could not recognize. In the two hundred years since Kant's death (February 12, 1804), we can find him worshipped as a savior,[8] a second Jesus, but also dismissed as a guardian of petit bourgeois values, defender of a guilt-ridden, and life-denying slave morality.[9] In our own day, some of the most interesting and important work being done in ethics and political philosophy shows his influence, but I have heard distinguished philosophers blame Kant for authoring the worst mistakes in the history of philosophy.[10]

Given this multiplicity of readings and responses, and the complexity of his thoughts and writings, any claim about what is of enduring value in Kant should be taken as a subjective expression of hope, not as a confident verdict. I have already indicated some of the things Kant stands for that have enduring value for me. They include the ideas of moral equality, of human beings as entitled to respect, and the limitation of human knowledge, a limitation that rules out claims of revelation or insight into divine intentions. As I have suggested, Kant articulates, in secular rather than religious terms, a way of looking at human beings that has been traditionally associated with theism. The metaphor of human beings as "children of God" expresses what the Categorical Imperative demands, in one of its formulations: that we treat the "humanity" in us and in others as an "end in itself."[11] Kant's formula captures a view of humanity that refers us not only to actions but also to their motivating reasons: the principles on which we act must take into account the special value of persons. Kant defends this demand sometimes with teleological claims about nature's purposes, claims that I find unconvincing and that seem to me to violate his own strictures on the use of such metaphysical ideas as purposiveness. But he also offers a relatively simple and clear presentation of the same basic moral commitment when he contrasts things that have a "price" and things that have an "inner worth," a worthiness of respect that he calls "dignity" (G 4:434). Whether Kant is successful in defending this distinction and the "sanctity" and irreplaceability of human beings, independently of traditional theological and metaphysical claims, is a matter of controversy. If one is not already persuaded that people are radically different and "superior" to non-human animals and that the "consciousness of the moral law" raises human beings infinitely above nature, Kant's argument that we are "ends" because we have the capacity to "legislate" or set ends is not likely to convert those people to this position. Perhaps the idea that human beings should be regarded as radically different from "things," replaceable objects, is no more than a postulate. As I have indicated, it is far from universally acknowledged. Yet I believe it underlies such moral commitments as the unconditional rejection of slavery, of subjugation, of various forms of exploitation, and of most forms of violence and coercion. Kant ties this rejection to the claim that human beings are autonomous "persons" with special cognitive and conative powers. This view of human beings as possessing "rational wills" seems both obscure and unrealistic, and the argument that we are "ends" because we have the capacity to "legislate" or set ends is, as I have admitted, one that I cannot find convincing.[12] But I think Kant is right to claim that looking at human beings *as if* they were rational – capable of understanding and deliberating and choosing to act for reasons other than self-interest – is something we presuppose when we hold them accountable for their actions. While an ethic without such accountability is conceivable – Spinoza's is an example – it would entail a major revolution in our thinking and judging, a revolution that, from my perspective, forgives and forgets too much, letting tyrants and murderous fanatics off the hook. Though I have qualms about his arguments, I therefore sympathize with Kant's goal of vindicating accountability.[13]

The moral ideas I have mentioned, ideas such as accountability, respect for humanity in ourselves and others, equality and freedom of various kinds, are vague and highly general, leaving us with many questions that will need to be debated and decided. Who are the "others" whose "humanity" we must respect, and do they include those who do not share Kantian ideals of reason, reciprocity, universal rights? If treating people as ends in themselves entails acting only on principles to which they too could consent, how do we determine what people could or could not consent? What, concretely, does taking another person's interests into account involve and require, and who has what obligations to care for and about whom? How are such questions to be decided in the real world, in non-ideal conditions?

I do not have answers to these questions but moral and political philosophers influenced or provoked by Kant – including some of the contributors to this volume – are seeking to provide reasoned solutions to these issues.

It may be a good idea to recall Kant's own warning about the limitations of philosophy, and how one's expecting too much from it – as we sometimes expect too much of other people – can lead to depression and a hatred of reason.[14] Towards the end of the *Critique of Pure Reason* (A 837f. = B865f.) Kant contrasts mathematics, an "actually existing a priori science," with philosophy. He writes: "[P]hilosophy is a mere idea of a possible science which nowhere exists *in concreto*, but to which, by many different paths, we endeavour to approximate. . . . For where is it? Who possesses it, and how shall we recognize it? We can only learn to philosophize, that is, to exercise the talent of reason . . . always, however, reserving the right of reason to investigate, to confirm, or to reject these principles in their sources." The concept of "reason" that Kant assumes in this passage is not overtly ethical but it is an important part of his moral legacy. It is a faculty of criticism, and of self-criticism, not only of calculating utilities or how to get what we want. I believe there are people, even now, who share Kant's moral qualms about reducing moral deliberation to questions of how best to employ such instrumental rationality. The ideals of human rights and the general conception of human beings as entitled to be treated with respect even when doing so would conflict with utility, are still alive, and not only in philosophers' conventions. What those ideas concretely require in order to be implemented is not a simple matter, and one has to acknowledge that intense disagreements persist when terms like "equality" and "freedom," for example, are replaced by specific policies that confront issues of gender, ethnic identity, political borders, economic welfare, access to resources, and the means of satisfying human needs. But Kantian ideals and imperatives, whether potent in practice or only objects of hope, at least provide a framework that many find essential for thinking critically about these issues.

Notes

1   That all human inclinations and feelings are burdensome to "right thinking" people and are all reducible to self-love is asserted in Kant's *Critique of Practical Reason* (1788). *The Metaphysics of Morals* (1797) shows that this was not to be his settled view.

2   Silber (1985).

3   Admittedly he opposed rebellion (though not civil disobedience) even against an unjust regime, and argued that there can be no legal right of revolution; but his sympathy for the American and French revolutions was clear to many of his contemporaries, and he argued against groups seeking to re-install the deposed monarchy in France. A concise summary of Kant's political position is given in Allen W. Wood's General Introduction to the volume, Kant's *Practical Philosophy* in the Cambridge Edition of the Works of Immanuel Kant (1996).

4   Findlay (1981). I am grateful to my colleague Douglas Lackey for calling my attention to Findlay's assessment of Kant.

5 I am thinking of his condemnation of "self-abuse" as a vice so vile its name cannot even be uttered, or his comparison of infants born out of wedlock to contraband goods, having no license to enter the world.

6 For the other side of Kant on the issue of "moralism," see Hill (1992).

7 The position developed in Kant's *Critique of Pure Reason,* which saves him from determinism by making causality a principle true only of objects as "appearances," not as "things in themselves."

8 See, for example, the letter from Heinrich Jung-Stilling who saw Kant as a second Christ. Kant *Correspondence* 11:7ff., p. 287. Jung-Stilling venerated Kant for saving him from total despair engendered by the threat of determinism.

9 See, e.g., Nietzsche, *The Genealogy of Morality*, Second Essay.

10 These verdicts, possibly uttered in jest, seem to me to involve deep misunderstandings of Kant's position, so it would be ungracious to identify the speakers. One blamed Kant for the now popular idea that objects of human knowledge are "social constructs," another for the "misguided" belief that morality has something to do with "rational beings."

11 For a critical and novel discussion of what this means, see the chapter by Richard Dean in this collection.

12 I sometimes wonder, following Schopenhauer, whether the capacities for suffering and sympathy, which we share with some non-human animals, might not be more important than rationality in determining what to treat as an end in itself. Buddhist attitudes towards living things result in very different moral practices than those Kant saw as morally required. It may sound foolish to ask: "What's so great about rationality?" but the question can come up, and not only when "rationality" is taken in the usual "instrumental" sense.

13 Worries about "the specter of determinism" and the reduction of human beings to "puppets" were not just issues of speculative metaphysics for him. They were, as he states in one of his letters, what first motivated him to write a "critique of reason." To Garve, Ak 12:258. Kant *Correspondence*, p. 552.

14 See Kant's letter to Herz, Ak.10: 249, February 4, 1779, Kant *Correspondence*, p. 175.

Bibliography

Findlay, J. 1981: *Kant and the Transcendental Object,* Ch. 9. Oxford: Oxford University Press.

Hill, T. E., Jr. 1992: *Dignity and Practical Reason in Kant's Moral Theory.* Ithaca: Cornell University Press.

Kant, I. 1900: Correspondence, Ak 10–13.

Nietzsche, F. 1887: *The Genealogy of Morality.*

Silber, J. 1985: Kant at Auschwitz. In G. Funke and T. Seebohm (eds.), *Proceedings of the Sixth International Kant-Congress,* vol. 1, pp. 151ff.

Wood, A. 1996: General Introduction to Kant's *Practical Philosophy* in the Cambridge Edition of the Works of Immanuel Kant. Cambridge: Cambridge University Press.

Index